An Encyclopedia of Judaism and Chr

'A pioneering and successful effort at describing accurately and objectively the parallels and differences between Judaism and Christianity on a host of important topics. It will be of much help to students and adherents of both religions.'

Rabbi Dr Louis Jacobs

'I welcome this book. It will provide Christian students with a wealth of information that will help them to understand the origins of their faith and the meaning of Judaism as a living religion; it will also provide them with an admirable insight into the mind of a learned and devout Jew.'

Donald Coggan, Archbishop of Canterbury 1974–80

An Encyclopedia of
Judaism and Christianity

Dan and Lavinia Cohn-Sherbok

For Robert and Conor
with love,
Dan and Lavinia

DARTON·LONGMAN + TODD

First published in 2004 by
Darton, Longman and Todd Ltd
1 Spencer Court
140–142 Wandsworth High Street
London SW18 4JJ

First published as *A Dictionary of Judaism and Christianity* in 1991 by SPCK and Trinity Press International

ISBN 0–232–52564–1

A catalogue record for this book is available from the British Library.

Designed by Sandie Boccacci
Phototypset in 10/11.25 pt Times New Roman Condensed
by Intype Libra Ltd
Printed and bound in Great Britain by
The Cromwell Press, Trowbridge, Wiltshire

For
Joan Heath

Preface

For nineteen centuries Jews and Christians have lived alongside one another; nevertheless positive dialogue between these two communities has only recently taken place. This change has been brought about for two important reasons. First, there has been considerable scholarly exploration into the background of the New Testament. Jesus and Paul were Jewish figures: they kept the Jewish law and participated in Jewish feasts. Pioneering work by both Jewish and Christian scholars has broadened the Jewish and Christian understanding of their own religious inheritance and has gone a long way to counteract traditional misunderstanding and prejudice. Second, fruitful Jewish–Christian dialogue is more of a possibility today because it is being conducted on a personal level. Encounters between Jews and Christians are taking place in friendship and understanding in Europe, Israel and the United States. Such amicable discussion has resulted in the formation of numerous associations of Jews and Christians throughout the world.

Yet despite these positive developments, it is often the case that even those who are actively engaged in Jewish–Christian encounter lack basic knowledge about one another's beliefs and practices. The purpose of this work is to provide information about Judaism and Christianity. In a single volume the wealth of the Jewish and Christian heritages is uncovered in direct and simple language, and throughout important connections are made between the two faiths. This is a reference work for everyone who wishes to understand the differences and similarities between these two religions. It serves as an introduction not only for students and teachers, but also for anyone who is interested in the fascinating richness of these two ancient traditions.

DAN AND LAVINIA COHN-SHERBOK
July 2004

Acknowledgements

We would like to acknowledge our indebtedness to a number of important sources from which we have obtained information: *A Dictionary of Christian Ethics*, ed. John Macquarrie (SCM Press, 1967); *A Dictionary of Christian Theology*, ed. Alan Richardson (SCM Press, 1969); *The Encyclopedia of the Jewish Religion*, eds. R. J. Zwi Werblowsky, Geoffrey Wigoder (Holt, Rinehart and Winston, 1966); *Encyclopedia Judaica* (Keter Publishing House, 1972); *The Encyclopedia of Judaism*, ed. Geoffrey Wigoder (Macmillan, 1989); *A New Dictionary of Christian Theology*, eds. Alan Richardson and John Bowden (SCM Press, 1983); *A New Dictionary of Theology*, eds. Joseph A. Komonchak, Mary Collins, Dermot A. Lane (Gill and Macmillan, 1960); *The New International Dictionary of the Christian Church*, ed. J. D. Douglas (Zondervan, 1978); *The Oxford Dictionary of the Christian Church*, eds. F. L. Cross, E. A. Livingstone (Oxford University Press, 1988). Those who wish to discover more information about the topics covered in this volume are encouraged to consult these reference works. This book is not intended to be the last word on the subjects discussed; rather, its intention is to stimulate further reading and reflection. We would also like to thank the Very Rev. Dr Victor de Waal, formerly Dean of Canterbury Cathedral, who very kindly read through the manuscript and made numerous important suggestions.

A

Abortion

The Bible, Talmud, and various codes of Jewish law make little reference to abortion, probably because it was unknown in the Jewish world. The only implicit biblical reference is found in Exod. 21.22: 'When men strive together, and hurt a woman with child, so that there is a miscarriage, and yet no harm follows, the one who hurt her shall be fined, according as the woman's husband shall lay upon him; and he shall pay as the judges determine.' Here the Bible legislates that in an attack on a pregnant woman that results in the abortion of her unborn child, the attacker shall be liable for monetary compensation, provided no harm follows. If harm does ensue, the offender shall pay with 'life for life'. (The rabbis interpret this proviso as meaning that no payment is due if the mother dies, since the offender would then incur capital liability.)

On the basis of this biblical passage, Jewish law grants full human rights only to born and viable persons. Thus, if the foetus endangers the life of the mother, it may be killed so long as neither its head nor the greater part of its body has emerged from the womb (in which case, it would be regarded as a full human being). Some rabbinic Responsa decree that therapeutic abortion is permitted only where there is a physical or psychological hazard to the mother's life – not simply in the case of a forbidden union, but from fear of giving birth to abnormal children, or for social and economic reasons. Contemporary Reform Judaism has, however, adopted a more liberal stance.

Christian opinion from the earliest period was opposed to abortion. Nevertheless, all abortions were not considered equally sinful. St Augustine (4th–5th cent.), for example, distinguished between the abortion of an animate and an inanimate foetus (the foetus being viewed as animated with a soul after 60 or 80 days following conception). Present-day Roman Catholicism teaches that direct intended abortion is never justified. Yet if an abortion is the unintended result of some necessary moral action (such as when a hysterectomy takes place to remove a cancerous growth), then it is acceptable according to the law of double-effect. But it is not permitted to abort a foetus even if, in the doctor's opinion, the continuing pregnancy will result in the mother's death. This is because the abortion would then be a direct intended result of the operation.

Recently, a number of Christians within a variety of denominations have come to believe that it is morally permissible to procure an abortion to save the life of the mother. Here, then, there is a congruence between the traditional Jewish view and that of liberal Christianity. Nonetheless, there is considerable uncertainty as to what other circumstances would justify such an act. Some Christians, like many Reform Jews, maintain that the mother's health and well-being override responsibilities to the foetus; others would disagree with this view. In this regard, the status of the foetus is uncertain. Although regarded as a potential person, it is unclear what rights it should be accorded. Thus the moral dilemma of weighing the value of a foetus against other considerations has become a serious problem.

Abraham

The first patriarch. According to Gen., he was told to move his family to Canaan, where he would become the father of a great people. As a sign of his covenant with God, he was told to circumcise himself and all his descendants – thus the circumcision of all male children is mandatory in the Jewish religion (Gen. 12–25). According to legend, he was the first person to recognize the existence of only one God. The example of Abraham is used by St Paul (Rom. 4) to show that God's salvation is not earned by human effort, but is the gift of faith. Paul also contrasts God's covenant with Abraham with that of Moses, arguing that Christians rather than Jews are the inheritors of that free promise (Gal. 4.21–28).

Absolution *see* Forgiveness

Abstinence *see* Fasting

Adam

First man. According to Gen. 1.26–30, Adam (literally in Hebrew, 'man') was created by God in his own image on the sixth day. Both male and female were created – they were to be fruitful and have dominion over all creatures. Another account of the creation of Adam in Gen. 2–3 is more extensive. Here God is depicted as creating Adam out of earth and charging him with tending the Garden of Eden. Eve was created from Adam's rib in order to be his helper. Subsequently, both Adam and Eve disobeyed God and ate from the Tree of Knowledge. In consequence, they were banished from the Garden and punished.

Elaborations of this account are contained in the Pseudepigrapha and Apocrypha. In the Talmud, God's purpose in creating Adam as well as Adam's relations with the heavenly hosts and lower forms of creation are discussed in detail. A number of Jewish philosophers allegorized the story of Adam and Eve. In kabbalistic (mystical) literature, the concept of *Adam Kadmon* ('Primal Man') became a dominant motif. The divine emanations – the *sephirot* – are described as comprising a huge human-like figure. This representation of *Adam Kadmon* is found in numerous mystical texts. A number of kabbalists (mystics) in the Middle Ages and the early modern period emphasized either its mythical-anthropomorphic significance or used it to explore the hidden realms of the Godhead.

Within Christianity, Adam plays a central role in the doctrine of original sin. Developing the rabbinic concept of the evil impulse (*yetzer ha-ra*) inborn in man, Paul linked up the phenomenon of original sin with the story of the Fall in Gen. 3. According to Pauline theology, human beings were involved in the fall of Adam, but can be saved through Christ. Thus the full significance of Adam is revealed through Christ's redeeming power. In the patristic period, the notion of original sin was the source of considerable debate. Tertullian (2nd–3rd cent.) used the term 'concupiscence' to refer to the inborn evil desire. Augustine (4th–5th cent.) argued that all human beings subsisted in Adam when he sinned – thus his sin became theirs. Humanity therefore is condemned, through its very ancestry. Further, since the time of Adam the capacity to obey God's will has been lost, and therefore human beings cannot be virtuous through their own efforts.

By the Middle Ages, original sin tended to be understood as the absence of original righteousness rather than as concupiscence. The reformers, however, under Luther's influence, returned to the Augustinian theory, emphasizing that because of

Adam human beings incline to evil in everything they do. In more recent times, such debate about the nature of original sin has been superseded by other theological concerns. Nonetheless, the doctrine of Adam's fall has retained a central place in both traditional Catholic and Protestant theology.

Adultery *see* Sexual morality

Advent

The beginning of the Christian year which, in the West, is now celebrated as the Sunday nearest 30 November. It is used both as a time of preparation for Christmas (i.e. the first Advent of Jesus), and for Christ's Second Coming – when he will judge the world and bring this era to an end. No formal season of Advent is celebrated in the Eastern Church. In contrast, the Jewish spiritual year begins in late September or early October. Like Advent, Rosh Hashanah ('New Year') concentrates on the awesome judgement of man by God and is a time of repentance and self-examination.

Afternoon service

The afternoon service is recited in synagogue each day no earlier than half-an-hour after midday and before the sun sets. It is one of the three daily services and corresponds with the afternoon sacrifice in the Temple. It includes Ps. 145, as well as the Amidah, Alenu and Kaddish prayers. Afternoon services also take place in the Christian liturgical tradition. Nones and vespers are part of the daily office of the Western Church and involve prayers, psalms, a Bible reading, and a hymn. The Eastern Orthodox Churches follow a similar structure.

Agaddah *see* Homiletics

Aliyah *see* Pilgrimage

Allegory

In the Jewish tradition, allegory is understood as the presentation of particular subject-matter under the guise of another, either through figurative speech or extended metaphor. From the earliest stages of biblical exegesis, it was motivated by the intention to derive moral lessons from biblical texts and the belief that, since the Torah was revealed by God, Scripture must contain a hidden meaning.

Also, there was the desire to preserve allegiance to the text even if certain aspects of the Bible no longer had practical application (such as the passages describing the sacrificial system that ceased to function after the destruction of the Temple), as well as the wish to reconcile the Bible with other systems of thought that were apparently in conflict.

These factors led to various types of allegorical interpretation. In the Hellenistic period, philosophical allegorization of the Bible was used particularly in the Alexandrian school by Philo (1st cent.). In the late Talmudic period in Palestine and Babylonia, symbolic Midrash (biblical interpretation) was frequently employed. Again, in the late Middle Ages, Greco-Arabic philosophy gave rise to a new type of allegorical exegesis as used by Moses Maimonides (12th cent.) in his *Guide for the Perplexed*. During this period and later, kabbalists (mystics) employed a mystical form of allegorical interpretation of the Bible.

In Christianity, allegorical interpretations were used by the Gospel writers – as, for example, in the explanations of the parable of the sower (Mark 4) and by Paul to demonstrate the truth of the Christian message (Gal. 4.21–31). Similarly, in the early Church, allegory found expression in the writings of Clement of Rome (1st cent.), Irenaeus (2nd cent.), Tertullian (2nd–3rd cent.) and, as with Judaism, especially in the Alexandrian school. Later, an allegorical hermeneutic was used by Jerome (4th–5th cent.), Hilary (4th cent.), Ambrose (4th cent.), and Augustine (4th–5th cent.).

In the Middle Ages, this tradition was continued by such theologians as Bernard of Clairvaux (11th–12th cent.) and Thomas Aquinas (13th cent.), who took up the fourfold system of interpretation (literal, analogical, typological, and allegorical) and made it normative for Catholicism. Nonetheless, from the 3rd cent., a number of Christians, such as those of the Antiochene school, were opposed to the use of the allegorical method. Thus Theodore of Mopsuestia (4th cent.) wrote *Against the Allegorians*. During the Reformation, a similar attack was launched against allegorical exegesis by scholars who argued that meaning must not be imposed upon Scripture, but instead be extracted from it. In recent times, allegorical exegesis has been largely abandoned by Christian exegetes, who have generally adopted the methodology of modern biblical criticism. However, allegory has continued to be widely used in sermons and devotional works such as John Bunyan's *The Pilgrim's Progress*.

Almsgiving *see* Charity

Alphabet

In Jewish thought, the Hebrew alphabet plays an important role. According to rabbinic theology, God revealed the Torah to Moses in the Hebrew language. Mystic powers were thus ascribed to the actual letters of the Hebrew alphabet by the kabbalists (mystics). In mystical literature God is viewed as having created the universe by means of Hebrew letters. In imitation of this divine act, kabbalists engaged in the permutation and combination of letters in various magical practices. In Christianity, there is no comparable belief about the divine revelation of a particular language. Rather, it is Jesus Christ himself who is the Word made flesh. Nonetheless, Jesus has been referred to as the Alpha and the Omega (the first and last letters of the Greek alphabet) – a notion that signifies his all-embracing and timeless significance.

Altar

Traditionally, altars were used for sacrifice. The Hebrew Bible records the building of altars in high places and, later, the placing of the sacrificial altar in the Temple in Jerusalem. With the destruction of the second Temple in 70 CE, animal sacrifice ceased to play a part in Jewish worship and there was no further need for a central altar. Instead, the table in the Jewish home took on a new symbolism, and it was there that bread and wine were sanctified and the chosenness of the Jewish people reasserted. Within Christianity, many of the connotations of the old sacrificial system were transferred to Jesus; he was the priest (Heb. 9.11), the victim (Heb. 9.12) and the altar (Heb. 13.10). Within the context of the Eucharist, the Lord's Table served as the Christian equivalent of the altar and was perceived as a place of encounter between God and humanity. It was there that Christ's sacrifice was re-enacted and God's people were nourished.

Amen *see* Prayer

Angel

Supernatural, celestial being. In the Bible, various names are applied to angelic beings: 'messenger', 'sons of God', 'holy ones'. In addition, supernatural creatures (seraphim, cherubim, and ophannim) are portrayed as connected with the Divine Throne or Chariot. These heavenly spirits are depicted as lacking individuality, personal names, and hierarchical rank; as a rule, they act in a beneficent fashion. The Babylonian exile, however, had a marked influence on Jewish angelology – angels subsequently became individualized and were ranked in later biblical books.

This evolution of angelology progressed in inter-Testamental literature such as the Books of Enoch, Jubilees, The Testament of the Twelve Patriarchs, and the Sybilline Oracles. Here, angels serve as the means of revelation and as instruments by which God governs the world. Later Jewish mysticism elaborated these conceptions by devoting special attention to the divine chariot in Ezek. 1–3. A complex picture of angelology is also found in the Talmud, Midrash (biblical commentaries), the Palestinian Targums (Aramaic translation of Scripture), and kabbalistic (mystical) literature. Medieval Jewish philosophers, in contrast, adopted a rationalist view of angels. Ibn Daud (12th cent.), Maimonides (12th cent.) and Gersonides (14th cent.), for example, identified them with the Pure Intellects who govern planetary bodies. In modern Judaism, allusions to angels in Scripture and the liturgy are generally regarded as having symbolic rather than factual import.

The early Christian view of angels was based on prior Jewish beliefs. In the New Testament, they serve as messengers, guardians, and protectors, as members of the divine court, and companions of Christ as judge. In addition, they bear witness to acts of salvation such as the resurrection of Jesus; they also bring healing and destruction and offer worship to God. Pauline theology linked the hierarchy of angels with cosmic and social forces, some of which were hostile to the gospel. Nonetheless, these 'principalities and powers' were subordinate to Christ.

In subsequent Christian doctrine, angelology was more systematically structured. The speculations of Pseudo-Dionysius and Gregory the Great (6th cent.) profoundly influenced Christian angelology in the Middle Ages. In the 13th cent., Thomas Aquinas's synthesis of Aristotelian and neo-Platonic metaphysics and scriptural and patristic sources served as the basis for subsequent theological reflection. The modern period, however, has witnessed a decline of interest in angelology. A number of Christians have tended to interpret references to angels as having poetic rather than literal significance. However, in some quarters angels still have a strong following.

Anointing

Consecration by the application of oil. In ancient Israel it was a central part of the act of consecration of high priests and kings. When Aaron was consecrated as high priest, the altar, sanctuary vessels, and Aaron himself were consecrated with oil (Lev. 7.10–12). In Scripture, it refers to 'the priest from among Aaron's sons, who is anointed to succeed him' (Lev. 6.22).

According to the Talmud, after the anointing of Aaron and his sons, only high priests and the priests appointed for war were anointed. But from the time of Solomon onwards, kings of the Davidic dynasty whose succession was disputed or in doubt were anointed. If the succession was natural and undisputed, anointing did not take place. Thus Solomon (9th cent. BCE) was anointed because of the rival claims of Adonijah (1 Kings 1.39); Joash (8th cent. BCE) because of Athaliah (2 Kings 11.12); and Jehoahaz (8th cent. BCE) because Jehoiakim was two years older (2 Kings 23.30).

The process of anointing was said to have been done with oil poured from a horn. For Saul, who was the only non-Davidic king to be anointed, it was poured from a horn (1 Sam. 16.13). (Northern kings were anointed with balsam rather than oil.) When kings were anointed, the whole head was covered with oil, whereas in the case of a priest it was in the shape of the letter X on the head. The phrase 'lord's anointed' (*Meshiah Adonai*) is used for a king (1 Sam. 24.6). The term 'Messiah' is derived from this Hebrew term and indicates the long-awaited King, descended from David, anointed by God, who would rule over a new golden age. After the destruction of the second Temple in 70 CE and until the advent of the Messiah, anointing plays no part in Judaism.

The Christian conception of anointing is based

on biblical practice. The term 'Christ' comes from the Hebrew word *Meshiah* ('The Anointed One'). The Church has interpreted the baptismal account in Mark 1.9–11 as the Messianic anointing of Jesus by the Holy Spirit. In some Churches this act has been extended to each Christian in the ritual of baptism.

In the Catholic tradition, at the present time, three oils are used. First, the oil of catechumens is employed prior to baptism. Initially, the person was anointed all over, but now oil is only applied to the breast, hands or, in some cases, other parts of the body. This anointing is a type of exorcism – it symbolizes the need for God's help and strength prior to the sacraments of initiation. Secondly, the oil of the sick is used in the sacrament of anointing the unwell. Based on Jas. 5, this is part of a long tradition in the Church of interceding on behalf of those who are ill. Here the head and hands are anointed by the priest. Finally, chrism is employed in the sacrament of baptism, confirmation, and the ordination of priests and bishops. Just as priests and kings were anointed with consecrated oil in the Hebrew Scriptures as a prefiguration of Christ, so Christians share in the priestly and kingly ministry of Jesus through this act.

A ceremony of anointing still takes place during the coronation of the British monarch, following Biblical precedent.

Anthropomorphism

The attribution of human qualities to God. In the Bible, God is frequently described as having human-like characteristics. Thus such phrases as 'the hand of the Lord', 'his outstretched arm', and 'the eyes of the Lord' are frequently found in Scripture. Yet it is obvious that many of these descriptions were not meant to be taken literally. For this reason, Aramaic translations of the Bible (particularly the work of Onkelos (1st cent. BCE)) as well as the writings of Hellenistic philosophers (1st cent. CE) were anxious to interpret such anthropomorphic depictions figuratively. In rabbinic literature, anthropomorphic language was also used, but the sages were aware of the potential danger of taking these descriptions literally. They therefore used various expressions to warn against this possibility, such as *ki-ve-yakol* ('if it were possible to say this . . . [of God]'). They also used terms such as Shekhinah, *Gevurah*, and *Ha-Makom*

('The Divine Presence', 'The Omnipotent', 'The Omnipresent') as circumlocutions for God's manifestations.

In the medieval period, Moses Maimonides (12th cent.) in his *Guide for the Perplexed* stressed that all biblical anthropomorphisms should be understood figuratively. However, other scholars (such as Abraham ben David of Posquières (12th cent.)) disagreed, stressing that the words of the Bible ascribing physical proportions to the Divine should be understood literally. Kabbalists (mystics) also developed anthropomorphic theories and concepts to explain the nature of the Godhead and God's relation to the world. However, the mainstream of Jewish theology from the early modern period onwards has followed the Maimonidean view that God has no physical form. In Christianity, there has been similar reflection about biblical anthropomorphism. The writings of Thomas Aquinas (13th cent.) have been pivotal in the development of Christian doctrine. Unlike Maimonides, whose work he had read, Aquinas held that not all anthropomorphic language is metaphorical. Such anthropomorphism is metaphorical only when the words used contain imperfections. But anthropomorphic language must be taken more literally when perfections such as love or acts such as creating are ascribed to God. In such cases, these terms are analogies that can be ascribed to God. Imperfection is not of their essence. In fact, they are applied most correctly to God and only derivatively to human beings.

On this view, such analogical anthropomorphism is justified by the doctrine that human beings are created in the image of God. Obviously, qualifications have to be made when transferring such human attributes to the Divine, but there nonetheless exists a resemblance between God and man. Later, Scholastics such as Cajetan (15th–16th cent.) developed the theory of analogy further, separating it from metaphor. Although this doctrine had a profound influence on later Christian thought, a number of subsequent theologians and philosophers disagreed; in their view, no theory can extend human meanings to a transcendent level. In the modern period, Karl Barth (20th cent.) is arguably the strongest critic of the use of the doctrine of analogy in describing God.

Antinomianism

Opposition to law. Through the centuries, Judaism has embraced movements and sects that have been antinomian in character. Various early Messianic movements taught that, with the coming of the Messiah, the law would no longer remain in force. Later movements, such as that of Shabbetai Tzevi (16th cent.) and of Jacob Frank (18th cent.), not only rejected the law, but glorified in its violation. Special emphasis was placed on the virtue of the 'holy sinner' who deliberately transgressed those scriptural laws for which the punishment was *karet* (excision from the Jewish people). Indeed, a special blessing was formulated to be recited before performing such sins, which was adapted from the daily blessing recited in the morning service. The leaders of the Jacob Frank sect went so far as to hold orgies they believed were in accord with God's will. Such actions, they maintained, helped to bring *tikkun* ('repair') to the heavenly spheres.

Contemporary Reform Judaism has been viewed as antinomian in character. In the 19th cent., Reformers decreed that they recognized as binding only the moral commandments, as well as those rituals that they viewed as spiritually uplifting. Laws regarding diet, priestly purity, dress, and other matters were rejected as anachronistic. This antinomian spirit has persisted to the present day, although within certain Reform circles there has been a tendency to revert to the legal tradition. Nonetheless, Reformers continue to regard the Pentateuch as having been inspired by God but written by men – thus its laws and subsequent rabbinical interpretations are subject to re-evaluation in every age.

From the earliest period, a number of Christians also adopted an antinomian stance. In some New Testament circles, antinomian tendencies appeared in various communities and were addressed by Paul in his epistles. Rom. 3.3–31 and 6.12–23 illustrate his struggle with critics who believed that antinomianism followed from his views on justification. In the early centuries of the Church, marginal groups such as the Adamists, the Satanists and the Cainites held strongly antinomian views. Again, in the Middle Ages, the Brethren of the Free Spirit held similar opinions.

During the Reformation, the views of Johann Agricola (15th–16th cent.) evoked Martin Luther's (15th–16th cent.) defence of the Ten Commandments and his denial that the suffering of Christ and the doctrine of justification by faith were sufficient to bring repentance and guide human conduct. It was Luther himself who coined the term 'antinomians' (*anti*, against, *nomos*, the law) to characterize Agricola's position. In the 17th cent., a number of sects emerged in England that also espoused antinomian views, such as the Ranters. Like the Frankists in Judaism, they acquired a reputation for acts of licentiousness. At the same time, Anne Hutchinson became the centre of an antinomian controversy in North America. In the modern period, Christian Situation Ethics has been charged with antinomianism in its rejection of a moral code.

However, despite the commonly held opinion that Judaism is a religion of law and Christianity is one of grace, this is an over-simplification. On the one hand, by no means all Jews regard the law as divinely inspired in every particular; and, on the other, the mainstream churches have firmly advocated a moral code and constructed their own systems of canon law.

Anti-Semitism *see* Racism

Aphikoman *see* Passover

Apocalyptic literature

Eschatological writings about the mysteries of a transcendent world where secret knowledge is revealed through supernatural figures. Such speculation is found in the Book of Daniel and writings from the second Temple period including 4 Ezra, 2 Baruch, and sections of 1 Enoch. Such works were dominated by the idea of dividing history into divinely ordained epochs, at the end of which the Messianic era would dawn. Angelology also plays a central role in these writings: angels are frequently depicted as guides in apocalyptic journeys and visions, and as active in the celestial court. Heavenly ascents also feature in apocalyptic texts, as does dualism – which posits Satan as the leader of a band of angels who rebel against God's supremacy.

These features of apocalyptic in the intertestamental period were appropriated by Midrashic (biblical interpreters) and Talmudic sages, although the ancient rabbis were wary of the influence of Christian and Gnostic apocalyptic texts. From the beginning of the 7th cent, until the end of the 10th cent. CE in Israel and the Near East, apocalyptic literature embodied Messianic speculation and was characterized by a preoccupation with the upheavals of world empires and the final vindication of the Jewish people in the Messianic age. In later centuries, popular works such as *Sefer Zerubbavel (Book of Zerubbabel)* influenced Midrashic literature, liturgical poetry, philosophical thought, and *Merkavah* ('Chariot') mysticism. In the 16th cent., Messianic apocalyptic again appeared in the Mediterranean region and led to the appearance of Shabbateanism (a Messianic movement based on the life and teaching of Shabbetai Tzevi).

Similar apocalyptic expectations play a fundamental role in the development of Christianity. Among the early Christians, Jesus' resurrection was viewed as part of an apocalyptic unfolding of history. Thus Paul saw Christ as 'the first fruits of those who have fallen asleep' (1 Cor. 15.20), the forerunner of a general resurrection. According to the Gospels, Jesus was the Son of Man as proclaimed in Daniel's vision, who would come on the clouds of heaven for the final judgement. The Book of Revelation also depicts God's deliverance of his people and the establishment of his Kingdom.

Largely as a result of the unsuccessful revolt against Rome in the 1st cent., Judaism ceased to regard inter-testamental Jewish apocalyptic literature as a central feature of its religious tradition. Christianity, however, preserved many of the Jewish apocalypses in Ethiopic, Syriac, Latin, and Old Church Slavonic, and also produced its own apocalyptic texts, such as those of Joachim of Fiore (12th cent.). Apocalyptic has thus occupied a central place in Christian thought, but it has not undergone the later development as found in Jewish literature – probably because Jesus has been understood as ushering in God's Kingdom. In Judaism, on the other hand, the expectation of a Messiah who will redeem the world has not yet been fulfilled, and this has led to renewed apocalyptic speculation through the centuries.

Apocrypha and pseudepigrapha

Corpus of Jewish literature written between 2nd cent. BCE and 1st cent. CE. It was not judged to be part of the canon of Scripture by the rabbinical synod of Jamnia (*c*. 100 CE). The 14 books of the Apocrypha contain historical, legendary, apocalyptic, and didactic material, whereas the pseudepigraphical literature is almost entirely apocalyptic. These books were largely preserved through the agency of the Christian Church. The Apocrypha was inserted between the text of the Hebrew Scriptures and the New Testament, although Protestants have returned to the Jewish tradition and deny its canonical validity. The Pseudepigrapha in their entirety have never been accepted by any Church.

Various other early Christian texts have also been preserved that contain a mass of legendary material about Jesus and his apostles. They have much the same status as most of the Jewish Pseudepigrapha – they are interesting, but are not regarded as authoritative.

Apologetics and polemics

Defence of a credal position and the rebuttal of attacks. The beginning of Jewish apologetics dates from the Hellenistic period, when writers sought to defend Judaism from the criticism of Hellenism and paganism. Philo's (1st cent. CE) *Apology on Behalf of the Jews* and Josephus' (1st cent. CE) *Against Apion* were among the earliest vindications of the Jewish faith. Apologetics are also found in Midrashic (biblical commentaries) and Talmudic literature, often in the form of arguments between rabbis and pagan philosophers and rulers.

The emergence of Christianity led to the development of anti-Christian polemics in rabbinic literature, notably in the Talmud. During the medieval period, Jewish apologists responded to the attacks of certain Jewish heretical sects such as the Karaites; Saadiah Gaon (10th cent.), in particular, attempted to show the errors of Karaite doctrine. In the Middle Ages, Jews were also forced to engage in disputations with Church officials about Christian doctrine, as well as about references to Christ and Christianity in the Talmud. Apologetics of this period are also found in the writings of various Jewish scholars such as Judah Ha-Levi, whose *Kuzari* consists of a disputation between a Christian, a Muslim, and a Jew. Among the Marrano community in the early modern period, an apologetic literature appeared which sought to illustrate the superiority of Judaism to Christianity. With the greater freedom of thought of the 19th cent., the need for similar apologetic or polemical works diminished, but recently many books have been produced to encourage secular late 20th cent. Jews to return to the customs and beliefs of their forefathers.

After the advent of Christianity, theologians in the early Church wrote apologies for Christianity (such as Justin Martyr's *First and Second Apology* and *Dialogue with Trypho the Jew*). Such works followed the pattern of apologetics adopted by Hellenistic Jewish writers. Against the Jews, these apologists argued that Christ had fulfilled the prophecies in Scripture. In the 3rd cent., writers such as Clement of Alexandria and Origen continued this tradition. In the 4th cent., Eusebius' *Preparation of the Gospel* and *The Proof of the Gospel* replied to philosophical and historical criticisms against Christianity.

In the medieval Church, apologetics were directed primarily against Islam and Judaism. The post-Reformation period, however, witnessed internal disputes between Roman Catholics and Protestants. In the following centuries, various apologetic defences of Church doctrine appeared as responses to alternative religious systems (such as deism). The Enlightenment and the French Revolution later led to the development of an apologetic political theology that stressed the importance of authority, tradition, and revelation. The modern period has seen the demise of the apologetic and polemic as literary forms. Nonetheless, as in Judaism, a number of writers within various Christian denominational traditions have attempted to demonstrate the viability of Christianity in the contemporary world in the face of increased secularism.

Apostasy

Abandonment of one's own faith and the acceptance of another. In the Bible, the prophets preached against idolatry, but the first account of organized apostasy dates from the 2nd cent. BCE. At this time, a number of Jews became Hellenized and abandoned their own religious traditions. In this milieu, sacrifices were even offered in the Temple to foreign gods. In response, the Hasmoneans drove out the Hellenized invaders of the country (the

Seleucids) and brought the nation back to the worship of the God of Israel.

The next challenge to Judaism was presented by the Christian faith, which attracted a number of Jews to its ranks. Initially, these Jewish Christians remained loyal to Judaism, but in time they separated from the Jewish people. In response, the sage Samuel ha-Katan (1st cent.) composed a petition against heretics and apostates; this was added to the 18 benedictions of the *Amidah* prayer.

During the Middle Ages, Jews were pressurized under the threat of death to convert to Christianity. Some of those who embraced the Christian faith subsequently engaged in disputations with their former co-religionists or were recruited to censor Jewish books. In the 14th and 15th cent., many Spanish Jews who were forced to convert to Christianity maintained their allegiance to the Jewish tradition in secret. These *Conversos* (or 'New Christians') were called Marranos (a derogatory term meaning 'swine'). Eventually, they became the primary victims of the Inquisition in Spain and Portugal. In the medieval Islamic world as well, Jews were forced to embrace Islam like the Christian *Conversos*; many of these individuals remained loyal to their former faith.

During the Enlightenment, a number of Jews converted to Christianity to improve their status in society. In modern times, this process of conversion to Christianity (as well as to other faiths) has continued, but generally for spiritual reasons, rather than out of a desire for advancement. In terms of Jewish law, however, such converts still remain Jews, but are regarded as sinners and outcasts.

In the New Testament there are warnings, parallel to what is found in the Hebrew Scriptures, against apostasy. According to 1 Tim. 4.1–3, apostasy is depicted as a departure from the true faith; 2 Pet. 3.17 declares that it is the result of being carried away by the error of lawless men. In Heb. apostasy is regarded as a falling away from the living God (Heb. 3.12). Again, Heb. 6.4–6 and 10.26 emphasizes the serious consequences of straying from the true faith. According to Matt., such an act takes place through the subverting influence of false teachers (Matt. 24.11), or because of persecution and stress (Matt. 24.9, 10).

Within the history of the Church there are frequent allusions to the activities of apostates, as well as discussion of suitable punishments for the lapsed. In the Middle Ages, civil power was used by both Catholics and Protestants to punish those charged with abandoning Christianity. In this connection, the Christian treatment of Jews who had been forcefully converted, but remained loyal to Judaism, constitutes a tragic episode in the history of Jewish–Christian relations. In the modern period, unlike Judaism, Christianity has adopted a more lenient attitude to those individuals who have abandoned their faith for another religion. However, both Judaism and Christianity have lamented the loss of adherents to secular humanism and agnosticism.

Aristotelianism

The writings of the Greek philosopher Aristotle (4th cent. BCE) were translated into Arabic during the Middle Ages and exerted an important influence on medieval Jewish thought. In particular, the Arabic philosopher Al-Farabi's (10th cent.) treatise, *The Philosophy of Plato and Aristotle*, had a crucial impact on the work of Moses Maimonides (12th cent.).

In his *Guide for the Perplexed*, Maimonides attempted to harmonize various Aristotelian ideas with the biblical text. Relying on Aristotle's arguments to demonstrate such religious doctrines as the existence of God and God's unity, he went on to argue that divine intervention operates on behalf of the human species rather than the individual. Here he abandoned the traditional notion of individual providence in favour of Aristotle's views. Nonetheless, Maimonides was critical of certain features of Aristotle's thought – such as the belief in the eternity of the universe and the concept of God as the Unmoved Mover. For Maimonides, Judaism's doctrine of creation *ex nihilo* (out of nothing) was dependent on prophetic faith.

After the 12th cent., Hebrew translations of the Arabic commentaries of Averroes (12th cent.) served as the basic Aristotelian source for Jewish theology. However, a number of Jewish thinkers were highly critical of Maimonides' Aristotelian approach, and formed an anti-intellectual counter-movement. In time, Aristotelianism ceased to have a significant impact on Jewish thought, and, from the early modern period onwards, Jewish writers have generally looked elsewhere for metaphysical theories on which to base their views about God and the universe.

In Christianity, interest in Aristotle existed in the patristic period. Such writers as Origen (3rd cent.) and Gregory of Nyssa (4th cent.) utilized Aristotelian logic to establish their doctrinal positions. In the 6th cent., John Philoponus commented on Aristotle's logic, and in the same century Boethius translated various works of Aristotle into Latin adding his own commentary. Nonetheless, most of the Church Fathers were highly suspicious of Aristotle, because of his view that providence only operated on the superlunary sphere and because of his rejection of the doctrine of the immortality of the soul.

In the Middle Ages, knowledge of Aristotle was derived from the work of Boethius, as well as from Arabic philosophers who were acquainted with Aristotle through Syriac translations. A number of Muslim writers translated most of Aristotle's works into Arabic, and these writings were themselves translated by Christian scholars into Latin by the 12th cent. In addition, William of Moerbeck, Archbishop of Corinth (13th cent.), translated Aristotle's works at the request of Thomas Aquinas, whose own philosophy was profoundly influenced by Aristotelianism. Like Maimonides before him, Aquinas integrated Aristotle's ideas into his own religious system, although he remained critical of a number of features of his thought.

Despite Aquinas's influence, his general acceptance of Aristotle did not immediately receive approval in the universities of Europe. In 1227, Thomism was condemned in Paris by Stephen Tempier, Bishop of Paris, and later in the same year by Robert Kilwardby, Archbishop of Canterbury. Subsequently, however, Aristotelianism was accepted as authoritative in the Church. Yet the resurgence of Platonism during the Renaissance, as well as Martin Luther's attack on Scholastic theology, weakened its position. Eventually, as in the Jewish faith, it lost its hold on Christian thought as Christian writers looked to other metaphysical systems as a basis for their theology.

Ark

According to the Book of Exodus, Moses was

instructed to build an ark to house the tablets of the law (Exod. 25). It was portable and accompanied the Israelites in their wanderings. Ultimately, it was placed in the Holy of Holies in the Temple in Jerusalem, which was visited annually by the high priest on the Day of Atonement. Its final fate is not known, but its significance and appearance is discussed at length in the Talmud.

Later, the term 'ark' was used for the closet set in the eastern wall of a synagogue which contained the scrolls of the law. It forms the focal point of the building and is frequently decorated. An eternal lamp (*ner tamid*) is often hung in front of it; this symbolizes the eternal watchfulness of God.

In contrast, the focal point of a Christian church is almost invariably the altar with its accompanying lights. The lectern (or reading desk), on which the Bible is placed, is of secondary importance. This reflects the emphasis in Christian theology on Jesus as the final sacrifice and means of salvation, as against the Jewish conviction that it is in hearing and obeying the scrolls of the law that the people become acceptable to God. Just as the altar is the scene of the enacted sacrifice, so the ark is the resting place of the law of God.

Ascension day

This festival is celebrated by Christians on the fifth Thursday after Easter and commemorates Jesus' ascent to heaven. The Acts of the Apostles (1.4–11) states that after his resurrection from the dead, Jesus appeared to his disciples for 40 days before he was removed from their sight. His return to the Father opens the way for his universal presence in the Church through the Holy Spirit. Christians believe that he will return again in glory to judge the world at the end of time.

There is no similar festival in Judaism, although the prophet Elijah is described as ascending to heaven in a fiery chariot (2 Kings 2). Since he never died, the belief grew up that he would return and bring peace to the earth (Mal. 4.5–6). It was widely believed that he would come at Passover time. It therefore became a custom to place a cup of wine for him at the Passover Seder (meal) table, and the front door was opened in the hope that this would be the year of his return.

Asceticism *see* Fasting

Atonement

(Expiation) (Penance) (Penitence) (Repentance): State of reconciliation between a sinner and the offended party prior to forgiveness. According to Jewish teaching, it can only be attained after a process of repentance involving the recognition of sin. It requires remorse, restitution, and a determination not to commit a similar offence. Both the Bible and rabbinic sources emphasize that God does not want the death of the sinner, but desires that he return from his evil ways. Unlike Christianity, God does not initiate this process through prevenient grace; rather, atonement depends on the sinner's sincere act of repentance. Only at this stage does God grant forgiveness and pardon.

With regard to unwitting offences against ritual law, a sin-offering was required in the biblical period as a sacramental act that restores the relationship between God and the transgressor. Following the destruction of the second Temple in 70 CE, prayer took the place of sacrifice. In addition, fasting, kindly acts, and the giving of charity were also viewed as means of atonement.

In the Jewish yearly cycle, a 10-day period (Ten Days of Penitence) is set aside, commencing with Rosh Hashanah (The New Year) and ending with Yom Kippur (The Day of Atonement), which is devoted to prayer and fasting. An echo of the ancient scapegoat ritual is observed by some traditional Jews on the Day of Atonement, whereby an individual's sins are expiated by the death of a white fowl. The Day of Atonement alone, however, only brings forgiveness for sins committed against God; for sins against others, atonement is granted only after the sinner has made final restitution and sought forgiveness from the offended party.

The Christian doctrine of atonement is based on the Jewish view of sacrificial death. According to Paul, at Calvary Christ was delivered for offences and raised for our justification (Rom. 4.25). Through his death, sinners could become 'at-one' with God (Rom. 5.1–10). In Heb. 10.19, Christ is viewed as the high priest who had performed the rites of absolution whereby sinners could enter God's presence through the blood of Jesus.

In the early Church it was proclaimed that the Son of God had come down to earth to share human nature; he had lived a life of perfect obedience and emerged victorious, thereby enabling his followers to partake of the divine nature. In this way, 'at-one-ment' was achieved. In the Middle Ages, Anslem (11th cent.) argued that human beings had disobeyed God, and it was impossible for adequate amends to be offered – only God could achieve what man was incapable of accomplishing. This was attained through Jesus' life and death.

On the other hand, Martin Luther (15th–16th cent.) concentrated on Paul's concept of the forgiveness of sins and the access to God through the atoning work of Christ. Calvin (16th cent.) insisted that Christ endured a substitute suffering, which otherwise would have been the lot of humanity. In the modern period, a shift has taken place in Christian thought away from the atonement of humanity as a whole to a concentration on individual repentance. Yet, despite the evolution of Christian reflection about atonement within the Christian faith, the belief in Christ's atoning act of sacrifice has been a central motif. Unlike Judaism, where the repentant sinner stands alone before God seeking forgiveness, Christianity has conceived of atonement only through the mediating influence of Jesus. Nonetheless, as in Judaism, forgiveness is not automatic. The Christian has to repent and actively accept the benefit of Christ's death. Where relevant, restitution to others is also required – as is the willingness to forgive others for their transgressions.

Attributes of God *see* God, attributes of

B

Baptism *see* Initiation rites

Bar Mitzvah *see* Coming of age

Bath, ritual *see* Immersion

Benediction

Blessing. The Hebrew term *berakha* ('blessing') is derived from the same root as 'knee', since bending the knee accompanied worship in ancient Israel. Various formulae were used from biblical times to the Mishnaic period; these were often introduced by the words *Barukh* ('Blessed'), *Barekhu* ('Bless'), or *Odekha* ('I will praise you'). In the Jewish liturgy the formula *Barukh Attah Adonai* ('Blessed are You, O Lord') (Ps. 119.12, 1 Chron. 29.10) was incorporated in the Jewish liturgy.

In the Talmud, Rabbi Meir (2nd cent.) decreed that a Jew should recite 100 benedictions daily. In the Middle Ages, Moses Maimonides (12th cent.) outlined three categories of blessing: (1) *Birkhot Ha-Nehenin* ('Blessings for Enjoyment') to be recited before and after eating or drinking and before inhaling spices and perfumes; (2) *Birkhot Ha-Mitzvot* ('Blessings on the Performance of Commandments') to be uttered when fulfilling a commandment; (3) *Birkhot Hoda'ah* ('Blessings of Gratitude and Thanksgiving') to be recited on witnessing natural phenomena (such as lightning, shooting stars, a sunrise, high mountains, great deserts and rivers) and on special events. By reciting such benedictions, the believer is reminded of his religious duties, his dependence on God, and the marvels of God's creation.

Following Jewish practice, Jesus blessed children, food, the apostles, and the bread and wine at the Last Supper. The Greek term for such acts of blessing – *eucharistia* – means essentially the same thing as the Hebrew *berakha*. In the Christian tradition, the Eucharist is the central act of worship, but its root meaning is blessing and praise. In the history of the Church many types of blessing were established – in various forms they are accompanied by the sign of the cross over a plate, object or person. Often, holy water is sprinkled or incense is used. Yet, despite these Christological features, the formulae of prayer have retained their original Jewish elements: praising God for what he did for his people, asking him for favour, and warding off evil.

As the Church developed, it became customary to end most services with a blessing. Frequently, this was the priestly blessing contained in the Hebrew Scriptures, which was initially recited by priests in the Temple and subsequently was introduced into the synagogue service: 'The Lord bless you and keep you: The Lord make his face to shine upon you, and be gracious to you: The Lord lift up his countenance upon you, and give you peace' (Num. 6.24–26). In the Roman Catholic and Greek Orthodox Churches, objects are frequently blessed;

in Reformed Churches, however, this has been generally eliminated, although there has been no hesitation about dedicating objects. Christianity and Judaism thus share the same biblical inheritance regarding blessing. There are strong liturgical parallels between both traditions, although the Christological elements introduced into Christian worship have separated it from its Jewish roots.

Beth Din *see* Courts

Bet Hamidrash *see* House of worship

Bible

(Canon of Scripture) (New Testament) (Old Testament) (Pentateuch) (Septuagint) (*Tanakh*) (Vulgate): In Hebrew, the Bible is referred to as *Tanakh*, a term formed from the initials of the three divisions of Scripture: Torah ('Law'), *Neviim* ('Prophets'), and *Ketuvim* ('writings' or 'Hagiographa'). The Torah consists of Genesis, Exodus, Leviticus, Numbers, and Deuteronomy. The *Neviim* are composed of the Former Prophets (Joshua, Judges, 1 and 2 Samuel, 1 and 2 Kings) and the Latter Prophets (Isaiah, Jeremiah, Ezekiel, Hosea, Joel, Amos, Obadiah, Jonah, Micah, Nahum, Habakkuk, Zephaniah, Haggai, Zechariah, and Malachi). The *Ketuvim* consist of liturgical poetry (Psalms and Lamentations), love poetry (the Song of Songs), wisdom literature (Proverbs, Job, and Ecclesiastes), historical books (Ruth, 1 and 2 Chronicles, Esther, Ezra, and Nehemiah), and apocalypse (Daniel).

The process of canonization took several centuries. The Torah in its present form possibly received scriptural status in the 5th cent. BCE, and the content of the prophetic books was, in all likelihood, compiled by the beginning of the 2nd cent. BCE. The compilation of the Hagiographa was probably decided at the synod of Yavneh in the 1st cent. (Nonetheless, during the next century, controversy took place about the status of Ezekiel, Proverbs, the Song of Songs, Ecclesiastes, and Esther.) The Greek translation of the various books (the Septuagint) was completed by 100 BCE.

In traditional Judaism, all the books of the Bible are viewed as sacred and inspired, yet the Torah is of pre-eminence since it is viewed by the Orthodox as revealed directly by God to Moses on Mt Sinai.

This means that all the words of the Torah are regarded as true, even though their meaning is interpreted in a variety of ways. Modern critical study has been rejected by Orthodox Judaism, since the Torah is viewed as sacrosanct. Non-Orthodox movements, however (such as Conservative, Reconstructionist, and Reform Judaism), have dismissed this objection as they regard the Pentateuch as inspired by God but written by human beings.

Jesus was perceived by his followers as the fulfilment of the Jewish tradition. Consequently, Christians have accepted the Hebrew Scriptures as canonical, although they appear in the Christian Bible in a different order from that found in Judaism. In addition to these scriptural books, the Church has added 27 writings which are also seen as inspired by God. These works emerged from living communities that bore witness to Jesus. The letters of Paul are the earliest of these works; traditionally, 14 letters were ascribed to him. But today it is widely accepted that authentic Pauline epistles are: 1 Thessalonians; 1, 2 Corinthians; Galatians, Romans, Philippians, Philemon. In all likelihood, 1, 2 Timothy and Titus are pseudepigraphical and, increasingly, 2 Thessalonians, Colossians, Ephesians and Hebrews have been regarded as written by someone other than Paul.

New Testament scholars differ widely on these matters, but traditionally Mark has been viewed as the earliest Gospel, written in Rome in about 65 CE. Most scholars believe that Matthew was written in *c.* 80–90 CE by an individual who made a synthesis of Mark and Q (a collection of Jesus' sayings); he may also have had access to other material (M). Luke and Acts are generally regarded as two parts of a single work possibly written *c.* 80–85 CE. The Gospel of John was probably written in *c.* 90–100 CE, although some scholars are inclined to give the work an earlier date. In addition to these books, the New Testament also contains the Book of Revelation, a work of apocalyptic. Many other books were produced by the early Church, but the New Testament canon of Scripture was established by the end of the 4th cent. Translations into other languages were also produced, the most famous being the Latin Vulgate (completed in 404).

Like the Hebrew Scriptures, the New Testament grew out of the life of a people who believed themselves to have been chosen by God. For the Jews,

God had revealed himself in their history. As a covenanted nation, they had received the law and had committed themselves to following God's commands. For Christianity, the Hebrew Scriptures constitute the Old Testament – a prelude to the New. Jesus was perceived as the Word made flesh, and in his life and death he was thought to have presented the Jewish community with a new perception of God's demands. According to the Christian Church, it is in the New Testament that the Old Testament promise of salvation for all people is fulfilled.

Biblical interpretation

(Midrash) (Targum): In the Jewish tradition, Ezra has been viewed as the Father of scriptural interpretation. Subsequently, two major exegetical trends manifested themselves: (1) interpretation based on the plain sense of the text, termed *peshat*; and (2) a homiletical method termed *derash*. In the rabbinic period, the latter type of interpretation, which sought to draw legal or religious teaching from the text, was referred to as Midrash. Halakhic Midrash was concerned primarily with legal and ritual matters, whereas homiletical Midrash was directed at non-legal (*agaddic*) exposition. Eventually, 7 hermeneutical rules were formulated by Hillel (1st cent. BCE), later expanded to 13 by Ishmael ben Elisha (2nd cent.), and eventually extended to 32 principles by Eliezer ben Yose (2nd cent.).

The preoccupation with the plain meaning of Scripture – *peshat* – is, on the one hand, evidenced in early biblical translations such as the Targums (Aramaic) and the Septuagint (Greek). In addition, the Masoretes (6th–10th cent.) attempted to provide a standard Hebrew text of the Bible. *Derash*, on the other hand, is found in both halakhic and *aggadic* Midrashim, and in the Talmud. In addition, mystical texts provide an esoteric interpretation in the attempt to uncover hidden meanings in Scripture. The account of creation in the first chapter of Ezek., in particular, served as the basis for extensive kabbalistic (mystical) speculation.

Simultaneously with the development of these various forms of biblical exegesis, Jewish philosophers of the Hellenistic period (such as Philo (1st cent.)) and those of the medieval period (including theologians such as Moses Maimonides (12th cent.)) provided a philosophical form of scriptural interpretation. A different type of exegetical tradition emerged among French and German scholars (such as Rashi (11th cent.)), who provided extensive commentary on Scripture combining both *peshat* and *derash*. In the modern period, the Enlightenment provided a framework for a renewed interest in scriptural commentary, as evidenced by Moses Mendelssohn's (18th cent.) *Biur*. Eventually, non-Orthodox Jewish scholars embraced the findings of biblical criticism, although traditionalists refused to accept the methods of modern biblical scholars.

In the early Church, a number of exegetical approaches were adopted by various biblical scholars. Origen (3rd cent.), for example, employed an allegorical method, believing that Scripture contains many levels of meaning. In the West, Augustine of Hippo (5th cent.) employed a parallel approach. Largely because of the influence of these two writers, as in Judaism, the Churches in the East and West accepted the notion of the multi-dimensional sense of Scripture.

In the Middle Ages, Jewish and Christian biblical scholars embraced a similar interpretative approach, yet Christian exegetes found within the Hebrew Scriptures Christological formulations. During the Reformation, the interpretation of Scripture altered course. No longer did exegetes hold to the view that the Bible contained multifarious meanings; instead, the text was interpreted along literal lines. Allegory was excluded, and the original meaning was sought. In this light, Luther and Calvin (both 16th cent.) attempted to elucidate the literal meaning of the Scriptures through philological exposition.

In the aftermath of the Reformation, Protestants and exponents of the Counter-Reformation utilized scriptural texts to demonstrate the validity of their doctrinal positions. Nonetheless, some scholars continued to be interested in the Bible for its own sake, and their studies paved the way for the modern approach. Today, both the Old and New Testaments have been subjected to scientific study by Christian exegetes from across the religious spectrum.

Bimah *see* Dais

Birth

In the Book of Genesis, Adam and Eve's disobedience resulted in a curse being imposed on Eve and her female descendants to suffer the pain of childbirth. Nonetheless, the first commandment in Scripture is to be fruitful and multiply (Gen. 1.28). During the biblical period, women gave birth in the kneeling position (1 Sam. 4.19) or sitting on a special stool (Exod. 1.16). Women with many children were viewed as blessed, whereas barrenness was seen as a curse.

The Bible imposes various laws of purity and impurity on mothers. When a male child is born, the mother is regarded as ritually impure for 7 days (14 for a girl). During the next 33 days (66 for a girl), she was not allowed to handle sacred objects or enter the Temple precincts. After these days of purification ended, she had to bring a burnt offering and a sin-offering to the Temple. In modern times, a woman who has given birth is obliged to follow the laws of *Niddah* (ritual uncleanness), including immersion in a ritual bath once she has become clean.

In accordance with Jewish folklore, amulets and talismen were frequently placed above the bed of the expectant mother to ward off evil. After the birth, family and friends often gathered at night to pray that the child be protected from evil spirits (such as Lilith, the female demon). After a male child was born, he was named at the circumcision ceremony. For girls, it was customary to be named in the synagogue when the father could be called to a reading of the Torah. It was also the practice to name the child when her mother entered the synagogue for the first time after giving birth.

Following the Jewish rite of purification in Lev. 12.6, a form of thanksgiving that Christian women could make after childbirth was adopted in the Church. This custom is mentioned in a letter of Augustine of Canterbury (7th cent.) to Gregory the Great (7th cent.), but the oldest extant form of service dates from the medieval period. In the Roman Catholic, Eastern, and Anglican Churches, it is held shortly after the birth of a child. Referred to as 'churching of women', its customs vary, but the usual date for churching is the 40th day after confinement. This is in accord with the biblical account of Mary's presentation of the child Jesus at the Temple (the redemption of the first-born).

Initially, it was almost certainly a ritual of purification from uncleanness as in the Jewish faith, since the woman customarily wore a white veil. In so far as the service still survives, it is now perceived as a thanksgiving after childbirth.

Birth control

Childlessness has been considered a great misfortune among the Jews – God's first command to Adam was: 'Be fruitful and multiply' (Gen. 1.22). Nonetheless, the practice of contraception was known from biblical times. Onan, who spilled his seed upon the ground (Gen. 38.9–10), was punished by death, and there are references to birth control in the Talmud. In general, Orthodox opinion condemns the practice except for health reasons and, even then, will only countenance female methods. The oral contraceptive pill is the most acceptable because it interferes least with the natural sexual act. (However, some authorities do allow birth control when a couple has produced at least one son and one daughter). Reform Jews permit contraception for social as well as health reasons, and argue that family size should be a matter of choice.

The question of birth control hardly arises in early Christian literature. Traditionally, the Church regarded sexuality with suspicion. Celibacy was the ideal; marriage was for those who could not attain this ideal, and the procreation of children was viewed as the only justification for sexual relationships. Thus, abstinence was perceived as a virtue and was the obvious and only form of permitted birth control. In theory, this remains the position of the Eastern Churches. With the increased emphasis on mutual love and comfort as the basis of marriage, the Roman Catholic Church has accepted the legitimacy of the rhythm method of contraception, but has remained steadfast in its opposition to any form of mechanical birth control. The Protestant Churches, however, generally teach that husbands and wives are free to use the gifts of science for the spacing or prevention of births as they wish, and their viewpoint is very similar to that of Reform Jews.

Bishop *see* Episcopacy

Blasphemy *see* Profanation of God's name

Body

The biblical view of the human person is of a single psychosomatic unit. The Hebrew words such as *nefesh, ru'ah* and *neshamah*, which are usually translated as 'soul' or 'spirit', are not used to refer to a disembodied spiritual element. Rather, these terms denote particular aspects of the human person. Later books of the Bible, however, do contain passages that appear to refer to a spirit or soul separated from the body (see 1 Sam. 25.29; Eccles. 3.20–21).

In rabbinic Judaism, however, the soul came to be seen as separable from the body – thus, during sleep the soul departs and is refreshed from on high, and at death it leaves the body altogether. It is unclear in rabbinic literature, however, whether the soul is able to sustain an independent, fully conscious existence away from the body after death. But in any case, the rabbis believed that the body and the soul form a harmonious unity in this life on earth.

Such a view implies that the body is sacred and must be respected. The Gnostic concept that the body is a prison of the soul is absent in rabbinic sources; instead, the body is conceived of as a sacred vessel. But it is not only in this earthly life that the body is of vital significance – the belief in physical resurrection came to be a basic principle of the Jewish faith. The concept of the resurrection of the dead is thus an extension of the biblical notion that human beings constitute a psychosomatic whole of body and soul, mind and matter, the spiritual and the physical.

In the modern world, Jews across the religious spectrum continue to regard the body as sacred and part of a harmonious whole. With increasing scientific knowledge, there has been a tendency to dismiss the doctrine of the physical resurrection in favour of a belief in the immortality of the soul.

Influenced by rabbinic Judaism, early Christian theologians adopted the view that the human person was composed of body and soul. Like the sages of the Midrash (biblical interpretation) and Talmud, they subscribed to a belief in the resurrection of the body in the world-to-come. However, in contrast with Judaism, these writers tended to denigrate the human body, making use of the Pauline contrast between 'flesh' and 'spirit'. For Paul, flesh referred to the whole person as oriented to sin, whereas spirit designated human beings as oriented to God. Such an attitude frequently led to ascetic practices that seem to imply an enmity between the body and the soul, and it is in this context that the Christian suspicion of sexuality – as against the Jewish attitude – can be understood. As in Judaism, despite Jesus' own physical resurrection, there has been a shift away from belief in the resurrection of the body. The tendency to identify the earthly body with sinful flesh has encouraged the conviction that it is only the immortal soul that survives death.

Bread

Bread plays a central part in both Jewish and Christian ritual. As a staple food, it came to represent the believer's livelihood or way of life, and was often presented in the Temple as an offering to God. During the festival of Passover, only unleavened bread is eaten. On the Sabbath, two white loaves, symbolizing the double portion of manna (Exod. 16), are blessed and shared out around the family table. This ceremony also takes place at home during other festivals, although then only one loaf is necessary.

At his Last Supper before his arrest, Jesus performed this bread ritual with his disciples. He transformed the traditional ceremony by indicating that the bread was his body which was given for humanity, and he instructed his followers to continue to share bread together in his memory (Luke 22).

From the beginning, meeting to break bread was a feature of Christian worship and this has developed into the liturgical celebration of the Eucharist. Unlike the Jewish ritual, this is not a domestic ceremony. It takes place not within the family, but within the congregation. Nonetheless, its Jewish roots are clear and the symbolism of the two rituals is not dissimilar; both are stressing the participants' commitment to a particular shared religious way of life.

Bris *see* Initiation rites

Burial *see* Funeral rites

15

C

Calendar

In the Jewish tradition, the act of creation constitutes Year 1 in the calendar. The calculation is based on genealogical tables in the Bible. On this basis, the year 2004-5 is 5765 in Judaism. The calendar itself is based on a lunar year composed of 12 months, each of which is 29 or 30 days. Since there is a discrepancy of 11 days between the lunar and solar years, a 13th month is added in certain years.

In ancient times, the Sanhedrin in Jerusalem fixed the date of the new moon as well as the addition of the 13th month to avoid the possibility that festivals would be observed on different days in various communities. Initially, the beginning of the new month was decided by eyewitnesses – distant communities were informed by a means of fire signals from one hilltop to another. Since communities in the Diaspora might still be in doubt about the exact beginning of the month, a second-day observance of festivals was instituted. In 358 CE, Hillel II introduced a permanent calendar based on mathematical and astronomical calculations.

In the Jewish calendar, the day begins at sunset and ends at nightfall on the next day. Thus the Sabbath begins at sundown on Friday night and ends with the appearance of three stars on Saturday night. The same calculation applies to all holy days. The major festivals in the Jewish calendar are: 15 Nisan – first Day of Passover; 5 Iyyar – Israel Independence Day; 18 Iyyar – Lag ba-Omer; 6 Sivan – Shavuot (Weeks); 17 Tammuz – fast of 17 Tammuz; 9 Av – fast of the ninth day of Av; 1 Tishri – first Day of Rosh Hashanah (New Year); 10 Tishri – Yom Kippur (Day of Atonement); 15 Tishri – first day of Sukkot (Booths); 25 Kislev – first day of Hanukkah (Lights); 10 Tevet – fast of the tenth day of Tevet; 15 Shevat – New Year for Trees; 14 Adar – Purim (Feast of Esther).

When Christianity began, the Julian Calendar, developed by Julius Caesar in 46 BCE, was in use. This calendar calculated the years almost accurately, but by 325 CE the error in determining the length of the year had become serious enough to cause the vernal equinox to fall on 21 March instead of 25 March. In 1582, the system was reformed by Gregory XIII, who caused 10 days to be omitted from that year to balance the error, and altered the leap-year cycle to prevent its recurrence.

The beginning of the Christian era begins with the date of the incarnation. The calendar begins from 25 March 1 CE, the alleged date of the annunciation, which was taken to be New Year's Day. The Gregorian Calendar restored New Year's Day to 1 January.

The Christian liturgical calendar is rooted in the Jewish tradition. The weekly Lord's Day (Sunday) reoriented the Jewish week. According to the Gospels, the resurrection occurred during the Passover season and the giving of the Holy Spirit took place on the festival of Shavuot (Weeks). This led to the continuing celebration by the Church of Passover and Weeks, but by the 2nd cent. these were transformed into Easter and Pentecost. Other festivals were later added to these holy days. To the weekly Lord's Day, fast days have been attached, and to the annual cycle the Church included Epiphany as a celebration of the visit of the wise men and of Jesus' baptism; Christmas as a celebration of Christ's nativity; and Ascension Day as commemorating his return to heaven. The season of Lent is also observed as a preparation for Easter, and Advent looks forward to Christmas. Yet, despite the Christological focus of the Christian calendar, its Jewish origins are clear.

Candles

(Menorah): The seven-branched candlestick (menorah) was a central feature of the sanctuary in the Jerusalem Temple, and candles have, from early times, been an important part of Jewish worship. In every home, at least two candles must be lit before sunset on the eve of Sabbath and festivals. Traditionally, this is done by the mother of the household and it symbolizes the light and joy of Holy Days. A special candle is also used to celebrate the ending of the Sabbath. It is made of at least two intertwined wicks and, when it is extinguished on Saturday evening, the Sabbath is over. Candles are often used at the Jewish festival of Lights (Hanukkah) and to search for leaven on the eve of Passover (Pesah). Candles are also lit in a house of mourning for seven days after the time of death, and in some communities they are used to accompany the bride and groom at their marriage ceremony. The symbolism of candles in Judaism is many-layered, but involves the perception of God's Word as a lamp to the feet and a light to the path (Ps. 119).

Christians traditionally put candles on or beside the altar during church services and, in some denominations, votive candles are set in front of statues of saints. In addition, the early Church traditionally lit a candle at the evening service of vespers. The festival of Candlemas, celebrated in February, commemorates the presentation of Jesus in the Temple (Luke 2). As in Judaism, the candles, which are distributed, symbolize God's Word as the Light of the World. But according to Christian teaching, it is no longer the Torah but Jesus Christ who is the light for revelation to the Gentiles, and for glory to the people Israel.

Canon of Scripture *see* Bible

Cantor *see* Music

Capital punishment

According to the Bible, capital punishment is to be administered for various crimes including kidnapping, murder, idolatry, blasphemy, adultery, incest, and violating the Sabbath. Stoning appears to have been the standard form of execution, but burning was also employed. To heighten the deterrent effect of this punishment, Deut. 21.22 prescribes that the body of anyone executed should be impaled on a stake and left for public display.

The Talmud adds two additional forms of execution to those mentioned in Scripture: slaying (by the sword) and strangling. Nonetheless, Talmudic law circumscribed the court's ability to convict those accused of capital offences. Such limitations included: (1) capital crimes could only be tried by a court of 23 individuals; (2) conviction was dependent on the testimony of two eyewitnesses; (3) circumstantial evidence and hearsay were inadmissible; (4) witnesses related to one another or the accused (by blood or marriage) were disqualified; (5) conviction could not be obtained unless the accused had been warned and acknowledged the warning verbally. Such restrictions rendered capital punishment practically impossible.

Initially, the Church found biblical justification for capital punishment. Lactantius (3rd–4th cent.) was one of the few Church Fathers to oppose it, and he was subsequently followed by a minority of Christians. Today, however, there has been a general shift in the Church in favour of its abolition. Nonetheless, there are a number of Christians who favour such a form of punishment since, in theory, it can act as a deterrent. In addition, they maintain that retribution is a central aspect of justice. Other Christians, however, reject capital punishment on the grounds that revenge is never justifiable, and because they believe that rehabilitation is always possible.

Casuistry

(*Pilpul*): A method of applying legal and moral principles to particular cases. In Judaism, the system of legal hermeneutics is based on Hillel's (1st cent. BCE) seven methods of interpretation. Later, these were expanded by Ishmael ben Elisha (1st–2nd cent.) and subsequently expanded by Eliezer ben Yose (2nd cent.) to 32. These exegetical principles were used to draw out the implications of the Written Law.

In addition to this standard method of legal interpretation, there later developed a systematic approach to the study of Talmudic and rabbinic texts known as *pilpul*. This term is derived from the Hebrew word for 'pepper', indicating that its methods were used by the sharper scholars. Initially, it was regarded as a praiseworthy approach involving the application of common hermeneutic principles in order to derive further prescriptions from the Written Law. However, it eventually became a hairsplitting methodology and was derided by numerous sages.

In the 16th cent., the use of *pilpul* at the rabbinical academy of Jacob Pollak in Cracow led to its adoption by students throughout Eastern Europe. During this period, it was regarded as a tool for sharpening the analytic powers of rabbinic students. Frequently, unrelated texts were juxtaposed and forced into a relationship with one another. Yet despite its popularity, *pilpul* aroused considerable criticism. In modern times, it is still practised, but is denigrated as unnecessary hairsplitting.

Despite the Gospel criticism of the Pharisees, Jesus is described as adopting rabbinic patterns of interpretation in dealing with such issues as Sabbath observance. Paul also dealt with specific cases by using Jewish methods of exegesis. Later, the

Church Fathers developed a type of casuistry in dealing with such issues as military service, persecution and wealth. From the 6th to 11th cent., a casuistry of sins and penances was developed in penitential books. This culminated in 1215 at the Fourth Lateran Council, when it was determined that annual confession and communion be obligatory.

In the 16th cent., the Council of Trent required the penitent to confess sins according to number, species, and circumstances. In consequence, a new type of literature was produced, *Institutiones Theologiae Moralis*. These texts dealt with such matters as sin, conscience, and law, and focused on specific cases. The method involved posing a question, citing authorities on both sides, and presenting a solution. This became the model for textbooks of moral theology which were produced up to modern times. Despite the popularity of such an approach, casuistry evoked criticism and was attacked for its legalism, minimalism, and individualism. Nonetheless, it is still often employed in discussing various spheres of ethical consideration.

Cathedral *see* House of worship

Catholicism

(*K'lal Yisrael*): The quality of being universal. In the New Testament, the Church is described as 'the fullness of him [Christ] who fills all in all' (Eph. 1.23). In Matt. 28.19–20, the Church is depicted as having a mission to all nations and generations. The Pauline and Deutero-Pauline letters celebrate Christianity's capacity to overcome all divisions in society.

In the Apostles' Creed, Christians confess: 'I believe in the holy Catholic Church', and in the Nicene-Constantopolitan Creed: 'I believe . . . in the Church, one holy, catholic, and apostolic.' Such a view was reiterated by the Church Fathers. Vincent of Lérins (5th cent.) defined doctrine as Catholic which has been believed 'everywhere, always and by everyone'. Cyril of Jerusalem (4th–5th cent.) taught that the Church had a mission to all peoples, and Augustine (4th–5th cent.) stessed the geographical and ethnic universality of the Church. During the Middle Ages, the concept of catholicity was developed by a number of theologians such as Thomas Aquinas (13th cent.), who argued that the Church has unlimited spatial and temporal extension, and includes all people who accept the salvation offered in Christ.

In Roman Catholic apologetics in the 16th–19th cent., catholicity was viewed as a mark of the true Church in opposition to heretical and schismatic sects. Protestant Churches in particular were seen as lacking catholicity because they were deficient in unity. Eastern Orthodox theologians understood the Church's catholicity as adherence to the full apostolic heritage as expressed in liturgies, creeds and dogmatic teaching. A number of Anglicans similarly looked on catholicity as a matter of preserving the patristic tradition. Yet despite such diversity of interpretation, which has continued to the present day, the catholicity of the Church has been a central feature of Christian self-understanding. It is an assertion of diversified unity rooted in Christ, an eternal community of belief that knows no barriers.

In the Jewish faith, the term *K'lal Yisrael* is a similar concept meaning 'the Jewish community as a whole'. However, unlike Christian catholicity, the unity of the Jewish people is not only a religious and historical concept, but also a current social reality embracing all Jews whatever their beliefs. According to tradition, all subsequent generations of Jews are viewed as having been present at Mt Sinai and are bound by the convenant. And at the end of time, the righteous of all generations will be reunited in the resurrection of the dead during the Messianic era.

In *aggadic* (narrative) literature, the concept of the community of Israel is used as a personification of Israel in its dialogue with God. Israel praises God, and the community is praised in turn. In Jewish mystical literature, God and the community of Israel are one when united in the Holy Land. According to this view, the people of Israel in exile are not united with God until they emerge from captivity and return to their land.

In modern times, the notion of *K'lal Yisrael* was developed by Solomon Schechter (20th cent.) in defining change and development within Jewish law. In his view, the collective community of 'Catholic' Israel as embodied in the universal synagogue is the only true guide for determining contemporary law. Today, the idea of *K'lal Yisrael* has served to animate Jewish consciousness, and functions as a central element in Jewish support for the State of Israel despite the various religious divisions within the Jewish world.

Celibacy

The priests and deacons of the Eastern Church may marry, but bishops must be unmarried. In the Western Church, all clergy in the major orders must be celibate, although this rule was abolished in the Reformed Churches. We know that some of the disciples were married (1 Cor. 9), but the idea that the unmarried state is preferable appears early in the history of the Church. Paul, who believed that the end of the era was near, argued that celibacy allows freedom from worldly care and greater concentration on spiritual matters (1 Cor. 7). This argument is still used in the Roman Catholic Church.

Judaism rejects celibacy, and traditionally bachelors were not allowed to occupy leadership positions. The commandment 'Be fruitful and multiply' (Gen. 1) is taken to mean that procreation is a duty. There have been very few exceptions, though Josephus (1st cent.) describes some Essene monastic communities as practising celibacy.

Charity

(Almsgiving): The Hebrew term for charity is *tzedakah*, a word derived from the root for justice. In the Pentateuch there are numerous provisions for the poor. The landowner, for example, is obligated to leave his gleanings, grain forgotten in the field, and the corner of each field for the destitute. Similarly, in the third and sixth years of the sabbatical year cycle, a tithe had to be given to the poor. In addition, all financial debts still owing in the sabbatical year were cancelled.

In the rabbinic period, the sages decreed that the way charity is bestowed adds to the merit of the act. Thus Moses Maimonides (12th cent.) outlined eight degrees of charity – the highest was to enable a person to become self-sufficient. The next highest is to give charity anonymously. The lowest form is when one visibly shows resentment in giving. The amount to be given is ⅒ of one's capital, and ⅒ of one's earnings; otherwise, it is possible to become destitute and require charity oneself.

The Talmud decrees that a person is not entitled to charity unless his total assets do not exceed a certain amount. The sum an individual is entitled to receive is related to his particular circumstances. Nonetheless, a person should make every effort to avoid receiving charity. Such rabbinic teaching about the importance and nature of charity has served as a framework for Jewish communal welfare services through the centuries, and in the modern world this tradition of philanthropy continues to serve as a keystone of Jewish life.

In Christianity, the word 'charity' has a specific theological meaning. The term 'agape' in the New Testament was translated in Latin as *caritas*, and then into English as 'charity'. It is found only twice in the Synoptic Gospels (Matt. 24.12; Luke 11.42), but it occurs often in the Fourth Gospel, the Pauline epistles and the Johannine epistles to denote the love of God or Christ for humanity, or the love of Christians for one another.

Within Christianity, charity is usually understood as the principle of God's love and human response. Love is the bond between the Father and the Son, and was particularly associated by Augustine (4th–5th cent.) with the Holy Spirit. The scriptural commandments that a person should love God (Deut. 6.5) and neighbour (Lev. 19.18) are joined together by Christ (Mark 12.29–31) as a single commandment. Love is viewed as the greatest of the theological virtues, and its manifestations are described in 1 Cor. 13.1–8. Later, theologians discussed the nature of love, and mystics stressed the importance of love in prayer. Because of the command to love one's neighbour, supporting the poor is as much a duty for Christians as it is for Jews. As far as tithing is concerned, in the early Church the clergy were maintained by ¼ of the offerings of the laity – the remaining ¾ went to the upkeep of the church, the relief of the poor, and the bishop. Later, this system was superseded by the biblical concept of tithes – ⅒ of all the produce of the land. According to tradition, the payment of such tithes is part of natural and divine law. Nonetheless, in modern times tithing has partly fallen into disuse, but many Christians are active in providing for those in need of assistance in a wide variety of spheres.

Chastity *see* Sexual morality

Choir *see* Music

Chosen people *see* Israel

Christmas

This festival commemorates the birth of Jesus, although there is no historical evidence that this event took place on 25 December. The Armenian Church celebrates it on 6 January, the same date as Epiphany. The date of the Roman pagan festival for the birthday of the unconquered sun was 25 December, when light began to increase after the winter solstice. This was spiritualized by the Christian Church to mean the birth of the Son of righteousness. Many of the traditional Christian customs, such as feasting, presents, lights and greenery, have their origin in the older pagan festivals and were thus disapproved of by the Puritans. Since the early 19th cent., the celebration of Christmas has become increasingly popular and is the subject of much commercial exploitation.

Jews also celebrate a festival of Light at much the same time of year. The feast of Hanukkah, which commemorates the rededication of the Temple in the time of the Maccabees, is traditionally a minor festival and there is no obligation to stop work. In view of the enormous impact of Christmas, however, Hanukkah has recently taken on increased importance with parties, games, songs, and presents.

Christology

The study of the person of Christ. The word 'Christ' is the Greek translation of the Hebrew *Mashiah* ('Anointed'). The term appears first in Lev. 4.3–5 as the anointed priest. In Scripture, it was initially used as the designation for anyone with a divine mission – such as priests, prophets, and kings. Eventually, the concept was associated with the idea of the end of days. Interwoven with the belief in the days of the Messiah are the notions of the resurrection of the dead, reward and punishment, the Last Judgement, and heaven and hell.

Messianism became a central element in the literature of the second Temple. The doctrine of the arrival of the Messiah and the resurrection of the dead was a major feature of Pharisaic belief, and dominated the literature of the Apocrypha and Pseudepigrapha. Although the Messiah was now viewed as an ideal human person who would rescue the nation, there was no expectation that he would be in any way divine.

When the Temple was destroyed in 70 CE, the belief in a Messiah helped the nation to endure, and penetrated all aspects of Jewish life. According to Moses Maimonides (12th cent.), Messianic hope is one of the 13 principles of the Jewish faith. In the kabbalah (mystical doctrine) of Isaac Luria (16th cent.), the Messianic era will be characterized by a period of *tikkun* (repair). During these times of catastrophe, Jewish scholars made calculations based on the numerical values of Hebrew words to determine the date of the coming of the Messiah. Such Messianic expectations gave rise to the belief in various false messiahs throughout history.

In the modern world, belief in the arrival of the Messiah has dwindled in the face of increasing secularization. Some non-Orthodox movements (such as Reform and Conservative Judaism) have translated belief in the Messiah into a belief in a Messianic period. In this light, Zionism too can be viewed as a secularization of the Messianic idea. Nonetheless, there still exist Jewish traditionalists who eagerly await the coming of the Messiah.

Within Christianity, Christology has focused on the nature of Jesus. The New Testament presents various facts about Jesus' person and ministry, but, unlike the Jewish Messianic expectation, the early Church quickly perceived Jesus to be divine as well as human. Christian theologians were concerned to explore how divine and human attributes could reside in one person. From the 2nd cent., these writers were anxious to explain how the Word, which is the expression of God, appeared on earth as the historical person of Jesus Christ.

Many theologians struggled to make sense of this doctrine of the incarnation, some emphasizing the human side of Christ's nature, and some the divine side. Arius (3rd–4th cent.), for example, argued for the unity of the Godhead, thereby denying that the Son is truly God. While insisting that Jesus was fully human, he maintained that there are not two natures in Christ. Instead, he believed that the nature of the Son took the place of the human soul in the historical Christ. Rejecting this interpretation, the Creed of the Council of Nicaea in 325 used the phrase 'being of one substance with the

Father', and 'became man'. Apollinarius (4th cent.) contended that the divine nature took the place of Christ's human spirit so that Jesus was truly God, but less than fully man. Other scholars, however, were anxious to separate Jesus' divinity and humanity, and in maintaining both they almost implied he was two separate persons.

The Council of Ephesus (431) asserted that he who was born of Mary is God. Subsequently, Eutyches (5th cent.) maintained that the union of the human and divine took place in a pre-existent state, but later coalesced into one. In response to this, the Council of Chalcedon (451) decreed that there is one Christ in two natures without division.

During the Reformation, Lutheranism stressed the unity of Christ's person, tending to argue that, in becoming human, Christ generally abstained from the use of divine attributes. Reformed theologies generally emphasized the difference between the divine and the human. Subsequent theological reflection has continued to focus on the true nature of Christ, and this issue still vexes Christian thinkers today.

Church *see* House of worship

Circumcision *see* Initiation rites

Clergy *see* Ordination

Clothing

(Headcovering) (*Kippah*) (*Shatnes*) (*Sheitel*) (Skull Cap) (*Tsitsit*) (Wig) (*Yarmulke*): In the Bible there are various references to different kinds of dress. On many occasions, clothing emphasized a person's status or rank; for example, a hairy cloak was worn by ascetics and Nazarites. During the period of mourning, widows wore characteristic dress, and prisoners had a special type of clothing. According to the Bible, various articles of clothing were appropriate to specific parts of the body. Yet despite such diversity of dress, the Bible lays down specific laws regarding the mingling of fabrics (*shatnes*) and the wearing of fringes (*tsitsit*). Garments containing mixed wool and linen are forbidden (Lev. 19.19). Fringes were also to be appended to each of the four corners of a garment (Deut. 22.12).

Women and men were also forbidden to wear each other's clothes (Deut. 22.5).

In Talmudic and Midrashic (biblical commentary) literature, there are also numerous references to men's clothing. On the upper part of the body a sleeveless tunic was worn, which was covered by a shirt. Over this was an outer tunic, and this was covered by a cloak. A hollow money belt was also worn. The lower part of the body was covered by breeches, over which trousers were worn. Socks and shoes covered the feet. In addition, a girdle (belt) was tied around the waist and an apron was also worn. A felt hat covered the head and a hat was worn over them. Finally, a scarf was also worn. Apart from the *tsitsit* and the prohibition against mixing fabrics, the dress of Jews during this period resembled that of other peoples. The scholar, however, wore distinctive garments, including a particular type of hat. It was against Jewish custom for women to wear their hair loose; this led to the practice of married women covering their hair or, from the 15th cent. on, shaving their hair and wearing a wig (*sheitel*).

Originally, there was no specific rabbinical dress, but among Eastern European Jews dinstinctive rabbinical garments came into fashion. By the 19th cent., the typical European rabbi wore a beard and a Polish-style costume which included a fur-trimmed gown and hat; this hat was exchanged for a wide-brimmed hat made of fur on the Sabbath (*streimel*). Through the centuries, Jews in Christian countries were forced to wear distinctive articles of clothing (such as badges and hats) to indicate their Jewish identity. In modern times, distinctive Jewish dress has largely disappeared, with the exception of a skull cap (known as *kippah* or *yarmulke*) worn as headcovering particularly in the synagogue, and a prayer shawl (tallith). Only the most Orthodox Jews such as the Hasidim continue to wear Eastern European dress.

Since Christianity rejected the Old Testament ritual laws, there have been no characteristic garments worn by the laity, except that, following the instructions of Paul (1 Cor. 11.5), women have traditionally covered their heads in church. Distinctive dress was worn by clergy when performing their liturgical duties. Such vestments originated in the ordinary clothing of antiquity. During the first centuries of the Christian era, a better type of dress was set aside for sacred functions, and the development of a priestly costume did not occur until the 4th–9th cent. By the 10th cent., the main liturgical vestments were established in the West.

In the 10th–13th cent., other additions were made. The surplice was used as a substitute for the alb on many occasions; the chasuble was reserved for the Mass; the tunicle became the distinctive vestment of the subdeacon. During this period, bishops used additional vestments such as sandals, mitre, and gloves. Later, the Liturgical Movement advocated a return to medieval models. The principal vestments of the Eastern Churches are similar to those of the West. In addition to such liturgical garments, various distinctive types of habits emerged within the religious orders (monks, friars, and nuns). They normally consist of a tunic, belt, scapular, hood for men, a veil for women, and a mantle for use in church and out of doors. In the modern period, clerical collars have become a common characteristic feature of clergy within a broad spectrum of religious denominations.

Codes of law

According to traditional Judaism, Moses received both the Written Law (Torah) and the unwritten or Oral Law on Mt Sinai. The doctrine of the Oral Law, embodying the explanation of the precepts contained in the Torah, was developed by the Pharisees. Through their interpretation of Scripture they were able to formulate biblical precepts in greater detail and also to apply scriptural law to changing circumstances. Initially, the Oral Law was not written down, but eventually it was recorded in the Mishnah and further developed in the Talmud.

The first code of law that embraced earlier precedent was Yehudai Gaon's (8th cent.) *Halakhot Pesukot*, which arranged its material according to topic. This work served as a basis for a number of later abbreviations and expanded reworkings, including the *Halakhot Gedolot* of Simeon Kayyara (9th cent.). The next important code was the codification of law by Isaac Alfasi (11th cent.). This was followed by Moses Maimonides's (12th cent.) *Mishneh Torah*, which included all Talmudic law arranged according to subject-matter. French scholars in the same period also produced legal codes in imitation of Alfasi's code.

In the 14th cent., Jacob ben Asher produced the *Arbaah Turim*, in which he divided the law into the topics of daily conduct, dietary requirements, family matters, and civil concerns. Here he presented the views of the Talmud as well as other codifiers. This work served as the basis of the *Shulhan Arukh* of Joseph Karo (16th cent.), which has become the standard Code of Jewish Law with additions by Moses Isserles (16th cent.) in the modern Orthodox world. The non-Orthodox branches of Judaism, however, have not reached a consensus concerning what are the minimal requirements of Jewish law – thus there are no authoritative codes in these movements.

Given their rejection of the legal requirements of the Hebrew Scriptures, there has not been a similar preoccupation with law among Christians. Nonetheless, from the earliest period there has been an awareness of natural law. Thus Paul in Rom. 2.15 wrote that Gentiles 'show that what the law requires is written on their hearts, while their conscience also bears witness . . .', although they do not have the Torah of Moses. Through the centuries, such a conviction has animated Christian consciousness.

As far as canon law is concerned, the corpus of law developed slowly. In the 4th cent., the canons promulgated at Nicaea gained authority in both the East and West. Eventually, the canons of other councils were formulated and, by the 5th cent., canonical collections began to appear. Simultaneously, the decrees of bishops served as another source of ecclesiastical legislation. From the 4th cent., special authority came to be attached to letters of the popes. In the 4th–5th cent., collections of canons were also ascribed to fictitious authors. Under Charlemagne (8th–9th cent.), some standardization took place.

In the Middle Ages, Gratian issued his collection of law *Decretum*, which was a turning point in the history of canon law. In the Roman Catholic Church, the *Corpus Iuris Canonici* came to enjoy authority through the centuries; the standard text is now *Codex Iuris Canonici*. Yet, despite such collections of law as well as local canons, law within Christianity never attained the binding authority of the legal heritage within traditional Judaism.

Cohen *see* Priesthood

Coming of age

(Bar Mitzvah) (Confirmation): Within the Jewish tradition, a boy reaches religious adulthood at the age of 13. From this point, he is counted as a member of the quorum for prayer (minyan). Prior to the 15th cent., there was no evidence of a 'bar mitzvah' ('son of the commandment') ceremony. Eventually, however, the rite of bar mitzvah emerged, when a boy reaching the age of adulthood was allowed to pray with tephillin (phylacteries) and read from the Torah.

Among Eastern European Jews, a boy was usually called to the Torah on the first Monday or Thursday after his 13th birthday. In Western Europe, the ceremony took place at Sabbath morning services, when the boy would recite Torah blessings, chant a portion of the Torah, and read the Haftarah (a section from the Prophets). This has now become the prevailing custom throughout the world. It also became customary for the bar mitzvah boy to deliver a discourse.

In recent times, a girl who has attained her religious majority can have a 'bat mitzvah' ('daughter of the commandment'), a ceremonial equivalent of the bar mitzvah but designed for girls. This celebration appeared in the 19th cent., but the ceremony did not take place during the synagogue service. More recently, it has become a common procedure. The nature of this ceremony varies considerably. In some Orthodox synagogues the bat mitzvah girl is allowed to participate in a limited way in the service, but in non-Orthodox congregations a bat mitzvah resembles a bar mitzvah in every particular. The service of confirmation in non-Orthodox synagogues has been borrowed from the Church, and introduced as a ceremony for boys and girls who have finished the course of instruction in religion school; it normally takes place at the age of 15.

In the Church, the rite of confirmation dates from the early Church. Some theologians find instances of it in the imposition of hands by the apostles on the Samaritan converts (Acts 8) and by Paul on the disciples at Ephesus (Acts 19). Subsequently, washing with water, anointing with oil, and laying on of hands came to be associated with initiation into Christianity.

In the Eastern Church, the custom of conferring confirmation at the same time as baptism, even with infants, was retained. However, confirmation was often delayed in the West until the candidate could be presented in person, and the service was always conducted by a bishop, following the biblical precedent of the apostles. In the Roman Catholic Church, the ceremony is essentially a renewal of baptismal vows and is independent of first communion. In the Church of England, as in many Protestant Churches where there is emphasis on instruction, confirmation is a necessary step before Holy Communion can be received. So for Anglicans, confirmation is similar to bar mitzvah in that both are rites of passage enabling young people to become full members of their respective religious communities. For members of the Roman Catholic and Orthodox Churches, however, confirmation is really part of baptism.

Commandments *see* Law

Communion, Holy *see* Eucharist

Community

In ancient times, the Jews were organized into clans. Eventually, as they began to settle in towns, the structure of the community became urbanized. Throughout the period of the monarchy, the population was organized into territorial or tribal units. Later, after the Babylonian exile in the 6th cent. BCE, the foundations were laid for self-governing communal institutions. Outside Israel, the synagogue served as a house of prayer, as a school, and as a study hall for adults. It was the focus of communal activities.

In the 2nd cent. BCE, Jews in Alexandria were allowed to have their own corporation with a council, which was empowered to conduct communal affairs. In the Roman Empire, the Jewish community conducted their own courts. By the end of the second Temple period, both Israel and Babylonia were headed by central authorities. The patriarchate with the Sanhedrin had such a role in Israel. In Babylonia, the *exilarch* was the head of the community together with the *geonim*, who were the supreme religious authorities. In North Africa, and in Spain, the head of the community was the *nagid*.

In the Franco-German region during the Middle Ages, communal leadership was exercised by rabbinic authorities, and the congregation (*kehillah*) was often located in a special part of the town. Wherever Jews lived, life was regulated by Jewish law which was enforced by a court consisting of a panel of religious judges. Often the community's president was recognized by the secular or Church authorities as the head of the community. In the Ottoman Empire, central authority was vested in a chief rabbi.

After the Enlightenment, Jews became full members of the larger societies in which they lived, thereby removing the necessity of the communal organization. In the modern world, the traditional pattern of communal life has been superseded by local communal organizations. Often the synagogue or Jewish community centre functions as a mini-community. Yet, despite such changes, Jews throughout the world feel themselves to be part of a world-wide Jewish community sharing a common cultural and religious heritage. Everyone who is born of a Jewish mother or who has joined the community by conversion is a member. Religious belief is not a necessary condition of belonging.

Unlike the Jewish community, which is based largely on a shared ethnic and historical tradition, the Church essentially constitutes a sacramental community of believers. In the New Testament, the primitive Church is depicted as the inheritor of the promises made to Israel. It was the body of Christ on earth, its different members working together in harmony animated by God's Holy Spirit. This conception was elaborated as time passed. Increasing emphasis was placed on the corporate nature of believing Christians. The Church was to be a holy, world-wide and apostolic body. Its membership, orders and ministry are all constituted by participation in the sacraments of baptism and Holy Communion.

After the schism between the East and the West, the Roman Catholic and Eastern Churches maintained that the other was in schism: each Church believed itself to be the true inheritor of the visible Church. The Reformation intensified such confusion about which groupings constitute the true Church. In modern times, however, there has generally been a more constructive and less polemical attitude to differences that have heretofore divided Christendom. Today, there is a growing awareness of the unity of all believers. A heightened interest in Christian ecumenism has led Christians in all denominations to a greater recognition of the universality of the Church and the participation of each Christian in the body of Christ.

Compassion

Compassion is one of the most important virtues in Judaism. It is an attribute of God, who is himself frequently described in rabbinic literature as 'the Compassionate One'. Since God shows compassion, human beings should follow his example – not only to each other, but also to the animal world. Compassion is equally prominent in Christianity. Jesus is shown in the Gospels as feeding and healing people out of his compassion. Since the ideal Christian life is seen as an imitation of Christ, compassion remains an essential quality.

Confession

In Judaism, confession of sin is an essential part of atonement. The sin must be acknowledged, confessed, and a new resolution made. There are many examples of confession in the Scriptures, such as the one made by Saul (1 Sam. 15) and David (2 Sam. 12). On the Day of Atonement, the high priest used to confess the sins of himself, the priests and the people in the Temple. The Day of Atonement services still contain prayers of confession, and these are spoken in the first person plural: the whole community is acknowledging its sin. Confession of sin is also made in private prayer and during other congregational services.

Judaism does not require an intermediary between the sinner and God. Christianity, however, has a long tradition of auricular confession – that is, private confession to a priest who is authorized in God's name to forgive the sins mentioned. In Roman Catholic churches, for example, confessional booths are constructed so that the penitent can be heard privately, and it is also an opportunity for spiritual direction. At the same time, communal confession is part of the Church liturgy and a general confession is made at most services, particularly before Holy Communion is celebrated. In this respect, the Jewish and Christian practices are very similar.

Confirmation *see* Coming of age

Congregation

(Minyan): According to Orthodox Judaism, public worship can only take place if 10 adult males are present (minyan). No rabbi or professional leader is necessary and the service does not have to be in a synagogue. The emphasis on having enough people reflects the Jewish stress on the importance of religious community, even though private prayer is still recognized as valuable. Non-Orthodox Judaism counts women in the minyan or does away with the concept altogether.

'Congregation' can also refer to the members of a particular synagogue, and this is the normal use of the term among Christians. In the Christian liturgy, a distinction is made between the words of the priest or religious leader and the responses of the congregation, but there is no minimum number required before a Christian public service can take place.

Conscience

Within traditional Judaism, morality is based on revealed law. According to rabbinic teaching, the corpus of legal precepts contained in the Pentateuch was given by God to Moses on Mt Sinai. Thus the norms of correct behaviour were addressed to the nation as a corporate entity. The prophetic books reinforce the importance of the moral code, particularly in spheres of social concern. The immorality of the people consisted in their transgression of divine decrees. Within this biblical framework, individual conscience and decision-making was replaced by adherence to covenantal obligations.

Biblical law was developed and expanded through rabbinic interpretation. Here the role of conscience was subordinated to a hermeneutical system based on a number of formal principles. Social legislation was motivated by the desire to expand the scope of law to cover as broad a range of situations as possible. As Judaism developed through the centuries, moral debate took place within the confines of this system of rabbinic jurisprudence, and legal decisions were recorded in various codes of Jewish law. However, the rabbis did accept the notion of people having good and evil inclinations. The function of the good inclination was to overcome the evil inclination and impel the individual to keep the law in its entirety. So, for the rabbis, conscience was not used to decide what was right, only to encourage the believer to do what was right.

In modern times, traditional Jewish moral thinking has evolved along similar lines. As in the past, the function of conscience has been subordinated to the system of Jewish law. However, within non-Orthodox religious movements, such as Reform Judaism, the concept of personal conscience plays a fundamental role. The human conscience is viewed within these movements as a complex capacity to live in conformity with those principles it judges to be good. Given the rejection of the biblical and rabbinic corpus of law, non-Orthodox Jews feel at liberty to utilize their own individual responses to decide which courses of action and thought are morally acceptable in contemporary society.

As for the non-Orthodox Jew, the conscience for the Christian serves as the foundation of the moral system. In the New Testament, the word *syneidesis* (conscience) was adopted from the Stoics and used in various contexts. Paul employed the term to refer to an interior judge of past actions – as a moral capacity it could either condemn or approve (Rom. 2.14f.). During the Middle Ages, it was usual to distinguish between the general knowledge of moral principles and their application to particular cases. The former was based on a moral discernment unaffected by the Fall, but opinions differed as to whether its source resided in the affections and the will or in practical reason. Reformers, however, reacted against the theory of an uncorrupted natural ability to distinguish between good and evil. Instead, they stressed the dependence of the Christian conscience on faith.

In the period of the Enlightenment, some theologians suggested that conscience can be identified with God's voice. In modern times, a number of writers have stressed that conscience serves as the mediator between the law of God and the will of human beings. But since conscience is liable to error, most Christian moralists have been reluctant to identify its pronouncements with divine law. Instead, it is viewed as the means by which individuals can learn the will of God within church fellowship, assisted by the grace of God in response to prayer. Given Christianity's view of biblical law, it is not surprising that there has been this shift away from traditional Jewish ethical legalism to an individualistic approach to ethics in which personal decision-making guided by conscience plays a decisive role.

Conversion

Within Judaism, conversion is the decision of a non-Jew to become a member of the Jewish people. Traditionally, the rites of conversion for the male involve circumcision and immersion; for women, immersion is the essential ritual. During the Temple period, the convert was also required to bring a sacrifice. In modern times, the educational process preceding conversion, as well as the ritual requirements, vary according to the religious movement supervising the procedure.

Among Jews, conversion has had a long history. In biblical times, Ruth was a Moabite proselyte who subsequently was viewed as a model convert. In the 2nd cent. BCE, John Hyrcanus forced the Idumeans to convert. In the Greco-Roman era, some of the greatest rabbinic scholars – such as Shemayah (1st cent.), Avtalyon (1st cent.), and Akiva (1st–2nd cent.) were reputed to be descendants of converts; others such as Onkelos (2nd cent.) had themselves converted to Judaism. In rabbinic sources, there are numerous expressions praising converts and their contribution to the Jewish people (although a minority among Talmudic sages expressed some opposition to converts). During this period, Jewish missionizing took place, but disappeared after Christianity became the official religion of the Empire. Subsequently, Jews refrained from active proselytizing, partly for fear of Christian persecution and partly because they believed that pious Gentiles could also be pleasing to God.

In modern times, a number of non-Jews have embraced Judaism, but the Orthodox rabbinate has refused to accept the validity of conversion under non-Orthodox auspices. In addition, Orthodoxy denies the Jewishness of offspring of non-Orthodox female converts. When asked to conduct a Jewish religious service for such converts (such as a wedding), Orthodox rabbis require a new Orthodox conversion. There is thus considerable friction in the Jewish world about the nature of conversion

and the status of those individuals who have been converted.

Unlike Judaism, where there has been a general reluctance to seek converts and where potential converts are initially discouraged, the call to conversion is a central theme of Christianity. In the New Testament, the Greek words for conversion or repentance are *metanoia* and *epistrophe* – both terms signify a reorientation of the whole person. Paul's conversion as recorded in Acts and his epistles has been regarded as a model of the conversion experience. Augustine's (4th–5th cent.) has also been viewed in a similar way. In both cases, Christ's redeeming power was seen as providing a new life, free from the guilt of past shortcomings.

During the Scholastic period, reflection about the nature of conversion waned, but later became a central aspect of Martin Luther's (15th–16th cent.) theology. Subsequently, there are frequent references to conversion in the writings of Ignatius Loyola (15th–16th cent.), the Pietists in Germany (17th–18th cent.), John Wesley (18th cent.), and Jonathan Edwards (18th cent.). In modern times, a number of scholars have utilized aspects of the biblical understanding of conversion to develop a systematic treatment of this topic. Other Christians, who describe themselves as 'born again', have emphasized the centrality of conversion in the evolution of their own religious faith.

In the past, it was generally thought among Christians that there could be no salvation for those who were outside the body of Christ. Support for missionary activity was therefore an essential duty, and this contrasts sharply with the Jewish idea that it is not necessary to be Jewish to be acceptable to God. In recent years, however, the Christian attitude towards other faiths has become more ecumenical, and many Christians would now disapprove of trying to convert adherents of other religions to Christianity.

Courts

(Beth Din) (Sanhedrin): In the Bible, Moses judged the people (Exod. 18.13); eventually Jethro, his father-in-law, advised him to create a system of judges. Later, when the Israelites entered the land, judges served as leaders of the people. A number of kings, such as Solomon (10th cent. BE), also acted as judges.

During the period of the second Temple, courts were established consisting of 3, 23, or 71 judges. Each locality had a court of three judges (Beth Din) which ruled on civil matters. All towns with a population of 120 or more male adults had a court of 23 judges which could rule on offences that merited corporal or capital punishment.

According to tradition, Jerusalem had three courts of 23 judges – one was located at the entrance of the Temple Mount, another at the entrance to the Temple courtyard, and the third was in the Chamber of Hewn Stones. In addition, the Sanhedrin consisted of 71 members and ruled on questions of Jewish law and acted in trials. With the fall of Jerusalem in 70 CE, Johanan ben Zakkai moved the Sanhedrin to Yavneh. Later, its authority was challenged by other Jewish centres, particularly in Babylonia. By the 5th cent., the Sanhedrin was dissolved.

For many centuries, Jews lived in their own autonomous communities. In this environment, the Beth Din ruled on all judicial questions. However, with the Emancipation, secular state courts were opened to Jewry and the previous authority of the Beth Din diminished. In modern times, Jewish courts deal primarily with matters of religious divorce and personal religious status.

The Christian rejection of the system of legislation contained in Scripture meant that religious law has not served the same function in Christianity as in Judaism. Instead, from the very beginning of the Church, Christ was viewed as the master whose teaching and ministry set the pattern for the Christian life. Nonetheless, order and discipline were required for the community.

The earliest documents that purport to come from the apostles are manuals of liturgical and disciplinary regulations such as the *Didache*. Eventually five regional councils held in Asia Minor and Syria during the 4th cent, constructed the nucleus of canon law. Topics dealt with include Church structures, the dignity of the clergy, public penance, liturgical rules, and the readmission of schismatics. As time passed, later councils issued further decrees, and collections of ecclesiastical law were produced by numerous scholars which, in modern times, have served as the basis for contemporary canon law. Throughout its history, Church law was supervised by a system of ecclesiastical courts that ensured that the rules of the Church were enforced. These courts still exist, but, like the Jewish Bet Din, their influence is much diminished. They are primarily concerned nowadays with Church property and clergy discipline.

Covenant

Contract between two parties. For example, in Gen. 6.18 God informed Noah that he would be granted a covenant and be saved by means of the ark. After the flood, God made the covenant in which he promised never to destroy all life by a flood (Gen. 9.8–17). Covenants between human persons were also common in the Bible.

The formation of a covenant was frequently marked by a symbolic act. In Gen. 26.31, it was accompanied by a meal and an oath; Jer. 34.18 refers to passing between two halves of a calf cloven in two. Frequently, symbols such as the rainbow (Gen. 9.13), or the monument of stones erected by Jacob and Laban (Gen. 31.51), were used to mark the formation of a covenant. The Bible also records God's covenant with Abraham; this involved circumcision for Abraham and his descendants (Gen. 17).

The Sinaitic covenant in Exod. 19–24 is the covenant par excellence between God and human beings. A voluntary act, it was accompanied by the bringing of sacrifices, the sprinkling of their blood upon the people, and the meal consumed by Moses and the elders. After the covenant was finalized, Moses ascended the mountain to receive the tablets of stone on which divine laws were inscribed.

In subsequent Jewish thought, the concept of the covenant has played a central role. Contemporary Jewish theologians continue to regard the agreement between the Jewish people and God as a fundamental aspect of the Jewish heritage. Yet within non-Orthodox Judaism, allowances for revisions to the original convenant are allowed on the basis of belief in progressive revelation.

In the early Church, the belief that the covenant established with the Jewish nation would be superseded by a new order became a central feature of the Christian faith. Through the death of Jesus, the old Sinaitic covenant was abrogated and a new covenant was instituted. For the Christian, this new covenant was focused in baptism and Holy Communion, and was brought about by the death of

Jesus. Gal. 4.21–28 contrasts the covenant of promise made to Abraham with the covenant of law made on Mt Sinai; the former is understood as a foreshadowing of the new covenant made in Jesus, since it is grounded in faith rather than law.

As Christian doctrine developed, the biblical concept of the covenant has received attention within Protestantism, beginning with the writings of J. H. Bullinger (16th cent.), continuing with the reflections of theologians of the Genevan tradition, and culminating in the theology of English Puritans of the 16th–17th cent. From such roots, the concept of covenant was of particular importance in the thinking of the early settlers in the New World. Interest in covenant theology continued into the 18th–19th cent., but in a diminished form. In recent times, it has been overshadowed by other theological concerns.

Creation

The Hebrew Scriptures begin with two creation stories. In the first, God created the universe in six days and rested on the seventh (Gen. 1.1–24). In the second (Gen. 2.4–24), Adam is formed from the earth, animated by God's breath, and serves as the source of Eve (who was created from his rib). Adam and Eve are then placed in the Garden of Eden, but are banished after disobeying God. In the Wisdom literature of the Apocrypha, the Wisdom of God is seen as the agent of creation (Wisd. 7.22). In rabbinic literature, the biblical narrative has served as the basis of considerable speculation. This was particularly acute in mystical sources, where attempts were made to penetrate the meaning of creation. According to this tradition, God's first step was an inward withdrawal of *En Sof* (the Infinite) into this hidden depth. This was followed by the emanation of the *sephirot* (channels of God's manifestation). In the thought of Isaac Luria (16th cent.), this process was accompanied by the 'breaking of the vessels', whereby the sparks of the primeval light of creation spilled on to the lower *sephirot*. They are to be restored to their original state through Messianic repair (*tikkun*) of the cosmos.

In the history of Jewish philosophy, speculation about the nature of creation also played a major role. In the 1st cent., Philo attempted to reconcile the Greek doctrine of creation with the scriptural account of *creatio ex nihilo*. During the medieval period, Saadiah Gaon (10th cent.) maintained that the world was created in time out of nothing and is separate from the Creator. In the next century, neo-Platonists such as Isaac Israeli and Solomon ibn Gabirol described a timeless emanation of primary matter. Later, philosophers of the Middle Ages debated the question whether matter is eternal or created. Within modern Jewish thought, the belief in a literal understanding of the creation account has been largely rejected. Instead, most Jewish theologians have attempted to harmonize the biblical narrative with the theory of evolution.

In the New Testament, Paul describes Jesus as the 'wisdom of God' (1 Cor. 1.24), 'in whom are hid all the treasures of wisdom and knowledge' (Col. 2.3). He taught that the creation of the world was planned with Christ in mind – God's intention was to bring everything to unity in him. Christ is the acme of creation, and through him all things are restored. The writer of the Fourth Gospel identified Christ with the Logos, the divine Word of God, through whom all creation came into being (John 1.1–8).

During the patristic period, some Church Fathers such as Justin (2nd cent.) and Clement of Alexandria (2nd–3rd cent.) argued that God used pre-existent matter in forming the universe. Other theologians, however, maintained the doctrine of *creatio ex nihilo* (creation out of nothing), which eventually became the central teaching of the Church. In the Middle Ages, Thomas Aquinas (13th cent.) asserted that although creation can be rationally understood, it is incapable of proof, 'being credible but not demonstrable'. Such a view was echoed by the philosopher Immanuel Kant in the 18th cent.; he held that reason was incapable of proving (or disproving) the creation of the world or its contrary.

In modern times, scientific knowledge has caused considerable confusion in Christian circles concerning the nature of creation. Many 19th-cent. Christians were profoundly disturbed by Darwin's theory of evolution. Nonetheless, some theologians such as Teilhard de Chardin (19th–20th cent.) have attempted to find a synthesis between science and faith. For Teilhard, the cosmos is a process that mirrors the inner life of God – all life is evolving towards convergence and unity. For a number of

Process theologians, God is conceived of as compassionately concerned with the developing cosmos. Rather than standing apart from his creation, God is viewed as intimately involved with its evolution. More recently, other Christian thinkers have formulated a theology of creation in which ecological concern is of major importance, and this emphasis can also be found in the work of modern Jewish theologians.

Creeds

(Dogma) (Principles of Faith): In the Torah there is no formulation of the central principles of the Jewish faith, although Deut. 6.4, 'Hear, O Israel: The Lord our God is one Lord', is the essential tenet of Judaism. Attempts subsequently were made to present the essential beliefs of Judaism. In the 1st cent., Philo stressed that the acceptance of Scripture commits one to the belief in the existence and unity of God, divine providence, and the eternity of the law.

In the Middle Ages, numerous Jewish theologians attempted to present a credal formulation of the Jewish faith. The most important presentation was that of Moses Maimonides (12th cent.), who argued in his commentary on the Mishnah that there are 13 basic principles: (1) God's existence; (2) God's unity; (3) God's incorporeality; (4) God's eternity; (5) God alone is to be worshipped; (6) belief in prophecy; (7) Moses was the greatest of the prophets; (8) God revealed the Torah to Moses; (9) the Torah is unchangeable; (10) God's omniscience; (11) reward and punishment; (12) the Messiah; (13) resurrection of the dead. Maimonides's principles were later included in the prayer book as the hymn *Yigdal*, and as a supplementary reading after the morning service.

In later centuries, a number of Jewish theologians, such as Hasdai Crescas (14th–15th cent.) and Joseph Albo (14th–15th cent.), disputed Maimonides's formulation. The lack of consensus among these scholars was a result of the fact that there is no universally recognized system of belief within Judaism. Some thinkers went so far as to reject the entire notion of differentiating between principles and non-principles. In modern times, there has been a general acceptance within Orthodoxy of Maimonides' formulation, but there are differing views as to how these beliefs are to be interpreted. Within non-Orthodox Judaism, a number of Maimonides' principles have been set aside, and there is no consensus as to what constitutes the cardinal tenets of the faith.

Unlike Judaism, Christianity has always been a credal faith. In the New Testament, creed-like statements appear in the Gospels (Mark 8.29) and in Paul's epistles (1 Cor. 12.3; 8.6; 15.3–7; 2 Cor. 13.14). The best known of the creeds are the Apostles' Creed, the Nicene Creed, and the Athanasian Creed. The Apostles' Creed had its origin in the baptismal creed used in Rome at the beginning of the 3rd cent. The Nicene Creed was proclaimed by the Council of Nicaea in 325 – its intent was the rejection of Arianism (a doctrine that Jesus Christ was God by courtesy but not in fact). The creed that is now known as Nicene is related to the Council of Constantinople (381) and contains an affirmation of the deity of the Holy Spirit. It is arguably the most universal of all the creeds. The Athanasian Creed was composed by an Augustinian theologian after the middle of the 5th cent.

The development of theology in the Middle Ages led to the formulation of other creeds. In the 16th cent., the Council of Trent promulgated canons and decrees that shaped Roman Catholicism until the Second Vatican Council. In the Protestant world, confessions constituted comprehensive statements of the Christian faith. In the modern period, the writing of creeds and confessions has become common practice within various Christian groups, but no credal formulation has had the same influence as the three ancient creeds. Thus, unlike Judaism where the issuing of creeds was of marginal importance, credal formulation has occupied a central role in Christian self-understanding through the centuries.

Cremation *see* Funeral rites

Criminal law *see* Law

Cross *see* Symbolism

Crucifix *see* Symbolism

D

Daily prayer

The practice of praying three times a day is found in the Bible: Dan. 6.10 states that Daniel got down on his knees three times a day and prayed and gave thanks before God. In ancient times, daily sacrifices were offered in the Temple in Jerusalem. After the destruction of the second Temple in 70 CE, these sacrifices ceased and fixed morning (*Shaharit*) and afternoon services (*Minhah*) were established by the rabbis for synagogue worship which corresponds with the daily morning and afternoon sacrifices. The evening prayer (*Maariv*) corresponds with the nightly burning of fats and limbs.

The morning service is the most extensive of the three daily prayer services (the other two services resemble it in form). It consists of: (1) the morning benedictions; (2) *Pesuke de-Zimra* ('Verses of Song'); (3) *Barekhu* (the reader's summons to prayer); (4) the Shema (consisting of Deut. 6.4–9; 11.13–21; and Num. 15.37–41) and its benedictions; (5) the *Amidah* (18 benedictions) and its repetition by the reader; (6) *Tahanun* (prayers of supplication); (7) reading of the Law on Mondays and Thursdays; (8) *Alenu* (prayer proclaiming God's sovereignty over Israel and the world); and (9) mourners' Kaddish. During the daily morning prayer, a prayer shawl (tallit) and phylacteries (tephillin) are worn by men. For all three daily services, the ideal is to pray with a minyan (a quorum of 10 adult men). Without this number, certain parts of the service cannot be recited. The non-Orthodox movements have altered or suspended this traditional requirement.

In the Church, the practice of saying prayers at fixed times during the day was taken over from Jewish worship. The monks of Palestine, Egypt, and Gaul appear to be the first to have constructed a complete office with specifications for what was to be said. They established formulae that included the recitation of the entire Psalter. Meanwhile, in cathedrals and parish churches a simpler office developed.

From the late 5th cent., however, the traditional monastic office of seven daily hours (lauds, prime, terce, sext, none, vespers and compline) and a night office (matins) developed. Eventually in the West, the arrangement of the office was fixed by Benedict (6th cent.). This use was introduced into England in the 7th cent., the Frankish kingdom in the 8th cent., and Spain in the 11th cent. This usage continued in the Roman Catholic Church until recently. All eight hours consist of psalms, hymns, lessons, antiphons, responses and versicles, and prayers. At the Reformation, monastic offices largely disappeared in the Protestant Churches. Their place was taken, for example in the Church of England, by the two offices of morning and evening prayers (matins and evensong), which were laid down in the Book of Common Prayer.

Dais

(Bimah) (Pulpit); The custom of reading the Torah publicly from a raised platform dates back at least as far as the time of Ezra (5th cent. BCE). A bimah, or dais, is a feature of every synagogue. It is situated either in the centre of the building, or against the western wall, opposite the ark, or, as in most Reform temples, at the eastern end, next to the ark. Its purpose is to enable the reader or preacher to be heard by everyone. A bimah is still used in the Syriac churches, and churches built on the basilica plan have two ambos, or raised platforms. In churches constructed in the cruciform pattern, the reader or preacher speaks from an elevated stand of wood or stone, known as the pulpit, which is generally at the north side of the nave. In a few Protestant churches where preaching is considered the most important part of the service, the pulpit is situated at the east end of the church, instead of the altar.

Damnation *see* Judgement

David

King of Israel in 11th–10th cent. BCE. Born in Bethlehem, he was the great-grandson of Boaz and Ruth, and the son of Jesse. Initially he was a shepherd, but later joined King Saul's entourage. When Saul was dejected, David played him music. His victory over Goliath made him a national hero, and he subsequently married Saul's daughter, Michal. Eventually Saul viewed David as a threat to the succession of his son Jonathan, and attempted to kill him. After Saul and Jonathan were killed in a battle with the Philistines on Mt Gilboa, David became king over Judah (2 Sam. 2.4).

He then defeated the forces of Saul's other son, Ishbosheth, and became ruler over the entire country. Realizing the need to create a neutral administrative centre, he conquered Jerusalem and established it as his capital. There he installed the ark of the covenant. However, his desire to build a temple was thwarted by Nathan, who told him that no person involved in war should do so (1 Chron. 22.8). His son, Solomon, eventually became his heir.

In the Jewish tradition, David became idealized, and the Psalms were attributed to him. On all occasions in the Jewish calendar he is recalled in prayer; in addition, the *Amidah* prayer, grace after meals and blessings following the reading of the law are regarded as invalid if the prayer for the House of David is omitted. The blessing for the New Moon contains the declaration: 'David, King of Israel, lives on'. During the festival of Tabernacles, he is mentioned as one of the seven guests. Moreover, it was believed that the Messiah would emerge from the House of David; this became the subject of numerous stories in the *aggadah* (narrative).

In the New Testament, the evangelists accept the tradition that the Messiah would be of Davidic descent. The birth stories of Jesus emphasize this and, according to Matt. 21.9, it is as the 'Son of David' that Christ was welcomed before his passion. His ancestry is also emphasized in Rom. 1.3; 2 Tim. 2.18; and Rev. 5.5; 22.16. In patristic sources, the idea of David as the type of Christ is frequently found. According to Augustine (4th–5th cent.), David's victory over Goliath parallels that of Christ over Satan. Again, Cyril of Alexandria (5th cent.) argued that David's sling foreshadows the cross of Christ. For Gregory the Great (6th cent.), the victory of David in his weakness foreshadows that of the Church and the Christian martyrs. Thus David's role in the Church is linked to the Jewish concept of a Messiah, but is interpreted in the light of Christ's ministry.

Day of atonement

(Yom Kippur): This is observed on the tenth day of the month of Tishri and is the holiest day in the Jewish year. It is kept as a strict fast from sunset until nightfall of the next day, and its purpose is to atone for sin, obeying the biblical injunction to 'afflict yourselves' (Lev. 16.29–31). Since atonement cannot be made until forgiveness has been sought from the one sinned against, it is usual to spend the day before Yom Kippur seeking reconciliation from enemies. Also, a chicken is sometimes killed, symbolizing the transfer of guilt from human to fowl. Five services are held in the synagogue, all emphasizing the confession of sin and the expression of penitence, and the day ends with the blowing of the shofar (ram's horn), indicating the end of the fast.

Although the Christian Church observes fast days, such as Ash Wednesday and Good Friday, there is no real equivalent to the Day of Atonement. This is because Christians do not believe that atonement can be made through fasting. Instead, forgiveness is a free gift of God, brought about by the sacrificial death of Jesus which can be freely appropriated by baptism, Holy Communion, and through living the Christian life.

Days of awe

(10 Days of Repentance): This is the name given to the 10 days beginning with the Jewish New Year (Rosh Hashanah) and ending with the Day of Atonement (Yom Kippur). These 10 days, 1–10 Tishri, make up the most solemn season of the Jewish year. The new year is traditionally the day when all humanity pass before God and are judged for the coming year; the final verdict is made on the Day of Atonement, and then supposedly the Book of Life, the heavenly ledger, is closed. The prayer, 'Inscribe us in the Book of Life', is a recurring theme of these 10 days.

There is no need for Christians to observe a similar period because they believe that Jesus has made atonement on the cross, once and for all, for the sins of the world. Eternal life is thus guaranteed for all who truly accept the gift in faith.

Death

According to Gen. 3.19, God informed man that he would return to earth from which he came. A number of biblical passages indicate that after death human beings dwell in a netherworld known by various names (such as She'ol). Although there is no clear statement of the resurrection of the dead in

Scripture, the rabbis were anxious to demonstrate this was a biblical doctrine.

Jewish law discusses the exact moment of death. The Talmud, for example, notes that death takes place when respiration has ceased. However, with the advance of medical knowledge, this definition has been refined. It is now possible to determine respiration in persons who previously would have been considered dead, or to resuscitate those who have stopped breathing. Thus some scholars have argued that death occurs when there has been both respiratory and cardiac arrest or when the brain stem is dead. A person who is critically ill, hovering between life and death, is considered to be alive. It is forbidden to hasten such an individual's death, but it is permitted to remove an external obstacle that may be preventing his or her demise.

Judaism decrees that no effort should be spared to save a dying patient. Yet, in the face of death, the devout are to accept God's decree. The utmost regard should be shown to a person who is dying. They are not to be left alone, and should be encouraged to confess their sins. All those who are present at the moment of death are to recite the blessing 'Blessed be the True Judge'.

After death has been determined, the eyes and mouth should be closed and, if necessary, the mouth should be tied shut. The body is then to be placed on the floor, covered with a sheet, and a lighted candle put close to the head. In the house of the deceased, mirrors are customarily covered and any standing water is poured out. Sitting with the body is considered a good deed, and it is desirable to recite psalms in the presence of the corpse. Before burial, the body is to be cleansed and clothed in shrouds.

In the New Testament, death is viewed as part of creation and essential to the nature of human beings (John 12.24; 1 Cor. 15.36; 1 Tim. 6.16). Other passages emphasize that death can be used positively in God's service (John 15.13; Phil. 2.17; 2 Tim. 4.6). Yet despite such a view, death is seen as the last enemy (1 Cor. 15.26, 55). It blights all human life (Matt. 4.16), and needs to be destroyed by Christ (Heb. 2.14f.). The power of Christ over death is linked with his combat and victory over the powers of evil (Rev. 20.14). Christ breaks the connection between death and sin and he himself has tasted its pangs (Acts 2.24; Heb. 2.9). He is the first-born of the dead (Rev. 1.5, 18), so that human beings may be saved from experiencing its sting (John 6.49; 8.53; 1 Cor. 15.55f.).

In the early Church, the practice of burial followed the customs of Judaism. Early Church sources do not forbid cremation, but the custom of burying was preferred. Because of the Church doctrines of the resurrection and the Second Coming as well as the emphasis on martyrdom, funeral services were occasions of celebration. However, from the 8th cent., the liturgy stressed praying for purification from purgatory and deliverance from hell. The ceremonies came to include vespers (the night before the funeral), matins and lauds (the dirge during the night), and the requiem mass (with prayers for absolution in the morning). At the graveside, committal prayers were offered. In the Protestant Churches, practices are generally less formalized.

Decalogue *see* Ten commandments

Deceit

Deceit is roundly condemned in both the Jewish and the Christian tradition. The Ten Commandments condemn bearing false witness (Exod. 20.16) and any form of lying is perceived as an offence to God. The rabbis taught that liars would not see God's glory, and Jonah of Geronah (13th cent.) classified nine different types of lie. Similarly, Jesus is described as saying that the devil is the father of lies (John 8.44). However, the Church Fathers – like the rabbis – conducted many debates over the centuries as to whether it was ever right to conceal the truth, and accepted that some forms of deceit were worse than others.

Demons

Evil spirits. The term *shedim* ('demons') appears only twice in the Bible (Deut. 32.17; Ps. 106.37) – in both cases, Israel is criticized for sacrificing to them. Arguably, Azazel – to whom the scapegoat was sent during the Day of Atonement ritual – was viewed as a prince of the demons. Subsequently, a complex demonology emerged in the Pseudepigrapha, Midrash (bibilical commentary) and Talmud.

In Midrashic literature and the Talmud the term *mazzikin* ('harmful ones') is used in addition to *shedim*. They are like the ministering angels in that they have wings, are invisible, and know the future. But they are similar to human beings in that they eat and drink, procreate, and die. In number, they far exceed the human race. According to legend, there are a number of precautions that can be taken to avoid such demonic beings. One should not venture out at night for example, particularly on Wednesdays and Fridays. Various incantations and adjurations were frequently used to ward off their influence.

During the Middle Ages, belief in demons was commonly accepted. Judah He-Hasid's (11th cent.) *Sefer Hasidim* frequently refers to their existence, and records how to stem their influence. In the Zohar (mystical commentary on the Pentateuch), the doctrine of divine emanation embraces 'the other side' (*sitra ahra*), a dimension of evil inhabited by the demons. When the two sides of the Divine are held in balance, they cannot exert their influence. But when they are torn apart, the side of impurity influenced by the demons is ascendant. In such a context, the wearing of amulets (often inscribed with the names of mystical angels) became a widespread practice.

Despite such beliefs, scholars from the Middle Ages to the present day have denied the existence of demons. Maimonides (12th cent.) identified them with wild animals and forbade the wearing of amulets. Abraham ibn Ezra (11th–12th cent.) denounced those who believed in their existence. In modern times, the belief in demons has largely disappeared within the various religious groupings in the Jewish community.

In the New Testament, there are frequent references to the devil, demons, and unclean spirits. Demons were allied with Satan's fallen angels (cf. Matt. 25.41; 2 Pet. 2.4; Jude 6; Rev. 12.4, 8). Heathen divining spirits were also viewed as demonic – they turned believers away from the gospel through wonders and false promises (1 Tim. 4.1; Rev. 16.14).

Paul envisaged the demonic opposition to Christ in terms of angelic principalities, authorities and powers, and thrones and dominations. Nonetheless, such forces were brought under control through the death and resurrection of Christ (1 Pet. 3.22; 2 Pet. 2.10–11).

In the Synoptic Gospels, Jesus triumphs over Satan's kingdom by expelling demons. In the early Church the act of ritual exorcism was frequently practised. Often, disturbed persons were prayed for by the entire congregation. However, it was only in the Middle Ages and post-Reformation era that such rituals were expanded. In the modern period, exorcism still takes place, but the belief in demons has been largely abandoned by most believers in response to the growth of scientific knowledge.

Devil

(Satan): In the Bible the term 'Satan' means an adversary. Thus in 1 Kings 11.14, 'The Lord raised up an adversary [Satan] against Solomon, Hadad the Edomite'. In later books of the Bible the term came to mean a supernatural being who accused man before God in the heavenly assembly. This is Satan's role in Job 1–2, where he challenges Job's loyalty to God. Here and in Zech. 3.1–2, Satan can act only within the limits set by God.

In the Apocrypha and Pseudepigrapha, the function of Satan is enlarged as it is further expanded in Midrashic (biblical commentary) literature and the Talmud. Previously, he was subordinate to God, but in these later sources he acts independently in encouraging human beings to disobey God's will. Thus in the Book of Jubilees he is called *Mastemah* ('Enmity'); in the Testament of the Twelve Patriarchs he is referred to as 'Belial'; in the Dead Sea Scrolls he is called the 'Angel of Darkness'. Subsequently, he played an important role in Jewish folk beliefs as well as in kabbalistic (mystical) texts (where different names are used), and is occasionally referred to in the liturgy.

Drawing on Jewish sources, the New Testament views the devil as an alien personal force in the universe. He attempts to destroy what God has created, and brings chaos where previously there was order. Although the New Testament adheres to the doctrine of fallen angels, the demonic kingdom is united under one head (Rev. 12.7–8). Jesus' life is a struggle against Satan, and the hour of his agony is the climax of this struggle (Luke 22.53).

As with Judaism, the belief in Satan became a central feature of Christian theology. In patristic sources there is considerable speculation about his nature and activity. Throughout the Middle Ages numerous theologians discussed the concept of the devil and formulated various theories about his origin and function. In modern times, however, such reflection has receded as other important issues have come to the fore.

Diaspora *see* Dispersion

Dietary laws *see* Food

Dispersion

(Diaspora) (Exile): Communities of Jews have lived outside the Holy Land since the time of the Babylonian exile (6th cent. BCE). After the destruction of Jerusalem by the Romans in 70 CE, the temple ceased to be the focus of the Jewish religion and the synagogue took its place. Inevitably, the different communities of the Diaspora (or dispersion) were influenced by the host country. Yet the emphasis on study of the law as a meritorious activity, coupled with an undying hope for the return of Jerusalem, enabled the Jews to maintain their separate identity. With the establishment of the State of Israel, the term 'Diaspora' is used to differentiate between Jews who live in Israel and those who live elsewhere.

Because Christians constitute a belief, rather than an ethnic community, there is no nostalgia for a particular native land or the sense of being an exile from a geographical place. Nonetheless, Christians have a strong desire to visit the sites associated with Jesus' ministry, and to make pilgrimage to other holy places. Jerusalem came to symbolize the Christian spiritual home, the city of peace, God's dwelling, and heaven. From this came the idea that the whole earth is a place of exile and a training ground through which the Christian pilgrim struggles before finally achieving the true home in heaven.

Divine names *see* Names of God

Divorce

(*get*): Deut. 24.1–4 decrees that, 'When a man takes a wife and marries her, if then she finds no favour in his eyes because he has found some indecency in her, and he writes her a bill of divorce and puts it in her hand and sends her out of his house . . .' Jewish law interprets this passage as granting the power of divorce exclusively to the husband. In the Mishnah, the rabbis debated the grounds of divorce, coming to differing conclusions. Yet despite the fact that divorce is allowed in Judaism, it is frowned upon in prophetic and Wisdom literature; such an attitude was later stressed in the Talmud.

During the Talmudic period, the law of divorce underwent a number of changes which granted the court the right to compel a husband to grant his wife a divorce. It is usual practice for a couple who intend to seek a divorce to draw up a legal agreement (dealing with custody of children, property settlement, and support) prior to applying to the rabbinical court. If these matters cannot be resolved by the couple themselves, the court should take over jurisdiction.

The bill of divorce (*get*) is to be drawn up by a scribe following a formula established in the Mishnah. This document, largely in Aramaic, must be signed by two witnesses. It is to be given to the wife, and is then retained by the rabbi who oversees the procedure. The rabbi gives the wife a document stating that she has been divorced and may remarry.

In the Middle Ages, Rabbenu Gershom (10th–11th cent.) promulgated an enactment stating that a husband may not divorce his wife without her consent; henceforth, divorce could only be by mutual consent. A century and a half later, Jacob Tam issued an ordinance declaring that in certain emergencies the enactment requiring mutual assent could be set aside. In modern times, considerable discussion has taken place regarding a number of problems connected with the Jewish law of divorce. In the Reform Movement, however, the Jewish regulations regarding divorce have been set aside, and couples are allowed to be divorced solely through the civil courts.

Departing from Jewish tradition, Christianity has adhered to Jesus' teaching in Matt. 5.31–32: 'It was also said, "Whoever divorces his wife, let him give her a certificate of divorce." But I say to you that every one who divorces his wife, except on the ground of unchastity, makes her an adulteress; and whoever marries a divorced woman commits adultery.' Jesus' disciples understood this pronouncement as instituting a new attitude towards marriage – husbands and wives have the duty to remain faithful for life. From the beginning, this was the view of the Church in the East and West.

From the second millennium, the Eastern Church accepted that Matt. 5.32 and 19.9 referring to 'unchastity' constituted an exception and, in the case of adultery, divorce and remarriage is allowed. However, the Western Church did not accept this interpretation, and developed a theory of marital indissolubility. Nonetheless, it decreed that divorce with freedom to marry can take place if the marriage has not been sexually consummated (as well as in certain other special cases). In recent times, the Orthodox Church has extended the right of divorce to individuals who are victims of other types of misbehaviour by their spouses. Within other Churches, an even more lenient attitude has developed. Some theologians even argue that Jesus' words were intended to express the ideal and were never meant to be taken literally. In any event, there is always room for repentance and forgiveness. The Churches that follow this line of thought will celebrate second marriages and their attitude to civil divorce is similar to that of Reform Judaism.

Dogma *see* Creeds

Door-posts

(Mezuzah): According to Deut. 6.9, Jews are commanded to inscribe God's words upon the door-posts of their houses. This has been understood to mean that a mezuzah, a small scroll of parchment containing selected biblical verses (Deut. 6.4–9; 11.13–21), should be attached to the door-posts of every Jewish home. Over the years, many rules evolved for the fixing of the mezuzah, and it is the custom among traditional Jews to touch it as they pass in or out of the house. Because the Church has rejected the ritual commandments of the Hebrew Scriptures, attaching a mezuzah has no place in Christianity.

E

Ear-locks

(*Païs*): Lev. 19.27 forbids rounding off the hair on the temples. Among some Orthodox Jews this has been taken to mean the lock of hair growing in front of the ears should not be cut. Because Christians do not regard the ritual laws of the Pentateuch as binding, this regulation is ignored.

Easter

The festival of Easter commemorates the resurrection of Jesus and is the most important feast of the Christian year. It is the climax of Lent and Holy Week and the Church celebrates Jesus' conquest of death, the overcoming of the power of sin, and God's gift of eternal life. Its date depends on that of the paschal full moon, and the name 'Easter' probably derives from that of the pagan goddess Eostre. Like Christmas, Easter takes the place of an ancient nature festival and the traditional giving of eggs symbolizes not only the new life of the resurrected Jesus, but also the new life of spring.

There are clear parallels between the Christian Easter and the Jewish festival of Passover. According to the Gospels, Jesus died at Passover time and the early Christians understood his death as a sacrifice for the sins of the world. In the same way as the Passover lamb died (Exod. 12) so that the angel of death would spare the first-born of the Israelites, so Jesus died that his followers would be spared the death and damnation that is the inevitable consequence of sin. Thus both festivals celebrate freedom. Christians rejoice in their liberation from slavery to sin and death, while Jews give thanks for their liberation from death when the angel of death 'passed over' their houses and from their life of misery as slaves in Egypt. Like Easter, Passover is also a nature festival, since it marks the beginning of the barley harvest.

Ecumenism

Throughout history there have been numerous schisms within the Jewish community, resulting in the formation of various religious groupings (such as the Essenes, Pharisees, Sadducees, Karaites, Hasidim, Reform Jews, etc.). In each instance, considerable hostility was evoked between the different movements, and little attempt was made at reconciliation. Nonetheless, all Jews – whatever their affiliations – have felt bound together by a common heritage. The notion of Catholic Israel (*K'lal Yisrael*) links Jews everywhere into an indivisible unity. This notion of a single body is not based on belief, but rather on a sense of shared identity, culture, and history. In this respect, Jewish ecumenism has been central to Jewish self-understanding through the ages.

As far as other religions are concerned, inter-faith activities have been conducted primarily with Christians. During the growth of the Church through the Middle Ages, Jews and Christians engaged in heated disputations about the merits of their respective faiths; such confrontations often provoked attacks on Jewish communities. From the time of the Emancipation, however, Jewish theologians (such as Moses Mendelssohn (18th cent.)) began to show an openness to the Christian faith. These attitudes culminated in the teachings of Franz Rosenzweig (20th cent.) and Martin Buber (20th cent.), who viewed Judaism and Christianity as separate valid roads to God.

The Holocaust has had a profound effect on Jewish–Christian relations in the last 50 years. Increasingly, Christian thinkers have attempted to formulate a more positive attitude to Judaism. Both the Catholic and Protestant Churches have tried to eliminate the anti-Semitic features of Christian teaching and foster positive Christian–Jewish relations. Such changes have provoked various Jewish responses. Generally, Jews have welcomed such openness, but within the Orthodox world reservations have been expressed about inter-faith activities. As far as discussion with other faiths is concerned, there has been very little activity in the Jewish world. Dialogue with Muslims does occasionally occur, but there is very limited inter-faith encounter with the members of other religions. Thus the notion of global inter-faith ecumenism is not part of the Jewish agenda in contemporary society.

Within Christianity, the aspiration for Christian unity can be found in the New Testament and has been expressed through the centuries. All Christians are viewed as part of the body of Christ. In the modern period, such an attitude was expressed by the evangelical revivals of the 18th and 19th cent., which crossed national and denominational boundaries. Added to this was the missionary expansion of the 19th cent., which stressed inter-denominational co-operation.

In 1910, the Edinburgh Conference led to the creation of the International Missionary Council; in 1927, the World Conference on Faith and Order at Lausanne addressed itself to the issue of Christian unity. Later, the World Council of Churches was formed to advance these initiatives. Parallel with these developments, the Appeal for Reunion was issued by the 1920 Lambeth Conference. With the next two decades similar activities were taking place within Eastern Orthodoxy and the Churches of Asia and Africa, and the World Council of Churches was founded in 1948. In the 1970s, the Roman Catholic Church undertook initiatives to explore the possibilities for Christian ecumenism. More recently, the quest to recover the unity of all believers in Christ has continued apace.

As with Judaism, the Christian community has also been anxious to encourage positive Jewish–Christian encounter. Eschewing its past anti-Jewish policy, Christians have attempted to forge positive links with the Jewish community in a wide range of areas. For the Catholic Church, the adoption of *Nostra Aetate* by the Second Vatican Council in 1965 heralded a new vision of Jewish–Christian relations. Within the Protestant world, similar statements have also been formulated. But in contrast with Judaism, the Church has emphasized the importance of world-wide ecumenical dialogue with all religious faiths. This aim is not to missionize, but to engage in a mutual quest for spiritual truth and discovery. Thus both Christian as well as inter-faith ecumenism has become a major concern of contemporary Christianity.

Education

(Yeshiva): The Bible states regarding Jewish law: 'You shall teach them diligently to your children' (Deut. 6.7). Again, the Pentateuch proclaims that fathers should tell their children about the Exodus from Egypt (Exod. 10.2; 13.8, 14; Deut. 6.20–21). These injunctions highlight the parental duty to provide religious instruction for their children. This training was largely informal, but Levites had the special duty of teaching the people (Deut. 33.10). After the return from the Babylonian exile, Ezra brought the people together and expounded the Torah to them (Neh. 8).

The Mishnah carries on this tradition by insisting that parents are to ensure that a child receives an education beginning from an early age. In the 1st cent. CE, Joshua ben Gamla organized the Jewish educational system, and this process of instruction was later formalized by the Talmud. Subsequently, academies were established in Babylonia where sages lectured on the Jewish law. Twice a year during the months of Adar and Elul, special study sessions were held for a lay audience.

From the completion of the Talmud *c.* 500 CE until the Emancipation of the Jews in the 18th cent., most male Jews received some type of educational training in sacred texts. Young boys entered the *heder* (elementary school), where they were taught the rudiments of Hebrew and basic religious sources by a single teacher. In certain communities there was a Talmud Torah (School), which had various classes. In some cases, secular subjects were introduced as well. In general, in the Middle Ages Jews were better educated than their Christian neighbours.

Through this system of training, the majority of Jewish males became literate, at a time when the vast majority of people could neither read nor write. However, only a small minority pursued their religious studies to an advanced level. In the 19th cent., organized yeshivot (Talmudic academies) flourished in Eastern Europe in such centres as Tels, Ponevezh, and Slobodka. In these academies, students progressed from one level to another.

With the Emancipation of Jewry, however, many Jews were influenced by the Enlightenment movement (*Haskalah*), and secular studies were gradually introduced into the curriculum. In the 19th cent., Samson Raphael Hirsch was a pioneer in formulating a modern Orthodox curriculum along these lines. Eventually, most Jews entered public secular schools, but their studies there were supplemented by Jewish education under religious auspices. In recent decades, Jewish day schools have undergone considerable growth in both the Orthodox and non-Orthodox communities. Both secular and religious education is highly valued in the Jewish community.

The Church also emphasized the importance of religious education from the beginning. The first Christian churches met in homes, and parents taught their children the rudiments of the faith. As Christianity developed, formal education became widespread; by the second century, the catechume-nate (instruction in Scripture, worship, and conduct) was introduced as a preparation for baptism and membership in the Church. In addition, Christian schools were founded during this period which provided both religious and secular education.

During the Middle Ages there may have been a general decline in learning, but Christian studies continued to flourish in monasteries. Within this context, there was a rediscovery of Greek philosophy, and various scholars attempted to reconcile Aristotelian philosophy with the Christian faith. In the medieval period, universities were founded in Bologna, Paris, Oxford, and Cambridge; however, such educational activities were reserved for a small Christian male elite. In many places, however, the common people, unlike the Jews, seem to have been frequently illiterate and dependent on the Church for all instruction.

During the Reformation, however, education became more widespread and Christian learning was revitalized. As with Judaism, the rise of secularism in the modern period impelled most Christians to seek education in publicly funded schools. Religious education was thus relegated to an extra-curricular activity taking place outside of school (usually on Sunday), except in those cases where pupils were instructed in religion during school hours as part of the regular curriculum.

Elder

According to Num. 11, Moses was commanded to gather together 70 elders to experience God's presence and to be leaders of the Jewish people. Community elders seem to have existed throughout the biblical period. According to the Mishnah, the religious tradition was preserved by the elders after the death of Joshua until the time of the prophets. Elders are mentioned in the Talmud and throughout medieval literature; the title seems to have been given to scholars and leaders of the community. The idea was taken up in anti-Semitic literature such as the influential 19th-cent. *Protocols of the Learned Elders of Zion.*

Jesus also appointed 70 to preach the gospel (Luke 10), but elders first appear in the Church as local supervisors (Acts 20.17). There is much scholarly debate as to the exact relationship of these elders (presbyters) with bishops (*episcopoi*), and the tradition of elders rather than bishops has been maintained in many Protestant Churches to this day. Many Eastern and Western Churches, on the other hand, believe bishops were a separate order and maintain a threefold ministry of bishops, presbyters, and deacons.

Election *see* Israel

Elijah

(John the Baptist): A 9th-cent. Israelite prophet. He lived during the reign of Ahab, king of Israel, as well as his son Ahaziah (1 Kings 17–19, 21; 2 Kings 1–2). During this period, he struggled against the worship of Baal which had spread under the influence of Ahab's wife, Jezebel. The most notable clash took place on Mt Carmel when a contest was held between Elijah and the prophets of Baal. These prophets were unable to bring down fire from heaven to ignite their burnt offerings (1 Kings 18.16ff.) but, in response to Elijah's prayer, fire consumed his offerings and the people proclaimed: 'The Lord, he is God.'

During Ahab's reign, Elijah continually rebuked the king for his immorality, particularly after Ahab had seized Naboth's vineyard. When the time came for Elijah to leave the earth, Elisha (whom he had appointed as his successor) did not want to be separated from him. But a fiery chariot with horses appeared, and Elijah ascended to heaven in a whirlwind (2 Kings 2).

In rabbinic sources, Elijah plays a central role – he is to answer unresolved questions that in the Talmud conclude with the word *teku* (meaning 'it will stand'), which is also interpreted as an acronym of 'the Tishbite [Elijah] will solve queries'. Furthermore, since Elijah came to the aid of those in difficulty, many legends have been told of his reappearance in times of danger to save the Jewish community. In addition, Elijah is conceived in Jewish sources as heralding the period of Messianic redemption as foretold by Malachi: 'Behold, I will send you Elijah the prophet before the great and terrible day of the Lord comes' (Mal. 4.5). This expectation is symbolically reflected in the practice of placing a fifth cup of wine on the Passover Seder (meal) table; it is hoped that Elijah will arrive and bring redemption on Passover eve.

This longing is also echoed in various Sabbath songs and liturgical poetry.

The Church followed Jewish teaching concerning the coming of the Messiah. In this context, John the Baptist was modelled on the figure of Elijah. Ministering in the region of the Jordan, his description echoes that of the prophet; he was clothed in camel's hair, with a leather girdle around his waist. He was an ascetic, eating locusts and wild honey (Mark 1. 1–16) and he preached 'a baptism of repentance for the forgiveness of sins' (Mark 1.4), a message that embodied an expectation of the Messianic age. John the Baptist thus served as an important bridge between Judaism and Christianity. As he acted out Elijah's role as the forerunner of the Messiah, he paved the way for Jesus' teaching and ministry.

Later in Jesus' life, three of his apostles saw Jesus transfigured. His clothes became dazzling white and he was seen talking with Moses and Elijah (Mark 9.2–12). Just as Moses represents the law, Elijah here represents the prophets, and Jesus is thus seen as the culmination of the whole Jewish tradition. Christianity therefore took over the Old Testament figure of Elijah and saw him as the ultimate prophet. He not only brought the nation back to God in the time of King Ahab but, in the person of John the Baptist, he also heralded the new age of the Messiah.

Enlightenment

(Modernism): Within the Jewish world this movement in the 18th–19th cent, encouraged Jews to acquire secular knowledge and culture. Referred to as the *Haskalah*, it was part of the general process of the European Enlightenment. It was a time when educated Jews attempted to promote the process of emancipation among Jewry, fostering cultural consciousness by emphasizing Hebrew as a literary medium.

The nature of the Enlightenment varied in different countries. In Eastern Europe it was synonymous with Westernization, and there were attempts to replace traditional religious schools with a modern system of education. This was virulently opposed by the Orthodox; their criticisms were countered by followers of the *Haskalah* who composed satires attacking rabbinic and Hasidic obscurantism and superstition. In addition, these modernists promoted historical research in scholarly periodicals, established secular schools, and issued manuals of educational instruction.

The proponents of the *Haskalah (maskilim)* actively encouraged the return to nature as well as manual work. They were also sympathetic to liturgical reform. In literature, they were drawn to ancient Israelite heroes and advocated romanticism and hedonism. Orthodox opponents of this new movement argued that the *maskilim* endangered the survival of the Jewish heritage. However, by the end of the 19th cent., many progressive ideas were firmly established. Nevertheless, a number of Jewish thinkers remained unconvinced that the new modernism would stem the rise of anti-Semitism. Some of these thinkers began to look beyond the Emancipation of the Jews to a vision of a Jewish homeland in Israel. Zionism, they believed, was the only hope for the Jewish community in contemporary society.

The Enlightenment of the 18th–19th cent, also affected the Christian community. The fashionable criticism of the authority of tradition led to increased secularism and rationalism – in this context, even the stories of the Bible were subject to investigation. Biographies of the historical Jesus were produced. Scepticism about miracles, the resurrection, and priestcraft was widespread. In addition, the awareness of the non-Christian religions led to a growing sense of the cultural relativity of the Christian faith.

Although the thought of the Enlightenment was generally hostile to Christianity, its adherents varied in their views, ranging from deistic beliefs to materialistic atheism. Parallel with the Jewish *Haskalah*, some modernists attempted to provide a rational version of the Christian religion for the contemporary age. Yet, despite such a critical attitude, traditional Christianity continued to survive and foster evangelical revivals in various parts of the world later in the 19th cent.

Epiphany

This Christian festival, which is celebrated on 6 January, commemorates the visit of the Wise Men to the baby Jesus and, in the Eastern Churches, Jesus' baptism by John in the River Jordan. The name of the feast comes from the Greek *Epiphaneia*, which means 'manifestation'. Christians celebrate their belief that Jesus was not only the Messiah for the Jews, but for everyone. There is no equivalent festival in Judaism. Although the Jewish tradition recognizes the sovereignty of God over all peoples, it also emphasizes the role of the Jews as the ones chosen uniquely to receive God's revelation.

Episcopacy

(Bishop): The system of Church government known as episcopacy refers to the rule of bishops. In the New Testament, the terms *episcopos* (bishop) and *presbuteros* (elder) seem to have been used interchangeably. Nonetheless, almost all the Churches that practise episcopacy stress the continuous spiritual line that derives from the commission of the 12 apostles. This is seen as a guarantee that the Church's beliefs and practices are identical and continuous with the faith of Jesus' disciples. At his consecration, the new bishop becomes part of this apostolic succession. Unlike a priest, a bishop can ordain clergy and administer the rite of confirmation. Besides these, he has the responsibility for supervising his diocese and his throne (cathedra) is in the cathedral. Most Protestant Churches do not have an episcopal organization, but rely either on a system of elders or on each congregation being completely autonomous.

Judaism has no diocesan structure. Before the destruction of the Temple, the high priest was the acknowledged leader, and through the Middle Ages, the *exilarch* (head of Babylonian Jewry) was the representative of the Jews of Babylonia. In many communities, however, the position of chief rabbi has evolved. The holder of this office is seen as the community representative and, except in Israel, is supported by the voluntary contributions of the congregations. In Israel, the chief rabbinate is an established government agency with total authority over marriage, divorce, and conversion to Judaism. Because the hereditary priesthood largely disappeared with the Temple, there is no idea that the chief rabbi of any community is in a long unbroken spiritual line, so in this respect there is no similarity with the office of bishop.

Eschatology

The concept of a perfected world that will be brought about by divine providence. During the biblical period, such expectation focused on the final destiny of the Jewish people who were to be the bearers of God's promise. A key element in Jewish eschatology was the concept of a Day of the Lord, when God would express his wrath against the wicked and reward the righteous. Amos decreed that such a day will be a time of doom (Amos 5.18–20). For the prophet Zephaniah, it will be an era of destruction for non-believers followed by the establishment of glory for the remnant of Israel (Zeph. 8–13). Isaiah declared that at this time God will be King and all nations will serve him (Isa. 11.10).

When the Jewish people returned to Israel after their exile in Babylonia, it was assumed that this would lead to the realization of the nation's hopes of restoration. When this did not occur, apocalyptic speculation about the end of the world became a central motif of Jewish thought. In the Book of Daniel, God's reign on earth was linked with the concept of the Messiah. Subsequently, the Pharisees included eschatological elements in their writings, as did the Essenes.

The destruction of the second Temple in 70 CE curtailed certain features of this eschatological hope; nevertheless, eschatology continued to serve as a central motif in Jewish thought through the centuries. In the Middle Ages, Moses Maimonides (12th cent.) incorporated the belief in the coming of the Messiah and the advent of the world-to-come as fundamental principles of the Jewish faith. In modern times, Jewish eschatology still survives in the traditional liturgy, but it has receded in importance as more pressing religious and social concerns have taken precedence. For many Jews, the commitment to the survival of a Jewish state has replaced the desire for the dawning of a Messianic age when all nations would live in harmony and peace.

The Church inherited Jewish teaching about the Messianic hope. In the New Testament, the belief in the final destiny of each individual and humanity in general is the subject of a number of Christ's parables. Paul also deals with eschatology in 1 and 2 Thess., and it is the main subject of the apocalypses in the Book of Revelation. However, when the eschatological predictions of the first Christians were not fulfilled in a literal sense, biblical teachings were interpreted in figurative and allegorical terms.

Traditional Christian thought continued to apply the passages in Daniel, Zechariah and Isaiah, Christ's teachings in parables, Paul's message, and apocalyptic passages in Revelation to a vision of a new heaven and earth. Some liberal Protestants, however, have interpreted eschatology differently. Albert Schweitzer (20th cent.), for example, argued that eschatological expectations were of central importance for Jesus. Yet when history did not come to an end, he felt he must offer himself as a ransom to God to inaugurate the new age. His statements on the cross, however, led Schweitzer to doubt whether he continued to maintain this conviction to the end. Schweitzer's views have had an important impact on 20th-cent. scholarship, although many critics have resisted his conclusions. Other scholars have formulated alternative concepts of Christian eschatology. Yet despite this debate, the doctrine concerning last things – including the resurrection of the dead, the Second Coming of Christ, the final Judgement, and God's Kingdom – continue to activate contemporary Christian thinking within all branches of the Church.

Esther, Book of *see* Lots, festival of

Esther, feast of *see* Lots, festival of

Eternal life *see* Judgement

Ethics *see* Morality

Etrog *see* Tabernacles, feast of

Eucharist
(Holy Communion) (Lord's Supper) (Mass): The central act of Christian worship, its name is derived from the Greek word for thanksgiving. In the New Testament, its institution is referred to in Paul's first letter to the Corinthians (11.23–25), and in the Synoptic Gospels (Matt.26.26–28; Mark 14.2–24; Luke 22. 17–20). Acts records that it was celebrated by the early Christian community in Jerusalem (Acts 2.42, 46), as well as by Paul on his visit to Troas (Acts 20.7).

According to tradition, the Eucharist conveys to the Christian the body and blood of Christ. From the 4th cent., it was held that a transformation of bread and wine took place. Subsequently, the belief in transubstantiation became a central tenet of the faith. However, in the early 9th cent., controversies took place about the nature of the Eucharistic presence. Paschasius Radbertus (9th cent.), for example, questioned the identity of Christ's Eucharistic body with his body in heaven. In the 11th cent., Berengar opposed the doctrine of the Real Presence, but later retracted his claims. At the Fourth Lateran Council (1215), the transubstantiation of the elements was affirmed, and later teaching explained how such changes occurred.

During the Reformation, controversies continued unabated. Martin Luther (15th–16th cent.) formulated the doctrine of consubstantiation, whereby after the consecration both the bread and the wine and the body and blood of Christ coexisted. Ulrich Zwingli (15th–16th cent.), on the other hand, held that the Lord's Supper should be viewed as a memorial rite. According to John Calvin (16th cent.), the body of Christ had ascended to heaven; nevertheless, the Holy Spirit could raise the soul to heaven to feed there by divine mystery on Christ himself. In subsequent centuries, considerable attention was paid to Eucharistic doctrine throughout Christendom. Yet despite the variety of interpretations, the celebration of the Eucharist was generally understood as a means by which Jesus' presence is made manifest to the Christian community.

The Eucharistic rite in the Church was based on Jewish precedent. In Gen., Melchizedek, king of Salem, brought out bread and wine (Gen. 14.18), and flour and wine were offered to the Lord according to Lev. (Lev. 2; 23.13). Most importantly, bread and wine played a central role in the kiddush and the Passover meal. The kiddush is the Jewish ceremony for the sanctification of the Sabbath or a festival. On Friday afternoon, families gather together for the evening meal, and the head of the household says the blessing over a cup of wine. This same ceremony is observed on festivals when a reference is made to the specific festival as well as the Sabbath. In addition, two loaves of bread, which symbolize the double portion of manna gathered by the Israelites in the desert, are blessed on the Sabbath, and at least one loaf on the other festivals.

At Passover, which commemorates the Exodus from Egypt, unleavened bread is blessed to symbolize the haste required to flee the Egyptians. It was also customary for Jews to say blessings over four cups of wine at the Passover meal (Seder). Some scholars have argued that the Last Supper took place at Passover time, and thus Jesus' blessing of the cup at the institution of the first Eucharist was the kiddush of the Passover celebration. Such a view is supported by the phraseology found in the Eucharistic prayers of the early Christian Church. Other scholars, however, prefer the Johannine dating of the Last Supper before the Passover. On this view, the blessing over the cup was the ordinary blessing recited at a fellowship meal. In any case, there are clear links between the Jewish practice of blessing bread and wine and the Eucharist, although what is understood in Judaism as a form of thanksgiving has taken on pivotal sacramental significance for Christians.

Euthanasia

Mercy killing. The term is derived from the Greek words *eu* and *thanatos*, meaning easy or gentle death. According to Judaism, life is God's supreme blessing. Thus Deut. declares: 'I have set before you life and death, blessing and curse; therefore choose life, that you and your descendants may live' (Deut. 30.19). Because of this central principle, all laws – except those concerning idolatry, bloodshed, and adultery – can be set aside if there is danger to life.

Because of this conviction, the infinite value of life is affirmed by the Jewish faith. Hastening death by even one minute is viewed as tantamount to bloodshed. Active euthanasia is therefore ruled out, whether it is voluntary or involuntary. In this context, the Code of Jewish Law states: 'A patient on his deathbed is considered as a living person in every respect . . . and it is forbidden to cause him to die quickly . . . or to move him from his place . . . and whoever closes his eyes with the onset of death is regarded as shedding blood.'

According to traditional Jewish law, killing any innocent person is viewed as murder. However, some rabbinical responses allow the cessation of artificial means to prolong life without the possibility of recovery. Withdrawing such treatment is justified on the basis of permission to remove an extraneous impediment from a dying person. Within non-Orthodox Judaism, there has been some discussion of the validity of voluntary euthanasia, but generally the traditional attitude has been adopted.

As with Judaism, traditional Christianity teaches that life is God-given; it is forbidden to take the life of an innocent person either with or without the individual's consent. To do so would be to commit an act of injustice towards the dying person and an act of impiety to God. Such an action is considered tantamount to murder.

Recently, a number of liberal Christians in various denominations have argued that voluntary euthanasia should be permitted in certain extreme cases. Nevertheless, attempts to legalize euthanasia in England have been repeatedly defeated on the grounds that it would constitute a violation of the sixth Commandment, as well as a denial of the Christian attitude to suffering. Euthanasia was condemned by the Pope in 1943 and 1948, by the Archbishops of Canterbury in 1936 and York in 1950; and by the Protestant Episcopal Church in America in 1952. Thus in both Judaism and Christianity there has been a common response through the ages about deliberately taking innocent life. Both faiths insist that human beings have the right to preserve and prolong life, but not the right to deny it.

Evening prayer

There was no evening sacrifice in the Temple in Jerusalem, but it was believed that the patriarch had instituted the regular practice of an evening prayer service (Gen. 28.11). This should take place between just before sunset and midnight and consists of blessings, prayers, and psalms. In Reform congregations, the Friday evening service has become of central importance, and sometimes the weekly Torah portion is read then. The two evening offices recited in monasteries are known as vespers and compline. The evening service held in churches is largely based on these two services, and includes prayers, readings, psalms, and a canticle. Recently, evening communion services have become more popular, particularly on the eve of major festivals. Like the Reform Jewish Friday evening service, this is popular since it is more convenient for modern congregations since it leaves the following day free.

Evil *see* Theodicy

Excommunication

(*Herem*): Exclusion from membership of the religious community and denial of rights and privileges. In Judaism it is employed as a form of punishment for sins or as a communal sanction. Regulations concerning excommunication are detailed in the Talmud. The mildest form is *neziphah* (rebuke), which lasted for only a day in Babylonia and seven days in Israel. Those excommunicated in this way were forced to remain in their dwelling and refrain from social contact. After expressing regret, the offender was allowed to live normally.

A more serious form of excommunication is *niddui* (banishment), which was usually instituted for 30 days. During this time, the offender is viewed as a pariah and is to be ostracized by everyone except for the immediate members of his family. In addition, his children could be denied circumcision, education, and synagogue attendance. If such restrictions are unable to bring the transgressor to penitence, the most serious form of excommunication – *herem* (ban) is to be imposed.

This extreme punishment is enforced for an indefinite period and denies the sinner all access to Jewish religious and social life. During the medieval period, this ban became the underlying sanction for communal enactments. Thus the phrase 'the *herem* of Rabbenu Gershom' (in relation to decrees concerning such a case as polygamy) meant that anyone transgressing his enactments without a legitimate legal excuse would be placed in *herem*. Although excommunication took place through the centuries (including the invocation of *herem* against Uriel Acosta and Baruch Spinoza in the 17th cent. by the Sephardi congregation in Amsterdam), it came to lose its force in the modern world. With increased secularization Jews were less dependent on the synagogue for their social world, and therefore the threat of exclusion became less serious.

As in the Jewish community, Christianity employed similar censure for wayward individuals. In the early Church, excommunication varied in degree. The more serious form deprived an offender from the right to administer or receive sacraments, maintain social contact with other

Christians, and obtain rights and privileges within the Church. The less extreme form of excommunication deprived an individual of the right to administer or receive sacraments.

In the Roman Catholic Church, this lesser form of excommunication is rarely enforced. However, a new distinction has been made between those excommunicate *vitandus* and those *toleratus*. The former case corresponds to a transgressor under the more serious form of excommunication – he may not attend religious services, hold ecclesiastical office, or have sustained contact with other Christians. No one is under such a ban unless he has attempted to cause physical harm to the Pope or is pronounced *vitandus* by the Holy See. Any other excommunicated offender is *toleratus*, and thereby deprived of the right to adminster or receive sacraments, or attend public worship. As in Judaism, such bans have largely lost their significance in contemporary society and are rarely employed.

Exile *see* Dispersion

Exodus

(Manna): The flight of the Israelites from slavery in Egypt. The Bible relates that the Jews were slaves there for 430 years. In response to God's command, Moses appeared before Pharaoh demanding their release. When Pharaoh refused, God afflicted Egypt with 10 plagues. After the last plague – the death of all Egyptian first-born sons – Pharaoh allowed the Israelites to leave. The Red Sea miraculously parted for them, but closed on Pharaoh's army which had chased after them.

In the Bible, the Book of Exodus relates the events of this deliverance from bondage; Exod. 1.1–2.25 gives an account of the enslavement of the Israelites and the early career of Moses. This is followed by a description of the call and mission of Moses (3.1–7.13), the first nine plagues visited upon Egypt (7.14–11.10), and the paschal sacrifice and the tenth plague (12.1–13.16). Chapters 13.17–16.27 provide a narrative of the Exodus from Egypt, the Song at the Sea, the complaints of the Israelites, the feeding of the people with manna, the battle with Amalek, and Jethro's visit and advice. There is then an account of the giving of the law on Mt Sinai (19.1–20.18), and a list of statutes

and laws (20.19–23.37). There follows the ceremony of the covenant (24.1–18). The Book of Exodus concludes with a description of the golden calf, the replacement of the broken tablets (32.1–34.35), and the building of the sanctuary and its utensils (35.11–40.38).

Throughout Jewish history the Exodus has symbolized the concept of freedom, God's intervention in history, and the fulfilment of divine redemption. Every day each Jew is to remember this primal act of deliverance, and the Exodus is frequently linked to biblical laws. The festival of Passover is specifically tied to this pivotal event in the life of the nation, and the Seder ceremony is devoted to retelling the story of God's act of salvation.

For Christians, the Book of Exodus is part of Holy Scripture, and the account of the Exodus from Egypt is also regarded as a central act of deliverance and favour to his chosen people. Yet from New Testament times the Passover was understood in Christological terms. Thus John 1.29 declares that Jesus is the Passover Lamb whose death brings salvation to the world. For Paul, God's action in Jesus is a Passover sacrifice inviting a new journey from death to life. Christians are urged to celebrate the feast with the fresh, unleavened dough of sincerity and truth (1 Cor. 5.8).

For Christians, then, Jesus Christ brings to the Passover of the Hebrew Scriptures a new order. As the bringer of the new covenant with God, Jesus is the true sacrificial offering, taking the place of the paschal offering in the Temple; the death of Christ on the cross is the full reality of all the promises connected with the Jewish Passover. Here, then, is a Christian transformation of the meaning of the Exodus, a revision of the Jewish symbolism in the light of Jesus' ministry and death. In recent times, the motif of the Exodus has also been employed by Christian theologians who are working for political liberation from oppressive regimes. In this, these Christian liberation scholars come close to their Jewish counterparts in perceiving the Exodus as a prototype of all freedom from slavery.

Exorcism

Expulsion of foreign spirits from individuals. In the Bible, Saul was possessed by an evil spirit; it was exorcised by David's playing the harp (1 Sam. 16.14–23). Exorcism is also found in the Book of

Tobit and occasionally in the Talmud. Later, it became a central kabbalistic (mystical) theory related to the doctrine of the transmigration of souls.

According to the kabbalah, the phenomenon of *ibbur* involves the joining of the soul of a dead person to someone who is alive. This occurs when the soul of the righteous person is joined to the soul of another individual to strengthen his good qualities and aid the Jewish people. Subsequently, the kabbalists developed this theory to embrace the entry of the soul of an evil person into the body of someone who has committed a sin.

In Jewish literature this evil spirit is referred to as a *dibbuk* – it speaks through the mouth of the person who is possessed and brings about spiritual disturbance. From the 16th cent., descriptions of such foreign entities were common, and form the basis for various literary works such as the play *The Dibbuk* by S. An-Ski (20th cent.). In modern times, however, the belief in exorcism has largely disappeared from Jewish life.

The tradition of expelling evil spirits was practised from the time of the New Testament. In Scripture, the casting out of evil spirits by Christ and the disciples is frequently mentioned. In the early Church it was usual to exorcise converts from Jewish and pagan backgrounds before baptism. During the Middle Ages, exorcism formed part of infant baptism; it was the custom to breath three times on the face of the infant while reciting: 'Depart from him, thou unclean spirit, and give place to the Holy Spirit.' This was later condensed in the *Rituals Romanum* (1614). In Lutheran baptismal services, as well as in the first Prayer Book of Edward VI (1549), a brief exorcism is mentioned.

In the early Church, the title of exorcist referred to a minor order of the ministry whose office included laying hands on the insane, exorcising catechumens, and helping at Holy Communion. In the modern Roman Catholic Church, the order has been retained as a stepping-stone to the priesthood. The Eastern Churches, however, have no order of exorcists. In the Pentecostalist movement, exorcism is often practised by charismatics, and licensed exorcists exist within the Church of England. Nonetheless, as is the case within Judaism, exorcism has receded in importance in contemporary Christianity.

Expiation *see* Atonement

F

Faith
Both the Jewish and Christian traditions distinguish between faith meaning 'Believing in' (*Emunah, Fides*) and faith meaning 'Trusting in' (*Bittahon, Fiducia*). Nonetheless, the Hebrew Scriptures' use of *Emunah* does not imply merely the conviction that God exists, since that was taken for granted. Rather, it indicates the belief that the promises of God would be fulfilled. In the Middle Ages, however, when the rabbis met unbelief, they used the term *Emunah* to affirm their ideas about God in such statements as Maimonides' (12th cent.) Thirteen Principles of the Jewish Faith. At the same time, it was accepted by such philosophers as Judah Halevy (11th-12th cent.) that the basis of the Jewish religion was not cognitive belief, but a unique religious relationship with God. A similar distinction is to be found in Christian theology. In the Catholic tradition, faith signifies mental assent to divinely revealed truths (such as are to be found in the creeds), while in Protestantism it means the attitude of trustful obedience to God as he is revealed through his Word. Nonetheless, as in Judaism, belief in propositions about God inevitably implies a pre-existing trusting relationship with God.

Fasting
(Abstinence) (Asceticism): Abstention from food, drink and physical pleasure. Within Judaism, fasting is viewed as a religious discipline – its purpose is to intensify the religious experiences of atonement, to commemorate national tragedies, or to reinforce the act of intercessory prayer.

As far as atonement is concerned, the most important example of fasting takes place on the Day of Atonement. Jews are commanded to afflict their souls (Lev. 16.31) by fasting and through various acts of abstention. During the biblical period, it was common to rend one's garments and put on sackcloth and ashes. Tragic events of Jewish history are also commemorated in this way on particular dates connected with the sieges of Jerusalem and the destruction of the first and second Temples. Fasts of petition are represented in enactments by the rabbis at times of national danger.

Various Jewish laws are associated with fasting. Obligatory fasts must be observed by all males over the age of 13 and females over the age of 12. Younger people are to observe partial fasts. However, sick people, women in advanced stages of pregnancy, and nursing mothers are not required to fast. Where there is a danger to health, fasting is prohibited. Despite the variety of fasts within Judaism, the spiritual intention in all cases is paramount. Fasting involves complete abstention from food and drink.

Following Jewish precedent, fasting was recommended by Jesus (Luke 4.2. Matt. 6.16–18; Mark 2.20). It was also observed by the apostles (Acts 13.2; 14.23; 2 Cor. 11.27), and regular weekly fast days were instituted in the early Church. The fast of Lent was initially connected with Easter; it originally lasted only two days but was later extended to 40. In the Eastern Church, three further periods of fasting were introduced while the Western Church developed vigil fasts before great feasts and the fasts of the Ember Days. For Christians, fasting only involves abstention from certain types of food, generally animal products.

Within the different branches of Christendom, various requirements for fasting have been specified. Yet in all cases it is a penitential practice, designed to strengthen the spiritual life. Unlike Judaism, fasting in the Christian tradition is not seen as a means of atonement, because atonement for sin has already been made through the sacrificial death of Jesus. Instead, it is understood as a religious act that strengthens the spiritual life of the believer.

Despite the common tradition of fasting, Jews and Christians have a different attitude to ascetic practices. Christians have a long history of monastic asceticism which includes vows of celibacy and extreme simplicity of life. In biblical times, various individuals, such as Samson, took a Nazerite vow which involved abstention from wine and from cutting the hair, but this only applied in Israel while the Temple stood. There have also been occasional Jewish sects – such as the Essenes – who seem to have lived in monastic communities, but the tradition of extreme asceticism has disappeared from modern Judaism.

Fasts

Both the Jewish and Christian traditions regard fasting as an important discipline, and fast days are part of the annual cycles of both religions. The most important Jewish fast is the Day of Atonement (Yom Kippur), which is ordained for the atoning of sin. There are four fast days commemorating events in Jewish history: 10 Tevet (*Asarah be-Tevet*) is a reminder of the Babylonian siege of Jerusalem in 586 BCE; 17 Tammuz (*Shivah Asar be-Tammuz*) commemorates the capture of the city by the Babylonians; on 9 Av (*Tishah be-Av*) the destructions of the Temple in both 586 BCE and 70 CE are remembered; and on 3 Tishri (the Fast of Gedaliah) the assassination of Gedaliah is commemorated (Jer. 40.4–41.3). On the Day of Atonement and 9 Av, no food or drink is to be consumed from the sunset of the previous day until the evening, and bathing, anointing, wearing leather shoes, and all sexual relations are forbidden. On the three minor fasts, fasting only begins at dawn and there are no other prohibitions.

The early Church observed Wednesday and Friday as fast days. The 40 days of Lent were regarded as a fast period, and the Western Church added Advent, the period from Pentecost until the Feast of St Peter and St Paul, and the two weeks before the festival of the Assumption. Originally one-day fasts meant the complete abstention from food, and fasting periods meant the abstention from all animal products except fish. In recent times, the rules have become less stringent. In the Roman Catholic Church, the only obligatory fast days are now Ash Wednesday (the first day of Lent) and Good Friday (commemorating Jesus' death on the cross), but the custom of giving up something for Lent persists even in fairly secular circles.

Fate *see* Providence

Feminism

After the Enlightenment, Jewish women attained a degree of emancipation and began to assume a more influential role in communal affairs. Nonetheless, they did not attain full participation in religious life and often occupied volunteer or low-paid positions in society. It was only in the late 1960s that Jewish women re-examined their role in Jewish affairs and the community generally; and it was during this period that various gatherings of Jewish women were held and specific publications dealing with Jewish feminism emerged. In 1972, the Reform Movement ordained a female rabbi, a policy that was later adopted by the Reconstructionist and Conservative movements.

Despite this revolution in Jewish life, Orthodoxy remained unmoved by women's demands. In consequence, some women left Orthodox Judaism; others refrained from participating in public worship where they were obliged to pray behind curtains or in balconies out of the sight of men. Some Orthodox women formed their own prayer groups, and by 1976 the Women's Tephillah (Prayer) Network had over 700 members in North America and Israel. These groups provide a means by which women are able to lead services, read from the Torah, and celebrate bat mitzvahs and baby namings. Orthodox women have also regarded religious study as central to their activities.

Despite this development, the Orthodox rabbinate has been unwilling to address the criticisms made of the traditional religious system. In particular, they have been firmly opposed to instituting changes to the Jewish legal system. Within the ultra-Orthodox world, considerable resistance has also been exerted against the demands of Jewish feminism. Ultra-Orthodox Jews have been anxious to stress the significance of the traditional woman's role in the home, and they have condemned the establishment of separate women's prayer groups as a contravention of this.

This conservative response has not deterred Jewish feminists from their activities. Some have attempted to reclaim women's rituals and holidays. Others have rejected all patriarchal associations. A number of feminist theologians have attempted to invest Jewish practices with feminist insight and interpretation. In addition, new rituals and blessings suited to the experiences of women have been introduced, and liturgical change involving the abolition of sexist language has been championed. All these have transformed Jewish life – they have widened and deepened the experiences of women, offering them new challenges and opportunities in the modern world.

Within Christianity, feminist criticism of biblical exegesis and Christian theology began in the 17th cent., with the work of such women as Margaret Fell. In 19th-cent. America, Quakerism served as an important source for feminist leaders. These writers argued for women's rights, criticized patriarchalism, and condemned the use of the Bible as an instrument of male domination.

In the modern Church, these views have been elaborated by feminist theologians, particularly from the 1960s. One of their central themes is the critique of the masculine bias of Christian theology. This prejudiced stance, they believe, has excluded women from the ordained ministry, as well as from higher theological education. Christian feminist theology aims to evaluate the effect of this exclusion on the development of traditional Christian thinking about God and the world.

Another central preoccupation of Christian feminism is the attempt to discover alternative historical traditions supportive of women. In this quest, some feminist theologians have given up on the Judeo-Christian tradition altogether; others, however, seek to affirm the possibility of a feminist tradition within this context. Their desire is to uncover the meaning of such concepts as God, Christ, discipleship, sin and redemption within a feminist framework. In so doing, they believe they will restore the wholeness of the Christian message which has been lost through patriarchal attitudes and masculine distortion.

Although there is considerable debate in Christian feminist circles about the results of this re-examination of Christian thought, Christian feminists are united in their desire to reformulate Christianity in the light of their experiences as women. For many of these writers, this enterprise is linked to the quest for the ordination of women – a demand met only by some sections of Christendom, but strongly resisted by Roman Catholicism and Eastern Orthodoxy.

Modern feminism is thus of far-reaching significance in both Judaism and Christianity. The movement has profoundly altered the conception of women and their position in both religious communities, and has had far-reaching repercussions for traditional theology. Both religions, being essentially patriarchal, have had difficulty accommodating the insights of feminism, and it is notable that it is the liberal wings of both traditions that have found the adjustment easiest.

Festivals

Both Jews and Christians celebrate festival days throughout the year. In Judaism, three pilgrim festivals (Yom Tov or Holy Days) are observed which have both historical and agricultural importance: Passover (Pesah, 15–22 of the month of Nisan) commemorates the Exodus from Egypt and the beginning of the barley harvest; the festival of Weeks (Shavuot, 6 Sivan) celebrates the giving of the law to Moses on Mt Sinai, the end of the barley harvest and the beginning of the wheat harvest; and Tabernacles (Sukkot, 15 Tishri), which is a reminder of the Israelites' 40 years in the wilderness and celebrates the bringing in of the grain to the barns. Traditionally, pilgrimages were made to the Temple in Jerusalem on these three festivals. In addition, Scripture forbids work on the New Year (Rosh Hashanah, 1 Tishri), on the Day of Atonement (Yom Kippur, 10 Tishri) and on the Day of the Solemn Assembly and Rejoicing in the Law (Shemini Atseret, 23 Tishri). All these festivals except the Day of Atonement are celebrated for two days because of doubts as to the date of the new moon from which the beginning of the month was counted. In each case, special liturgies are followed in the synagogue and other traditional customs are observed at home. Other festivals were ordained by the rabbis: the Feast of Esther or Lots (Purim) and the festival of Lights (Hanukkah) both commemorate events in Jewish history, as does Israel Independence Day. There are also other minor festivals such as those celebrating the monthly new moon, the new year for trees and the 33rd day of the Omer.

Christian festivals are centred round the life of Jesus, although several have older, agricultural roots. Advent Sunday, near the beginning of December, looks forward to the coming of Jesus; Christmas Day (25 December), which originally was connected with the passing of the winter solstice, commemorates the birth of Jesus, and Epiphany (6 January), the coming of the Wise Men. Ash Wednesday (in February or March) is the start of the season of Lent when Christians think of Jesus' 40-day sojourn in the wilderness; Palm Sunday in late March or April marks the beginning of Holy Week and Jesus' triumphant entry into Jerusalem; Good Friday is the day of Jesus' crucifixion, and on Easter Sunday (originally a pagan spring festival) Jesus' resurrection from the dead is celebrated. Forty days later, Jesus' ascension into heaven is remembered on Ascension Day, and the giving of the Holy Spirit is commemorated 10 days later on Whitsunday or Pentecost. Various days connected with the saints are also regarded as festivals, but Harvest Thanksgiving, although popular, is unofficial, and is celebrated on different days in different churches. On each festival, the church is appropriately decorated and there are special readings and prayers.

Thus both Christians and Jews punctuate the year with a cycle of festivals. Many of these have their roots in old nature celebrations, but they have been transformed to commemorate the history of the central features of each tradition and are celebrated accordingly.

Font

(*Mikveh*): Both the Jewish and Christian traditions use water to initiate new adherents into their religion. Most churches are equipped with a small stone or metal basin which is filled with water and used to baptize new Christians. Since in general it only involves pouring water on the head, this font need not be large. Some Protestant denominations such as Baptists require baptism by total immersion, and such churches use a baptismal pool and do not have a font. This, in fact, was the tradition of the early church, and it was only in the Middle Ages that baptism by pouring or sprinkling became the norm. Gentile proselytes to Judaism are also expected to immerse themselves completely in a ritual bath (*mikveh*), which has to fulfil the rabbinic requirements laid down in the Mishnah. The source of the water must be spring or rain-water, and the built-in or hewn-out pool must contain at least 77 gallons. Besides conversion, the *mikveh* is used to wash away all the ritual impurity including that arising from menstruation; a monthly visit is thus a regular commitment in the life of Orthodox Jewish women. Because the laws of purification are so vital in Judaism, traditionally the duty of building a *mikveh* comes before the duty of building a synagogue. Among Reform Jews, however, the *mikveh* is not used, except occasionally for converts, because the notion of menstrual impurity is perceived as being degrading to women.

Food

(Dietary laws) (*Kashrut*): The system of dietary laws (*kashrut*) in Judaism is based on Lev. 11.44: 'For I am the Lord your God; consecrate yourselves therefore, and be holy, for I am holy.' According to the Torah, the purpose of the dietary laws is to attain the ideal of holiness. Thus food served must be in accordance with God's decrees as laid down in Scripture.

According to the Book of Leviticus, only cattle or beasts that chew cud and have a cloven-hoof are permitted. Lev. also states that only fish having fins and scales are allowed. Insects must not be eaten, nor any creeping thing. The milk of unclean animals and the eggs of unclean birds are also forbidden, as is the sinew of animals and the blood of beasts and birds. In rabbinic literature, these and many other laws dealing with *kashrut* are further expanded.

The dietary laws not only deal with permitted and forbidden food, but also with the slaughter (shehitah) of animals. The ritual specified method consists of a rapid slitting of the throat of an animal with a knife. After this act, the slaughterer must perform an inspection of the animal to determine if the internal organs show any sign of injury or death that would have been likely to cause the animal's death within one year. In such a case, the animal is forbidden. Various procedures are then undertaken to ensure that the blood is drained from the meat.

Different types of food have been traditional for Jews through the centuries, though they differ from community to community. Sabbath meals open with a sanctification over a cup of wine followed by the blessing over bread. At the New Year (Rosh Hashanah), loaves of bread are usually baked in round or in different shapes, each with a symbolic meaning. Culinary practices for Tabernacles (Sukkot) vary considerably. Latkes (pancakes made of grated potatoes and fried in oil) are distinctive festival of Lights (Hanukkah) food among azi (Eastern European) Jewry. On the Feast of Esther (Purim) *humantashen* (the 3-cornered poppyseed buns representing Haman's hat) are common. Passover (Pesah) laws require the abstinence from leaven and the eating of matzah (unleavened bread). At the Passover Seder (meal), four cups of wine are drunk, and bitter herbs, haroset (paste made of apples, cinnamon, nuts, and wine), and green vegetables are eaten – all these have symbolic significance related to the Exodus from Egypt. Dairy dishes are served on the Feast of Weeks (Shavuot). In addition, Jewish communities throughout the world have evolved their own distinctive types of food.

After the early Church had made the decision to admit Gentiles as full members, Scriptural food laws were no longer observed by Christians. Paul argued that since Christians are saved by faith rather than by works of the law, it was not reasonable to insist on eating separately from Gentile converts (Gal. 2.11–16). Therefore, the Church observes no laws connected with forbidden food except on fast days when, as a matter of discipline, traditionally all animal products were forbidden.

In Christian circles, certain foods are also connected with particular celebrations. Bread and wine are consecrated at the Holy Communion service to share among the faithful, symbolizing the body and blood of Jesus. At his Last Supper, which was the origin of the Christian ceremony, Jesus performed the traditional Jewish rite of sanctification (Kiddush) over bread and wine. Because according to the Synoptic Gospels the Last Supper was a Passover meal and thus unleavened bread was used, many churches use specially baked wafers rather than normal bread. Christmas, as a time of feasting, is associated with celebratory meals. Shrove Tuesday (the day before the fast of Lent) is known in the Anglo-Saxon world as 'Pancake Day'. This is because the eggs, butter, and milk were used up on that day before the season of Lent began. From earliest times, eggs have been exchanged at Easter. These symbolize the new resurrected life of Jesus, but the custom goes back to pagan times when Easter was a festival to celebrate the coming of spring.

Forgiveness

(Mercy): Forgiving transgression is one of God's 13 attributes in the Bible (Exod. 34.6–7). In the sixth blessing of the *Amidah* prayer, God is addressed three times daily as 'The one who forgives abundantly'. Throughout Scripture, God's forgiving nature is repeatedly asserted. Thus, for example, when the Israelites turned against the Lord and worshipped the golden calf, God heeded Moses prayer and overcame his anger (Exod.

32.11–14). A central theme of the prophetic books is the need for repentance – an act made possible by God's capacity for forgiveness.

In the Middle Ages, Maimonides (12th cent.) asserted that divine forgiveness is dependent on confession, repentance, and the determination not to repeat the offence. In the Jewish faith, these stages are highlighted and reflected in the liturgy, particularly on the Day of Atonement. Each individual is to seek forgiveness from God and from his neighbour. God is conceived as ready to forgive at the first sign of repentance, and human beings are urged to follow his example. However, it is understood that when one has committed an offence against another person, restitution is necessary and the offender must seek the injured party's forgiveness. Hence, on the eve of the Day of Atonement, it is customary to ask forgiveness from those whom one has wronged and to offer to make amends.

Underlying the Jewish view of forgiveness is the belief in God's mercy. According to Ps. 145.9, 'His compassion is over all that he has made'. Human beings too must adopt this quality. In the tradition, God is referred to as the Merciful One, yet he is continually forced to weigh the attribute of mercy against his attribute of justice. Thus, Jews also feel compelled to take into account the demands of justice in assessing the extent to which mercy should be shown. The relative priority of these concepts in rabbinic thought is illustrated by the legend where God is depicted as praying that his qualities of mercy and forgiveness should override the demand for strict justice.

In the New Testament, the theme of repentance as a central feature of Jesus' ministry is introduced by John the Baptist (Mark 1.4). In Jesus' conception of God's Kingdom, forgiveness of sin was of major importance, and through his death forgiveness was made available for all. According to the New Testament view, God does not demand a prior restitution from the offender; instead, God takes upon himself the act of reparation. In this way, the sinner can be restored to a true relationship with God. In Rom., Paul argues that the acceptance of this act of pure divine love is the moment of initiation into the Christian life (Rom. 5.5–8).

God's love is thus wholly unconditional, free, and unmerited, and as such it naturally calls out repentance from human beings. When Christians see God's reconciling love in Christ, their hearts are moved to repentance towards God and forgiveness towards others. Forgiveness is thus from God, and by God through Jesus' teaching and ministry. Just as God forgives transgressors, so too must human beings forgive those who offend against them. In the Lord's Prayer, Christians are taught to pray: 'Forgive us our trespasses, as we forgive those who trespass against us.' In this way, the gift of forgiveness and repentance is available through the person and mission of Jesus Christ.

Thus in contrast to Judaism – with its emphasis on individual repentance, restitution, and reconciliation – the Church has understood forgiveness primarily as a gift, mediated through the life and death of Christ. Within the Jewish faith, the offender is to take the first step towards forgiveness through a change of heart. In Christianity, forgiveness is freely offered by God to sinners; God takes the initiative in drawing to him those who have fallen into sin, and the individual Christian is to forgive transgressors with the same loving spirit as God. In so doing, the way to repentance and reconciliation is opened through a vision of God's unconditional love. Jews therefore only feel the need to forgive those who repent, while Christians feel obliged to forgive their enemies unconditionally.

Free will

According to the Bible, each person has the freedom of choice to obey God. In Gen., Cain was told by God that he can master his inclination to sin (Gen. 4.7). Later, Moses told the Israelites that the destiny of the nation rests on personal choice: 'I have set before you life and death, blessing and curse; therefore choose life' (Deut. 30.19). Throughout the Pentateuch the concept of repentance (*teshuvah*) is emphasized, and was reinforced by the prophets – a notion that presupposes freedom of the will.

Despite such biblical teaching, not all Jews in the Hellenistic period accepted this doctrine: the Essenes believed in divine predestination, whereas the Sadducees denied divine providence and maintained that everything was the result of chance. Nevertheless, the belief in free will became a central principle of rabbinic Judaism, and Jewish theology sought to reconcile personal decision-making with the concept of God's omniscience. Maimonides (12th cent.), for example, argued that God's knowledge is utterly different from human knowledge – this implies that since God is outside time, his omniscience is not, strictly speaking, foreknowledge. God perceives past, present, and future simultaneously; hence his knowledge is not in conflict with human freedom. Even when God acts in history, this does not interfere with human volition.

In the modern period, the belief in free will has continued to serve as a central feature of the Jewish faith – it is the basis of the Jewish conviction that all individuals have the capacity to shape their own lives. Some Jewish thinkers have been aware of the challenge of contemporary psychology which conceives of the human mind as causally determined. Yet, in accordance with biblical and rabbinic thought, they assert that moral responsibility is an inherent part of the created order. Just as God created the universe out of nothing, so each person can act as a self-originating creative force.

The belief in free will is also a dominant element in Christian thought. The New Testament emphasizes the biblical conviction that each person is free to make moral and religious choices, and this belief animated the quest of the early Church to spread the gospel. Nonetheless, Christian theologians were acutely aware of the conflict between human responsibility and divine providence. In *De libero arbitrio*, Augustine (4th–5th cent.) contended that although God has foreknowledge, human beings are not deprived of freedom since God foreknows what they will freely choose. Later theologians have sought various ways of resolving this seeming contradiction. In the 5th–6th cent., Boethius (like Maimonides six centuries later) argued that God's knowledge is outside time, and is thus of a different order from human prediction.

Within Protestantism, some theologians were less accepting of the doctrine of free will. John Calvin (16th cent.), in his famous doctrine of double predestination, maintained that some are ordained for heaven and some for hell, and there is little space for human free will. Jonathan Edwards (18th cent.), on the other hand, although he adopted a negative view of human freedom, still maintained that human beings are responsible agents. Other theologians accepted the belief in human liberty,

but their commitment to the doctrines of grace, foreknowledge, and predestination made it more difficult for them to give significance to the traditional doctrine of human freedom. However, recent Protestant theology has tended to be more accepting of the role of personal choice, and some theologians have sought to redefine divine omniscience in order to give more scope to free will. Thus in both the Christian and Jewish traditions, there has been a common acceptance of human freedom, although theologians in both faiths have wrestled with the seeming conflict between this belief and divine providence.

Fundamentalism

The term 'fundamentalist' first became current in the late 19th cent. in Christian Protestant circles. It was an expression of discontent with liberal theology, stressing the inerrancy and literal interpretation of Scripture. The findings of biblical scholarship were rejected and believers were expected to accept the virgin birth of Jesus, his miracles, and his bodily resurrection as historical facts. In recent years, such opposition to cultural and religious liberalism can be found in all Christian denominations, and in the other great world faiths. In Judaism, followers of traditional Orthodoxy are perceived as being fundamentalist by non-Orthodox Jews because they believe that the Written Law (Torah) was directly given by God to Moses on Mt Sinai, and should thus be obeyed in every particular. The conjectures of liberal scholars about the sources of the Pentateuch are dismissed out of hand. In addition, they insist that the process of formulating the Oral Law was also guided by God, and so must be seen as of equal validity to the Written Law. Thus fundamentalism must be seen as a traditionalist response to modern liberalism. Adherents regard the written Scriptures as being God-given, and therefore reject unconditionally the insights of liberal theological modernity.

Funeral rites

(Burial) (Cremation) (Kaddish) (Mourning) (*Shiva*) (*Yahrzeit*): In ancient times it was regarded as a travesty to leave a corpse unburied (1 Kings 14.11; 16.4; Jer. 22.19). Caves, catacombs, and various types of sepulchre were used for this purpose. Until the Middle Ages it was the custom to put the bones of the dead in sarcophagi; a year later they were exhumed and buried in a crypt or ossury. Subsequently, it became the practice to bury the dead in Jewish cemeteries.

The responsibility for burial rests on the immediate relatives of the deceased, but in their absence this duty became a communal responsibility. Most Jewish communities have their own burial society (*hevrah kaddisha*). Burial should take place as soon as possible after death, but no burial may take place on a Sabbath or the Day of Atonement. Burial in the land of Israel was favoured, but it was usual for burial to take place in a local cemetery. After members of the burial society have taken charge of the body, they wash it and dress it in a white linen shroud. The deceased is then placed in a coffin before the funeral service. Orthodox Jews only permit the use of a plain wooden coffin and cremation is abhorrent to them, being associated with paganism and conflicting with the doctrine of the resurrection of the body. Among Reform Jews, funeral practice differs from this traditional pattern. Embalming and cremation are permitted, and the dead are buried in normal clothing.

Mourning rites are undertaken for immediate relatives (father, mother, son, daughter, sister, and spouse). During the first seven days, (*shivah*), the mourner is forbidden to leave his home, study the Torah, bathe, shave, cut his hair, engage in business activities, or have sexual relations. It is obligatory to sit on the floor or a low stool. From the 7th to 30th day (*sheloshim*), the mourner is also under various restrictions. If a parent has died, the mourner is to recite the Kaddish prayer at each service for 11 months (for 30 days in the case of other relatives). The day of death is observed yearly (*yahrzeit*), and it became customary to kindle a light on such occasions.

In the early Church, the pattern of burial followed Jewish precedent, although a positive note was introduced in the funeral service since death was seen as a prelude to resurrection. By the 4th cent., burials were occasions of joy in which participants were dressed in white. However, from the 8th cent., the emphasis shifted; services became 'black' and prayers were offered for purification and deliverance from hell. By the medieval period, burial practices were formalized. The burial was preceded overnight by vespers, after which matins and lauds were said in the night. Requiem mass was then held in the morning with prayers for the absolution of the dead. Requiems were also recited on the 3rd, 9th and 30th day after death, as well as on anniversaries.

The first Christian cemeteries were in the area of Rome; later cemeteries became consecrated ground and churches were constructed on or near gravesites. Because of the doctrine of the resurrection of the body, cremation was not generally practised until the early 20th cent, by Protestants, and the late 20th cent, by Roman Catholics. At both burials and cremations special committal prayers are offered, although Protestant procedures are less liturgical. The belief in and hope for the resurrection of the dead is firmly expressed.

In both faiths, the funeral rites were grounded in biblical practice. For Christians, Christ's deliverance from death and corruption has served as the central focus of religious activities dealing with the dead, while in Judaism, the emphasis is on the grief of the mourners and the fulfilment of their ritual duties.

Future world *see* Heaven; hell; judgement; messianic age

G

Garden of Eden *see* Heaven

Gehenna *see* Hell

Gentile

(*Ger*): A non-Jew, that is someone not born of a Jewish mother, or who has not been converted to Judaism. Gentiles are believed to have a place in the world-to-come, provided they keep the Seven Laws of Noah – belief in one God; the avoidance of blasphemy, murder, theft, sexual immorality, and eating from a living animal; and the compulsion to set up courts of law. Jews feel no obligation to encourage Gentiles to take on Jewish status, since they already have the capacity of achieving salvation. Most commentators accept that Muslims and Christians are *Ger Toshav* – literally, a resident alien, but meaning one who keeps the Noachide Laws. Other Gentiles, polytheists, and atheists are regarded as *Akum* – pagans – and for them there is no hope. The Talmud contains many laws restricting intercourse between Jews and Gentiles, but since the time of the Enlightenment there has been much greater freedom. This is the cause of some concern today, since it inevitably leads to some degree of assimilation of the Jewish community into the mainstream and the increased threat of inter-marriage. The term *Ger* originally referred to the non-Jews living within the Jewish community, but is now used to describe a Gentile who has converted to Judaism. Orthodox Jews only accept such converts if they have fulfilled their own stringent conversion requirements; the vast majority of converts, however, are attached to the non-Orthodox movements and they are not recognized as Jews by the Orthodox – they and their children (if they are female) remain Gentiles.

In the early days of Christianity when the early Church was still a sect within Judaism, there was an initial reluctance to accept Gentile converts. Acts of the Apostles 10 and 11 describes how this was overcome. Since salvation was no longer to be found in keeping the law, but only in the grace offered through Jesus Christ, there could no longer be a distinction between Jew and Gentile. Thus Christianity, unlike Judaism, perceives itself to be a universal religion, transcending all tribal and ethnic barriers. Because of this, and because traditionally there was believed to be no salvation outside the Church, Christians have felt a strong compulsion to convert adherents of other faiths to Christianity. In recent years, however, with the increased knowledge of other religions, many Christians believe there are many equally legitimate paths to God and there is as much as interest in inter-faith dialogue in missionary work.

Ger *see* Gentile

Get *see* Divorce

Ghetto

The term has its origin in the name given to the Jewish quarter of Venice in 1516 – the *geto nuovo*. In the Middle Ages, the Church insisted on the segregation of the Jews from the Christian population, and this pattern was followed by the Muslim rulers. Wild stories about the Jews were circulated; they were accused of murdering Christian children for the Passover ritual, of poisoning wells, and of torturing the consecrated host. These tales encouraged anti-Semitic pogroms and the Jews were compelled to live in a restricted area of the town. The ghetto was often surrounded by a wall, and life inside was regulated by Jewish civil law. With the declining power of the Church in the 18th and 19th cent., Jews increasingly lived outside the ghetto. This resulted in the lessening influence of the Jewish authorities over the community, and many Jews assimilating into the Gentile world. The Nazis reintroduced ghettos into many European towns during the Second World War in order to maintain control over the Jewish population, prior to deportation to the death camps.

Ghosts *see* Exorcism

Glory *see* God, attributes of

Gnosticism

System of belief shared by various sects in the Roman World in the 1st and 2nd cent. According to some scholars, the movement originated in Jewish and Samaritan circles which came under the influence of Oriental ideas. Although these groups differed in numerous ways, Gnosticism as a movement adopted the belief in a Supreme Being as well as in a demiurge. This secondary power was responsible for creation and intervened in the material world. In addition, most gnostic systems embraced a dualistic philosophy characterized by the conviction that the universe is ruled by two opposing powers. The Supreme first Principle was understood as an all-powerful force, whereas the demiurge was conceived as a lower, imperfect being.

Within Christianity, some Gnostics identified the first Principle with the New Testament God of Love and the demiurge with the God of the Hebrew Scriptures whom they viewed as evil. In this context, they refuted the biblical conviction that creation is essentially good; rather, they believed that the material world resulted from a primordial fall from a pure spiritual state. Moreover, they thought that the soul is in exile in the material universe in which it has fallen, but that it can be redeemed by means of secret knowledge.

The early Church struggled against Christian forms of Gnosticism. Similarly, Jewish sages combated the influence of gnostic ideas, and their reaction is reflected in the liturgy as well as in rabbinic pronouncements against the *Minim* (heretics). Nonetheless, gnostic concepts influenced Jewish mysticism and appeared in medieval kabbalistic (mystical) works such as the Zohar, as well as in the teachings of Isaac Luria in the 16th cent.

God, attributes of

(Attributes of God) (Glory) (Holiness) (Omnipotence) (Omnipresence) (Omniscience) (Oneness of God) (Trinity): The Bible presupposes the existence of God, who is the creator and sustainer of the universe. Although concerned with all people, God established a special relationship with Israel. Bound to God by the covenant given to Moses on Mt Sinai, the nation is to serve as God's witness to all peoples. The purpose of God's law (Torah) is to make Israel a holy nation; however, if the Jewish people transgress God's decrees, punishment will be meted out in accordance with divine justice. God is a transcendent holy God, but his immanent glory is experienced in the world. Thus the hymn of the seraphim (Isa. 6.3), 'Holy, holy, holy is the Lord of hosts; the whole earth is full of his glory', is an expression of his total transcendence and constant immanence.

In the post-biblical period, Jewish thinkers engaged in philosophical speculation about the nature of God. The earliest reflections are found in the Apocrypha. In the Aramaic (Targum) and Greek (Septuagint) translations of the Bible, there are attempts to avoid anthropomorphisms in describing God's nature and activity. In Philo's (1st cent.) writings there is a sustained attempt to reinterpret the biblical view of God in philosophical terms. Under the influence of the Arab rediscovery of Greek philosophy, medieval Jewish writers utilized the insights of Aristotelianism and neo-Platonism in formulating their theological views. During this period, philosophers were particularly concerned with the attributes of God, the relationship between divine foreknowledge and human freedom, and the problem of evil. Their primary aim was to reconcile biblical and rabbinic views of God with rational

thought. In their writings, thinkers such as Maimonides (12th cent.) emphasized the oneness of God as well as his omniscience, omnipotence, and omnipresence. Other thinkers, however (such as Judah Ha-Levi, 12th cent.), stressed the importance of God's activity in the world.

In medieval mysticism, God was conceived as the infinite mystery of hiddenness whose presence was manifested through the ten *sephirot* (channels) of divine manifestation. After the Enlightenment, Jewish religious writers were concerned with issues other than harmonizing revelation and reason. Hermann Cohen (19th and early 20th cent.), for example, produced a synthesis between Kantianism and Judaism. In the existentialist philosophy of Franz Rosenzweig (early 20th cent.), the interconnections between God, man, and the world are explored. Martin Buber's (20th cent.) dialogical system stresses the significance of the I–Thou relationship, whereby human beings address God in full personal relationship. In Mordecai Kaplan's work (20th cent.), supernaturalism has been rejected in his formulation of Jewish civilization, a view that is echoed in the works of several Holocaust theologians such as Richard Rubenstein (20th cent.). Nonetheless, through the ages, Jews have declared their belief in the one God – 'Hear, O Israel, the Lord our God, the Lord is One.'

The Hebrew view of God is presupposed in the New Testament: God is viewed as almighty, holy, loving, faithful, and glorious. It is he who is made manifest in Jesus Christ. For the evangelists, God's purposes are revealed in the life and death of Jesus, who was perceived in the Church as the Son of God and the second person of the Holy Trinity. The Trinity as well as the oneness of God is a central doctrine of Christian theology: the one God is perceived as being in three Persons – Father, Son, and Holy Spirit – but is nonetheless of one substance. As Greek thought began to penetrate Christian theology, Christian writers attempted to define the nature of God's being and activity in the world. A number of writers stressed the ineffableness, omnipotence, and impassability of God; others elaborated his simplicity, indivisibility, and providence. By the time of Nicaea (325), such divine attributes as eternity, immutability, omniscience, and omnipotence had become central beliefs of Christendom.

The speculations of the Fathers were gathered together in a great synthesis by Augustine (4th–5th cent.), which was later elaborated by medieval schoolmen. In Augustine's writings, the three ways of conceiving God – by affirmation, negation, and eminence – were combined. Medieval scholars later began to investigate the nature of God by using the methods of rational proof independent of revelation. Reformers, however, abandoned this method of speculation and concentrated on personal religious experience in conceiving of God's nature and action. Such an approach continued in the modern period in the writings of Søren Kierkegaard (19th cent.) and F. D. E. Schleiermacher (18th–19th cent.); it is also reflected in modern religious existentialism.

A major trend in 20th-cent. Christian theology has been the reaffirmation of divine transcendence, a view found in the writings of Karl Barth and Emil Brunner. Nonetheless, 'Death of God' theologians have also had an important impact on Christian thought. More recently, there has been a revival of Process theology, emphasizing God's continuing changing activity in the world, as well as the emergence of liberation theology, which has focused on God's primary concern with the plight of the oppressed. Thus in both Judaism and Christianity, reflections about the nature and activity of God are rooted in the Bible. Jews have vigorously rejected the doctrine of the Trinity to the extent that some Jewish philosophers such as Maimonides (12th cent.) did not recognize Christians as monotheists. Even so, Jews and Christians subscribe to the same belief in a transcendent and immanent God who providentially guides human history; and through the ages, both faiths have been anxious to interpret such a conviction in the light of alternative and challenging systems of thought.

Golden rule

In Lev. 19.18, God commands the Israelites to 'Love your neighbour as yourself'. When asked by a Gentile to teach him the law in the time he could stand on one foot, Hillel (1st cent. BCE) responded, 'What is hateful to you, do not do to your fellow.' Jesus put forward the same idea in positive terms, 'So whatever you wish that men would do to you, do so to them; for this is the Law and the prophets' (Matt. 7.12). Thus both Christians and Jews accept that altruism rather than selfishness is the basis of good conduct.

Good Friday

Known as Great Friday in the Greek Orthodox Church, this is the day on which the crucifixion of Jesus is commemorated. It is traditionally kept as a fast day and, in recent times, a three-hour service is held in many churches. This lasts from noon until 3.00 pm, the hours that Jesus hung on the cross, and seven sermons are preached based on Jesus' seven sayings from the cross. Churches are usually stripped of all decorations, which are not renewed until the feast of Easter, two days later. According to the Synoptic Gospels, Jesus' death occurred at Passover time, and St Paul associated the sacrifice of Jesus with the Passover sacrifice (1 Cor. 5.7). In the same way as the original Passover lamb died to free the Israelites from slavery to the Egyptians, so Jesus died to free his followers from the chains of sin and death. Good Friday is the most solemn day in the Church's year. Despite the Passover connection, the nearest equivalent fast in Judaism is the Day of Atonement. Jews spend the whole day in solemn prayer and fasting, believing that in this way atonement is made for wrong-doing. Christians believe that Jesus' death brought about atonement for the sins of the whole world. By keeping Good Friday, Christians are vicariously sharing in Jesus' death so that, on Easter Sunday, they also share in the joyful benefits of his resurrection.

Good work

(Merit): The Hebrew word for righteousness, *tzedakah*, implies both legal justice and ethical conduct. The biblical prophets, in particular, stressed that God was not satisfied solely by ritual observance and they emphasized the importance of morality. Merit (*zekhut*) was attainable only through performing deeds of righteousness, and it was also believed that the good deeds of ancestors could store up merit for future generations. A Midrash (biblical interpretation) on Ps. 104.44 declares that the merits of the fathers will hasten the redemption of Israel.

Christians disagree as to whether human achievements can have merit before God. Paul wrote that no person will be justified in God's sight through works of the law (Rom. 3.19). Augustine (4th–5th cent.) insisted that because all good comes from God, in rewarding human virtue God is really only acknowledging his own works. This line was followed by the Protestant reformers in the 16th cent., who maintained that sinners are justified through Christ alone, not through any good deeds of their own. On the other hand, many Roman Catholic scholars have argued that those who use their natural powers for the glory of God will attain merit because it is fitting that their efforts should be rewarded. The virtue of the saints in heaven serves as an inspiration for living Christians, and the saints are making intercession for the sins of the world.

There is thus a real difference of opinion between Jews and Christians about the idea of attaining merit. Jews think that human beings are capable of righteousness and that they are rewarded by God for their good deeds. Christians, however, do not believe that people can be virtuous without the grace of God (yet it should be noted that some theologians do accept the possibility of God rewarding human actions, whereas others feel that this minimizes Christ's role in salvation). As far as storing up merit is concerned, there is a convergence of views within both traditions. The Jewish doctrine of fathers storing up merit for future generations is paralleled by the role of Christian saints who, through intercession, are able to contribute to redemption for the world.

Gospel

The English word 'gospel' is a translation of the Greek *Evangelion*, meaning good news. Jesus, in preaching the gospel (Mark 1.14), was preaching the good news of the Kingdom of God, which his life and ministry was bringing into effect. Later, the first four books of the New Testament that are ascribed to Matthew, Mark, Luke and John, were called Gospels – because they contained the good news of God's salvation. Most scholars believe that Mark's was the earliest work, and that Matthew and Luke used it as one source for their own versions. The Fourth Gospel is generally thought to come from a different tradition. In addition, there are various apocryphal Gospels containing other material about Jesus, but these are of a later date. A passage from the Gospels is always read at the Eucharist,

and it is the custom for the congregation to stand, indicating the centrality of the Gospels for the Christian faith.

The equivalent reading for Jews comes from the five books of Moses (the Pentateuch), which occurs every week at the Sabbath morning service. The scroll is brought out of the ark while the congregation stands, and a prescribed passage is read with great solemnity. In the same way as the life of Jesus Christ is the basis of Christianity, the words of the Torah are the foundation of the Jewish religion.

Grace

In the Hebrew Scriptures, God's grace or free favour is shown in his choice and care of the Israelites, as, for example, in 'The steadfast love of the Lord never ceases, his mercies never come to an end' (Lam. 3.22). Christians believe that the greatest manifestation of God's grace is to be found in the life and work of Jesus Christ: Paul, for example, begins his first letter to the Corinthians by saying, 'I give thanks to God always for you because of the grace of God which was given you in Christ Jesus' (1 Cor. 1.4).

The concept of divine grace has been a source of conflict between Christians. Augustine (4th–5th cent.) taught that it was only through the grace of God that the sinner achieved justification, while the heretic Pelagius (4th–5th cent.) argued that human beings could accept salvation through their own human faculties, grace merely makes the process easier. Even today, Roman Catholics tend to stress the availability of grace through the Church's sacraments, while Protestants emphasize the role of individual faith in the reception of grace. However, both groups agree that redemption is only available through God's grace – without it, human beings are inevitably condemned.

In contrast, while Jews believe and rejoice in the grace of God, they maintain that it is ultimately revealed in the gift of the Torah, or law. Through following the path of the Torah, individual Jews can be acceptable to God through their own efforts.

Grace at meals

Both Christians and Jews follow the tradition of saying grace at meals. The rabbis thought it was forbidden to enjoy the good things of the world without a blessing. Before meals, bread is blessed

(*Ha-motsi*) and shared out among the diners. After the meal, a series of blessings and prayers are recited; different communities follow different traditions. The Gospels describe Jesus blessing food (for example, at the feeding of the 5,000, Matt. 14.19), and the Church has continued the custom to the present day. In contrast to Judaism, there are no universally accepted forms of words and, increasingly, an extempore prayer is said.

H

Hair and beard

(Haircovering): According to Lev. 19.27, 'You shall not round off the hair on your temples or mar the edges of your beard.' This was later interpreted to mean that all shaving was forbidden and, in Eastern Europe, to remove the beard was seen to be symbolically breaking with the tradition. In fact, it is not breaking the law to get rid of the beard with depilatories, scissors or two-edged electric razors, so nowadays many Orthodox men are clean-shaven. Nonetheless, merely to trim the beard and hair in honour of the Sabbath is regarded as a pious act. In biblical times, shaving off all the hair and beard was part of a purification ceremony (Lev. 14.8), and also a sign of mourning (Job 1.20). Those who took a Nazarite vow, such as Samson or Samuel, refrained from cutting their hair at all, but the rabbis agreed that such a vow could only be made in the land of Israel. The wearing of uncut forelocks at the edges of the beard, however, continues in some religious groups to this day. Jewish married women were traditionally commanded to cover their hair and, from the 15th cent., they were expected to shave their heads at marriage and to cover their hair with a wig (*sheitel*). Among the very Orthodox, this practice is still followed, but the majority of secular Jews ignore all these laws and customs and appear indistinguishable from their Gentile neighbours.

Because Christians do not follow the ritual laws of the Hebrew Scriptures, there are no commandments or prohibitions for them concerning hair or beard. Paul did insist that women covered their hair in church (1 Cor. 11.5), but this clearly reflected his Jewish roots. Monks and priests have traditionally shaved all or part of their heads (tonsure) to indicate their religious calling. Similarly, nuns had their hair shaved off when they were admitted into their new life and from then on they covered their heads with a veil. All these customs have largely disappeared in the 20th cent., as they have in the secular Jewish community.

Hands, laying on of

In the Hebrew Scriptures, a manner of blessing was used that involved the laying on of hands (for example, Gen. 48.13, 14). When Moses transferred his authority to Joshua, this was symbolized by Joshua standing before the whole congregation and Moses laying his hands upon him (Num. 27.18–23). This tradition has continued until the present day in the ordination of rabbis. The ordinand's teacher lays his hands on the rabbinical candidate and invests him with judicial authority.

The laying on of hands was also used in the Christian Church. The early Church employed it at Antioch to evoke the Holy Spirit (Acts 8.14–17), and in ordination (Acts 13.1–3). Jesus himself laid his hands on those he was healing (for example, Mark 6.5), and this tradition has also been continued in the Church's ministry of healing.

Hanukkah *see* Lights, festival of

Harvest celebrations

The three Jewish Pilgrim festivals, Passover (Pesah), Weeks, (Shavuot) and Tabernacles (Sukkot), were all originally harvest festivals. Passover celebrated the beginning of the barley harvest and the offering of the first sheaf in the Temple. The festival of Weeks, which occurred at the end of the seven weeks of counting the *Omer* (barley sheaves), commemorated the conclusion of the grain harvest. The festival of Tabernacles is also called the 'Feast of Ingathering', when the people rejoiced that everything was stored away in barns. Traditionally, harvest times were occasions of merrymaking (Isa. 16.10, Jer. 48.33). Nowadays, the festival of Tabernacles has become the main harvest festival. The faithful live in the *sukkah* (booth), which is decorated with flowers and fruit and the four species (the palms, the myrtle, the willow, and the citron) are waved in the synagogue.

Like Passover and the festival of Weeks, Tabernacles has a connection with Israel's history – namely, the 40-year sojourn in the wilderness – but it remains the festival that has most faithfully retained its agricultural origins.

Harvest thanksgiving is an unofficial festival in Christianity. It is celebrated in September or October, at much the same time as the Jewish festival of Tabernacles. Churches are also decorated with fruit and vegetables, flowers, and plants. Special hymns of rejoicing are sung and the harvest offerings are given to charity. It is one of the most popular services in the Church's year. In the Western Church there are fixed dates, known as Rogation Days, on which prayers for the harvest are said. In the Middle Ages, on 1 August or Lammas Day, bread made from the first-cut corn was consecrated to God – a clear reminiscence of the Temple offering of the first barley sheaf at Passover. Both Lammas and Rogation Days have receded in importance since the Industrial Revolution.

Hasidim *see* Pious

Havdalah
The word *havdalah* means separation, and the Havdalah ceremony marks the passing of a sacred day, a Sabbath or festival, and the advent of a secular week-day. The Havdalah is primarily a home ritual. It generally consists of four blessings, the first over wine, the second over spices, the third over a plaited candle, and the final one, which contrasts the sacred and profane, light and darkness, Israel and the nations. Different communities follow different customs regarding drinking the wine, breathing in the smell of the spices, and lighting and extinguishing the candle. There is no parallel ceremony in Christianity, perhaps because, despite the efforts of Sabbatarians, the distinction between work-days and the Sabbath is less pronounced than in Judaism.

Hazzan *see* Music

Headcovering *see* Clothing; hair and beard

Healing *see* Miracles

'Hear, O Israel'
(Shema): 'Hear, O Israel: The Lord our God is one Lord' (Deut. 6.4). This is the fundamental statement of the Jewish faith, which is to be pronounced daily by all adult Jewish males, 'when you lie down, and when you rise' (Deut. 6.7). The full prayer – the Shema, which means 'Hear' – is composed of three sections: Deut. 6.4–9, Deut. 11.13–21, and Num. 15.37–41. The mezuzah, which is hung on the door-post of every Jewish house, contains the first two passages, as do phylactery boxes (tephillin). It is the prayer that should be recited at the moment of death, and the ideal is to die while saying it. The Shema is an affirmation of faith in the God of Israel and his law, and it is addressed to fellow Jews. In contrast, the central Christian prayer, the Our Father, which Jesus taught to his followers (Matt. 6.9–13), is spoken to God. It looks forward to the future Kingdom of God on earth and asks for the safety of the petitioners. Both prayers stress the communal nature of the respective religious faiths ('Hear, O Israel'; 'Our Father'), but the different emphases repay close attention.

Heathenism *see* Paganism

Heaven
(Future World) (Garden of Eden) (Paradise): In the Bible there is no fully developed belief in an afterlife or future world, but under Persian and Greek influence the doctrine of reward and punishment became a central feature of rabbinic theology. Jewish literature of the Hellenistic period contrasts the world-to-come (*Olam Ha-Ba*) with earthly life, and the concept of the immortality of the soul was developed in the writings of Philo (1st cent.). Rabbinic belief in reward and punishment is grounded in the conviction that God will meet out his justice in a future world. Nonetheless, the rabbis held differing views about the nature of this state. Referred to as the 'Garden of Eden' or paradise, it was described in terms of an earthly garden. According to the Babylonian scholar Rav (3rd cent.), in the world-to-come there is no eating, drinking, begetting, bargaining, hatred, jealousy, or strife. Instead, the righteous sit with crowns on their heads and enjoy the emanation of God's presence. In later writing, the righteous in heaven are depicted as

engaging in the study of the Torah. In the Middle Ages, neo-Platonic philosophers believed that the souls of the righteous ascend to God and commune with Wisdom. In contrast, Aristotelian theologians argued that in eternity there is a conjunction of the acquired intellect with the universal Active Intellect. In this regard, Maimonides (12th cent.) maintained that in the Messianic age souls would return to their bodies, but in the world-to-come disembodied souls of the righteous will enjoy spiritual bliss. Jewish mystics in the medieval period outlined the nature of the resurrected soul's existence in the hereafter. In the Zohar (mystical commentary on the Pentateuch), the three parts of the soul have different fates. The first two (*nefesh* and *ruah*) are susceptible to sin, and thus subject to punishment. But the pure soul (*neshamah*), which existed before the body among the *sephirot* (divine emanations), ascends again to their heights.

Despite this development of rabbinic speculation about the nature of the hereafter, there has been an increasing reluctance in the modern period to accept the notion of divine reward and punishment. Within Orthodoxy, such beliefs retain their centrality in the liturgy, yet they have lost most of their compelling urgency. For Reform Jews, the concept of heaven as an abode for the righteous has largely lost its force. Instead, believing Jews across the religious spectrum have generally substituted the concept of personal immortality for traditional eschatology. In most cases, there has been a tendency to emphasize this-worldly obligations instead of speculation about a future world.

In the New Testament, biblical and inter-testamental imagery penetrated Christian thought about the world-to-come. For Christians, heaven was conceived as a place of bliss where the faithful would be rewarded; there the believer is united with Christ. The characteristic feature of New Testament belief is the transformation of scriptural hope into the vision of God, and the reunion of the righteous around Jesus who leads the pious to the Father.

Early Church creeds usually included a reference to eternal life, but the most important texts about the nature of heaven emerged in the 14th cent. The Benedictus Deus of Benedict XII affirmed the existence of a beatific vision of the divine essence; such an experience was envisaged as occurring after death and continuing for ever. The Council of Florence asserted that the intensity of this vision will be experienced in accordance with a diversity of merit. Scholastic and neo-Scholastic reflection about heaven was primarily concerned with this concept of the beatific vision, and has continued until the modern period.

Despite such debate, there has been widespread agreement within the Church that souls, who having died in a state of grace and been purged of their sins in purgatory, pass into heaven where they enjoy eternal bliss. There they wait for reunion with their bodies at the general resurrection of the dead after which they enjoy heaven in an embodied state. Traditionally, Christians have believed that heaven was reserved only for those who believed in Christ, but in recent years a number of Christians have wished to include righteous believers of other faiths; this parallels the traditional Jewish view that righteous Gentiles who have accepted the Noachide Laws have a place in the world-to-come.

Although some Christians today would disagree about various details of this eschatological scheme, most would subscribe to a belief in a heavenly state that is the fulfilment of humanity's deepest longings. There is thus considerable divergence between Judaism and Christianity in the modern world concerning belief in the hereafter. Although officially the doctrine of heaven has been a major feature of Jewish theology, it has receded in importance in contemporary society as other concerns have come to the fore. For the Christian, however, the belief in heavenly reward continues to animate religious consciousness.

Hell

(Future World) (Gehenna): In the Bible there are several references to an abode of the dead, but it is not described as a place of punishment or reward. Located under the earth, at the bottoms of mountains, or under the waters, it was at times personified as a monster with a wide-open mouth. There all are equal including kings and subjects, as well as masters and slaves. Although God's sovereignty extends there, no communication takes place between him and the dead. In early rabbinic literature the term 'Gehenna' is used to refer to the biblical conception of the netherworld. This name is derived from Gei Ben Hinnom, a valley south of

Jerusalem where children were sacrificed to the god Moloch. Gehenna was identified with the region where the wicked would be punished for their misdeeds in a future world. In the Talmud, Joshua ben Levi (3rd cent.) referred to Gehenna by seven names, which were subsequently used to designate its divisions. In rabbinic sources, reflections of foreign elements widespread in the Hellenistic world are found in depictions of this accursed place. Thus the punishment of a wicked person whose tongue hangs out to lap the water of a river but is unable to reach it, is reminiscent of the punishment of Tantalus in Hades. Other descriptions concentrate on the size, entrances, gates, and divisions of Gehenna.

Some rabbinic texts portray the fire of Gehenna; others focus on its darkness. There are also depictions of rivers of fire as well as the sufferings of the unrighteous – including hanging by various limbs, roasting by fire, and suffocating by smoke. Opinion differed as to the duration of such punishment. According to the school of Shammai (1st cent.), those who are utterly wicked remain there for ever, whereas individuals who have been less wicked descend to Gehenna, are purged, and ascend after purification. The school of Hillel (1st cent.) adopted a more lenient stance. In rabbinic literature there are also various legends of visits to Gehenna, in which these torments are outlined in detail. Although the concept of hell became a central feature of rabbinic eschatology, it has been largely abandoned in modern times. Instead, most Jews have set aside such a notion as other spiritual concerns have come to the fore in Jewish life.

In the New Testament, Christian writers presuppose earlier Jewish traditions concerning Gehenna, a term that appears 11 times in the Synoptic Gospels. It is a place of fire, darkness, worms, howling, and gnashing of teeth. Although Paul does not use such imagery, he speaks of eternal destruction and banishment (2 Thess. 1.9; Rom. 9.22; Phil. 3.19). In the Book of Revelation 21.8, apocalyptic imagery is used to portray the torments of hell, and Jude 6–7 utilizes images of eternal chains, gloom, and fire.

In various creeds the concept of eternal damnation is mentioned, and numerous councils dealt with the subject of hell. It has also been the inspiration for such literary work as Dante's *Inferno*, (13th–14th cent.). Officially, the Church has subscribed to the belief that those who die in mortal sin will be punished eternally after death. In 1979 the Sacred Congregation for the Doctrine of the Faith published a *Letter on Certain Questions concerning Eschatology*, which reaffirmed the traditional teaching of punishment for sinners; they will be deprived of the sight of God for ever.

Despite such official teaching, there has been considerable discussion through the centuries about the nature of such punishment. A number of patristic writers interpreted the fires of hell in a symbolic sense, whereas other theologians held that fire is real. Various thinkers argued that there would be an end to punishment in hell, and this view has had an increasing number of adherents in modern times. There is, however, a wide body of Christian opinion today that seeks to reject the doctrine altogether, a shift within liberal Christianity that parallels a similar transformation in contemporary Jewish thought.

Hellenism

Term referring to the cultural and religious influences on Europe and the Near and Middle East from the 4th cent. BCE. It constituted an amalgam of elements from classical Greece, as well as the societal and cultural features of peoples of the East conquered by Alexander the Great. Hellenism was a serious threat to traditional Judaism, and numerous Jewish apologists emphasized its inadequacies in various literary works of the Greco-Roman period. Such texts extol the glories of Judaism as against pagan polytheism.

Despite such apologetics, Jewish communities from Italy to Babylonia and Persia were profoundly affected by the social, cultural, and political currents of Hellenistic thought. Within Palestine, upper-class segments of Jewish society came under the spell of Hellenism, and Jerusalem was reconstituted as a Greek *polis* (city) with a gymnasium. Such a transformation of Jewish life was resisted by the Hasmoneans, who staged a successful revolt against the Seleucids and eradicated pagan practices in the Holy Land. Their victory is celebrated by the annual festival of Lights (Hanukkah). Nonetheless, Judaism continued to be subject to Hellenistic influence. The Talmud contains numerous Greek and Latin loan words, phrases, and concepts. In addition, the hermeneutical principles of Talmudic reasoning have a Hellenistic basis. Herod's Temple was constructed along Greco-Roman lines, and archaeological remains of this period testify to the influence of Hellenistic culture.

Christianity emerged within such a Greco-Roman milieu. The Greek language was used by Jews in the Diaspora in pre-Christian and New Testament times, and was the common language at the beginning of the Christian era. Paul was a Diaspora (dispersion) Jew from Tarsus, whose theology contains numerous Hellenistic elements. Various aspects of Hellenistic culture profoundly affected the development of Christian thought and the prevalence of the Greek language enabled the Christian message to spread quickly around the Mediterranean area. When the Christian faith became the religion of the Empire, Christians were exposed to the education of the Greek world, and Christian thought was shaped by prevailing literary and cultural modes. Thus, both Judaism and Christianity were deeply influenced by the prevailing patterns of social, political, economic, and cultural aspects of Hellenism. Yet within both faiths there was a fervent rejection of pagan features, and an insistence on the sole reality of the God of Israel.

Herem *see* Excommunication

Heresy

Beliefs considered to be contrary to authoritative teaching. Although neither the Bible nor the Talmud contain a systematic credal formulation, certain religious beliefs are fundamental to the Jewish faith. In the 12th cent., Moses Maimonides listed what he believed to be the 13 central principles of Judaism. According to Maimonides, if someone denied any of these beliefs, he would thereby forfeit his portion in the world-to-come. Later, Simeon ben Tzemah Duran (14th–15th cent.), while agreeing with Maimonides' formulation of the principles of the Jewish faith, argued that a person would not lose eternal life if he denied any of these principles through incorrect teaching or erroneous reasoning. Other Jewish thinkers offered different formulations of the central Jewish beliefs, whereas some sages asserted that every detail of the Torah must be maintained since it is all essential.

Despite this debate, the Mishnah itself specifies certain heresies that cause a person to lose a place in the hereafter (including denying the resurrection of the dead and the divine origins of the Torah). The Talmud defines a heretic (*epikoros*) as one who scorns the rabbis or deprecates others in their presence. The 16th-cent. Code of Jewish Law (*Shulhan Arukh*) decrees than anyone who holds the sages in contempt has no portion in the world-to-come. Maimonides also defined other terms that refer to individuals who hold incorrect beliefs: (1) a *min* – one who does not believe in God, thinks there is more than one God, conceives of God as corporeal and limited in time, or worships stars and other objects: (2) a *mumar* – one who intentionally does not observe a commandment in the Torah or abandons the Jewish faith under duress; (3) a *kofer* – one who denies the Torah, resurrection of the dead, and the coming of the Messiah.

In rabbinic sources, a person who is guilty of heresy is referred to as *kofer ba-ikkar* (a denier of basic principles), a term that designates an individual whose beliefs and actions illustrate a rejection of the divine origin of the Torah and Jewish law. Throughout Jewish history, certain groups have been designated as heretics, such as the Karaites (8th–12th cent.), who did not accept the validity of the Oral Law, as well as non-Orthodox Jews of today because of their departure from traditional Jewish belief and practice. In addition, various individuals, such as Uriel Acosta (16th–17th cent.) and Benedict Spinoza (17th cent.), have been condemned for heresy and sanctioned by the community. Nonetheless, such individuals who do not hold Orthodox beliefs are still regarded as Jews. Despite this tradition of rooting out heresy, Judaism has within limitations always accepted differing theological views, and a variety of opinions are recorded in Jewish sources.

The term heresy (*hairesis*) is used in the New Testament to refer to divisions within the Church that threaten its unity. The problem of heresy is also referred to in 2 Pet. 2.1, where the term designates false teachers who introduce destructive heresies in their denial of Christ. The letters of Paul and John also reflect pressure on the early Church to resist doctrinal error within the ranks, as well as from outside influences. Initially, heresy and schism were not distinguished in the Church, but the concept of heresy as theological error eventually gained currency. From the 2nd cent., the term designated doctrinal error or departure from the rules of the faith, whereas 'schism' implied dissent from the Church for any reason.

In time, numerous councils sought to define the true Christian faith in order to root out heterodox theological opinions such as those espoused by Arius (3rd–4th cent.), Nestorius (5th cent.), and Pelagius (5th cent.). According to the early Church Fathers, heterodoxy was sinful because it indicated an inflexibility of the will, and this position influenced subsequent medieval Scholastic thought on this subject. In more recent times, the term has come to mean doctrinal heterodoxy deserving of censure. Yet the growth of biblical scholarship and the recognition of religious plurality in the modern world has made the identification of heresy a more disputable process. However, because the Christian Church is a belief community rather than a shared ethnic heritage, differing theological opinion has been traditionally less acceptable and more readily condemned than in Judaism.

Hermeneutics

Method of Bible exegesis. The process of expounding Scripture began in the 5th cent. BCE with the teaching of Ezra (Ezra 7.10). At his instigation, the Torah was read and explained. As time passed, the process of interpretation (Midrash) became formalized into a set of principles (*middot*). In the 1st cent. BCE, Hillel formulated seven methods of interpretation: (1) *Kal va Homer*: deduction from a minor to a major case; (2) *Gezerah Shavah*: drawing a conclusion by word analogy; (3) *Binyan Av mi-Katuv Ehad*: application of a principle derived from a single verse to a wider range of cases; (4) *Binyan Av mi-Shene Ketuvim*: application of a principle, that may be derived from two specific verses, to a wider range of cases; (5) *Kelal u-Ferat u-Ferat u-Kelal*: a restriction on a general principle from a specific case, or an expanded application of specific cases by a subsequent general principle; (6) *Ka Yotse Bo be-Makom Aher*: drawing conclusions on the basis of a similarity between passages; (7) *Davar Ha-Lamed mi-Inyano*: drawing a conclusion from the context.

Later, Nahum of Gimzo (1st–2nd cent. CE) formulated an alternative system of exegesis, which was further developed by Akiva (1st–2nd cent. CE). In the 2nd cent., Ishmael ben Elisha expanded Hillel's 7 rules to 13; these were eventually further expanded by Eliezer ben Yose Ha-Gelili (2nd cent.) to 32. These exegetical principles were used to introduce new legal rulings, as well as expound the meaning of the biblical text.

Other methods of biblical hermeneutics were subsequently developed, including gematria, a calculation of the numerical value of Hebrew words and the search for other words or phrases of equal value. This method became a central feature of kabbalistic (mystical) exposition, as well as of magical practice.

In addition, the system of *notarikon* also came into vogue, whereby the separate letters of a word were viewed as initials for other words. Such interpretation was utilized in moral and homiletical lessons. In modern times, these various principles of biblical hermeneutics have continued to be employed within traditional Jewish circles. However, because of the belief that the Torah was given by God to Moses on Mt Sinai, Orthodox scholars have been unwilling to apply modern critical methods of interpretation to the biblical text. Within non-Orthodox Judaism, however, such interpretive procedures have been widely accepted.

In the New Testament, the term *hermeneuein* and its cognates are used in connection with the translation of significant terms and proper names, as well as the interpretation of tongues. In Luke 24.27 Christ is described as interpreting all things concerning himself in Scripture. The first major Christian interpreter, Origen (2nd–3rd cent.), stressed the importance of understanding the scriptural text in its literal and spiritual sense. Augustine (4th–5th cent.) later provided philosophical support for such a method, and this model served as the authoritative method of biblical interpretation that emerged in the Church – literal, allegorical, analogical and prophetic. In all cases, interpreters were anxious to understand Scripture in the light of their conviction that, in Jesus Christ, God's promises had been fulfilled.

During the Reformation, the new importance given to Scripture encouraged individual believers to read and understand the Bible for themselves.

This impetus freed scriptural interpretation from the formal authority of the magisterium. After the Enlightenment, and largely through the writings of F. D. E. Schleiermacher (18th–19th cent.), Christian hermeneutics were put on a new footing. According to Schleiermacher, all extra-textual authorities constitute illegitimate impositions on the individual act of understanding Scripture – the text must be allowed to speak for itself. In time, the concept of a hermeneutical circle developed within Christian thinking. On this view, the Bible cannot be approached neutrally; rather, interpreters work within a circle of shared assumptions and need to reflect on the historical conditions affecting them. Such an approach has been widely influential, and has recently been embraced by a number of liberation theologians.

Added to this approach are the contributions of literary studies including generative grammar, semiotics, genre research, structural analysis, and inquiry into the formation of the canon of the Bible. Such an openness to modern forms of scriptural interpretation throughout Christendom contrasts sharply with modern Orthodox Jewish scholarship, which remains rooted to the methods of the past. It is only within non-Orthodox Judaism that contemporary hermeneutical methods have been employed in recent times.

Holiness, *see* God, attributes of

Holy places *see* Pilgrimage

Holy Spirit

In Judaism, the Holy Spirit is conceived as manifest in creation and in the lives of individuals. In the Bible – where it is referred to as *Ruah Ha-Kodesh* (the Holy Spirit), *Ruah Elohim* (Spirit of God), or *Ruah Adonai* (Spirit of the Lord) – there are 80 allusions to such a Spirit. When it rests on an individual, that person experiences prophetic visions, utters inspired speech, or is enabled to perform divinely appointed tasks. According to the rabbis, the Holy Spirit rested on the high priest when he consulted the Urim and Thummim, on David when he wrote the Psalms, and on Solomon when he wrote Proverbs, Ecclesiastes, and the Song of Songs.

The Talmud asserts that the Holy Spirit ceased inspiring human beings after the last of the prophets (Haggai, Zechariah, and Malachi) died. Nevertheless, in Midrashic (biblical narrative) literature, the Holy Spirit is conceived as resting on pious Jews in every generation, enabling them to see into the future, bring down blessings on those in need, and perceive the spiritual source of the created order. Religious perfection can be achieved only by *tzaddikim* (righteous individuals) in every generation, but even ordinary persons can feel the Holy Spirit on special occasions such as the Sabbath and festivals.

In the Middle Ages, Moses Maimonides (12th cent.) viewed the Holy Spirit as one of the lower orders of prophecy. Such a prophetic spirit, he argued, rests only on a person who is great in wisdom, strong in moral character, and whose passions never overcome him. When inspired by the Holy Spirit, he is able to contemplate the wisdom of God as reflected in his creatures and knows from this his greatness. Such a view was echoed by other writers who viewed the Holy Spirit as a degree of spiritual perfection. The Holy Spirit is a gift of God, but in no case is it envisaged as a separate divine entity or part of the Godhead.

In the New Testament, the biblical notion of the Holy Spirit plays a central role. The early Christians, following the prophecy of Joel 2.28, 'And it shall come to pass afterward, that I will pour out my spirit on all flesh; your sons and your daughters shall prophesy', believed that the Holy Spirit was the sign of the Messianic age. At his baptism, the Holy Spirit descended on Jesus (Mark 1.10) as it had descended on the kings of old at their anointing (1 Sam. 10.1–13). In the desert it supported him in his conflict with Satan (Mark 1.12), and through his ministry it was an operative power in his healing and preaching (Luke 4.18). In the Fourth Gospel, the full mission of the Holy Spirit in the Church is seen as lying in the future after Jesus has been glorified. It will teach the disciples and guide them into all truth (John 16.13). Acts 2.1–13 describes the impact of the Holy Spirit on the disciples: it appeared as flames of fire and was marked by the gift of tongues. In addition, the early Christians believed that they received direct communications from the Holy Spirit, as in the instruction to baptize the Gentile Cornelius (Acts 10.44–48), and it was seen as an active power in their deliberations (Acts

15.28). The gift of the Holy Spirit could also be conveyed to others by baptism and the laying on of their hands (Acts 8.15–17).

For Paul, the Christian life was understood as a life in the Spirit, and this is contrasted with his pre-Christian life in the flesh. The Holy Spirit is humanity's intercessor with the Father (Rom. 8.26f.) In Gal. 5.22f., the fruits and gifts of the Spirit are outlined. They are love, joy, peace, patience, kindness, goodness, faithfulness, gentleness, and self-control. Through possession of the Spirit, a Christian at baptism becomes a member of the Church, the body of Christ on earth (1 Cor. 12.13) and, in the future, will share in Christ's resurrection (1 Cor. 15.20–24). The Church Fathers elaborated the doctrine of the Holy Spirit, and from 360 CE it became a source of serious controversy. The Macedonians, while maintaining against the Arians the full divinity of the Son, denied the divinity of the Holy Spirit. In 381 at the Council of Constantinople, Macedonianism was rejected and the full doctrine of the Holy Spirit was accepted in the Church. Later, this doctrine was elaborated by Augustine (4th–5th cent.) in *De Trinitate*. In time, a serious dispute concerning the question whether the Holy Spirit proceeds from the Father and the Son – *procedit ex patre filioque* – (the Western view), or solely from the Father (the Eastern position), divided Christendom. However, despite this controversy, Christians are united in understanding the Holy Spirit as a co-equal, co-eternal person of the Trinity, a view that is vehemently rejected by Jews who see the Holy Spirit as simply an outpouring of God's presence on selected individuals.

Holy week

This week, which has its climax on Easter Sunday, is celebrated by Christians in the spring and is a time of devotion to the suffering, death, and resurrection of Jesus. It begins with Palm Sunday when Jesus' triumphal ride into Jerusalem is celebrated (Mark 11.1–11). Maundy Thursday commemorates the washing of the disciples' feet (John 13.1–20) and the institution of the Eucharist (Mark 14.22–25). Good Friday is the anniversary of the crucifixion (Mark 15.42–47). Easter Sunday is the day of Jesus' resurrection, and the most joyful festival of the Church's year. Services are held every day of Holy Week when the relevant gospel stories are read, and appropriate hymns and psalms are sung.

The Jewish festival of Passover occurs at about the same time as Holy Week. At the Passover Seder (meal), the tale of the miraculous deliverance of the Jewish people from misery in Egypt is retold in the same way as the story of Jesus' passion is read in churches. Both seasons (Passover also lasts a week) commemorate liberation; for the Jews, it is freedom from the bonds of slavery, and for the Christians, it is from the chains of sin and death. In Judaism, another holy period begins in the autumn with the Ten Days of Repentance. This starts with the New Year (Rosh Hashanah) and ends with the Day of Atonement (Yom Kippur). These days are a time of penitence in preparation for the prayer and fasting of the Day of Atonement, which will secure the forgiveness of sins. In the same way as Holy Week culminates in Easter which for Christians is the guarantee of absolution and future resurrection, the Ten Days of Repentance find their climax in the atonement effected by the great fast of Yom Kippur.

Home

The home, as well as the synagogue, is a focus of Jewish life. Traditionally, a mezuzah is placed on the door-post and various religious objects are kept for home rituals. There are Sabbath candlesticks, a Kiddush cup for blessing the wine, a *Havdalah* (ceremony at the conclusion of the Sabbath) candle, spice box, and an eight-branched candlestick for the festival of Lights (Hanukkah). Generally, there is a small collection of Hebrew books such as the Bible, Prayer Book and perhaps a copy of the Talmud and *Shulhan Arukh*. The kitchen is arranged in accordance with the rules of *kashrut* (dietary laws), with separate areas for preparing milk and meat dishes. The laws of family purity are kept and the annual festivals honoured. The Passover has many home rituals, such as the search for leaven and the Seder meal. A booth is built for the family to live outside during the festival of Tabernacles. The candles are lit on each day of the festival of Lights. Children dress up and play games on the feast of Lots. Every Friday night, the Sabbath is welcomed and the whole family eat together. Grace is said before and after meals and guests are welcomed. At life-cycle events, there are gatherings. At the circumcision ceremony on the eighth day after the birth of a boy and at the redemption of the first-born on the thirtieth day, there is a party. When a boy or girl becomes bar or bat mitzvah, there is rejoicing at home. A marriage calls for a week of feasting, and family and friends visit to console the bereaved while they mourn for seven days. Above all, Jewish values are transmitted in the home across the generations. Inevitably, in the 20th cent., this model of the Jewish home is under threat, and non-Orthodox Jews in particular have modified these features in numerous ways. In addition, there are more one-parent families, less Jewish education, and more secular influences. Nonetheless, the Jewish home is still seen as an essential component of Jewish life, and the strength of the Jewish family is much admired by Christians.

There are fewer ritual objects in a Christian home. Certainly, the family would own a Bible, and there might be a crib that comes out at Christmas. Grace is still sometimes said at meals, but the custom of family prayers has largely disappeared. There are no laws governing the preparation of food or family purity. Christmas and Easter are celebrated, but largely by secular customs such as decorating the house, exchanging presents, or giving eggs. The focus of the family's religious life is the church rather than the home, and it is there that the religious activities of Holy Communion, preaching, Sunday school, and hymn-singing take place. Although Christians approve of the home-centredness of the Jewish religion, it is less important within Christianity. This may be because marriage and raising a family are not regarded as the ideal in Christianity. Jesus said, 'If any one comes to me and does not hate his own father and mother and wife and children and brothers and sisters, yes, and even his own life, he cannot be my disciple' (Luke 14.26). This has been understood as an example of hyperbole, stressing the ultimate importance of the Kingdom of God. None the less, in contrast to Judaism, Christianity traditionally approves of the idea of celibacy. Although marriage is perceived to be crucially important in the transmission of Christian values and the relationship between a husband and wife is seen as analogous to the relationship of Christ and his Church (Eph. 5.21–30), Christians, unlike Jews, recognize other models of domestic organization besides family life.

Homiletics

(*Agaddah*) (Preaching) (Sermon): Traditionally, biblical commentary (*agaddah*) constituted the subject-matter of sermons delivered on Sabbaths, festivals and special occasions – these addresses dealt with religious faith, theology, and morality. The institution of preaching originated in biblical times. Thus the Book of Deuteronomy contains speeches uttered by Moses, and in Judg. 9.7–20 Jotham delivered a sermon to the people of Shechem. The Book of Ecclesiastes consists of a series of sermons, and homiletical material is found in both the Targums (Aramaic versions of Scripture) and the Apocrypha. In the Tannaitic (1st cent. BCE–2nd cent. CE) and Amoraic (2nd–6th cent.) periods, a number of scholars specialized as preachers, and their sermons were subsequently incorporated into a vast body of homiletical literature.

Such writing continued into the early Middle Ages (10th–11th cent.), but evolved into a new form in the Mediterranean communities that emanated from the traditional centres in Palestine and Babylonia (where the writing of Ahia of Shabha originated – the first sermonic work by a known author on Halachic (legal) and *agaddic* (narrative) topics. From the 12th cent., a number of preachers issued their sermons in popular form. In Spain, in particular, homiletics were apologetic in nature, serving to defend Judaism from Christian attacks. In the 13th cent., Moses ben Jacob of Coucy, a wandering preacher, was highly critical of Moses Maimonides (12th cent.), whereas his contemporary Jacob Anatoli wrote *Malmad Ha-Talmidim* in the spirit of Maimonides. In Germany during this period, the Hasidei Ashkenaz (mystics of the Rhineland) utilized mystical homiletic in their literary productions. The Karaites also produced homiletical material, as did Jews during the Renaissance in Italy and Bohemia. In the 17th cent., the life of the pseudo-messiah Shabbetai Tzevi had an important impact on Jewish preaching and, from the following century, the Hasidic movement created a new, popular form of homiletics.

In the modern period, preaching has continued to be a vital force in Jewish life. In Eastern Europe, leading rabbis and itinerant preachers added to this tradition, as did Reformers who emphasized the importance of the sermon in synagogue worship. Usually, modern sermons are based on quotations from the Bible and Jewish sources, but no longer could preachers, whether Orthodox or non-Orthodox, assume an extensive knowledge of Judaism among their congregants. Jewish homiletics has thus been a constant feature of the Jewish faith from biblical times until the present, undergoing a variegated development resulting in a large body of literary products.

The New Testament continued the biblical tradition of preaching. John the Baptist preached the prophetic message of the coming of the Messiah and the Kingdom of God, and much of Jesus' ministry was devoted to preaching. His disciples were instructed to preach (Matt. 10.7) and their words would cause the spread of God's Kingdom until the end of the world (Matt. 24.14). After Jesus' resurrection, the disciples believed that Jesus continued his ministry through their preaching, and that through their teaching salvation was being offered to all people. In the apostolic Church, preaching took the form of an exposition of Scripture in the context of an assembly of believers, especially on the Lord's Day (Rom. 15.4; Acts 18.24–28.; 20.7f). Such a practice continued into the next centuries.

The earliest preaching was in the form of a practical and pastoral homily – it was based on the text that had been read, and was usually delivered extempore. Often it followed the various topics in the text in the order in which they arose. The primary duty of the bishop was to preach, seated while the congregation stood. The first important discussion of homiletics was Augustine's (4th–5th cent.) *On Christian Doctrine.*

During the Middle Ages, excerpts of sermons of the Church Fathers were circulated to help preachers with their own sermons. The Dominican and Franciscan friars encouraged a revival of preaching, and various homiletical aids were produced. In the 13th cent., a new form of thematic preaching from a short text with an introduction, transitions, and conclusion under three headings became current in university circles. During the Reformation, John Calvin (16th cent.) and Martin Luther (15th–16th cent.) returned to older patterns of preaching, and among the reformers the importance of preaching was particularly emphasized; salvation was to be found in responding to the

Word of God rather than in the Catholic sacraments of the Church. In the modern period, the art of preaching has continued and is still regarded – as in Judaism – as a central dimension of worship and religious life.

Homosexuality *see* Sexual morality

Hospitality

The duty of hospitality has always been stressed in Judaism. Gen. 18 describes how Abraham entertained three travellers who turned out to be angels. The Talmud describes how guests should be treated and, at the beginning of the Passover meal, the invitation is made, 'Let all who are hungry come and eat.' This injunction to hospitality has been particularly important because so many Jews have been forced to wander from place to place as a result of religious persecutions or economic or social pressure. The same emphasis exists in Christianity. The writer of the epistle to the Hebrews, with a clear reference to the story of Abraham, warns his readers not to neglect to show hospitality to strangers 'for thereby some have entertained angels unawares' (13.2), and this tradition has been continued to the present day.

House of worship

(*Bet Hamidrash*) (Cathedral Church) (Synagogue) (Shul) (Temple): In ancient Israel the Temple was the central sanctuary of Jewish worship. Situated on Mt Moriah in Jerusalem, it was constructed by Solomon in the 10th cent. BCE. In its erection he enlisted the aid of Hiram, king of Tyre; the building began in the fourth year of Solomon's reign, and took seven years. The Temple itself was 100 cubits (165 feet) long, and 50 cubits wide. The main building was divided into an inner room (the Holy of Holies), and an outer room on the east. The entrance to the Temple was through the porch, on each side of which stood bronze pillars.

The ark was installed in the Holy of Holies in which were placed the two tablets of the covenant with the Ten Commandments. Two wooden cherubs with outspread wings surrounded the ark, symbolizing the divine presence. In the other room stood an incense altar, the table for shewbread, and 10 lampstands. In front of the Temple there was a bronze water basin supported by 12 bronze cattle.

65

A bronze altar also stood in the courtyard; this was employed for various sacrifices.

Within the Temple locality were three enclosures for priests, male worshippers, and female worshippers. During Solomon's reign, the Temple was the focal point of Jewish ritual, but eventually, when the Kingdom was divided, two other temples were located at Dan and Bethel in the north. In 586 BCE the Temple was destroyed by Nebuchadnezzar; the second Temple was rededicated (c. 52 BCE), rebuilt by Herod the Great (1st cent. BCE), and destroyed by the Romans under Titus in 70 CE.

After the destruction of the second Temple, the synagogue (shul) became the central religious institution of Judaism. Of ancient origin, it served as the centre for public prayer as well as religious and communal activities. Prayer was viewed as the replacement for sacrifice, and services were established to conform to regular communal offerings that could no longer be brought to the Temple. Unlike the Temple where the priest carried out ritual practices, the only stipulation for a synagogue service was a quorum (minyan) of 10 men, and any layman was allowed to lead the service.

Within the synagogue there are various features reminiscent of the Temple. The ark, representing the Holy of Holies, is built on the eastern wall and contains the Torah scroll (the five books of Moses). The eternal light (ner tamid) hangs before the ark and represents the lamp that burnt continually in the sanctuary. In addition, synagogues contain a raised platform (bimah) for the reading of the law, as well as a gallery for women. Instrumental music is forbidden on Sabbaths and Holy Days as a reminder of the destruction of the Temple. Many synagogues have a small room attached to them, known as a house of study (bet ha-midrash), where courses in rabbinic studies take place. It is customary for traditional Jews to pray three times a day, but this pattern, as well as the traditional liturgy, has been modified in non-Orthodox movements in the modern era.

In the New Testament, Jesus and Paul are portrayed as worshipping in the synagogue, and Jesus is depicted as making a pilgrimage to the Temple on Passover. The early Church was formed by his band of disciples who, on the day of Pentecost, received his spirit which empowered them to witness to Jesus as the risen Christ (Acts 1.8).

Governed by elders after the analogy of the synagogue, this body took the forms of believers meeting in various places for worship. The primitive Church believed it was the inheritor of the promises made to Israel. According to tradition, it was established by Christ as the new Israel and endowed by him with the Holy Spirit. Thus Church has two meanings – the body of all Christian people, and the place where Christians worship.

The Church in the first sense is perceived as a unified body, a holy, world-wide, visible community; its members, orders of ministry, and unity are all constituted by participation in visible sacraments, such as baptism, confirmation, ordination, and Holy Communion. Separation from the Church is the sin of schism; the rejection of its apostolic doctrine is heresy. After the schism between Roman Catholicism and the Eastern Orthodox Church, Christendom was divided, and this fragmentation was further intensified by the Reformation. Yet despite such division, churches as houses of worship contain a number of common features.

The earliest buildings for Christian worship were simply the houses of the faithful, but churches began to be built from the end of the 3rd cent. Early churches were simple in character but, with the publication of the edict of Milan (313 CE), places of worship were built following the pattern of the basilica. The bishop's throne was placed in the apse (in cathedrals), and surrounded by seats of the elders (presbyters). In addition, there developed the baptistery and the martyrdom housing the tomb or relics of a martyr. In both East and West, the altar on which the sacrifice of Holy Communion was enacted by the priest became more distant from the worshipper and, like the synagogue ark, lay by the eastern wall. It was traditionally customary in the East to separate it from the rest of the church by a solid screen (iconostasis), adorned with icons of the saints. In the West, the basilica plan was retained. The nave (for the laity) contained a pulpit for preaching, a lectern or reading stand, and sometimes a second altar. The baptismal font was placed at the western end near the entrance to the church. In many churches a light burns, signifying the presence of the blessed sacrament, and this is reminiscent of the Jewish eternal light. These arrangements continued throughout the Middle

Ages and still influence Church architecture. In Christian worship – as in Judaism – both the construction of the house of worship and the liturgy echo back to the ancient Temple, and in this way both traditions are linked to the same biblical roots.

Hymnology *see* Music

I

Iconography

Traditionally in Judaism there has been ambivalence about pictorial art. Exod. 20.4 forbids the making of graven images 'or any likeness of anything that is in heaven above, or that is in the earth beneath, or that is in the water under the earth'. This was clearly a prohibition against idolatry – 'You shall not bow down to them or worship them' – and through the ages the rabbis have interpreted these words more or less leniently. Archaeology has uncovered mosaic floors and frescoes of biblical scenes dating back to the 4th cent. CE, and ritual objects, manuscripts, and synagogues have been decorated from early times with patterns, stylized Jewish motifs and, to a lesser extent, realistic images. Nonetheless, the fear of idolatry persisted, and such eminent authorities as Moses Maimonides (12th cent.) refused to allow the portrayal of a human figure in the round. In the same century, Eliakim ben Joseph of Mainz ordered the removal of a synagogue stained-glass window on the grounds that it was distracting for worshippers.

Despite the Second Commandment (Exod. 20.4), Christians have had less reservations than Jews about using art to express and teach the ideas of Christianity. From the 5th cent., icons of Jesus and the saints were used as an aid to worship in the Eastern Church. It was believed that through them the saints would exercise their kindly powers, and they were given every mark of adoration. In the 8th–9th cent., the veneration of icons was forbidden as idolatrous and users were persecuted. There was a popular outcry, however, and in 842 the worship of icons was restored. In the West, statues rather than icons were generally more popular, and Thomas Aquinas (12th cent.) argued that the hon-our paid to images was not idolatry because it passed back to the origins of the image. This was not the view of the 16th–17th-cent. Protestant reformers. Although Christian art is to be found in Protestant churches today, Protestants unconditionally reject any form of image-worship, and their position is very similar to that of Orthodox Jews.

Idolatry *see* Paganism

Illegitimacy

(*Mamzer*): The notion of illegitimacy in Judaism is different from that in secular use. If a child is the product of fornication, provided his mother is Jewish, he is fully Jewish in every respect. A bastard, or *mamzer*, is the child of any adulterous or incestuous union. Nowadays, in practice this means a child who is the product of a second marriage in which the mother has not been given a *get* or religious bill of divorce from her first husband. According to Jewish law, she is still tied to her first marriage and any subsequent unions are adulterous. Although a *mamzer* is expected to keep Jewish law, he is excluded from marrying a legitimate Jew and, if he does so, all children of the marriage will in their turn be *mamzerim*. The only lawful marriage is to another *mamzer* or to a proselyte to Judaism. The rabbis were aware of the harshness of these regulations and they tried to mitigate them. In commenting on Eccles. 4.1, 'I saw . . . the tears of the oppressed, and they had no one to comfort them', they wrote, 'This verse refers to *mamzerim* whose fathers sinned yet they are condemned to exclusion . . . by the authority of the Torah. Therefore the Holy One, blessed be he, says, "I will comfort them in a future life."' Illegitimacy has to be proved – a mere suspicion of it does not make someone a *mamzer* and probability is always on the side of legitimacy. The situation has been complicated in recent years. The Reform Movement does not issue religious bills of divorce since the procedure is regarded as being degrading to women and the movement has rejected the whole notion of illegitimacy. As a result, there are now thousands of children of second marriages in the Diaspora who are regarded by the Orthodox as *mamzerim*, but who can be married in Reform synagogues or by the civil authorities. In the State of Israel, however, all marriages and matters of personal status are in the hands of the Orthodox Ministry of Religious Affairs. Civil or Reform marriage is not permitted, so a known *mamzer* suffers a serious legal disability in Israel whatever his personal religious beliefs.

In Christianity, an illegitimate child is one born outside marriage. The Roman Catholic Church has clear rules about legitimacy and a bastard child can be legitimized for purposes of inheritance by a dispensation of the Pope. Although illegitimacy was traditionally a handicap in civil law, an illegitimate child can be a full Christian in every respect. In contrast to Judaism, the essential qualifications are faith and baptism, not physical descent.

Imitation of God

According to Gen. 1.26–27, God created human beings in the image of God. In Lev. 19.2 they were commanded to be holy 'for I the Lord your God am holy' and Deut. 11.22 requires the human race to walk in the ways of God. The idea of the imitation of God being a model for conduct was developed and explained by the rabbis – 'As he visited the sick, so you shall visit the sick: as he comforted mourners, so shall you comfort those who mourn . . .' and those who follow God's example will have a place in the world-to-come. The doctrine was preserved and elaborated by later Jewish writers, particularly among the kabbalists (mystics) of the 16th cent. and the Hasidim (19th–20th-cent). It has also been used by the influential 20th cent. theologian Martin Buber.

The concept was transformed by Christians into the imitation of Christ. Jesus called his disciples to 'follow' him (Mark 1.16–20) and Paul regarded the Christian Church as the body of Christ on earth, animated by his Spirit and continuing with his work (1 Cor. 12). However, the emphasis was not on a literal interpretation of Jesus' earthly life, but the imitation of Christ was seen instead as the work of the Spirit moulding the Christian into the likeness of Jesus' spiritual self-giving. This will result in sharing in the benefits of Jesus' death and resurrection both in this life and in the world-to-come. In the Middle Ages attempts were made to imitate the historical Jesus: the life of Francis of Assisi (12th–13th cent.) and Thomas à Kempis's spiritual classic, the *Imitation of Christ*, are obvious examples. The stations of the cross and the deliberate re-enactment of the Last Supper were incorporated into the liturgy. The reformers, however, were wary of the doctrine; Martin Luther (16th cent.), in particular, felt it concealed the notion that salvation could be attained by the believers' own efforts. Later, with the advent of biblical criticism, there was increased scepticism about the possibility of knowing the true events of Jesus' life anyway. However, the imitation of Christ in the Pauline spiritual sense has remained the ideal for many Christians.

Thus, for Jews, the imitation of God is essentially a moral duty, whereas for Christians, it is a sharing in the spiritual benefits of Jesus' death and resurrection. Nonetheless, for both, in their different ways, it is the path of salvation.

Immersion

(Bath, ritual) (Washing): If a Jew becomes ritually impure, he is commanded in Lev. 15.16 to 'bathe his whole body in water'. From very early times, each Jewish community has built a ritual bath (*mikveh*) to fulfill this regulation. It is used every month by menstruating women and as part of the conversion ritual for proselytes. Ultra-Orthodox men immerse themselves before festivals and even before morning prayer. According to tradition, the body must be completely washed and totally clean before it is immersed, so that there is nothing whatsoever between water and flesh. Cooking vessels that have become ritually unclean or that have been bought from non-Jews are also dipped in the ritual bath. In addition, the law requires partial washing. The priests in the Temple in Jerusalem had to wash their hands and feet before conducting the sacrifices. Nowadays, there are various occasions on which hands must be washed – such as before dividing bread, after visiting the lavatory, and on waking from sleep.

The New Testament records how John the Baptist urged his followers to immerse themselves in the River Jordan as a preparation for the coming Kingdom of God (Mark 1.1–8). When Jesus was baptized by John, he was filled with the Holy Spirit (Mark 1.9–11) and John made the distinction between his baptism with water, symbolizing ritual purity, and Jesus' baptism of the Holy Spirit, which was a sign of the arrival of God's rule on earth (John 1.24–34). The early followers of Jesus continued the practice of baptizing new converts and they expected the immersion to be accompanied by signs of the Spirit (Acts 8.14–17). This tradition has been continued, even though in most churches baptism is no longer by total immersion, but by water being poured or sprinkled over the head of the candidate. Christian baptism involves not only the ritual washing away of past sins, but also a spiritual incorporation into the body of Christ (1 Cor. 12.13). In contrast to Jewish ritual washing, it is a once-in-a-lifetime event. Christians also have the tradition of priests washing their hands before celebrating Holy Communion, in the same way as Jewish priests washed before performing Temple sacrifices. The Roman Catholic Church also uses water for blessings, dedications, burials, and exorcisms – in each case to symbolize ritual cleansing.

Thus total or partial immersion is used in both the Jewish and Christian traditions to symbolize cleansing from sin and ritual impurity. Both religions insist that new converts should undergo ritual washing, although Christian baptism and immersion also involve the reception of the Holy Spirit. Both groups also incorporate the washing of hands into their religious practices.

Immortality *see* Resurrection; soul

Incarnation
The belief that God has made himself present in human form. In the New Testament, the divine status of Jesus is recognized, primarily in the Fourth Gospel and in Paul's epistles. Traditionally, it is also viewed as implicit in the treatment of the birth narratives in the Synoptic Gospels, in the opening verses of the letter to the Hebrews, and in the Book of Revelation which conceives of Jesus (along with God) as the Alpha and the Omega. Over the first five centuries of the Christian era, these insights were refined and eventually crystallized in the ecumenical councils of Nicaea (4th cent.), Constantinople (4th cent.), Ephesus (5th cent.), and Chalcedon (5th cent.). Two further councils at Constantinople continued this debate into the 6th and 7th cent.

Through these discussions, the various councils rejected a number of heretical beliefs: Arianism (denial of the Son's eternal divinity), Appollinarianism (denial of Jesus' human spirit), Nestorianism (denial that the divine-human Christ should be conceived as a single person), Eutychianism (denial of Jesus' two natures), and Monotheletism (denial of the divine and human will in Christ). This development of the doctrine of the incarnation went hand in hand with Christian reflection about the nature of the Trinity, since both doctrines are inseparably linked and the final results of the deliberations are enshrined in the Christian creeds.

Despite the divisions that have separated Christians from one another over the centuries, there has been general agreement that the doctrine of the incarnation is central to Christian belief. By making himself known to humanity through Christ, Christians believe that God was able to bridge the gap between the human and the divine, reveal his will, and offer the experience of his presence to the faithful. Further, through the incarnation, God was able to subject himself to human suffering and evil; this involvement serves as the pattern of self-sacrificial love and is the basis for Christian moral commitment. The incarnation thus functions as the foundation of humanity's relationship to God and serves as the basis for the unfolding of God's promises for the reconstruction of the world.

In modern times, the traditional belief in the incarnation has undergone considerable development within Christian theology, and has even been challenged from various Christian quarters. Liberal and modernist theologians (primarily within the Protestant Churches) have questioned its intelligibility, as well as its historical foundation, in the primitive Church. Some writers have argued that the doctrine should not be understood literally; rather, it should be seen as a mythical expression of the religious significance of Jesus in the life of his followers. The recognition of the plurality of other faiths has added further stimulus to this reformulation of Christian belief. Nonetheless, for most Christians, the belief that God was in Christ continues to be the fulcrum of their faith.

Judaism does not contain a belief in the incarnation as it has been understood in Christianity. Nonetheless, there are frequent references to God's immanence in the world in biblical and rabbinic sources. In the Bible, the terms *Ruah Ha-Kodesh* (Holy Spirit), *Ruah Elohim* (Spirit of God) and *Ruah Adonai* (Spirit of the Lord) are used to refer to God's presence. Although the rabbis assert that the Holy Spirit departed from Israel with the death of the last three prophets (Haggai, Zechariah, Malachi), the term 'Shekinah' was employed in rabbinic terms to designate God's presence in the world. In the Targums (Aramaic translations of Scripture), it is frequently employed together with other intermediary terms such as *Memra Yakara* (noble word) in order to avoid the anthropomorphic implications of various biblical expressions.

In the Talmud and Midrash (biblical interpretation), the usage of 'Shekinah' does not have the same apologetic force as in the Targums – it is used generally to refer to a divine manifestation at a given place. Though the Shekinah is everywhere, it rests pre-eminently on Israel since the nation was chosen and sanctified to proclaim God's word. The Shekinah is also viewed as present in certain contexts, such as when 10 Jews are gathered for prayer; it is also associated with charismatic individuals such as outstanding Talmudic rabbis. Sometimes the term is employed simply as an alternative for God, but in other contexts it has overtones of something separated from the Godhead. From Hellenistic times, the kabbalists (mystics) have taught that the Godhead has manifested itself in 10 emanations (*sephirot*) which include power, wisdom, intelligence, charity, law, beauty, eternity, glory, force, and Shekinah. The whole was symbolized in a divine cosmic figure, the primeval man or Adam Kadmon. This is not dissimilar to Paul's concept of Jesus, as the last Adam ('"the first man Adam became a living being"; the last Adam became a life-giving spirit' (1 Cor. 15.45). Nonetheless, even the kabbalists never claimed that the emanations of God became a human being in history. The belief that the Word of God became flesh and 'dwelt among us' (John 1.14) is a uniquely Christian conviction that has been unequivocally rejected by Jews down the ages.

Incense

Traditionally, incense was burnt by the priests in the Temple in Jerusalem. Either it was made of pure frankincense or 11 ingredients mentioned in the Talmud. It accompanied the sacrifices and a special incense altar stood in front of the Holy of Holies. On the Day of Atonement, the one day of the year on which the Holy of Holies was visited, the high priest took a censer of incense in with him. It was forbidden for anyone but priests to offer incense to God. King Uzziah was struck down by leprosy when he attempted to burn incense in the Temple (2 Chron. 26.16). Consequently, the use of incense in Jewish worship disappeared with the destruction of the Temple in 70 CE.

The Evangelist Matthew records how wise men brought the gift of frankincense to the baby Jesus (2.11), thus hinting at his divine status. Christians have continued the tradition of employing incense since at least the 6th cent. It is considered to be symbolic of prayer rising to heaven and, as in the Temple of Jerusalem, it accompanies sacrifice – in this case, the re-enacted offering of Jesus on the altar of the Eucharist.

Infallibility

The inability to err when teaching divinely revealed truth. On the basis of John 16.13, 'When the Spirit of truth comes, he will guide you into all truth', some Christians believe that the Church's teaching is infallible. Yet even among such Christians there is disagreement as to whether it is infallible only in such doctrines as are accepted by the whole Church, or those accepted by the general ecumenical councils. In 1870, the first Vatican Council of the Roman Catholic Church declared that the Pope's *ex cathedra* (from the throne) pronouncements were infallible. This was not accepted by Protestants, who maintain that only God and his Word are infallible.

A similar conflict exists in Judaism. Orthodox Jews believe that the 613 Written Commandments of the Pentateuch are completely authoritative because they were revealed by God to Moses on Mt Sinai. In addition, the Oral Law, which was passed down by word of mouth, was decided by a majority decision of the rabbinic elders. Once decided, it had the authority of Halakhah (ruling). Through the ages, there have been groups within Judaism who did not accept this structure of authority. In the days of the second Temple, the Sadducees, or priestly families, did not accept the validity of the Oral Law. From the 8th to 12th cent., the Karaites rejected all law that was not directly based on Scripture. In the modern period, Reform and Conservative Jews do not believe literally the doctrine of *Torah mi-Sinai* (law from Sinai), and consequently feel free to interpret both the Written and

Oral Law according to modern ideals and conventions. Thus, as in Christianity, there is a fundamental disagreement within the tradition as to the origin and extent of religious infallibility in interpretation.

Initiation rites

(Baptism) (*Bris*) (Circumcision): In Judaism, circumcision (referred to as *bris* (covenant)) is performed on the eighth day of a child's life as a rite of initiation into the Jewish faith. The biblical roots of this ceremony are found in Gen. 17 where God decreed to Abraham: 'Every male among you shall be circumcised. You shall be circumcised in the flesh of your foreskins, and it shall be a sign of the covenant between me and you' (Gen. 17.10–11). Through the ages, this vital ritual came to be understood as a fundamental religious act for all male Jewish children as well as male converts. However, even if a boy is not circumcised, he is still a member of the community by virtue of his descent. Circumcision is merely a sign of his existing status as a member of the house of Israel.

The laws specifying the main aspect of ritual circumcision are based on biblical sources as developed through later rabbinical enactments. Traditionally, the ceremony is performed in the presence of 10 adult Jewish males (minyan). The infant is taken from his mother by the godmother, who hands him to the godfather (*sandak*). The godfather then carries the child into the room where the circumcision is to be performed and gives him to the person who will place the child on a chair referred to as the Chair of Elijah. The child is then taken from this chair and passed to the child's father, who places him on the lap of the godfather who holds the infant during the ceremony, which is performed by a *mohel* (person authorized to perform circumcision).

The circumcision itself requires the removal of the foreskin; formerly, blood was drawn orally, but now an instrument is used. The child is then handed to the person who will hold him during the naming ceremony – a special blessing is said over a cup of wine and the child receives his Jewish name. This initiation rite is observed by all segments of the Jewish community, although Reform Jews allow a medical doctor to perform the circumcision in

place of a *mohel*. Female babies are given their names in the synagogue after birth. Again, this is not an admission ceremony.

Male converts to traditional Judaism are also obligated to undergo circumcision as entry into the covenant of Abraham as well as the act of *tevilah* – the complete immersion in a ritual bath or other authorized body of water. If the male convert is already circumcised, it is sufficient to draw a drop of blood, but immersion is still required as it is for female converts. Prescribed benedictions are also recited. These formal acts constitute their adoption into the Jewish people and the immersion symbolizes the washing away or death of the former identity. (Reform Judaism, however, frequently dispenses with both circumcision and immersion for converts, and a simple admission ceremony is held instead.) Both male and female converts are given new names and are described as *ben Avraham* (son of Abraham) or *bat Ruth* (daughter of Ruth) – Ruth and Abraham being the most prominent biblical proselytes. Through the ages, *tevilah* has served as the means of formal admission into the Jewish faith – an act that symbolizes personal spiritual renewal and acceptance of a new way of life.

Although Christianity in the light of Paul's teaching dispensed with the Jewish requirement of circumcision, the process by which an individual comes to full membership in the Christian community is rooted in the Jewish tradition. According to John 3.5, Jesus announced the necessity of a spiritual regeneration by water and the Spirit – it is traditionally held that he instituted the sacrament of baptism before his death, or after his resurrection when he instructed his disciples to baptize in the threefold name of Father, Son and the Holy Spirit (Matt. 28.19). Though infant baptism is not explicitly referred to in the New Testament, it is possibly implied in a number of passages (Matt. 19.14; Acts 16.33). Paul, following the Jewish tradition, saw baptism as a symbolic death. The new convert died to his old life so he could share in the spiritual benefits of Jesus' resurrected life (Rom. 6.3–4).

In the early Church, the rites of baptism were developed. The *Didache*, for example, outlines the principle duties of candidates for baptism and the method of administering it by triple immersion. Conferred by the bishop, it was closely associated with confirmation and the Eucharist. From the 2nd to 4th cent., it was administered at Easter and Pentecost, but in the 4th cent. the Feast of the Epiphany became an additional baptismal date in the East. In Spain and Gaul, Christmas and other feasts were also added. In cases of necessity, however, it could be administered at any time by any Christian. Through the centuries, the theology of baptism was elaborated by numerous theologians.

Baptismal rites vary within the different branches of Christendom, but in the West it has assumed the most elaborate form in Roman Catholicism. After parents have undertaken to bring up children in the Christian faith, the priest reads from Scriptures and delivers a homily. A prayer of exorcism is followed by the anointing of the candidate's breast with the oil of catechumens. The priest then blesses the water; both parents renounce Satan and evil, and make a declaration of faith. The child is then baptized by immersion or affusion, anointed with chrism, and clothed in a white garment. The child's father lights a candle in the baptistery, and the ceremony is concluded at the sanctuary with a recital of the Lord's Prayer and a threefold blessing. The Church of England and other Protestant Churches have simplified the rite in various ways; in a few branches, total immersion of adults is required. In all cases, the new Christian is named with his or her Christian name. Yet despite the diversity of practices, all Christian communities regard baptism as an essential initiation rite into the Christian faith.

Thus in both traditions, the initiation rites involve the giving of a personal name, symbolizing the religious identity of the candidate. Christians have taken over the ceremony of baptism from the Jewish practice of initiating proselytes. However, children who are born of Jewish parents are not admitted into the religion and do not require immersion. Circumcision is merely a sign of what is already the case. Baptism, on the other hand, is an admission ceremony into a voluntary belief community, and is thus a necessary condition of membership.

Inquisition

A court set up by the Roman Catholic Church for the trial of heretics. It only had jurisdiction over Christians, so Jews were not affected unless they had formally adopted Christianity. From the 14th cent. until the early 19th cent., it existed in Spain and Portugal and their overseas possessions. The court was particularly indefatigable in its efforts in hunting down Marranos (forcibly converted Jews who secretly reverted to Jewish practices). Some 30,000 Marranos are estimated to have been burnt at the stake and another 16,000 burnt in effigy. The Inquisition is not a unique example of intolerance and persecution in the history of the Church. Christianity has traditionally claimed to be the only true faith and, in the Middle Ages when Church and State were closely connected, heretics were perceived as being a danger to society. Following Jesus' parable of the great feast (Luke 14.14–24), when those outside were 'compelled to come in', Church leaders saw nothing wrong in handing over obstinate dissenters to the secular power for torture and death. With the growth of religious diversity and indifference from the mid-17th cent. onwards, religious toleration became increasingly the norm. Judaism, on the other hand, does not teach that salvation is only available to the Jews. They believe that the righteous of all nations who keep the laws of Noah (Gen. 9.1–7) will have a place in the world-to-come. Consequently, the rabbis felt no compulsion to missionize. In any case, from post-biblical times, Jews have been a minority group living in an alien culture. They have not had much opportunity of compelling conversion or using the government of the time to punish religious dissent.

Inspiration

The condition of being filled with the Spirit of God. The Hebrew Scriptures contain several accounts of individuals being inspired, such as Bezalel the craftsman who was 'filled . . . with the Spirit of God, with ability and intelligence, with knowledge and all craftsmanship to devise artistic designs' (Exod. 31.3). Similarly, the prophets brought God's message to Israel through the Spirit (for example, Isa. 61.1, 'The Spirit of the Lord God is upon me, because the Lord has anointed me to bring good tidings to the afflicted'). The rabbis believed the Spirit ceased to appear in Israel with the deaths of the prophets Haggai, Zechariah, and Malachi, and one criterion of inclusion in the biblical canon was whether the particular book had been written under divine inspiration. It was accepted, however, that there were different degrees of inspiration. The Talmud says that Moses saw God 'through a clear glass', whereas the prophets only saw him through 'a glass darkly'. Later Jewish scholars debated the nature of this divine inspiration. Judah Ha-Levi (12th cent.) saw it as an entirely supernatural occurrence, a unique, non-rational gift from God. Moses Maimonides (12th cent.), on the other hand, saw prophecy as grounded in the conjunction between the human intellect and divine rationality. Nevertheless, the biblical commentators saw the Scriptures as an inexhaustible source of wisdom and they believed that different levels of meaning could be uncovered through different methods of exegesis. This process has continued until the present day, and Orthodox Judaism teaches that one way of encountering God's inspiration is through the study of the Torah. Thus even though the biblical writers were inspired by the one God, there is no single correct understanding of the meaning of Scripture. Modern non-Orthodox Jews go further than this. They are uneasy with the whole idea of divine inspiration and they do not believe that God literally spoke through the prophets. However, they do accept that in some sense the Spirit of God is to be found in the words of Scripture.

The early Church accepted that the books of the Hebrew Scriptures were inspired by God – as the writer of 2 Pet. put it, 'no prophecy of scripture is a matter of one's own interpretation, because no prophecy ever came by the impulse of man, but men moved by the Holy Spirit spoke from God' (2 Pet. 1.20–21) Jesus' earthly ministry began when he received the Holy Spirit at baptism (Mark 1.9–11), and through the Spirit the disciples continued his preaching and healing ministry after his ascension into heaven (Acts 1.1–11). Christians believe that the New Testament writers bore witness to the activity of the Spirit and were themselves inspired by it. However, their words are only received correctly if the reader is also inspired to understand them. This is not dissimilar to Maimonides' view of inspiration, and was particularly emphasized by the Protestant reformers – as John Calvin (16th cent.) put it, 'For as God alone can properly bear witness to His own words, so these words will not obtain full credit in the hearts of men until they are sealed by the inward testimony of the Spirit.' Therefore in some sense

inspiration is a continuous and progressive process, and it is generally accepted that Scripture can be understood in different ways at different times. As in Judaism, an enormous variety of interpretations of the biblical text can be found in the tradition, from allegory to literal fundamentalism. In addition, many modern Christians are uncomfortable with the whole idea of divine inspiration. They do not believe that the Bible is the inerrant word of God, and their views on Scripture are very similar to those of non-Orthodox Jews.

Intention

The Hebrew word *Kavvanah* refers to the religious intention behind an act. Jews are expected to keep the Written and Oral Law with the *Kavvanah* of obeying God's commandments. Their actions are not to be justified on utilitarian grounds, but because it is God's will that they should obey him. Christianity also emphasizes the importance of intention. A good intention is essential if an action is to be of moral worth, and a bad intention will devalue an action even if it has good results. However, in contrast to Judaism, the fundamental principle of Christian behaviour does not lie in following God's Written or Oral Commandments, but rather in imitating the selfless love of Jesus.

Israel

(Chosen People) (Election) (Jews) (*K'lal Yisrael*) (People of Israel) (Promised Land): Israel is the name given to Jacob after he wrestled with a stranger until dawn. There Jacob discovered that his antagonist was a divine being who asked to be released at daybreak. Before agreeing, Jacob insisted on receiving a blessing, and the angel renamed him *Yisrael*, 'for you have striven (*sarita*) with God and with men, and have prevailed' (Gen. 32.28). Later, his sons became known as *bene Yisrael* (sons of Israel), and the term Israelites came to designate his descendants.

In Genesis, God promised Abraham that he would inherit the land of Canaan (Gen. 12.7); for this reason, it was known as the 'Promised Land'. Under Joshua, the Jewish people conquered this territory from its Canaanite rulers, and it became known as the land of Israel. This territory is regarded as an inalienable divine gift for God's chosen people and was promised as part of the covenant. There, the 12 Israelite tribes lived until the northern kingdom of Israel was conquered in 722 BCE; in 586 BCE the southern kingdom of Judah was also devastated by invading enemies. Exiled to Babylonia, Jews returned to the land of Israel at the end of the 6th cent. BCE, and for the next six centuries they lived there under successive Persian, Syrian, and Roman rule. In 70 CE the Temple was destroyed by the Romans, and Jews were again sent into exile. Nonetheless, a number of Jews continued to live in the land of Israel for several centuries. However, under Christian persecution, most left for other countries. Yet the longing for the land was not forgotten. The annual Passover service ends with the hope of 'Next Year in Jerusalem'. At the end of the 19th cent., Zionism became a major force in Jewish life, and in 1917 the Balfour Declaration recognized a Jewish national home in Palestine. In 1948, in response to the Holocaust, the State of Israel was proclaimed.

According to tradition, the land of Israel has always been regarded as holy, and through the ages Jews have regarded it as their spiritual home. Often they wished to die there, or at least have a bag of soil from the Holy Land placed with them in their graves. In Jewish life and prayer, the land of Israel has also been of central importance. Although a number of Orthodox Jews were initially hostile to Zionism because they believed that a Jewish state could only be established through divine initiative with the coming of the Messiah, the vast majority of all Jews today are committed to the existence of a Jewish state. Indeed, for a number of religious Jews, the creation of modern Israel is viewed as part of God's providential plan. For secularists, a homeland is seen as vital to the safety of world Jewry in the face of anti-Semitism. The tradition asserts that all Jews are bound together into a single body (*K'lal Yisrael*), but in the modern world it is the Jewish allegiance to the State of Israel rather than loyalty to the principles of the Torah that has drawn together all segments of the Jewish community.

In the New Testament, the term 'Israel' refers to the Israel of old (Luke 4.25, 27; Acts 7.23) as well as contemporary Judaism (Matt. 8.10; Luke 1.16; 2.34; John 1.31; 3.10). Thus Jesus is described as coming as the consolation, glory, and redemption of Israel (Luke 2.24–26, 32; 24.21). Paul's reference to Israel according to the flesh (1 Cor. 10.18) implies that there is a different Israel 'according to the spirit'. Such a distinction is based on the conviction that the Christian community constitutes a new Israel that is due to inherit the privileges of ancient Israel.

For Christians, God established a new covenant with the followers of Christ. Jesus as the Messiah is seen as the fulfilment of the Messianic prophecies in the Hebrew Scriptures. The narrative of the Last Supper is told with covenantal terminology: 'This cup is the new covenant in my blood' (1 Cor. 11.25; Luke 22.20; cf. Matt. 26.27; Mark 14.24). In this way, the new covenant is sealed in the sacrifice of Jesus' death. In his letter to the Romans, Paul contrasts the old and new covenants. Originally, God had established a covenant with Abraham and those of his descendants who followed his example of faith. This occurred before he was circumcised. Abraham is therefore viewed as the father of the uncircumcised (the Gentiles) who believe, in addition to the circumcised (Rom. 4.1–25). According to Paul, the new covenant is superior to the old because of its dependence on the Spirit rather than the letter of the law (2 Cor. 3.1–18; Gal. 4.21–28); the law brings slavery to sin and death, but the Spirit enables believers to enjoy the freedom of the sons of God (Gal. 4.1–7).

In this light, Christianity views itself as the new Israel, taking the place of the old. Under the old covenant, Jews offered their imperfect righteousness in exchange for the promises of God; under the new covenant all human beings regardless of their merit can be forgiven in Christ. The new Israel is thus reshaped in a new relationship with God and the benefits of the gospel are available to the entire world. Israel is in this way conceived as a universal body embracing all people who have become followers of Christ. Given the universality of this new conception, for many Christians the land of Israel has receded in significance. Although it is associated with the events of the old covenant and was the setting of Jesus' ministry, the concept of Israel is no longer bound in space and time. The Jewish ethnic and historical associations of the land have thereby been transcended. However, Christian Zionists still maintain that the physical Israel has a crucial role in God's plan and they understand the recreation of the Jewish State as a fulfilment of God's covenantal promise.

J

Jehovah

(Tetragrammaton): English version of the Hebrew divine name. The tetragrammaton JHVH is considered too sacred to utter, so is normally read 'Adonai' (the Lord). The vowels of Adonai were used by English commentators to vocalize JHVH, making Jehovah. The original pronunciation was probably Yahweh.

Jerusalem

(Zion): Capital of Israel. Originally the city was called 'Jebus' for the Jebusites lived there. In the 11th cent. BCE, it was conquered by David; he moved his capital to the city after reigning in Hebron for over six years (2 Sam. 5.1–13). After David's conquest, it was also referred to in the Bible as 'the city of David'. According to 2 Sam. 6, David transferred the ark of the covenant there, and he was later told by the prophet Gad to establish an altar on adjacent land. David purchased the site from Araunah the Jebusite, although Araunah desired to give it to him as a gift (2 Sam. 24.18–25). According to tradition, this was the Temple Mount.

David's son Solomon later built the Temple in Jerusalem, and the city became the focus of pilgrimages undertaken three times a year (on Passover, the festival of Weeks, and the festival of Tabernacles). As the place chosen by God, Jerusalem or, as it was sometimes called, Zion, became a symbol of the nation's aspirations. Celebrated by the prophets and in the Book of Psalms, it was viewed by Isaiah as the city of righteousness from which God's Word would issue forth (Isa. 1.26; 2.3). Jeremiah prophesied that in the future all nations would assemble there (Jer. 3.17), and throughout Scripture its beauty and holiness are extolled. Such a view was reinforced in *agaddic* (narrative) literature. Thus the Talmud states that anyone who has not seen Jerusalem in her glory has not seen a beautiful city. The Midrash (biblical

commentary) asserts that its uniqueness was the result of its being the focus of atonement of Israel through sacrifice. The Halakhah (commandments) also emphasized the holiness of Jerusalem through a system of laws relating to the city.

After the Temple was destroyed in 70 CE, Jerusalem ceased to play a cultic role in the religious life of the nation; nonetheless, it retained its symbolic significance, and longing for Zion became a major aspect of the liturgy. Thus the grace after meals contains a prayer for the rebuilding of Jerusalem, and the psalm added to the grace on week-days includes the verse: 'If I forget you, O Jerusalem, let my right hand wither!' (Ps. 137.5). In addition, the *Amidah* prayer (recited three times a day in traditional synagogues) is said facing the east; it contains a prayer for God to return to Jerusalem, rebuild the city, and re-establish David's dynasty. During the year, three fasts are observed to mourn the city's destruction.

Although the control of the city has changed hands numerous times throughout history, there has been a Jewish settlement there over the centuries, and a portion of the western retaining wall of the Temple (Western Wall) became a site of prayer and mourning. With the rise of Zionism, increasing pressure was exerted by Jews to establish a permanent homeland in Palestine. In 1917, the country was taken over by the British who established a mandatory government with Jerusalem as the capital. During the 1948 War of Independence, the old city fell to the Jordanian Arab Legion, Jews were expelled, and the city was divided. However, on 7 June 1967, the city of Jerusalem was reunited during the Six Day War, and subsequently became the capital of the Jewish state.

The Christian history of Jerusalem begins with Jesus' ministry, culminating in his death and resurrection. The apostles lived and taught for some time in the city – later, they scattered to other places but met there with the elders of the Church for the first Christian council in *c.* 49 CE (Acts 15). Jesus' brother James presided over the local church in the city but, when Jews were banished from the area, the church became entirely Gentile in composition. In the 4th cent., Helena, mother of the Emperor Constantine, visited Jerusalem, and Christians began to venerate the holy places set by her visit. Until the 5th cent., the see was suffragan to

Caesarea, but at the Council of Chalcedon (457) the bishop was given patriarchal status.

When the Crusaders held the city in the 12th cent., the Eastern patriarch lived in Constantinople, and it has only been since 1845 that he has resided in Jerusalem. Since the first half of the 16th cent., the patriarch has always been a Greek. A Latin patriarch was in existence from 1099 until 1291, and nominally until 1374; in 1847, it was again constituted. There is also an Armenian patriarchate, and the Melchite patriarch of Antioch adds the title of Jerusalem to his other titles. Within the city there are numerous Christian sites, including the Church of the Resurrection (the Holy Sepulchre), and over the ages Christian pilgrims have been anxious to walk in the footsteps of their Lord. Nonetheless, unlike Jews, Christians have not been preoccupied with Jerusalem as a geographical locality – instead, they have focused on the idea of Jerusalem as a spiritual concept. From New Testament times, Jerusalem was the name given to the heavenly city (Heb. 12.22), and symbolized the faithful people of God. This idea has been very influential on writers of Christian hymns and devotional writings.

Jesus

Christians believe that Jesus of Nazareth (1st cent. CE) was the long-promised Jewish Messiah (the Christ). He is seen to have fulfilled the prophecies of the Hebrew Scriptures and, as Christianity became a world-wide religion rather than a Jewish sect, he was perceived to be the divine pre-existent Logos (Word), the second Person of the Trinity. The four New Testament Gospels contain all we know of Jesus' earthly life and teaching. In fulfilment of Isa. 7.14 and Mic. 5.2, he is said to have been born of a virgin in the town of Bethlehem (Matt. 2.1–12, Luke 2.1–20). At his baptism he received the Holy Spirit and God's assurance of his Sonship (Mark 1.1–11), and he began his preaching ministry in the region of Galilee. The essence of his message was, 'The time is fulfilled, and the kingdom of God is at hand' (Mark 1.15). The Jews believed that in the Last Days, God would intervene in history and establish his rule on earth. After the terrible Day of Judgement, God would create a new order of peace and harmony, presided over by the Messiah, the divinely anointed King. Jesus taught that this era had begun to arrive.

His healing miracles and exorcisms were signs of the Spirit of God at work (Luke 11.14–23). To his disciples, he emphasized that he was not the glorious kingly leader they were expecting, but that he would suffer many things. He identified himself with the son of man (Dan. 7.13) who was an agent in God's final judgement, and he insisted that he 'came not to be served but to serve, and to give his life as a ransom for many' (Mark 10.45). The Gospels, which have a strong anti-Jewish bias, record Jesus coming into conflict with the religious establishment of his time. He exalted the principles of charity and sincerity over a strict interpretation of the ritual law (Mark 2.15–3.6), and several of his sayings and parables imply that the religious outcast was more acceptable to God than the self-righteous leader (Luke 10.29–37). At his Last Supper with his disciples, he indicated that the old covenant with the Jews had come to an end and that God was instituting a new order, sealed with the sacrifice of his blood (Mark 14.22–25). He was put to death by the Roman authorities, crucified as a political rebel who had claimed to be King of the Jews. Two days later his tomb was found to be empty, and his followers insisted that he was alive and had been seen by them. They were convinced that God had raised him from the dead and that through his death and resurrection, evil and death had been conquered. The early Church also received the gift of the Holy Spirit which gave them the power to preach the gospel, and this was understood to be a confirmation of God's Kingdom on earth (Acts 2.16–21). Although the first disciples understood Jesus to be the Jewish Messiah, the Christian message quickly spread to the Gentile world, particularly once circumcision ceased to be a condition of membership (Acts 15.6–21). Paul (1st cent.) argued in his epistles that the old Jewish law was now superseded, and salvation was now only available through faith in Jesus (Rom. 8.1–17). Jesus came to be seen as the Word of God (John 1.1–18) – God's final revelation, co-equal and co-eternal with the Father, truly God as well as truly human.

A breach with the synagogue was inevitable and the Jewish community introduced a curse on the *Minim* (sectarians) in their *Amidah* prayer. In his lifetime, Jesus was one preacher among many in an obscure corner of the Roman Empire. The mention of him in Josephus (1st cent.) is almost certainly a later Christian addition, and references to him in the Talmud are late and polemical. Although Christians 'prove' Jesus' Messiahship by reference to the Hebrew Scriptures, the Jewish rejection of Christian doctrine is also based on biblical texts. Orthodox Jews still await the coming of the Messiah and a future age of universal peace and prosperity. In recent times, however, with more positive Jewish–Christian dialogue, Christian scholars have been increasingly interested in the Jewish background of Jesus and, conversely, Jews are more willing to see Jesus as a significant figure in the prophetic tradition.

Jews *see* Israel

John the Baptist *see* Elijah

Judgement

(Damnation) (Eternal Life) (Future Life): In the Bible, God is depicted as a moral being concerned with justice. As part of the covenant, God agreed to reward the Jewish people with wealth and prosperity if they observe his commandments; however, if they depart from his ways, God decreed that he would inflict punishment on the nation. This scheme of reward and punishment is a dominant theme of Scripture but, in the prophetic books as well as Wisdom literature, doubts were expressed about such a providential plan. Thus Jeremiah asked: 'Why does the way of the wicked prosper?' (Jer. 12.1.) Again, Habakkuk declared: 'O Lord, how long shall I cry for help, and thou wilt not hear ... For the wicked surround the righteous, so justice goes forth perverted' (Hab. 1.2, 4). In the Book of Job the problem of theodicy (divine justice) is explored in detail, and the Book of Ecclesiastes raises the same issue.

Seeking to resolve this dilemma, the Pharisees of the late second Temple (2nd and 1st cent. BCE) developed a comprehensive eschatological scheme. Since it was clear that God's promises of reward were not always fulfilled in this life, the dominant view was that justice would be meted out in the world-to-come. This solution alleviated the problem of the righteous who suffer, and the wicked who prosper, in this life. The afterlife was thus conceived as the opportunity for individual recompense. In their speculations about the hereafter, the rabbis spoke of *Gan Eden* (the Garden of Eden) as the place of reward and *Gehinnom* (Gehenna) as the place of punishment. In these two domains, those who have been resurrected will receive their due reward or suffer eternally after the period of Messianic redemption.

During the Middle Ages, various aspects of this eschatological system were debated by Jewish scholars. Saadiah Gaon (9th–10th cent.), for example, argued that after death the souls of both the righteous and the wicked are kept in separate places until the time of the resurrection of the dead. This will occur, he stated, after the coming of the Messiah. When the body and soul are reunited, judgement will take place, and then reward and punishment will occur in the world-to-come. Moses Maimonides (12th cent.), on the other hand, maintained that the ultimate reward consists of a spiritual disembodied existence in God's presence. The wicked, he believed, will simply be extinguished rather than endure eternal torment.

Despite such different interpretations of reward and punishment, judgement and belief in the hereafter are central tenets of traditional Jewish theology. In the modern period, however, rabbinic eschatology has ceased to play such a central role in Jewish thought. Increasingly, Jews have found it difficult to believe in a providential Lord of history who will send a Messiah to usher in a period of redemption, bring about the physical resurrection of the dead, and reward the righteous and punish the wicked in a future life. Instead, for most religious Jews across the denominational spectrum, a belief in the immortality of the soul without the consideration of divine judgement and damnation has replaced the complex system of theodicy found in rabbinic sources.

The writers of the New Testament inherited Jewish traditions about God's judgement in a future world. Like the Pharisees, Jesus took issue with the Sadducees and defended the doctrine of the resurrection of the dead (Mark 12.18–27). Throughout his ministry, he proclaimed the imminence of the reign of God and the dawning of salvation, and one of his parables describes the Day of Judgement when the wicked would go to eternal punishment and the righteous to eternal life (Matt. 25.31–46). According to the Fourth Gospel, Jesus should be understood as the Son of Man who comes from heaven and people are judged by their reaction to him (John 3.18). After his resurrection, he ascended to heaven to sit at the right hand of the Father (Mark 14.62). From there he will reappear as a judge at the end of time (Mark 8.38). In the New Testament, heaven is regarded as the place of final reward for the faithful, whereas hell is depicted as the realm where the wicked will receive punishment (Luke 16.19–31).

Reflecting on this eschatological scheme, Paul envisaged heaven as sharing in Christ's resurrected life (Phil. 3.21), whereas hell is conceived as banishment from the face of God (2 Thess. 1.9). Rom. 2.8–9 depicts the tribulation and distress of those who have performed wicked deeds. The early Christian creeds contain explicit articles concerning belief in an afterlife where the righteous will be rewarded and the wicked punished, and these teachings were later elaborated in the writings of medieval theologians. Throughout, the principle of retributive justice is affirmed, and the notion of judgement was socially useful in that it was an incentive to good behaviour and a deterrent to the wicked. As in Judaism, the Christian doctrine of the afterlife was a means of redressing the obvious injustices of this life and was seen by its critics as a means of keeping the underprivileged subservient and content with their lot.

In modern thought, the belief in traditional eschatology has given way to a reinterpretation of the Last Judgement, heaven and hell. Many Christians now understand the traditional doctrines of eternal reward and punishment as symbolic or figurative in character. Although the conviction that individuals will enter into a divine life and attain a beatific vision of God is still a central feature of Christianity, this state is generally conceived without the rich imagery of the past.

Justification

Judaism teaches that justification in the sight of God can only be achieved through righteousness. A righteous person is one who lives in accordance with Torah, the law of God. The purpose of God's covenant with Abraham was to do 'righteousness and justice' (Gen. 18.19) and, in the famous words of the prophet Micah, 'what does the Lord require of you but to do justice, and to love kindness, and

to walk humbly with your God?' (6.8.) It was recognized that keeping the law in every particular was not possible, but, through prayer and fasting, atonement for transgression could be made and justification achieved.

Christianity teaches that human beings are naturally sinful and incapable by themselves of righteousness. It is only through God's saving grace that justification is possible. Paul (1st cent.), writing from his own experience, declared, 'I can will what is right, but I cannot do it. For I do not do the good I want, but the evil I do not want is what I do' (Rom. 7.18, 19). Redemption can only be found through faith in the saving death of Jesus Christ which has effected a reconciliation between God and humanity. Although Roman Catholics and Protestants differ as to precisely how justification is achieved, they are agreed that it is through God's initiative rather than through human effort. In this, there is a radical departure from the Jewish tradition.

K

Kabbalah *see* Mysticism

Kaddish *see* Funeral rites

Kashrut *see* Food

Ketubah *see* Marriage

Kiddush *see* Grace at meals

Kiddush Ha-Shem *see* Martyrology

Kingdom of God

Eschatological reference to the End of Days (also called the 'Kingdom of heaven'). The term designates a period when the world will be perfected, suffering will cease, and humanity will live according to God's law. According to the prophet Isaiah, during this time the 'wolf shall dwell with the lamb, and the leopard shall lie down with the kid' (Isa. 11.6). The prophets decreed that the imperfect order of the world would end on the Day of the

Lord; God would then create a new heaven and earth when humanity and all nature will be at peace as they were in the Garden of Eden.

As time passed, the concept of the Kingdom of God and the doctrine of the Messiah were combined so that there was no distinction between the Kingdom of heaven and the Days of the Messiah. In the pseudepigrapha there are numerous descriptions of this future paradise, and the Dead Sea sect at Qumran believed that the Kingdom of God was at hand. By joining the sect, they claimed, one could be an active participant in the eschatological process by which this world is made anew.

In talmudic sources there are frequent references to the Kingdom of heaven. In some cases, the expression refers to the Days of the Messiah; at other times, it designates the *Olam Ha-Ba* (world-to-come) as distinct from Messianic redemption. The latter interpretation assumed that the Messianic era would be followed by the Kingdom of God. Once the Days of the Messiah had come to an end, a general resurrection would take place, and then God would judge all people. Subsequently, a new creation would be established devoid of unrighteousness. In medieval thought, this distinction between the Messianic era and the Kingdom of God continued. In this light, the political and social reformation of earthly life was seen as a temporary goal, to be superseded ultimately by a divine transformation of existence. The longing for the advent of this new age is reflected in the *Alenu* prayer, which concludes each daily service with the hope that 'all will accept the yoke of Your kingship, and You will soon rule over all of them eternally'.

In the New Testament, the Jewish idea of the Kingdom of God (referred to as the 'Kingdom of heaven' in Matt.) occupies a central role. In Mark 1.14–15, Jesus came into Galilee after John was arrested, proclaiming that 'The time is fulfilled, and the kingdom of God is at hand'. Jesus' actions reveal its fulfilment – thus he declared: 'if it is by the finger of God that I cast out demons, then the kingdom of God has come upon you' (Luke 11.20). Although the kingly rule of God was believed to have begun with Jesus' ministry as the Messiah, it would only be fully revealed at the end of time. The early Church, following Jesus' instruction, prayed for its arrival (Matt. 6.10) and expected its realization in the near future (cf. Mark 9.1). When this did not take place, the Kingdom of God came to be identified with the visible Church, as well as the rule of Christ in the life of the individual Christian. This teaching was adopted by patristic writers as well as the medieval Schoolmen, even though the doctrine of the Second Coming of Jesus and the final Judgement remained an essential element of the Christian message.

Reformers, however, objected to the identification between the Kingdom of God and any earthly organization. For Martin Luther (15th–16th cent.), the Kingdom of God is synonymous with the realm of divine grace. John Calvin (16th cent.) envisaged the Kingdom as primarily embodied in a theocratic society in which individuals could play an active role. The point at issue here was the question whether human efforts could contribute to the coming of the Kingdom, or if the Kingdom would be understood solely as a gift of grace. Pietists and evangelicals associated the concept of extending the Kingdom with missionary work. Many Christian thinkers envisaged the Kingdom as an ideal society that would be achieved by human progress, and this view dominated liberal theology in the 19th cent. Yet despite the influence of this interpretation, this view of the Kingdom of heaven has been subjected to serious criticism. The political and social disasters of the 20th cent. have led to the rejection of the concept of evolutionary idealism, and theologians such as Karl Barth (20th cent.) insist that God's Kingdom can only be revealed by God himself.

Nonetheless, since the 1960s, the idea of the Kingdom of God as an idealized society has come into prominence in the work of liberation theologians. Liberationists in both the Third and First World have understood Jesus as a liberator who struggled to bring God's Kingdom in his own time. In addition, programmes of social renewal have utilized the doctrine of the Kingdom of God as a central element of their policies. Such a this-worldly focus has parallels with the Jewish commitment to establishing God's Kingdom in anticipation of God's Messianic rule. Nevertheless, as distinct from Judaism, Christians of all religious persuasions believe that in some way Jesus as Messiah ushered in the heavenly Kingdom in his own lifetime. What is at stake is the degree to which God's Kingdom has already unfolded in history through the ministry of Jesus and through the activity of the Holy Spirit both in the Church and in the lives of individual Christians. However, both Christians and Jews recognize that the world has not yet reached perfection, and members of both groups look forward to a final transformation.

Kingship

According to Deut. 17.14–20, the ancient Israelites were commanded to appoint a king who would be a guardian of God's law. There is another tradition in the Hebrew Scriptures (1 Sam. 8) that is strongly anti-monarchist, but the idea of the hereditary kingship of the house of David is nonetheless fundamental to Judaism. The laws concerning kings were codified by Moses Maimonides (12th cent. AD) and prayers for the restoration of the Davidic line are still to be found in the liturgy. However, the idea of absolute monarchy is totally foreign to the Jews. The king was the king under God. When David broke the law in seducing Bathsheba and killing her husband (2 Sam. 11 and 12), he was punished, and the Deuteronomic historian was pitiless in his criticism of other monarchs who were less than virtuous. After the defeat of the Bar Kochba revolt by the Romans in 132 CE, the question of Jewish sovereignty became purely theoretical, but it was still believed that God's future anointed Messiah would be of the House of David and would establish peace, justice, and prosperity over all the earth. While living in the Dispersion, however, Jews accepted the kingship of the reigning Gentile monarch. The Talmud taught that the law of the land is the law, and prayers for the welfare of the national government are included in the daily synagogue services.

This tradition of obedience to the secular power was carried over into Christianity. The first letter of Peter instructs the Church to 'Be subject for the Lord's sake to every human institution, whether it be to the emperor as supreme, or to governors as sent by him' (1 Pet. 2.13–14). On the other hand, Jesus Christ as Messiah is exalted above all human rule and is the King of kings and Lord of lords (Rev. 19.16). From the late Middle Ages until the 18th cent., many Christians held the belief that kings ruled by divine right. The coronation ceremony often involves anointing with oil, and the king was sometimes perceived as having super-natural powers such as healing. All resistance, even to a tyrant, was seen to be quasi-blasphemous. However, this line of thought was vigorously criticized, and the general Christian opinion is directly in line with the Israelite view that the monarch rules justly only when he rules in accordance with the laws of God.

Kippah *see* Clothing

K'lal Yisrael *see* Catholicism; Israel

L

Laity *see* Ordination

Lamb of God

(Paschal Lamb): According to the Book of Exodus, before the Children of Israel escaped from Egypt, they were commanded to slaughter a lamb. When the angel of death killed all the first-born in the land, the blood of the lamb was smeared on the Israelites' door-posts and the angel 'passed over' their houses (Exod. 12.1–32). This ritual of sacrificing a lamb on the eve of the Passover festival continued throughout the Temple period, and is to be found today in the symbolic lamb shankbone on the Seder (Passover meal) table.

The Fourth Gospel describes John the Baptist calling Jesus 'the Lamb of God, who takes away the sin of the world!' (John 1.29). Similarly, the Book of Revelation identifies Jesus with a lamb (chs 5 and 6). In the same way that the Passover lamb saved the Israelites from physical slavery and destruction, Jesus' sacrifice on the cross at the Passover festival frees his followers from slavery to sin and saves them from spiritual death. A lamb with a cross is a common symbol for Jesus in Christian art.

Law

(Commandments) (Civil Law) (Criminal Law) (Decalogue) (*Mitzvot*) (Oral Law) (Rabbinical Law) (Torah) (Unwritten Law): Jewish law is based on the biblical commandments contained in the Pentateuch (Torah). According to tradition, God revealed the Ten Commandments (the Decalogue) as well as 603 other commandments (*mitzvot*) to Moses on Mt Sinai. These laws consist of 248 positive and 365 negative prescriptions.

During the Hellenistic period, the Sadducees maintained that these written laws contain the essence of Jewish legislation; the Pharisees, on the other hand, believed that they need to be supplemented by additional rulings. According to the rabbis there were two laws: the Written Law as revealed in the five books of Moses (*Torah she-bikhetav*) and the Oral Law (*Torah she-be'al peh*), which was handed down from one generation to the next. Thus the Mishnah proclaims: 'Moses received the Torah from Sinai, and handed it to Joshua; Joshua to the elders; the elders to the prophets, and the prophets to the Men of the Great Assembly.'

The method of interpretating Scripture (Midrash) took the form of expounding the text to support legal rulings. This system of exegesis was later systematized into a series of rules. In the 1st cent. BCE, Hillel employed seven hermeneutical rules which were later expanded into 13 by Ishmael ben Elisha (1st–2nd cent.) – these principles have been viewed through the ages as the standard rules of scriptural interpretation. According to tradition, laws derived from Scripture through the process of rabbinic interpretation (where there is a consensus or a majority of agreement) are regarded as part of the Oral Law revealed to Moses on Mt Sinai. Added to scriptural-based laws are customs (*minhagim*), which emerged within specific areas in the course of time – they, too, are regarded as obligatory prescriptions.

In the history of the evolution of law, the Mishnah was the first collection of the Oral Law. Compiled by Judah Ha-Nasi in the 3rd cent., it consists of legal traditions from *c.* 300 BCE–200 CE. Primarily, it contains the discussions and decisions of sages about the content of scriptural law. Its purpose was to supply teachers with an authoritative compilation of the Oral tradition. This process continued in subsequent centuries, culminating in the compilation of the Palestinian and Babylonian Talmuds. These two bodies of literature comprise the authoritative corpus of Jewish law accumulated from *c.* 200–500. Both these works incorporate the Mishnah and rabbinic discussions known as Gemara.

After the compilation of these Talmuds, leading rabbinical authorities issued decisions (Responsa) about specific legal questions. Beginning in the 8th cent., digests of Jewish law (containing religious as well as civil and criminal law) were composed to serve the needs of the community. Such writers as Isaac Alfasi (11th–12th cent.), Moses Maimonides (12th cent.), and Asher ben Jehiel (13th cent.) produced comprehensive codes of law. The most authoritative code is the *Shulhan Arukh* of Joseph Caro (15th–16th cent.), together with the glosses of Moses Isserles (16th cent.). This compilation has continued to serve Orthodox Jewry until the present day. However, after the Enlightenment in the 18th and 19th cent., non-Orthodox Jews ceased to view this corpus of law as binding – instead, they have subscribed only to those legal precepts that they regard as spiritually significant in the modern world.

Although Christianity sought to break away from the legal constraints of the Torah, Christians from the very earliest period recognized the existence of natural law. Thus Paul in Rom. 2 states that 'what the law requires is written on their hearts' (Rom. 2.15). In the writings of the Church Fathers as well as in the Roman legal tradition, the theory of natural right or law was transmitted to medieval Christian thinkers such as Thomas Aquinas. The Thomist approach to natural law stresses its dependence on right reasoning, practical experience, and the intellect. Later, Scholastics tended to envisage its operation as an act of will rather than a judgement of intellect. Eventually, Christian thinkers came to view natural law as a set of commands imposed on human beings by God. Yet despite this variety of interpretations, the concept of natural law still functions as an important aspect of Christian moral thinking.

Parallel with the development of natural law theory, a body of ecclesiastical rules dealing with matters of faith, morals, and disciplines evolved in the Church. Beginning with the practice of convening councils to resolve disputed issues, various *ad hoc* pronouncements were made. In the 4th cent., a series of canons promulgated at Nicaea came to be regarded as authoritative in both the East and West. Other sets of canons were subsequently added by later councils and, by the beginning of the 5th cent., canonical collections began to appear. Alongside the decrees of Church councils, individual bishops promulgated ecclesiastical legislation. In the 4th cent., special authority was attributed to papal letters and, in the 4th–5th cent., collections of canons were attributed to fictitious authors. Under Charlemagne (8th–9th cent.), considerable standardization took place, and in time a body of canonists appeared. In the Middle Ages, Gratian's (12th cent.) *Decretum* had an enormous influence; it was eventually supplemented by later collections. Despite this development, law in Christianity was never viewed in the same light as in Judaism. The resurrection of Christ introduced a new era of grace which freed Christians from the bondage of scriptural legislation. Through the ages, Christian thinkers have been pre-eminently concerned with the heart and soul of the individual Christian rather than the imposition of extraneous legal prescriptions.

Law books

(Mishnah) (Pentateuch) (*Shulhan Arukh*) (Talmud) (Written Law): According to tradition, God revealed 613 commandments to Moses on Mt Sinai; these laws (known as the Written Law) are recorded in the Five Books of Moses (Torah). These prescriptions, which are to be observed as part of God's covenant with Israel, are classified in two major categories: (1) statutes (*hukkim*) concerned with ritual performances characterized as obligations between human beings and God; and (2) judgements (*mishpatim*) consisting of ritual laws that would have been adopted by society even if they had not been decreed by God (such as laws regarding murder and theft). These 613 commandments consist of 365 negative (prohibited) and 248 positive (duties to be performed) prescriptions.

According to tradition, Moses received the Oral Torah in addition to the Written Law. This was passed down from generation to generation and was the subject of rabbinic debate. The first authoritative compilation of the Oral Law was the Mishnah composed by Judah Ha-Nasi in the 3rd cent. CE. This work is the most important book of law after the Bible; its purpose was to supply teachers and judges with an authoritative guide to the Jewish legal tradition. There are six orders of the Mishnah: (1) 'seeds' – dealing with benedictions, daily prayers, and agricultural laws; (2) 'appointed seasons' – on laws covering observances of the Sabbath, festivals, and fasts; (3) 'women' – specifying practices concerning marriage, divorce, and vows; (4) 'damages' – on civil and criminal law, punishments, and idolatry; (5) 'holy things' – about ritual slaughter, sacrifices, offerings, and the Temple; and (6) 'cleanliness' – which discusses ritual purity and impurity.

In subsequent centuries, sages continued to discuss the content of Jewish law; their deliberations are recorded in the Palestinian and Babylonian Talmuds. Both Talmuds incorporate the Mishnah and later rabbinic discussions known as the Gemara. The Gemara text preserves the proceedings of the academies in both Palestine and Babylonia, where scholars assembled to study the Mishnah. The central purpose of these deliberations was to elucidate the Mishnah text.

After the compilation of the Talmuds (6th cent.), outstanding rabbinic authorities continued the development of Jewish law by issuing answers to specific questions. These responses (known as Responsa) touched on all aspects of Jewish law and ensured a standardization of practice. In time, various scholars felt the need to produce codes of Jewish law so that all members of the community would have access to the legal tradition. In the 11th cent., Isaac Alfasi produced a work (*Hilkhot Ha-Rif*) that became the standard code for Sephardic Jewry. Two centuries later, Asher ben Jehiel wrote a code (*Hilkhot Ha-Rosh*) that became the code for Ashkenazi Jews. Moses Maimonides (12th cent.) also wrote an important code (*Mishneh Torah*) that had a wide influence, as did the code *Arbaah Turim* by Jacob ben Asher (13th–14th cent.), the son of Asher ben Jehiel. In the 16th cent. Joseph Caro published the *Shulhan Arukh*, which (together with glosses by Moses Isserles (16th cent.)) has served as the standard code of Jewish law for Orthodox Jewry until the present day. In the modern world, however, non-Orthodox Jews have rejected the belief in the divine origin of the Written and Oral Law. As a consequence, they do not regard any traditional compilation as authoritative, and there is no equivalent code of law within any of these movements. Instead, non-Orthodox Jews feel free to select from the tradition those laws that they believe are spiritually meaningful in the modern age.

From New Testament times, Christians did not feel obligated to observe the scriptural commandments. Paul taught that with the death and resurrection of Jesus, the era of the law was over and salvation was no longer to be obtained by keeping the commandments (Rom. 3.21–26). Nonetheless, the early Church found it necessary to introduce laws over and above Jesus' teaching. Documents exist that allegedly come from the apostles and are manuals of liturgical and disciplinary regulations (such as the *Didache*). In the 4th cent. Meletios of Antioch made a compilation of the canons of various councils, known as the *Corpus Canonum*, of Antioch. This was followed by the *Dionysiana Collection* (5th cent.), the most important Christian body of law produced during the first millennium. However, the Church never attempted to legislate for every aspect of the Christian life as the rabbis did for the Jews.

In the Middle Ages, Gratian (12th cent.) produced *Decretum*, which dominated the field of canon law. Other collections of law updated this corpus, and the *Corpus Iuris Canonici* (16th cent.) became the basis of Church law until 1917, when Pope Benedict XV promulgated the *Codex Iuris Canonici*. Within the various Protestant branches of Christendom, these collections of ecclesiastial law were largely overlooked, but each wing of the Church evolved its own procedures and practices to regulate Christian life. In this respect, these reform movements parallel the developments within modern Judaism of religious bodies that have attempted to free themselves from the legal constraints of the past.

Lectern

A reading stand that is used to support the Bible or other liturgical books in church. Often it takes the form of an eagle, the symbol of the Fourth Evangelist. The Jewish equivalent is the bimah (dais) from which the Torah scroll is read. However, the scrolls of the law are so highly venerated that they are kept in the ark, not, as in a Christian church, on permanent display. They are solemnly brought out to be read during the course of the service and then, with full ceremony, they are returned to their place.

Lent

A 40-day fast beginning with Ash Wednesday and ending with Easter Sunday. It commemorates Jesus' 40 days in the wilderness (Mark 1.12 and 13). Ash Wednesday is so called because, as a symbol of repentance, ashes were placed on the heads of the people during the service. The 40 days end with Holy Week, in which Christians remember the last week of Jesus' earthly life. It culminates in Jesus' crucifixion on Good Friday and his resurrection on Easter Sunday. Traditionally, the fast was kept strictly; only one meal a day was allowed, with no meat, fish, eggs, or dairy products. This has been considerably relaxed. In the Roman Catholic Church, only Ash Wednesday and Good Friday remain as obligatory fast days, and then only meat is forbidden. Lent is regarded as a time of penance. Purple vestments are used and the churches are left undecorated. Many Christians spend more time on religious exercises during this period; they may attend a course of Lenten addresses, for example, and even in fairly secular circles it is customary to give up some indulgence such as tobacco, alcohol, or sweets for the season. This is regarded as a matter of self-discipline.

The theology of fasting is different in Judaism. Jews believe that through fasting, atonement can be made for sin. Christians, on the other hand, believe that atonement has already been effected through the sacrificial death of Jesus, and that therefore fasting is merely a sign of their repentance. Jews have particular fast days throughout the year when no food or drink is taken at all. The nearest equivalent season to Lent is the Ten Solemn Days in the autumn, between the New Year (Rosh Hashanah) and the Day of Atonement (Yom Kippur). This is to be spent in preparation for the great 25-hour fast of the Day of Atonement, in the same way as Lent is a time of preparation for the great festival of Easter. Through prayer and fasting on the Day of Atonement, Jews believe that their sins can be atoned for and forgiven, in the same way that Christians believe that the burden of sin is removed by the atonement wrought in Jesus' death and that his resurrection on Easter Day is a guarantee of their forgiveness.

Levirate marriage

According to Deut. 25.5–10, if a man dies childless, it is the obligation of one of his brothers to marry the widow to raise up children in the name of his dead brother. If the brothers refuse to do this, the widow must perform the ceremony of *halitza* (drawing off). In front of a court of five, she must read the relevant biblical verses, take off the brother's right shoe, spit on the ground and say, 'So shall it be done to the man who does not build up his brother's house'. The custom of levirate marriage died out in Talmudic times, although it was supported by Moses Maimonides (12th cent.). However, widows were encouraged to continue to perform the ceremony of *halitza* so that there could be no question of the validity of any future marriage and the legitimacy of their subsequent children. Today, the State of Israel has forbidden levirate marriage and has made *halitza* compulsory. This is because marriage to a dead spouse's sibling is considered incestuous, and also because levirate marriage frequently clashed with the rabbinic prohibition against polygamy. Reform Jews have dispensed with both levirate marriage and *halitza* as customs of another age that conflict with the principle of equality between the sexes.

Jesus referred to the custom of levirate marriage in his discussion with members of the priestly party on the question of resurrection of the dead (Mark 12.18–27), but it has never been practised in the Christian Church. Marriage between a widow and her husband's brother and also a widower and his wife's sister are traditionally forbidden as being incestuous, but in many countries these provisions are overruled by the law of the land.

Liberalism

With the Emancipation of Jews in the late 18th cent., liberalism became a dominant force in modern Jewish life. For centuries the Jewish community was forced to live an isolated existence in ghettos but, at the end of the 18th cent., Gentiles began to champion the cause of Jewish liberty. Proclaiming a fundamental bill of rights for all people, they argued that Jewry must be allowed full citizenship in the countries where they lived. As restrictions against Jewish participation in social and cultural life diminished, Jews adopted a much more sympathetic attitude to the intellectual attitudes of their age.

The *Haskalah* (Jewish enlightenment) move-

ment was a product of these changes. Jewish *maskilim* (the enlightened) argued that secular studies should be an integral part of the Jewish education. Adopting a hostile attitude to Yiddish, they maintained that Jews must be fluent in the language of general society. Further, they insisted that the history of Judaism and the Jewish people should be pursued in depth and that the study of Hebrew be promoted. Some modernists also argued for the reform of the Jewish religion. Reform Judaism as a movement sought to modify religious belief and practice to suit the modern age. In a less extreme form, neo-Orthodoxy sought a modern adaptation of traditional Judaism to contemporary society. In particular, neo-Orthodox leaders such as Samson Raphael Hirsch (19th cent.) advocated the integration of secular and Jewish studies, more decorum in synagogue services, and the utilization of modern methods in the study of sacred texts.

The growth of Zionism was also a product of secular and liberal tendencies. The appreciation of secular values, the preoccupation with Jewish history, and the increasing importance of Hebrew led to the efflorescence of modern Jewish nationalism. The political Zionist movement under Theodor Herzl (19th–20th cent.) was a secularized version of the belief that the land of Israel is the eternal homeland of the Jewish nation. These various developments in Jewish life and thought were expressions of liberal acculturation. Although they set the tone for contemporary Jewish history, counter-assimilatory tendencies over the past two centuries (such as Hasidism) sought to draw the Jewish people back to traditional patterns of Jewish life.

Within Christianity, liberalism is often defined in opposition to conservatism and fundamentalism. As in Judaism, it refers to the attempt to be open to secular study, scientific investigation, and historical research. In the 19th and 20th cent., liberal Protestantism in particular championed the importance of such openness. According to liberal thought, Christianity must pursue the truth wherever it is found. Reason and experience, rather than authority, must serve as the guide. In this light, dogmatism and exclusivism are rejected, and Christianity is viewed not as the sole expression of God's revelation. Instead, divine encounter is understood as ongoing and present in all traditions. This has profoundly affected Jewish–Christian dialogue, and it is notable that inter-faith activity is pursued most actively by the liberal branches of Christianity and Judaism.

Christian liberal thinkers have also been sympathetic to the findings of modern biblical scholarship. In their studies of Scripture, they have attempted to distinguish between the authentic message of the gospel and those cultural accretions that form its context. Like non-Orthodox Jews, they view the Bible as a human document recording God's meeting with the Jewish people. The task of the Christian exegete is to interpret the Bible in the light of contemporary knowledge. Liberal Christians have also been anxious to point out the ethical implications of their faith. Christianity is not viewed simply as a system of belief; it is also a way of life. Social evils must be confronted, and liberals are frequently at the forefront of campaigns to reform public policy and to temper traditional ethical thinking with the insights of modern sociology and psychology; despite their influence, such liberal tendencies have not gone unchallenged. Traditional Christians argue that liberalism accommodates too easily to cultural trends, and in doing so loses sight of Christ's eternal message. Here, then, in both traditions, it is possible to see a common development of liberal thought, evoking parallel counter-movements that reject the assumptions of such an approach to religious faith.

Liberation theology

A Christian theological movement that emerged in Latin America in the late 1960s. It recognizes that Christianity should make a religious response to the situation of the poor. The Second Vatican Council, in its statement on the Church and the World, *Gaudium et Spes*, accepted that individual morality is inadequate to deal with widespread social problems and urged Christians to make use of the insights of the social sciences. Following this, the Latin American bishops held a conference in Medellín, Columbia in 1968 that committed the Church to liberation of the poor and the oppressed. In liberationist thinking, all human experience is seen as an encounter with God's grace. Jesus, with his concern for those who were marginalized in his society, reveals God's will for humankind. Living the gospel means living in solidarity with all

human beings, not just with the rich and powerful. The function of the Church is to reveal God's values and, by so doing, build up the Kingdom of God on earth. Liberation theology has been linked with Marxism in that it shares a similar analysis of the state of society and, like Marxism, proposes collective rather than individual solutions. Because of this, some liberationists have been regarded with suspicion by the Vatican. However, Latin American theology has been highly influential on other theological movements. With its emphasis on concrete praxis, rather than on theoretical conjecture, the insights of liberation theology have been used to develop distinctive Asian, black, and feminist theologies, all of which focus on the condition of the oppressed in 20th-cent. society.

Liberation theology also has close affinities with Jewish thinking and draws heavily on the insights and situations that are to be found in the Hebrew Scriptures. Liberationists have largely rejected the spiritualizing tendency of the Christian Church, which has traditionally understood the Exodus as a metaphor for spiritual freedom and the Kingdom of God as a heavenly state of mind. Instead, they see the Exodus as a prototype of liberation from grinding physical slavery, and they perceive the Kingdom of God as an earthly situation towards which it is the duty of all human beings to contribute. This has always been the Jewish reading of the biblical texts and the stress on praxis rather than theory is very much in the Jewish tradition. However, because the majority of Jews are members of the prosperous developed world, they are largely unconcerned with liberation theology and are unaware of its affinities with traditional Jewish thought. It is perhaps only through feminist theology that the mainstream Jewish community has been affected by liberationism.

Light, eternal (Ner Tamid)

According to Lev. 24.2, Moses was commanded to tell the Children of Israel 'to bring . . . pure oil from beaten olives for the lamp, that a light may be kept burning continually'. The light was arranged on the menorah (seven-branched candlestick) in the Temple sanctuary and was tended by the priests. This tradition was maintained in the synagogue after the destruction of the Temple in 70 CE. Nowadays, the Eternal Light (*Ner Tamid*) is suspended above the ark. The light has been interpreted both as a symbol of the Jewish people whose mission is to be a 'light to the nations' (Isa. 42.6), and also of God's word, which is described by the Psalmist as 'a lamp to my feet and a light to my path' (Ps. 119.105).

Similarly, Christians burn a perpetual light before the reserved sacrament either on the high altar or on a side-chapel altar. The symbolism is identical to that of the *Ner Tamid*. Jesus called his followers 'the light of the world' and commanded them to let their 'light so shine before men, that they may see your good works and give glory to your Father who is in heaven' (Matt. 5.16). According to the Fourth Gospel, Jesus also called himself the Light of the World – 'he who follows me will not walk in darkness, but will have the light of life' (John 8.12). The perpetual light therefore indicates the presence of Jesus in the sacrament. It is Jesus who lights the Christian path through the world in the same way as it is the Torah that illumines the way of the Jews. Similarly, the Jewish people should enlighten the world, as should the disciples of Jesus.

Lights, festival of (Hanukkah)

Jewish feast that commemorates the rededication of the second Temple by Judas Maccabee in 165 BC. The Temple had previously been desecrated by the Hellenizing Seleucid rulers who were driven out by the observant Judas. According to Talmudic legend, the festival is celebrated for eight days because one day's supply of oil miraculously lasted for eight. On each day of the festival, a candle is lit in a special eight-branched menorah (candlestick) – one candle for the first night, two candles for the second, and so on. Hymns are sung, children's games are played, notably the *dreidl* (spinning top), and it is a time of rejoicing. The festival occurs in December and was originally considered to be of minor importance. However, with the commercialization of Christmas in the Gentile world, it has become an alternative celebration for Jewish children. Presents are given on each of the eight days and certain Christian customs have been adopted in some communities – for example, Hanukkah bushes are decorated as substitutes for Christmas trees. It is notable that the adoption of customs is not just in one direction. Christians have taken over the Hanukkah method of lighting candles in the December season of Advent. On the first Sunday, one candle is lit, on the second Sunday, two, working up to four candles on the Sunday before Christmas. This is part of the preparation for the coming of Jesus, whom Christians see as the Light of the World.

Liturgy

During the period of the first Temple, a formal structure of public worship was unknown. According to the Mishnah, priests during second Temple times participated in a short liturgy composed of the Shema (Deut. 6.4), the Ten Commandments (Exod. 20.3–17), and the priestly blessing (Num. 6.24–26). In this context, public prayer responses were probably introduced – those present with sacrifices bowed and praised God after the officiating priests. During this period, the entire congregation began to pray at specified times according to a set order of prayers, and week-day services were held four times daily. These liturgies were called *Sharharit* (morning), *Musaf* (additional), *Minhah* (afternoon) and *Neilat Shearim* (closing of the (Temple) gates or evening prayer).

After the destruction of the second Temple in 70 CE, Gamaliel II established a standard order of service – these prayer services replaced the sacrifices that could no longer be offered and were conducted in synagogues wherever Jews lived. The essential features of this liturgy included the prayer formula 'Blessed are You, O Lord', the Shema ('Hear, O Israel') with its attendant blessings, and the *Amidah*, composed of 19 benedictions. The *Alenu* prayer and the Kaddish concluded the prayers of every service. On Sabbaths and festivals, a set reading from the Torah scroll took place. By the end of the Talmudic period, the prayer services were supplemented by liturgical hymns (*piyyutim*).

In the 9th cent., Amram Gaon composed the first ordering of prayer texts (*Seder Rav*). Subsequently, the first authoritative prayer book was produced by Saadiah (10th cent.). As time passed, various rites emerged in different Jewish communities, but despite their differences they shared a fundamental core of communal prayers. After the Enlightenment in the early 19th cent., however, an attempt was made by reformers to modify traditional Jewish practice. Modelled after Protestant worship, the Reform service was conducted largely in the vernacular, included a sermon, eliminated numerous aspects of the traditional liturgy, and introduced a choir and organ. Other non-Orthodox movements also modified Jewish worship to suit their religious needs. More recently, liturgical development in all Jewish denominations has pioneered creative liturgy, and historical events have inspired new liturgies (such as those that commemorate Holocaust Remembrance Day and Israel Independence Day). Jewish feminists have also encouraged the modification of liturgical practice, and some Orthodox Jewish women have formed their own prayer groups.

Christian worship arose out of Jewish practices in the Temple and the synagogue. Thus the Christian cycle of feasts and seasons was related to the observance of Passover–Pentecost and Sabbath services; the Eucharist was linked to the Passover meal; and the reading of Scripture derived from synagogue practice. Nonetheless, these Jewish features were modified to conform to Christian perceptions about the life, death, and resurrection of Jesus Christ. The new movement encouraged both Jews and Gentiles to reformulate their views about God's salvific activity and providential plan for humanity.

During the 2nd–4th cent., distinctive Christian liturgical patterns developed in major urban centres in the Mediterranean world, and this process of differentiation between areas continued through the centuries. In the early medieval period, reciprocal borrowing took place between the distinctive Eastern and Western rites. Yet in the 9th cent., Charlemagne imposed the Roman rite on the entire territory of the Holy Roman Empire. In the 16th cent., the Western liturgical tradition underwent another major development owing to the impact of the Protestant reformers. In response to the challenge of the Reformation, the Roman see issued uniform revised liturgical books to be used by all churches in communion with Rome, whereas the reformers' concern with public worship gave rise to the emergence of various Protestant forms of worship. More recently, creative liturgies have been encouraged by a wide range of denominations within Christendom, and Christian feminists in particular have advocated liturgical change in line with modern non-sexist thinking. Thus, like Judaism, the patterns of Christian worship have become increasingly diverse as a result of the activity of reformers and progressives. Nonetheless, liturgical practices in both faiths are radically different. Although both traditions are rooted in the practices of the Temple and early synagogue, Christian worship is primarily a memorial and invocation of the risen Lord and a public proclamation of faith in the saving power of Jesus' death and resurrection. Jewish liturgy, on the other hand, is a declaration of trust in God's providential care of and concern for his chosen people, whom he has sanctified by his commandments and who have a unique role among all the nations.

Lord's Prayer

(Our Father): The prayer taught by Jesus to his disciples (Matt. 6.9–13). As Jesus' early followers were all Jews, the prayer is very much in line with the Jewish tradition. It consists of an address ('Our Father, who art in Heaven'), three petitions for the coming of God's rule on earth ('Hallowed be thy name'; 'Thy Kingdom come'; and 'Thy will be done on earth as it is in Heaven'), and four petitions for fundamental human needs ('Give us this day our daily bread'; 'Forgive us our trespasses as we forgive them that trespass against us'; 'Lead us not into temptation'; and 'Deliver us from evil'). The doxology ('For thine is the kingdom, the power and the glory for ever and ever') was added later. Because the prayer was given by Jesus himself, it is regarded as particularly sacred. Tertullian (2nd–3rd cent.) called it *breviarum totius evangelii* (the essence of the whole gospel), and Augustine (4th–5th cent.) saw it as the basis of all other Christian prayers. It is said at almost every service and is the prayer that is known by all Christian believers. In this sense, it is similar to the Jewish Shema ('Hear, O Israel'), which is said by pious Jews every morning and evening. The Shema, however, is not strictly a prayer. It is addressed not to God but to fellow Israelites, and is a reminder of their particular status as a nation before God. The Lord's Prayer, on the other hand, while recognizing the unique holiness of God, addresses him in the context of a personal relationship and brings before him the needs that are common to all humanity.

Lord's Supper *see* Eucharist

Lots, festival of

(Esther, Book of) (Esther, Feast of) (Purim): A minor festival, celebrated on 14 Adar (normally in March), which commemorates the deliverance of the Jews of Persia from the wicked designs of the Grand Vizier, Haman. The story is found in the Book of Esther. Haman planned to massacre the Jews, who were only saved through the intercession of the Jewish Queen Esther and her Uncle Mordecai. The name 'festival of Lots' (Purim) refers to the lots Haman cast to find a suitable day to effect his plans. Although it is considered to be only a minor festival, it is celebrated with much merriment. Adults and children wear costumes; the scroll (*Megillah*) of the Book of Esther is read in the synagogue; and whenever Haman's name is mentioned, a great noise is made to 'blot it out'. There should be a festive meal and children are given little presents of money. The rabbis taught that it is permissible to become so intoxicated that one can no longer tell the difference between the names of Haman and Mordecai. In Israel, Purim is a time of carnival and the streets are crowded with revellers.

Since God is not mentioned in the Book of Esther, the religious message of Purim is unclear; it is really a time of national rejoicing for the deliverance of the Jewish people. Different communities also celebrate additional local Purims. For example, a Florence Purim used to be kept on 27 Sivan to commemorate the rescue of the Jews from the mob by a Christian bishop in 1790, and a Baghdad Purim took place on 11 Av to remember the defeat of the anti-Semitic Persians in that city. There is no similar festival in Christianity, since it is in no sense a national religion. The nearest equivalents are public holidays that celebrate historical events of importance to the nation – Trafalgar Day in Britain, Independence Day in the USA, and Bastille Day in France are obvious examples.

Love

According to Lev. 19.18, human beings are commanded to 'love your neighbour as yourself', and it is stressed that this includes the non-Jew as well as the fellow Israelite ('you shall love him as yourself; for you were strangers in the land of Egypt' (Lev. 19.34)). Hillel (1st cent. BC) summarized the whole law as not doing to others what you would not want to be done to you. He particularly instructed his listeners to love their fellow creatures. Jews are also commanded to love God with 'all your heart, and with all your soul, and with all your might' (Deut. 6.5). These injunctions were taken over unconditionally by the Christian Church. Jesus told a lawyer that if he loved God and his neighbour, he would live (Luke 10.27–28), and he summarized the law by saying: 'as you wish that men would do to you, do so to them' (Luke 6.31). In the Fourth Gospel, he is described as telling his disciples to 'love one another as I have loved you' (John 15.12).

The biblical prophets used the love between a husband and wife as an analogy of the feelings of God for Israel. As Hosea (8th cent. BCE) put it, 'I will betroth you to me for ever; I will betroth you to me in righteousness and in justice, in steadfast love, and in mercy' (Hos. 2.19). Paul took over this imagery, but applied it not to God and Israel, but to the relationship between Jesus Christ and his Church: 'Husbands, love your wives, as Christ loved the church and gave himself up for her' (Eph. 5.25). The idea of love as an attribute of God is fundamental in the liturgies of both traditions. Every day in the synagogue, before they say the Shema ('Hear, O Israel'), pious Jews recite the *Ahavah Rabbah* prayer which declares, 'With great love Thou hast loved us Eternal, our God . . . Be blessed O Eternal, who has chosen his nation Israel in love.' Similarly, Paul's farewell to the Corinthian Church, 'The grace of the Lord Jesus Christ and the love of God and the fellowship of the Holy Spirit be with you all' (2 Cor. 13.14), has been adapted as a regular prayer in Christian services. Thus both Jews and Christians perceive love as the highest religious quality, the one the most characteristic of the God both traditions worship.

Lulav *see* Tabernacles, feast of

M

Magen David *see* Symbolism

Mamzer *see* Illegitimacy

Man (Humanity)

In the Bible, man is part of the natural order; created last, he is to have dominion over 'the fish of the sea and over the birds of the air and over every living thing that moves upon the earth' (Gen. 1.28). Formed in the image of God, he is the Lord of creation. In the Bible, man is conceived as a psychosomatic unity – the terms *nefesh* (soul) and *ruah* (spirit) refer to the total reality of the human person rather than any disembodied part of the human personality. However, under the influence of Greek and Persian thought, the rabbis later distinguished between the body and soul.

According to rabbinic theology, the image of God in man is associated with the freedom of the will, the ability to use language, the creative use of intelligence, the capacity for reflective thought, and the recognition of moral responsibility. This divine link confers special dignity upon the human body, requiring that it be kept in a state of cleanliness. Moreover, the conception of a common humanity derived from God emphasizes the essential equality of all people and the infinite worth of each human being.

In the Bible, man's propensity to evil is highlighted in various ways – as is his inherent goodness. As a consequence, the rabbis taught that each person possesses a good inclination (*yetzer ha-tov*) and an evil inclination (*yetzer ha-ra*). According to rabbinic tradition, the evil inclination can be disciplined and pressed into the service of God, yet the conflict between these two aspects of man's nature is a continuous struggle. The identification of the good inclination with the Torah led to the view that the evil inclination is inherent in human beings from birth, but the good inclination originated when there can be a full acceptance of religious responsibilities. If the individual is able to live a life consonant with the demands of the Torah, he is able to receive divine reward in the hereafter where human beings can attain their ultimate destiny.

Inheriting Jewish traditions about the nature of man, the early Christians subscribed to the belief that human beings are created in the image of God, are composed of souls and bodies, and will attain their true fulfilment in an afterlife. Regarding human nature, they also subscribed to the rabbinic view that man is inherently sinful. Commenting on Gen. 3, Paul argued that just as mankind can be totally identified in and saved in Christ, so human beings are totally involved in the fall of Adam. The sins of all men are the unfolding of Adam's original sin of disobedience in the Garden of Eden: 'Therefore as sin came into the world through one man and death through sin, and so death spread to all men because all men sinned – sin indeed was in the world before the law was given . . . Then as one man's trespass led to condemnation for all men, so one man's act of righteousness leads to acquittal and life for all men' (Rom. 5.12, 18).

The doctrine of original sin became the focus of considerable theological debate in the history of the Church. Tertullian (2nd–3rd cent.) used the term 'concupiscence' to refer to man's inborn evil desire. According to Augustine (4th–5th cent.), the phrase in Rom. 5.12, 'because all men sinned', implies that all human beings subsisted in Adam when he sinned, and thus his sin is theirs. Therefore humanity is not condemned through personal choice, but by ancestry. Moreover, through the Fall, man has lost all ability to obey God's decrees. Pelagius (4th–5th cent.), on the other hand, rejected Augustine's view, arguing that human beings are born without virtue or vice and are free to make moral decisions.

In the Middle Ages, original sin was usually understood as the absence of original righteousness rather than as concupiscence. However, reformers under the influence of Martin Luther (15th–16th cent.) revived the Augustinian doctrine. In modern Christianity, there are widely diverse interpretations of the nature of personhood – ranging from strict Orthodox doctrine to radical reassessments of human anthropology in the light of contemporary developments in psychology and biology. Yet, as in Judaism, the Christian view of human nature is ultimately rooted in biblical and early rabbinic conceptions of God and man. Although the Christian doctrine of original sin differs in several respects from the traditional Jewish understanding of the *yetzer ha-ra*, there is a common recognition in both faiths of man's propensity to sin.

Manna *see* Exodus

Mariology

The study of the person and nature of the Virgin Mary and her role in the incarnation. According to the New Testament, Mary was a native of Nazareth. While still a virgin, through the Holy Spirit she conceived Jesus who was subsequently born in Bethlehem (Luke 1.35; 2.1–7). She is mentioned several times later in the Gospels and was a member of the early Church (Acts 1.14). Although Jesus is described as having brothers and sisters (Matt. 13.55), from the late 2nd cent., the doctrine of Mary's perpetual virginity was current and was formally accepted by the Church in the 5th cent. At the Council of Ephesus of 431, she was given the title of *Theotokos* (mother of God), and her role as the mother of the redeemer was understood as reversing the downfall of humanity caused by Eve's disobedience (Gen. 3.6). From the 6th cent., the Feast of the Assumption of the Blessed Virgin was celebrated. This recognizes that at the end of her bodily life, Mary was directly taken up into heaven. Increasingly in the Middle Ages, the doctrine of her immaculate conception was accepted. This maintains that Mary, alone of all human beings, was born without taint of original sin; and this was finally defined for Roman Catholics in 1854. Mary has been an important focus for popular Christianity since at least the 4th cent. Special prayers such as the Hail Mary and the Little Office of Our Lady are dedicated to her, and she is believed to be particularly effective at intercession. Throughout Christian history, particular individuals have had visions of her. The most famous of these occurred at Lourdes and Fatima, which have subsequently become places of pilgrimage. The Protestant reformers (16th–17th cent.) attacked the worship of the saints generally and the Virgin in particular, but in recent years there has been a tendency even among Protestant theologians to see the value of Marian doctrines. There is some criticism, however, among feminists. Mary is seen as a not entirely desirable model for women; she is meek and humble, and passive rather than active. In addition, virginal motherhood is an impossible state to emulate.

There is no equivalent female figure in Judaism. The rabbis did not accept the doctrine of the fall of man, so there was no need of another woman to reverse Eve's disobedience. In any case, perpetual virginity is not seen to be a meritorious condition; a wifeless man is said to be a deficient man. The matriarchs – Sarah, Rebekah, Leah, and Rachel (the wives of the patriarchs, Abraham, Isaac, and Jacob) – do have an honoured role in Jewish folk religion. They are invoked in the Sabbath blessing of daughters and in the prayer said after the birth of a child. Feminist liturgies also include them whenever the patriarchs are mentioned. However, they are never perceived as anything more than virtuous human beings, and worship of anyone other than God is completely rejected in Judaism.

Marriage

(Ketubah) (Monogamy) (Polygamy): In biblical and Talmudic times marriage was a two-stage process – it commenced with betrothal (*kiddushim*) and ended with marriage (*nissuim*). Traditionally, there were three forms of acquiring a wife by *kiddushim*: through money, by a written deed, or by cohabitation. Commonly this takes place through money (i.e. an object of value, usually a gold ring). In front of two witnesses, the bridegroom gives the bride a ring and states: 'Behold thou art consecrated to me by this ring according to the law of Moses and Israel.' The rite of *nissuim* imposes upon the partners the mutual obligations of marriage.

Although an unlimited time was allowed to elapse between betrothal and marriage, in modern times, *kiddushim*, the reading of a marriage document (Ketubah), and *nissuim* all take place under a *huppah* (marriage canopy) within the wedding service. During the ceremony, two benedictions for *kiddushim* and seven for *nissuim* are recited – they stress the religious nature of the marriage bond, thank God for the joys of the marriage state, and include prayers for the happiness of the bride and groom and the restoration of Jerusalem. Both *kiddushim* and *nissuim* begin with a cup of wine. At the end of the ceremony a glass is broken, probably to symbolize the destruction of Jerusalem. The wedding ceremony is then followed by a feast.

According to tradition, weddings are not allowed to take place on Sabbaths, holy days, or during times associated with memories of national tragedies (such as the three weeks ending with 9 Av and the period of counting the omer: the sheaf cut in the barley harvest). To marry, the bride and groom must be of marriageable age (13 and a day for boys; 12½ and a day for girls), and males are traditionally encouraged not to delay marriage beyond the age of 20. If the relationship between bride and groom disqualifies them as marriage partners, a wedding ceremony performed between them is void. According to Jewish law, marriages between Jews and non-Jews are forbidden. Although Jewish law does not require monogamy, in the 11th cent., Rabbi Gershom prohibited polygamy among Ashkenazi Jews, and in modern times polygamous marriages have all but disappeared from Jewish life. Although civil marriages are recognized as valid in all sections of the religious community, Jewish law requires the granting of a religious divorce before another marriage is allowed to take place. In contrast to Christianity, divorce is permissible and is seen as an occasional unfortunate necessity.

Non-Orthodox marriage practices follow the traditional pattern of marriage with certain modifications. However, within Reform Judaism the granting of a religious divorce is not required as long as a civil divorce has been obtained. Further, a considerable number of Reform rabbis are prepared to officiate at weddings between Jews and non-Jews, although they frequently stipulate conditions for the marriage to take place (such as the couple joining the congregation, raising children as Jews, etc.). Yet despite the variations that exist within the Jewish community, marriage is universally regarded as a sacred bond and a means of personal fulfilment. The prophets compared the relationship between a husband and wife with the relationship between God and Israel (Hos. 2.19–20), and even today marriage is invested with sanctity; it is seen as the natural and desirable state for every adult.

Following the Jewish understanding of marriage, in Mark 10.2–12 Jesus declared that marriage is part of the original order of creation. However, he differed from the traditional view by declaring it indissoluble (although he does give the possible exception of fornication as a basis for divorce in Matt. 5.31–32). Scholars still disagree as to whether he was describing the ideal or whether he was giving literal instructions to his followers. In the epistle to the Ephesians, marriage is compared by Paul to Christ's relationship to the Church (Eph. 5.22ff.). The author of Hebrews counselled:

'Let marriage be held in honour among all, and let the marriage bed be undefiled; for God will judge the immoral and adulterous' (Heb. 13.4).

Nonetheless, despite this recognition of the sanctity of marriage, Paul advocated celibacy for himself and others who wished to serve Christ. In 1 Cor. 7.32–34, he argued that the unmarried man is free to devote himself to the affairs of the Lord whereas a married man is inevitably anxious about worldly affairs – thus his interests are divided. He therefore encouraged the celibate state, but recognized that it is better to marry than be consumed by sexual passion (1 Cor. 7. 8–9).

Following Paul's teaching – which constituted a radical departure from the traditional Jewish conception of marriage – the early Church Fathers stressed that all sexual desire is undesirable and advocated celibacy or spiritual marriages. Augustine (4th–5th cent.), for example, argued that although matrimony is a sacrament instituted for procreation and to curb lust, sex within marriage is also evil. In the Middle Ages, Thomas Aquinas (13th cent.) followed Augustine's teaching about celibacy, and maintained that the very act of coitus transmits original sin. Thus continence should be practised as much as possible. Reformers such as John Calvin (16th cent.) departed from previous Church doctrine, and stressed that the primary purpose of marriage is social and not generative. The Puritans developed Calvin's views and gave greater equality and independence to women. However, Christian marriage continued to be seen as a lifelong commitment, a solemn promise sealed with the giving and receiving of a ring.

In modern times, Christian thinking about marriage has been influenced by the insights of modern psychology, encouraging a more positive attitude to human sexuality, and by modern birth-control techniques that liberate women from constant child-bearing. Further, within some branches of the Church a more liberal attitude to divorce and remarriage has been adopted. Yet despite these developments, Christians, like Jews, see marriage as an enriching relationship that is essential for the stability of society and a paradigm of God's relationship with his people.

Martyrology

(*Kiddush Ha-Shem*) (Persecution): According to

Jewish law, rather than commit an act of idolatry, murder, or sexual immorality, a Jew should choose to die. If he does so, this is described as *Kiddush Ha-Shem* (the Sanctification of the Divine Name). The concept of *Kiddush Ha-Shem* is derived from Lev. 22.32, 'You shall not profane my holy name, but I will be hallowed among the people of Israel.' To commit idolatry, murder, or sexual immorality reflects dishonour on God, and therefore death is preferable. Martyrdom is better than forced conversion. Throughout Jewish history, particularly in the Middle Ages, thousands of the faithful laid down their lives in obedience to this principle and a prayer is still recited every Sabbath, remembering 'the holy congregations who laid down their lives for the Sanctification of the Divine Name'. The names of these communities and their individual leaders were kept in a *Memorbuch* (Memorial Book) and they were read out when the prayer for the memory of the dead was recited.

The Church also suffered persecution before Christianity became the official religion of the Roman Empire in the 4th cent. The New Testament records how Stephen (1st cent.) was put to death, probably within five years of the crucifixion of Jesus (Acts 7.58–60), and many Christians died subsequently for the sake of their faith. As in Judaism, their names were remembered and official registers were kept. In monasteries, the names of the particular martyrs who had been killed on that day were read out in the morning service, and anniversaries of martyrdom were kept as local and national festivals. However, unlike Judaism, the Christian Church encouraged the veneration of martyrs; they were seen as powerful pleaders with God, and statues of famous ones (Catherine with her wheel, Sebastian shot through with arrows, for example) are to be found in many churches.

Mass *see* Eucharist

Matzah *see* Passover

Mehitsah *see* Screen

Menorah *see* Candles

Mercy *see* Forgiveness

Merit *see* Good work

Messiah

In the Bible, the term *Mashiah* (anointed) refers to individuals with a divine mission such as priests, prophets, and kings. In Isa. 45.1, the term is even used to refer to the Gentile king Cyrus of Persia. The prophets occasionally compared the corrupt leaders of the nation with their conception of an ideal, divinely ordained, righteous king. In post-exilic literature, the Messianic king was viewed as God's agent who would vanquish Israel's enemies and establish a reign of peace. When the Babylonian exiles returned to Jerusalem, Zerubbabel (6th cent. BCE) was seen in Messianic terms. Later, the Maccabean revolt against the Seleucids (2nd cent. BCE) had Messianic overtones, and a number of Jewish Messianic sects emerged during the Hellenistic period. The Dead Sea community, for example, expected the appearance of two Messiahs (a Messianic king and a high priest), whereas other groups expected a transcendental deliverer.

In the Pseudepigrapha, there are frequent references to the Messiah, and Josephus (1st cent. CE) describes several Messianic groups. A number of those who participated in the revolt against Rome (66–70 CE) believed that they were engaged in an eschatological struggle that would result in the advent of the Messianic age. After the destruction of the Temple in 70 CE, some Jews interpreted this calamity as the birth-pangs of the Messiah. In the next century, the revolt of 115–117 CE, as well as the Bar Kokhba uprising (132 CE), were viewed in Messianic terms; and some sages, such as Akiva (2nd cent. CE), believed Bar Kokhba (2nd cent. CE) to be the Messiah. In time, the concept of a warrior Messiah (Messiah ben Joseph) who would die in an eschatological battle became part of Jewish thought.

Eventually, Messianic expectations ceased to animate Jewish life; instead, they became a subject of theological speculation. The Messiah was conceived as a human figure who would bring about the resurrection of the dead, the ingathering of the exiles, and a golden age of history. During times of persecution, the Jewish community longed for Messianic redemption. Thus the collapse of the Persian empire before the Arab invaders in the 7th cent. led to the appearance of several pseudo-

Messiahs. In the next century, Messianic hope appeared among the followers of Serene in Syria and Abu Issa Al-Isfahani in Persia. During the Crusades, a number of pseudo-Messiahs emerged such as David Alroy (12th cent.), who led a Messianic movement in Persia and Kurdistan. Again, the expulsion of Jews from Spain and the Spanish Inquisition evoked Messianic expectations. In the 17th cent., Shabbetai Tzevi was widely recognized as the Messiah, and even after his conversion to Islam he retained a following. In the modern period, however, Messianic zeal has ceased to be a central element in Jewish thought, and within Reform Judaism the doctrine of a personal Messiah has been replaced by belief in a Messianic age.

In the New Testament, the Jewish belief in the Messiah served as the basis for Christian convictions about Jesus. From the very first, the title 'Christ' (Messiah) was used to refer to Jesus and his mission: 'And he asked them, "But who do you say I am?" Peter answered him, "You are the Christ"' (Mark 8.29). Although there is considerable scholarly debate about whether Jesus saw himself as the Christ, the conception of Jesus as the Messiah quickly became pivotal in Christian thought. In Paul's epistles, 'Christ' usually serves as Jesus' second proper name – this designation is possibly related to the inscription on the cross: 'The King of the Jews' (Mark 15.26). In Acts, Jesus is viewed as the anointed agent of God who was crucified: 'Let all the whole house of Israel know assuredly that God has made him both Lord and Christ, this Jesus whom you crucified' (Acts 2.36).

Some members of the early Church – the Ebionites – conceived of Christ as the traditional human Messiah to the neglect of his divinity. But in the first centuries of the Church, theologians attempted to explain how there could be a union in him of both the divine and the human. In their writings, they advanced the Logos doctrine put forward in the Fourth Gospel (John 1.1–18), arguing that the Word (Logos), an eternal expression of God, appeared on earth as Jesus Christ. Building on this conception, later Christian theologians struggled to make sense of Jesus' nature as Christ and Lord, and their discussions led to numerous divisions within the Church. Yet despite the variety of views about his nature, Christians through the ages have universally recognized Jesus as the Messiah. He is seen as fulfilling all the promises of the Hebrew Scriptures, and inaugurating a new era. Unlike Judaism, this new age is not generally understood as an alteration of this earthly life, but rather a complete spiritualized transformation. Because Jesus did not accomplish this during his lifetime, Jews have rejected him as the Messiah. But for the believing Church, Jesus is understood as having inaugurated the Kingdom of God in his lifetime; at present they are living in the Messianic age, and finally at the Second Coming he will return in glory to judge the living and the dead and to terminate human history.

Messianic age

(Future World): The era of peace and plenty at the end of history. The Jewish doctrine of the Last Days is linked with expectations about the Messiah. In the Hebrew Scriptures, the prophets described the gathering of the exiles to Jerusalem (Isa. 2.2–4) and a time of universal world harmony – 'nation will not lift up sword against nation, neither shall they learn war any more' (Mic. 4.3). By the time of the return from the Babylonian exile (5th cent. BCE), eschatological expectations were an important element in Jewish thinking, although there was considerable disagreement about them among the various religious parties. During the Roman occupation of Palestine (1st cent. BCE–2nd cent. CE), numerous Messianic groups appeared, including the Christians, and there was a widespread hope of the imminent deliverance of Israel. This would involve the resurrection of the dead, a time of judgement, and the establishment of God's rule on earth. In subsequent rabbinic literature, there was much discussion about the *Olam Ha-Ba* (the world-to-come). It was described as a time when earthly cares are no longer significant and the righteous will enjoy the brilliance of the Shekinah (Divine Presence). In his formulation of the Thirteen Principles of the Jewish Faith, Moses Maimonides (12th cent.) included beliefs in the coming of the Messiah, the resurrection of the dead, and reward and punishment. In recent times, the idea of the Messianic age has been reinterpreted in different ways. The Orthodox still look for the coming of the Messiah who will gather the faithful together in Israel, rebuild the Temple, and re-establish ancient religious rituals. However, Reform Judaism has abandoned the belief in a personal

Messiah, and teaches that it is through human effort that the world can move to an era of peace and justice. Zionism, on the other hand, is a secularization of the whole Messianic concept; the goal has become the establishment of a political rather than a religious Israel.

According to the Gospels, the central element of Jesus' teaching was 'The time is fulfilled, and the kingdom of God is at hand' (Mark 1.15). Jesus' miracles were seen as a fulfilment of the prophecy of Isa. 35.5–6, 'The eyes of the blind shall be opened, and the ears of the deaf unstopped . . .'. His resurrection was understood as the first-fruit of a general resurrection (1 Cor. 15.21). Consequently, the early Christians were puzzled and often discouraged by the delay in the arrival of the universal Messianic age, and the author of the second epistle to Peter is forced to conclude that it is because God's time is different from ours (2 Pet. 3.8–10). Nonetheless, Christians have retained the belief in the resurrection of the dead and the Day of Judgement at the end of time. Precisely how these beliefs have been interpreted has varied among different groups. On the one hand, millenarians such as Jehovah's Witnesses have interpreted the biblical texts so literally that they claim to be able to calculate the precise date of Judgement Day. This obviously has its parallels with Messianic movements in Judaism. At the opposite extreme, some theologians have understood the doctrine of the reign of God in purely metaphorical terms, expressing in some sense God's salvation of the world in the here and now and in the future. Liberal Protestants of the 19th-cent. and 20th-cent. liberationists concentrate on the this-worldly aspect of the Kingdom of God; like Reform Jews, they emphasize the importance of human effort in the transformation of the world. Most Christians, however, like most Jews, are content to accept the traditional doctrine without defining too precisely what it actually means.

Mezuzah *see* Door-posts

Midrash *see* Biblical interpretation

Mikveh *see* Font

Millenarianism

The belief that there will be a 1,000-year period of perfect order and peace when Jesus will reign over the world. In Jewish Pseudepigraphical writings the idea of a Messianic era is to be found, and some rabbis of the Tannaitic period (1st–2nd cent. CE) believed that the world, as we know it, would only last for 6,000 years. The seventh millennium (the Sabbath) would be the 1,000 years of the Messiah. This understanding is probably based on Ps. 90.4, 'For a thousand years in thy sight are but as yesterday'. If a day for God lasts 1,000 years, then a week must last 7,000, and a week was thought to be a suitable duration for the history of the world. The same conviction can be found in the New Testament Book of Revelation (Rev. 20.1–10). This describes the binding of Satan for 1,000 years while Jesus reigns with the Christian martyrs who have been raised from the dead. After 1,000 years, a second general resurrection will take place and there will be a great battle that will end in Satan being thrown into a lake of fire and sulphur to be tormented for ever and ever.

Through both Jewish and Christian history, there have been groups who have interpreted these ideas literally. Jews have followed particular Messianic claiments, such as Shabbetai Tzevi in the 17th cent. and Jacob Frank in the 18th cent.. Millenarian Christians, believing that Jesus is the Messiah, have formed sects based on precise calculations as to when the world will end; the Shakers (formed in the 18th cent.) and the Seventh Day Adventists (19th cent.) are obvious examples. However, the mainstream Jewish and Christian establishments have rejected millenarianism and interpret these colourful prophecies metaphorically.

Minyan *see* Congregation

Miracles

(Healing): Events that appear to violate the laws of nature. In the Hebrew Scriptures, there is no specific biblical concept of a miracle, and the term 'miracle' does not appear in the Hebrew Bible – instead, extraordinary events are designated in Hebrew as *gedolot* (great things) (2 Kings 8.4; Deut. 10.21), *niphlaot* (marvels) (Exod. 34.10–11), and *otot u-mophetim* (signs and wonders) (Jer. 32.21). Throughout the biblical narrative, God's activity is wondrous; he is capable of destroying Sodom and Gomorrah, enabling Sarah to give birth at an advanced age, bringing about the plagues in Egypt, and leading his chosen people into the Promised Land. In all such cases, these actions are viewed as expressions of God's infinite power, and those who witnessed them believed that they were the result of divine intention. Within this range of activity, there were some events that appeared to conflict with the order of nature – such as the parting of the Red Sea, the appearance of manna in the desert, and Elijah's ascent to heaven.

In Talmudic literature the rabbis used the term *nes* to refer to events caused by God – they were preordained and provided for in the act of creation. Rather than classifying them as violations of the laws of nature, they embraced everyday occurrences as well as spectacular happenings. Repeatedly, the sages stressed that human beings are continuously surrounded by miracles that reflect God's loving concern. Thus in the Midrash (biblical interpretation), Jews are admonished to observe God's miraculous power: 'Come and consider how many miracles the Holy One, blessed be He, performs for man, and he is unaware of it.' This idea is expressed in the formula of the thanksgiving prayer that is contained in the daily *Amidah* prayer: 'For Thy miracles which are daily with us, and for Thy wonders and Thy benefits, which are wrought at all times, evening, morning and night.'

In medieval times, the subject of miracles was one of the most important issues considered by Jewish philosophers. For neo-Platonists, miracles were viewed as the imposition of a supernatural order on the natural world. Aristotelian philosophers such as Maimonides argued that miracles are voluntary acts of God – they were predetermined at the time of the creation. For Maimonides, the difference between an act of nature and a miracle is a difference between a regular and a unique occurrence. In later Jewish thought, discussion about the nature of miracles continued, and a number of writers stressed the historicity of miracles recorded in the Bible. In modern times, there have been two tendencies in Jewish reflection about miracles: some thinkers have adopted the biblical concept of miracles – seeing them as a sign of God's presence; others have advocated a more rationalistic approach in line with modern scientific investiga-

tion. Yet despite these differences in interpretation, Jews through the ages have subscribed to the belief that God acts in the world and that the Bible testifies to his miraculous intervention.

In the Gospels, the biblical notion of a miracle as a divine intervention in human affairs was linked to Jesus' ministry. The life, death, and resurrection of Jesus were seen as the manifestation of God's plan to banish corruption, overcome death, and restore human life to its true destiny. In this context, the miracles brought about by Jesus (including acts of healing and exorcism) are allied to the proclamation of God's Kingdom, and the resurrection itself is depicted as a miraculous event that underscores Jesus' status as the long-awaited Messiah. As the Church expanded, there was a need to stress the miraculous aspects of the gospel, and apologists appealed to the miracles in the New Testament as a confirmation of Christian claims – the miraculous powers of Jesus were viewed as testifying to his divinity, and fulfilling the biblical prophecies about the Messianic age.

In the Middle Ages, biblical miracles continued to be seen as proofs of the truth of Christianity. Thus Thomas Aquinas (12th cent.) criticized Muhammad's inability to provide miraculous signs as evidence of the inferiority of Islam. Miracles are associated with the activities of the saints, particularly healing and exorcisms, and even today many churches continue to hold services of healing among their regular offices. After the Reformation, other thinkers continued to stress the necessity of miracles to establish the validity of Christian claims. Yet with the growth of modern physics, it has become increasingly difficult for many Christians to believe in the accuracy of the biblical account of events that appear to violate the laws of nature. In addition, some biblical critics have viewed reports of miracles in Scripture – including the resurrection – as mythological expressions of existential truths. Yet, as in Judaism, Christians of all denominations continue to affirm that God acts in history. For Christian believers across the religious spectrum, the Hebrew Scriptures and the New Testament testify to God's providential concern for Israel and the ultimate disclosure of his loving concern in the life and death of Christ.

Mishnah *see* Law books

Missionizing

According to Eleazar ben Pedat (2nd cent.), the Jewish people were scattered throughout the world in order that they might gain converts to their religion. Jesus (1st cent. CE) described the scribes and Pharisees crossing land and sea to make a single proselyte (Matt. 23.15), and the historian Flavius Josephus (1st cent. CE) remarked that Jewish observances had penetrated every city. The rabbis distinguished between two types of convert: the *ger toshav* (settler) who kept the Seven Laws of Noah, but who was not circumcised; and the *ger tzedek* (righteous proselyte), who accepted the whole Torah and who was regarded as a Jew in every respect. Once Christianity became the official religion of the Roman Empire (4th cent. CE), conversion to Judaism became a criminal offence and, for their own protection, the community strongly discouraged proselytes. In any case, the rabbis believed that Gentiles who kept the Noachide Laws against idolatry, blasphemy, sexual immorality, murder, robbery, cruelty to animals, and injustice would have a place in the world-to-come. In fact, it was easier for a Gentile to be pleasing to God than it was for a Jew; Jews had to keep all 613 commandments, whereas Gentiles only had to keep 7. There was thus no reason to encourage conversion, and this has remained the opinion of the Orthodox to this day. In the 20th cent., in order to combat the effects of intermarriage, Reform Jews have instituted outreach programmes, particularly to encourage Gentile spouses to convert so that the children of the marriage will be part of the community. However, the Orthodox do not accept Reform converts and insist that they (and, if they are female, their children) are still non-Jews.

From early times, Christianity has been a missionary religion. The Gospel of Matthew describes Jesus telling his followers to 'Go therefore and make disciples of all nations' (Matt. 28.19). The Acts of the Apostles tells the story of how the gospel travelled from Jerusalem to Rome. From the beginning, Christians felt the obligation to spread the good news of the salvation to be found in Jesus to the four corners of the world. Following Jesus' saying in the Fourth Gospel, 'I am the way, the truth, and the life; no one comes to the Father, but by me' (John 14.6), the Church taught that Christianity was the only path to salvation. Consequently, preaching was an urgent duty and through the centuries Christians have sent missionaries not only to pagans, but also to Jews and Muslims. There was particular emphasis on Christian expansion after the Reformation in the 16th cent. and in the 19th cent. In every country, a Christian network has been set up, and often the various denominations rivalled one another in their zeal for converts. In the 20th cent., the nature of missionary work has changed in that there has been more emphasis on self-determining native ministries. In addition, with increased knowledge and understanding of other religions, the Churches have embarked on more inter-religious dialogue; the conviction that there is no hope outside Christianity has in some cases been modified. Nonetheless, there is still a very real difference in attitude towards mission among Jews and Christians. Jews are largely content to let the other nations find their own path to God, whereas Christians are anxious to spread the good news and rejoice over each new convert.

Mitzvot *see* Law

Modernism *see* Enlightenment

Monasticism

Monasticism is almost unknown in Judaism. Flavius Josephus (1st cent. CE) records the existence of communities of Essenes, and Philo (1st cent.) mentions the Therapeutae of Egypt. Both groups seem to have been ascetic communities devoted to prayer and study. Nonetheless, the idea of withdrawing from the world to achieve sanctity is foreign to the world-affirming philosophy of Judaism, which emphasizes the sanctification of this life through keeping the law. Celibacy is also regarded with suspicion; marriage and children are seen as essential for a fulfilled existence.

Christian monasticism is generally thought to have been founded by Antony of Egypt (3rd–4th cent.). It rapidly spread through both the Eastern and Western Church, the most famous rule in the East being that of St Basil (4th cent.), and in the West being that of Benedict of Nursia (6th cent.). A monk's chief aim was to attain holiness through a life of prayer and work, withdrawn from the world. Vows of obedience, stability, and conversion of life were taken and the monk lived in an ordered community. Through the stability of the monasteries, the monks were able to spend much of their time in research, teaching, and copying manuscripts. Through their efforts, much of the learning of the ancient world was preserved through the turbulent Middle Ages. There were also communities of nuns as well as monks who followed similar rules. From the 12th cent., other monastic orders were founded, as well as orders of friars who were not committed to stay in one place and could therefore move to the areas of greatest need. The Protestant reformers were anxious to do away with all these groups, although religious orders continued to flourish in the Roman Catholic and Eastern Church. In the 19th cent., however, there was a renewed desire for the monastic life and some Protestant Churches do now support monks and nuns. There has been a general decline in vocations in all Churches which is a reflection of the increased secularism of modern times.

Monogamy *see* Marriage

Monotheism

(Oneness of God) (Theism) (Trinity): Belief in one God. In the Bible there are numerous references to belief in and worship of many gods (polytheism), worship of the God of Israel together with the worship of Canaanite gods (syncretism), and belief in a separate god for each nation (monolatry). According to some scholars, pure monotheism did not emerge in ancient Israel until the prophetic period. Other scholars maintain that the origins of monotheism go back to the time of the patriarchs. In any case, monotheism became a central feature of Jewish life in biblical times.

Biblical monotheism differs from polytheism in its understanding of God as above nature – the universe exists solely through his will. Unlike the Canaanite gods, the Lord of Israel was not born, nor did he beget divinities. He cannot be coerced by magic, nor is he dependent upon a sacrificial cult to sustain his being. Although transcendent, he acts in history and is concerned with each person.

In addition, he is regarded as 'a God merciful and gracious, slow to anger, and abounding in steadfast love and faithfulness, keeping steadfast love for thousands, forgiving iniquity and transgression and sin . . .' (Exod. 34.6–7).

In rabbinic literature, the sages continued the prophetic struggle against idolatry and polytheistic practices, and as a reaction to Christianity they laid stress on God's unity. Thus the Shema ('Hear, O Israel, the Lord our God, the Lord is One') was viewed as the most important confession of the faith. In this context, the rabbis were careful to reject any suggestion that there were two powers in heaven, and they insisted that God does not have a father or brother. In subsequent centuries, Jewish thought developed under the impact of the rediscovery of Greek philosophy by the Arabs. In the Middle Ages, Jewish philosophers directed attention to the concept of divine attributes, the relation between God's foreknowledge and human freedom, and the problem of human suffering. In wrestling with these issues, they developed the concept of the oneness of God, a being of absolute unity, free of all human and natural properties. Moses Maimonides (12th cent.), in particular, was anxious to stress God's transcendent nature in his presentation of classical theism. A different direction in theological speculation was taken by medieval kabbalists (mystics), who taught the doctrine of the two aspects of God: the infinite 'Mystery of Hiddenness' and the 10 *sephirot* of divine emanation. In contemporary Judaism, the medieval attempt to harmonize revelation and reason has been superseded by new currents of Jewish thought. Yet despite the varied approaches to Jewish theology through the ages, the belief in one God who is the creator of the universe and the Lord of history has served as the bedrock of the Jewish way of life.

The New Testament accepts the strict monotheism of biblical Judaism. Thus when asked to name the greatest commandment, Jesus quoted Deut. 6.4–5: 'Hear, O Israel: The Lord our God, The Lord is one; and you shall love the Lord your God with all your heart, and with all your soul, and with all your mind, and with all your strength' (Mark 12.29–30). Nonetheless, after his death, Christians desired to distinguish Jesus from God while identifying him with the Godhead. Thus Paul declared:

'May the God of steadfastness and encouragement grant you to live in such harmony with one another, in accord with Christ Jesus, that together you may with one voice glorify the God and Father of our Lord Jesus Christ' (Rom. 15.5–6). With the descent of the Holy Spirit at Pentecost, the elements of later Trinitarian doctrine became current in the early Church, so Paul could speak of 'The grace of the Lord Jesus Christ and the love of God and the fellowship of the Holy Spirit' (2 Cor. 13.14).

The term 'Trinity' was first used in its Greek form *trias* by Theophilus of Antioch (2nd cent.), and the doctrine was set out in creeds, doxologies, and individual confessions of faith. At the Council of Nicaea (325) and Constantinople (381), the dogma was outlined in detail. In the face of competing heresies, it was asserted that the three Divine Persons differ only in origin in that the Father is ungenerated. The Son, however, is generated from the Father, and the Holy Spirit proceeds from the Father through the Son. In the Eastern Church, the Spirit is viewed as descending in a straight line from the Son who came from the Father. In the West, this doctrine developed differently, the co-equality of the three Persons was asserted and the procession of the Holy Spirit was attributed equally to the Father and the Son. The symbol of the Trinity became not the straight line, but the triangle.

This theory of the Trinity was later elaborated by medieval Schoolmen, and Christian theology in the Middle Ages revived the doctrines of the Athanasian Creed (5th cent.) – this was most elaborately expanded by Thomas Aquinas (12th cent.). With modifications, this Scholastic doctrine has been the common inheritance of later Western Christian theology. Over the centuries, this central Trinitarian teaching of the Church about God's nature has been firmly rejected by Judaism. The doctrine of the Trinity is viewed as diluting the pure monotheism of biblical and rabbinic teaching. Christians, however, have been anxious to assert that Trinitarian theology is fully compatible with the belief in the unity of God, and most fully expresses God's nature in the Father's loving concern, the redeeming work of Christ, and the fellowship of the Spirit.

Morality

Ideas that prescribe how people ought to behave.

The historical narratives in Gen. and Exod. contain a variety of teachings about the moral life. Yet the moral law in the Pentateuch, which comprises an essential part of the covenant, constitutes the basis for Jewish ethics. These commandments range over a wide variety of situations and also stipulate punishments for disobedience. According to tradition, God revealed these laws to Moses on Mt Sinai; together with ritual precepts, they are binding on all Jews. In prophetic literature these moral prescriptions were applied to the social conditions of the times, and served as a basis for rebuking the leaders of the nation. In the Hagiographa, moral values also play an important role in a number of books such as Ruth, Esther, and Proverbs.

In rabbinic literature, biblical moral precepts were expanded to cover unforeseen circumstances not dealt with in Scripture. Here the rabbis used the same exegetical method they applied to ritual law. In addition, they employed the method of *agaddah* (commentary) to draw out the moral implications of the scriptural narrative. They also made role models out of heroes such as Abraham, Moses, and Aaron. In a section of the Mishnah (2nd cent. CE), the tractate *Avot* (*Sayings of the Fathers*), early rabbinic pronouncements were recorded in the style of the Book of Proverbs. In discussing ethical behaviour, the sages were anxious to stress that God is the source of goodness. As God is described in the Bible as 'merciful and gracious, slow to anger, and abounding in steadfast love and faithfulness, keeping steadfast love for thousands, forgiving iniquity and transgression and sin' (Exod. 34.6), human beings are to imitate him in their dealings with others. In their discussions of ethics, the rabbis were anxious to emphasize that morality is not restricted to the actions of men and women – it also includes their thoughts, emotion, intentions, attitudes, and motives.

In the Middle Ages, Jewish thinkers were not primarily concerned with the philosophy of ethics. Instead, they concentrated on abstract aspects of theology dealing with God's nature and activity. But in the 16th cent., Judah Löw of Prague discussed the essence of morality, arguing that moral action is the most direct way of cleaving to God. In the 19th cent., Samson Raphael Hirsch taught that justice is the central concept that the Torah seeks to convey. Subsequently, a number of Jewish writers accorded morality a central place in their philosophy of Judaism. Yet despite these different emphases in Jewish thought, Orthodox Jews have consistently maintained through the centuries that ethics are ultimately grounded in God's will as revealed in Scripture. Thus the Bible constitutes the bedrock of Jewish morality. Non-Orthodox thinkers, however, have rejected the belief in the divine origin of the 613 commandments in the Pentateuch, and as a result there is some uncertainty in non-Orthodox circles about a variety of moral issues.

Jewish teaching about morality provides the background for the understanding of ethics in the New Testament. Jesus is portrayed as the moral symbol of God and, by following his example and with the guidance of his Holy Spirit, human beings are able to live in accordance with God's will. This does not mean that the New Testament is bereft of specific moral prescriptions. On the contrary, Jesus gave many moral teachings to his disciples (Matt. 5–7), and Paul in Gal. condemns fornication, impurity, enmity, strife, jealousy, anger, selfishness, dissension, and envy; but praises love, joy, peace, patience, kindness, goodness, faithfulness, gentleness, and self-control (Gal. 5.19–23). Similar moral teaching is to be found in the pastoral epistles. The writings of the Church Fathers also did not present complete systems of moral teaching, but they did concern themselves with ethical issues. In their writings, a number of the Fathers utilized Platonic and Aristotelian ideas in presenting their views. In the 5th cent., Augustine dealt with various moral issues, including the nature of God as the sovereign good, the eternal law, the nature of sin, and the definitions of virtue and sin.

From 600 to 1200, moral theory did not make major advances in Christianity, although penitential books were issued that listed sins for which penances were prescribed. In the 13th cent., the Franciscan School expanded the treatment of morals, but it was Thomas Aquinas who systematized previous teaching, and his work gained considerable influence. In the 17th cent., moral theory was separated from the rest of theology and was concerned primarily with matters of conscience and moral doubt. The outstanding writer of the 18th cent. was Alphonsus Liguori, whose *Theologia Moralis* had an important impact on subsequent writers. The 19th cent. witnessed the dominance of ethical manuals in the Roman Catholic Church that became the basis for seminary moral teaching. In modern times, moral theology has become an ecumenical discipline focusing on pressing social problems, and liberation theology in recent years has gained a wide following. Despite this development of Christian reflection about ethics through the ages, Christians have universally viewed Jesus' life as the basis for moral living. Jesus himself, not the New Testament, is the Word of God. Unlike Jews, they do not subscribe to the belief that God revealed specific moral commandments that are applicable for all time – instead, they rely on the word made flesh as the paradigm of the moral life, and the guidance of the Holy Spirit which will 'guide you into all truth' (John 16.13).

Morning prayer

Traditionally, the morning service was instituted by the patriarch Abraham (Gen. 19.27) and morning sacrifices were made daily in the Temple. The full service can only be read in the synagogue if a quorum of 10 adult men (minyan) are present. Otherwise, certain prayers have to be omitted. The service consists of the morning benedictions, verses from psalms and songs, the Shema ('Hear, O Israel'), and the *Amidah* prayer. On Sabbaths, festivals, Mondays, and Thursdays, a prescribed portion from the Torah scroll is read, and the service concludes with the mourners' Kaddish and other prayers. At every morning service, except on 9 Av, men wear prayer shawls (tallith) and, except on Sabbaths and festivals, phylacteries (tephillin).

In the monasteries, services were said throughout the day. The first office, traditionally appointed for 6.00 a.m., was prime, followed by terce at 9.00 and sext at 12.00. The morning services of matins and lauds were sometimes said in anticipation the night before, and sometimes were recited in the middle of the night or very early in the morning. All these services consist of psalms, prayers, hymns, canticles, and readings. Matins is still retained as the Sunday morning service in many English churches; it consists of a mixture of the matins, lauds, and prime liturgies, and is not dissimilar to its Jewish counterpart. In most churches, however, both the week-day and Sunday morning services are Eucharists.

Mourning *see* Funeral rites

Music

(Cantor) (*Hazzan*) (Hymns): In the Bible, Jubal is described as the father of music, having invented the lyre and pipe (Gen. 4.21). Another instrument mentioned in Scripture is the tambourine (Gen. 31.27), which was associated with women's dance songs such as Miriam's song at the Red Sea (Exod. 15.20). In all likelihood, some of the poems in the Bible were chanted or sung. During David's reign, music came to play an important role in religious life, and he was traditionally regarded as the founder of music in the first Temple. As 1 Chron. records, David established 24 groups of musicians, consisting of 12 singers and instrumentalists (1 Chron. 25). In the Temple, psalms were sung antiphonally (between two groups of singers) or responsorially (between the soloist and congregation). In addition, some psalms were sung as litanies with a recurring short response. The Mishnah records that in the second Temple there was a choir consisting of 12 Levites, together with an instrumental orchestra.

From the 1st cent. BCE, synagogues were active throughout the Jewish world. No musical instruments were used, and the worship centred on reading Scripture and chanting prayers by the cantor (*hazzan*). The music consisted of three types of chant: psalmody, cantillation of Scripture, and liturgical recitative. After the destruction of the Temple in 70 CE, the rabbis ruled that in certain circumstances no singing or playing should take place in the synagogue. This ban was issued in order to ensure the sanctity of Sabbath worship, prevent promiscuity, and express mourning for the destruction of the Temple. After the 4th cent., new poetic prayers (*piyyutim*) were created to serve as artistic additions to the fixed prayers, and were sung by poet-singers (*paytannim*).

During the medieval period, Jews in Muslim lands were influenced by Arab culture and musical tradition, and a number of Jews became active musicians. In Spain, the coexistence of Jews and Gentiles helped to create songs in the Judeo-Spanish (Ladino) language. In addition, new songs were composed in the Balkans and Morocco dealing with romances, celebrations of Jewish holidays, and life-cycle events. Ashkenazi Jews also formulated their own synagogue songs based on forms of cantillation mixed with non-Jewish melodies. Subsequently, Ashkenazi musical forms were transferred to Eastern Europe, where they were influenced by Slavic music.

During the Renaissance, polyphonic music for the synagogue was created, and later Jews performed baroque-style Hebrew cantatas in synagogue and family celebrations. In the 18th and 19th cent., the Hasidim regarded music as of fundamental importance, and leaders encouraged the creation of new musical forms. Simultaneously, Reformers introduced Protestant chorals with organ accompaniment into the synagogue service. Unlike the Orthodox, Reform congregations made use of mixed choirs of men and women. In modern times, Jewish music has undergone considerable development in Israel, the USA and beyond, in both religious and secular contexts.

Influenced by Jewish liturgical forms, the apostolic Church sang hymns, and the Psalter was soon supplemented by the canticles of Luke 1–2 and the doxologies (such as Luke 2.14). Eventually, the Gregorian chant came into fashion; based on simple chant formulae inherited from the synagogue, it embodied other musical patterns. Essentially sacerdotal in character, it was used by trained singers, monks in the canonical hours of the abbeys and choirs and celebrants in chapels, churches, and cathedrals. Other systems of chant also included the Ambrosian chant of Milan, the Byzantine chant of the Greek Orthodox Church, and the Znamenny chant of the Russian Church. The Syrian, Armenian, and Coptic Churches also possessed other types of chant.

In the 9th cent., polyphonous music began to develop in Church circles, initially consisting of singing a plainsong with one or more voices duplicating the melody four or five scales below or above. In the 13th–14th cent., this new art evolved into complex musical forms. During this time, polyphonic settings of choral sections of the ordinary of the Mass also began to appear. In subsequent centuries, Church music reached great heights, and the innovation of musical printing and the introduction of copper engraving in the 16th cent. accelerated the dissemination of music throughout the Christian world. With the advent of the Reformation, the Lutheran Church developed a great musical tradition of congregational song and choral repertory, and a vast literature of organ music also appeared. In the 17th cent., both Lutheran and Catholic composers produced numerous compositions for the Church, and this tradition continued in later centuries. In the modern period, new music of a classical and popular form has appeared in the USA and elsewhere, which has enjoyed a considerable degree of freedom from official restraint. This evolution of Church music through the ages stands in marked contrast to the relatively limited musical development in Judaism, since the traditional prohibitions against instrumental and choral music severely constrained musical innovation.

Mysticism

(Kabbalah) (Zohar): In the Bible, the patriarchs, Moses, the Prophets, and others attained contact with God – in this sense, mysticism is a central aspect of biblical Judaism. Apocalyptic literature such as the Book of Enoch and IV Ezra also contains numerous mystical visions and revelations. However, in the narrower sense, Jewish mysticism was confined to small rabbinic circles who passed on traditions to the chosen few. According to tradition, the subject was divided into *Maaseh Bereshit* (work of creation) and *Maaseh Merkavah* (work of the chariot). The first type of mystical speculation was concerned with cosmology and cosmogony. Essentially, it consisted of an exposition of the first chapter of Gen. and led to the composition of the *Sepher Yetzirah* (Book of Creation), which expounds the powers of the Hebrew alphabet and the role of the 10 *sephirot* (manifestations of the divine) in creation.

Maaseh Merkavah, on the other hand, deals with the vision of divine majesty (*kavod*) on its throne of glory, as figuratively depicted in the first chapter of the Book of Ezekiel. This vision could be attained by an ascent of the soul in mystical ecstasy to the heavenly spheres; those who engaged in this type of mystical experience were called *Yordei Merkavah* (descenders of the chariot). Although the Talmud does not explain the nature of this experience, it is described as entering *Pardes* (paradise)

and is associated with danger. A Talmudic legend records that the sages Ben Azzai, Ben Zoma, Aher, and Akiva entered *Pardes* – Ben Azzai looked and died, Ben Zoma looked and went mad; Aher became an apostate; and Akiva came out in peace. In post-Talmudic writings of the 6th–8th cent. – known as Heikhalot literature – such ascents are described in more detail.

In the 12th and 13th cent., mystical traditions from Palestine and Babylonia penetrated Europe through Italy. During this period, mystics in the Rhineland – *Hasidei Ashkenaz* (the pious of Germany and Western Europe) – encouraged otherworldly asceticism, emphasized the importance of proper devotion during prayer, and focused on the mystery of the glory of God. Another mystical tradition – associated with the term 'kabbalah' (received tradition) – emerged in Provence; in this milieu, the *Bahir* (one of the oldest kabbalistic texts) had an important impact on doctrines dealing with the *sephirot*. Kabbalistic centres also emerged in Spain, where the Zohar was produced in the 13th cent. Attributed to the 2nd-cent. Palestinian scholar Simeon bar Yohai, it was the work of Moses de Leon (13th cent.). Dealing with a wide range of mystical topics, it influenced kabbalistic thought in the 14th and 15th cent. In the 16th cent., a mystical centre in Safed in Upper Galilee became the spiritual home of mystical Judaism, producing such luminaries as Moses Cordovero and Isaac Luria. In the 17th cent., Lurianic doctrine was developed by the followers of the pseudo-Messiah Shabbetai Tzevi, and in the 19th and 20th cent., Hasidim incorporated various mystical teachings into their theology.

In the New Testament, Jesus' mystical life unfolded as he experienced God's presence in his ministry. Paul's conversion to Christianity was the result of a mystical experience which he described in 1 Cor. 15.8–10. As with the Hebrew Scriptures, the New Testament can be understood as mystical in character. However, for the Church Fathers, mysticism in a narrower sense was viewed as a mode of scriptural interpretation. Thus Clement (1st cent.) and Origen (2nd–3rd cent.) spoke about the mystical or spiritual meaning of the biblical text. By the 4th cent., the term 'mystical' referred to Christ's hidden presence in Scripture as well as in the liturgy and sacraments. In the 5th cent.,

Pseudo-Dionysius utilized the term to denote the deeper meaning of Scripture and the sacraments through which Christ's love is revealed. In *Mystica Theologia* he described mystical contemplation as transcending concepts and symbols. In the 9th cent., this work was translated into Latin by John Scotus Erigena, and had an important impact on later Christian mystical thought.

In the 12th and 13th cent., schools of mysticism were founded, such as the Cistercian and Franciscan schools, and the Victorines. In the following century, Dominican mystics of the Rhineland made significant contributions to mystical theology. Meister Eckhart, for example, emphasized the otherness of God who can be approached through a 'letting-go'. In the 14th and 15th cent., Flemish and English mystics produced seminal mystical texts – for example, the anonymous *Cloud of Unknowing*. Spanish mystics of the 16th cent., such as John of the Cross, also made major contributions to Christian spirituality. In later centuries, mystical writers have carried on this tradition. Through the centuries, these mystical texts have provided a rich source for Christian reflection about the experience of God, yet, in contrast to Judaism, Christian mysticism was not a scholarly tradition reserved for the elect. Instead, mystical works were largely composed for ordinary Christians who wished to gain an awareness of God's mystery and enter into a relationship with him through contemplation and prayer.

N

Names

In the story of creation, the relationship of an object to its name is of crucial importance. Human beings have dominion over the beasts because they give them their names: 'whatever the man called every living creature, that was its name' (Gen. 2.19). Human names are also significant and convey a particular meaning; many biblical names, for example, refer to God – such as Jonathan (from *Yah*) or Elyakim (from *El*). Jewish boys are given their names at the circumcision ceremony, and girls are formally named in the synagogue. Among the

Ashkenazim (Eastern European Jews), it is often the practice to name a child after a close relative who has recently died. When a Gentile converts to Judaism, he or she is given a new name to symbolize a new allegiance and nationality. Similarly, there is a custom of changing the name of someone dangerously ill with the idea of giving them a new life and misleading the angel of death.

The full Hebrew name consists of the personal name followed by son (*ben*) or daughter (*bat*) of the father (for example Joshua ben Abraham), and this form is still used on all Hebrew documents. However, in the modern period it became customary for Jews to adopt surnames as did their Gentile neighbours. Sometimes the place of origin was used, such as Litvak (from Lithuania); sometimes description of descent, such as Cohen (priest), was employed; sometimes it was the occupation, such as Goldsmith; and sometimes a father's personal name was converted, as in Davidson or Mendelssohn.

Christians are also given their names at their initiation ceremony. The water of baptism symbolizes sharing in the death and resurrection of Jesus – the new Christian thus embarks on a new life. It is appropriate therefore to take on a new name and, in Christian countries where infant baptism is usual, personal names are commonly called 'Christian names'. These names can be biblical or secular in origin. In some Churches, it is also the practice to give a child a saint's name; the saint is seen as his or her special protector and someone who is a spiritual model. This is not unlike the Ashkenazic practice of naming a child after a dead relation.

Names of God

(Divine Names): In the Hebrew Scriptures there are various names for God. The most important is the tetragrammaton consisting of the letters 'Yod', 'He', 'Vav', 'He' (YHVH). In all likelihood, it is connected with the phrase 'I am that I am' – this was the name God revealed to Moses when he was asked what God should be called (Exod. 3.14). Because of its great holiness, the tetragrammaton was not pronounced – except once a year by the high priest on the Day of Atonement. The original pronunciation is now not certain, but it is read as 'Adonai' (my Lord). In vocalized texts, the tetragrammaton is given the vowels of 'Adonai'; this has led to the hybrid form 'Jehovah' in English translations.

Other personal names of God in the Bible are El, Eloha, Elohim, Shaddai, and Zebaoth. According to the rabbis, these different names express various aspects of God's nature. In addition to personal names, descriptive names were used to express divine attributes such as *Rahum* (Merciful) and *Elyon* (Most High). The sanctity attached to the names of God and the prohibition against taking God's name in vain led to a reluctance to use biblical names, and various circumlocutions were substituted. The most common in Midrashic literature are *Ha-Kadosh Barukh Hu* (The Holy One, blessed be He) and *Ribono Shel Olam* (Master of the Universe). Also used were *Ha-Makom* (the Place), *Ha-Rahman* (the All-Merciful), and Shekinah (Divine Presence). In philosophical and kabbalistic literature, technical terms such as *En-Soph* (first Cause) were used rather than biblical or rabbinic names of God. There are also rabbinic traditions referring to divine names composed of 12, 42, and 72 letters; combinations of these letters were used by kabbalists for magical purposes.

The doctrine of God in the Hebrew Scriptures was taken over by the early Church, and Hebrew terms denoting God were translated by New Testament writers into Greek. Jesus himself taught his followers to call God 'Abba', meaning Father. Because of the relationship between the Father and the Son, these terms were also applied to Jesus himself. As the gospel spread to the Gentile world, these names were translated into numerous other languages. In addition, because of the development of the doctrine of the Trinity, the Church utilized the threefold invocation 'Father, Son, and Holy Spirit' to refer to the triune God, and this was the formula by which newcomers were baptized. Yet, unlike Jews, Christians have not been reluctant to pronounce God's name, and there has been no evolution of terminology relating to God's name in a single sacred language. As a world-wide faith embracing believers speaking different languages, Christians did not engage in the same sort of reflection about the theological and mystical significance of the names of God.

Natural law

The law inherent in the natural order. According to

the Jewish tradition, seven laws were given to Noah; these Noachide Laws are viewed as the minimal moral duties that all people must follow. Jews are obligated to follow the entire corpus of Jewish law, whereas every non-Jew is conceived as a child of Noah and thus obligated to keep these minimal moral duties. In the early rabbinic period, the following seven laws were generally understood as constituting the Noachide Laws: the prohibition of (1) idolatry; (2) blasphemy; (3) bloodshed; (4) sexual sins; (5) theft; (6) eating from a living animal; and (7) the duty of establishing a legal system. Nonetheless, there was not complete agreement as to the number of these injunctions. Thus the *Tosefta* records four additional prohibitions against (1) drinking the blood of a living animal; (2) emasculation; (3) sorcery; and (4) the magical practices listed in Deut. 18.10–11. In the Talmud there is also a reference to the prohibition against the crossbreeding of animals of different types, and grafting trees of different kinds. In the Book of Jubilees there is a completely different list of injunctions given by Noah to his sons: (1) to observe righteousness; (2) to cover the shame of their flesh; (3) to bless their creator; (4) to honour parents; (5) to love their neighbour; and (6) to guard against fornication, uncleanliness, and iniquity.

In the Talmudic period, there was a difference of opinion as to whether the Noachide Laws should be viewed as natural law or were intended as rules to govern the behaviour of non-Jews living in a Jewish milieu. Some authorities declared that most of these laws would be mandatory even if they had not been revealed to Noah; others asserted that six of the seven laws were revealed to Adam and are therefore universalistic in character. However, the fact that the Noachide Laws could be enforced by rabbinic courts suggested to some sages that these laws are intended as means of regulating non-Jewish behaviour in areas where Jews are sovereign. Yet despite this dispute as to the status of the Noachide Laws, it was universally accepted that such precepts should govern the conduct of non-Jews.

The Jewish idea of law implanted by nature was taken up by Paul in Rom. 2.14–15: 'When Gentiles who have not the law do by nature what the law requires, they are a law to themselves, even though they do not have the law. They show that what the law requires is written on their hearts . . .' Through the Church Fathers as well as the legal tradition of the late Roman Empire, the theory of natural law was transmitted to Christian moralists in the Middle Ages. One of the most important expositions of natural law is found in the works of Thomas Aquinas (12th cent.). In the *Summa Theologica* he wrote, 'The rational creature . . . participates in eternal reason, through which he possesses a natural inclination to a fitting act and end. Such participation on the part of a rational creature in the eternal law is natural law.' According to Aquinas, natural law is dependent on both right reasoning and practical experience. Later, Scholastics tended to focus attention on the area of the will rather than the intellect.

In time, the Thomistic claim that the moral law can only be discovered through intellectual reflection was superseded by theories that emphasized the importance of personal volition. In Europe, Hugo Grotius (16th–17th cent.) and Pufendorf (17th cent.) wrote treatises on natural law in the voluntarist tradition. Among classic British moralists, natural law was viewed as a set of commands imposed on man by the will of God. Although the natural law tradition has continued into the modern period, a number of contemporary theologians have questioned its role in Christian life. Thus in both the Jewish and Christian faiths the doctrine of natural law has played an important role in moral thinking – yet it has been interpreted in widely divergent ways. Within Judaism, the theory of the Noachide Laws has served as a framework for understanding universal moral precepts and regulating the behaviour of non-Jews in a Jewish environment. For the Christian, on the other hand, the concept of natural law has been viewed as a central feature of ethical reflection.

Natural theology

Knowledge about God based on human reason. Although the Bible and rabbinic literature contain reflections about God's nature and activity, theology as a systematic discipline did not emerge until the time of Philo (1st cent. BCE–1st cent. CE). Influenced by Hellenistic philosophy, he developed the concept of the Divine Logos (or Wisdom of God), which he identified with the divine attributes of justice and mercy as well as the angelic realm.

After Philo, Jewish theology was not pursued again until the early Middle Ages, when Jews came into contact with Islamic theology and, through it, with Greek philosophy. During this period, contemporary philosophy was represented by the Islamic Kalam theologians, as well as neo-Platonism and Aristotelianism as mediated through Arabic commentators.

During the Middle Ages, numerous Jewish theologians such as Saadiah Gaon (9th–10th cent.), Solomon ibn Gabirol (11th cent.), and Moses Maimonides (12th cent.) engaged in philosophical speculation about the nature of God and the world. Common to all these writers was the conviction that God provided human beings with two sources of truth: Scripture and human reason. Since God is the ultimate source of all true knowledge, there can be no conflict between these two sources. Not all Jews, however, were content with this approach, and a major controversy took place about the work of Maimonides in the 13th cent. Some scholars rejected his views and maintained that his advocacy of rationalism would weaken the faith.

During the Enlightenment, Jewish theology took a new direction with the writing of Moses Mendelssohn (18th cent.). Rejecting the view that revelation is the source of both religious and rational truths, he argued that revelation presupposes rational truth which is available to all people in the universal religion of reason. In the 19th cent., Jewish theologians attempted to work out a way of reconciling a theology of Judaism with modern thought, and this process has continued into the 20th cent. in the work of such thinkers as Franz Rosenzweig (19th–20th cent.), Martin Buber (19th–20th cent.), and Mordecai Kaplan (19th–20th cent.). More recently, a number of Jewish theologians have endeavoured to give a rational explanation of God's presence and the evils of the Holocaust, and Jews as well as Christians are interested in the philosophy of religion.

In the first centuries of the Christian Church, a variety of attitudes to natural theology emerged. Tertullian (2nd–3rd cent.) was highly critical of a philosophical approach to the Christian faith. 'What has Athens to do with Jerusalem?' he asked. Augustine (4th–5th cent.), on the other hand, maintained that the Platonists were proto-Christians; nonetheless, he criticized the arrogance of philosophers and stressed that reason must be supported by faith. In time, both Platonism and Aristotelianism exerted an important influence on Christian thought, and the Middle Ages saw a flowering of philosophical theology parallel to that which occurred in Jewish circles. Pre-eminent among natural theologians was Thomas Aquinas (12th cent.), who systematized Christian theology along Aristotelian lines.

After the time of Aquinas, natural and revealed theology were viewed as the co-ordinating structure of all knowledge; theology was thought to be 'the Queen of the Sciences' and this attitude persisted until the Enlightenment when other disciplines came to the fore. In the modern period, natural theology has come to be understood primarily as philosophy of religion dealing with such topics as proofs for the existence of God, the rationality of religious belief, religious experience, and the relationship between religion and morality. In the 20th cent., such writers as Norman Malcolm and Alvin Plantinga have supported versions of the ontological argument for the existence of God. Process philosophers such as Charles Hartshorne have contributed to an understanding of divine power, knowledge, and perfection. Other writers such as Basil Mitchell and Richard Swinburne have maintained that theology is compatible with reason, and therefore intellectually respectable. Again, churchmen such as Bishop Ian Ramsey have been anxious to defend the use of religious language on philosophical grounds. Thus in both faiths from ancient times to those of the present day, natural theology has been viewed as a central religious task. Its aim is to offer a rational presentation of faith; in the words of Anselm (11th cent.), it is *fides quaerens intellectum* (faith seeking understanding).

Neo-Orthodoxy

Within the Jewish faith, neo-Orthodoxy refers to an ideological movement that seeks to combine traditional Judaism with a positive attitude towards modern culture. Among its first exponents were Isaac Bernays (18th–19th cent.) of Hamburg and Jacob Ettlinger (19th cent.) of Altona. Later, Samson Raphael Hirsch (19th cent.) promoted a religious and educational programme based on the principle that the Torah should be in harmony with secular culture (*Torah im Derekh Erets*). However,

he insisted on the divine origin of the law and would have nothing to do with the non-Orthodox Reform movement. Initially, he led a community in Frankfurt on this basis, subsequently guiding other congregations in Central Europe. This concept of neo-Orthodoxy insisted on the authority of the Written and Oral Law, while at the same time encouraging the promotion of German culture, the improvement of the position of women, the adoption of Western dress, the fostering of patriotism, and the advocacy of Jewish mission. Thus neo-Orthodoxy can be seen as a reaction to the liberalism of 19th-cent. Reform Judaism.

In time, other innovations were introduced into this religious approach, including preaching in the vernacular, the introduction of a cantor and choir in synagogue services, the publication of prayer books with translations and commentaries, and the encouragement of involvement in social, professional, and political life. Throughout the 19th cent., neo-Orthodox religious seminaries were established in major Jewish centres, and religious authority was centralized through the establishment of a chief rabbinate in various countries.

Despite such common ground, there were various divisions within the movement. Azriel Hildesheimer (19th cent.), for example, adopted a different attitude from Hirsch to Jewish communal affairs. Hirsch and his supporters established their own separate congregations – a move opposed by Hildesheimer, who believed that such a breach in Jewish unity would weaken the hold of traditional Judaism. In addition, Hirsch's camp opposed the Hibbat Zion movement (a forerunner of modern Zionism), which was supported by Hildesheimer and his followers. The supporters of Hirsch later joined the anti-Zionist Agudat Israel organization, whereas those who sided with Hildersheimer supported modern Zionism. Yet despite these divisions, neo-Orthodoxy has continued to flourish in the 20th cent. and has become the mainstream ideological position of the majority of Orthodox Jews.

Within Christianity, neo-Orthodoxy refers to various types of 20th-cent. Protestant theology that aim to recover the central precepts of the Reformation. As a reaction against the theological liberalism of the 19th and 20th cent., this movement stresses a number of biblical themes: the transcendence of God, the sinfulness of human beings, the uniqueness of Christ, and the importance of personal encounter with God. Pre-eminent among modern neo-Orthodox theologians is Karl Barth (19th–20th cent.), whose *Commentary on Romans* envisages God as the wholly other who breaks into human life in the person of Christ. According to Barth, full revelation only occurs in the risen Christ, who can be known through encounter rather than by means of historical investigation.

The work of Emil Brunner (19th–20th cent.) has also had an important impact on the development of neo-Orthodox thought. Brunner criticized Barth for asserting that human beings could have no knowledge of God, except for what is mediated through Christ. According to Brunner, it is possible to formulate a reformed natural theology. Associated with the work of Barth and Brunner were Rudolph Bultmann (19th–20th cent.) and Friedrich Gogarten (19th–20th cent.). Whereas Barth and Brunner based their positions on biblical theism, these writers interpreted biblical themes in the light of existential philosophy. Similarly, Paul Tillich (19th–20th cent.) grounded his neo-Orthodox views on existential thought. Further, Reinhold Niebuhr utilized biblical categories in his moral philosophy and interpretation of history. Despite the differences in their approaches, these neo-Orthodox writers were united in their conviction that the guiding idea of the Reformation should be applied to contemporary Christianity, and their views have had an important influence on modern neo-Orthodox circles. The neo-Orthodox emphases in Judaism and Christianity are thus widely divergent. In the Jewish community, the proponents of neo-Orthodoxy were anxious to harmonize traditional Judaism with contemporary culture. Neo-Orthodox Christians, on the other hand, sought to revitalize Christianity by applying the central insights of the Reformation to Christian life and thought. However, both movements arose as a corrective to the free-thinking liberalism of the 19th cent.

Neo-Platonism

The revival of Platonic thought in philosophy and theology between the 3rd and 6th cent. CE. The two philosophers most associated with neo-Platonism are Plotinus (3rd cent.) and Proclus (5th cent.). Plotinus taught that everything that exists emanates from the One, which is perfect. The One begets the *Nous* (mind), which in its turn begets the *Psyche* (world soul). The rest of the universe emanates from the world soul, and everything that is can return to the One by conversion and desire. The writings of Proclus, who taught similar doctrines, were put together in Arabic in the 9th cent. and were subsequently translated into Latin, the *Liber de Causis* in the 12th cent.

Jewish neo-Platonist thinkers, such as Solomon ibn Gabirol (11th cent.), identified the One with God and taught that God could be known through intellectual abstraction. Ibn Gabirol may have known the Arabic version of Proclus' philosophy. Certainly, the Latin translation of his own work, the *Fons Vitae*, was known to the Christian Scholastics, who did not realize that it was the work of a Jew. Although neo-Platonism was soon eclipsed by Aristotelianism in the Jewish tradition, the idea of emanation was very influential in mystical (kabbalistic) speculation from the 13th cent. onwards. Neo-Platonic elements can also be found in the work of the Christian Augustine of Hippo (4th–5th cent.), and in that of the medieval Schoolmen who drew on both the *Liber de Causis* and the *Fons Vitae*.

Ner Tamid *see* Light, eternal

New Moon

The Jewish calendar is lunar and each month begins at the time of the New Moon (*Rosh Hodesh*). The calendar was fixed by Hillel II in 325 CE and the date of each New Moon was decided by astronomical calculations. Previously, the authorities in Jerusalem had relied on observation. In early biblical times, the New Moon was a festival (2 Kings 4.23), but by the time the Jews returned from exile in Babylon (6th cent. BCE), it had become a normal day. Extra prayers are still included in the daily services, and an additional service is read which corresponds to the additional sacrifice that was made in the Temple. The new month is announced in the synagogue on the previous Sabbath. It is forbidden to fast or mourn on the New Moon but, particularly among the mystical kabbalists (16th–19th cent.), it was customary to hold a small fast on the eve of the New Moon. This was to emphasize that the new month would be a time of spiritual renewal. In a few very traditional communities, after the third day of the New Moon, but before the fifteenth when it began to wane, it was customary to hold a small joyous ceremony of Sanctifying the New Moon (*Kiddush Levanah*).

There are no celebrations of the New Moon in Christianity. Christians use the solar calendar originally devised by Julius Caesar and modified by Pope Gregory XIII in 1582. The first day of the month, therefore, does not correspond with a New Moon. The date of Easter is related to the lunar year and thus its date and the corresponding dates of Ash Wednesday, Holy Week, Ascension Day, and Whitsunday vary from year to year.

New Testament *see* Bible

New Year

(Rosh Hashanah) (New Year for Trees): The first day of Tishri is celebrated as the religious New Year (Rosh Hashanah) in Judaism. It is viewed as the birthday of the world and marks the beginning of the Ten Solemn Days of Penitence, which have their climax in the Day of Atonement (Yom Kippur). According to the Mishnah, Rosh Hashanah is the annual Day of Judgement and 'All that comes into the world pass before Him like flocks of sheep'. Lev. 23.23 contains the command, 'In the seventh month, on the first day of the month, you shall observe a day of solemn rest, a memorial proclaimed with blast of trumpets (*shofarot*), a holy convocation.' Traditionally, therefore, the blowing of the *shofar* – a trumpet made from a ram's horn – is a feature of the synagogue service. The liturgy emphasizes the solemnity of the festival; it is a day of self-examination and prayers are said for the establishment of God's Kingdom on earth. Various customs are observed at home. On the first night, it is usual to eat something sweet (cake or apples dipped in honey) in anticipation of a 'good and sweet year'. On the second night, a new fruit is eaten for the first time to rejoice in the freshness of the season. In Orthodox circles, it is also customary to visit a river or sea-shore to recite Mic. 7.19, 'He will again have compassion upon us, he will tread our iniquities under foot. Thou wilt cast all our sins into the depths of the sea.' This goes back to the Middle Ages and may be based on the ancient superstition of casting sins into the sea. For this reason, it is rejected by some authorities. As with all Jewish festivals, except the Day of Atonement, it is celebrated in the Diaspora for two days because of traditional uncertainty as to which night is that of the New Moon. Rosh Hashanah, however, is the only festival that is commemorated for two days in Israel.

The Mishnah mentions three other New Years in the Jewish calendar: the New Year for Kings (1 Nisan), the New Year for Tithing Cattle (1 Elul), and the New Year for Trees (15 Shevat). Only the last of these is still celebrated. Originally, it was the date on which the tithe was levied on fruit trees, but with the destruction of the Temple in 70 CE this was no longer relevant. The festival survived primarily as a remembrance of the Land of Israel, and it was renewed with the founding of the nation in 1948. Nowadays, saplings are planted and Israeli schoolchildren are particularly encouraged to take their part in the forestation of the land.

According to the Julian Calendar, the New Year begins on 1 January and the day was celebrated with the pagan Saturnalia. Christians were forbidden to take part in these licentious and idolatrous parties, and the Church's year began on different days in different countries. In England it began with the Feast of the Annunciation on 25 March, because traditionally that is when the new era began in 1 CE, with Jesus' conception. In Germany it began with Christmas, and in France with Easter. However, Advent Sunday is now generally accepted as the day when the ecclesiastical year begins and, interestingly, it has clear theological connections with the Jewish New Year. Both are solemn days of self-examination which look forward to the Day of Judgement, and both focus on subsequent festivals (the Day of Atonement and Christmas Day) which will bring God's redemption.

Since the Gregorian reform of the calendar in 1582, 1 January has gradually come to be accepted as the beginning of the secular year. It is not a religious festival, and is celebrated even by many Christians and Jews in a way that is not dissimilar to the old Saturnalia.

New Year for Trees *see* New Year

O

Oaths

(Vows): In general, the rabbis took a negative attitude towards vows and oaths – as it is written in the Talmud, 'He who makes a vow, though he fulfil it, is called wicked.' Nonetheless, solemn undertakings were made either to God or to fellow human beings; Gen. 28.20–22 describes Jacob making a vow to God in a time of distress, and the author of Ps. 116.16–19 promised sacrifices of thanksgiving and the fulfilment of vows. A husband could nullify the vows of his wife and unmarried daughters (Num. 30.3–8) but, in general, oaths and vows must be kept. The opening prayer on the evening of the Day of Atonement is the *Kol Nidrei* (All Vows) and is a declaration that all vows made rashly during the year are cancelled. This only applies to vows made to God, but has been widely misunderstood in the Gentile world. As early as the 6th cent., the Emperor Justinian would not accept Jewish testimony against Christians because it was thought that Jews could absolve themselves from their oaths. In many countries up until the beginning of the 20th cent., a humiliating Jewish Oath was extracted in the law courts from Jewish witnesses on these grounds. In fact, vows between human beings can only be cancelled by mutual consent, and Jews take vows and oaths very seriously indeed. The Third Commandment stresses, 'You shall not take the name of the Lord your God in vain; for the Lord will not hold him guiltless who takes his name in vain' (Exod. 20.7). Taking God's name lightly, as in a neglected vow, is thus sacrilege.

Jesus shared the rabbis' disapproval of oaths (Matt. 5.33–37) and some Christians have interpreted his words to mean that no oath should be taken under any circumstances. Generally, however, the Church has only forbidden frivolous oaths, and it is permitted to swear to speak the truth in a court of law. To fail to tell the truth when under oath is a great sin, that of perjury. As in Judaism, a valid vow, such as on marriage or when becoming a member of a religious community, creates a real obligation. Although an individual can be released from his vows in particular circumstances, this is not done lightly.

Old Testament *see* Bible

Omnipotence *see* God, attributes of

Omnipresence *see* God, attributes of

Omniscience *see* God, attributes of

Oneness of God *see* God, attributes of; monotheism

Oral Law *see* law

Ordination

(Clergy) (Laity) (*Semikhah*): In the Bible, God gave authority to Moses who passed it to Joshua. Thus Scripture records that God said to Moses: 'Take Joshua the son of Nun, a man in whom is the spirit, and lay your hand upon him ... You shall invest him with some of your authority, that all the congregation of the people of Israel may obey' (Num. 27.18, 20). In conformity with this act, laying on of hands became part of the ceremony of ordination (*semikhah*). According to the Mishnah, the transmission of authority was passed from Joshua to the men of the Great Assembly, and subsequently ordination was practised on behalf of the Sanhedrin by the ordinand's teachers. The person ordained received the title 'rabbi' (my teacher) and possessed judicial authority. Ordination could only take place in Israel; in Babylonia the academies conferred the title *rav* (great).

After the second Temple was destroyed in 70 CE, the ceremony of *semikhah* continued at the Sanhedrin reconstituted by Johanan ben Zakkai. However, after the Bar Kokhba revolt in 135, ordination was officially suppressed by Hadrian; nonetheless, it continued until about the 4th cent. Once this chain had been broken, it was no longer possible to ordain rabbis. In the 12th cent., Moses Maimonides encouraged the re-establishment of ordination by the unanimous decision of all the rabbis in the land of Israel. On this basis, Jacob Bernay made an attempt to reintroduce ordination in Safed in 1538. This led to a heated controversy, and the attempt failed. Subsequent discussions about the possibility of reconstituting the Sanhedrin so as to confer ordination have taken place up to modern times, and became a real possibility after 1948 with the founding of the State of Israel. Nonetheless, no agreement has as yet been reached.

The *semikhah* conferred on candidates after the Sanhedrin disappeared was not the same as ancient ordination. Laying on of hands did not generally take place, nor was there the conferring of judicial authority that resided in Talmudic *semikhah*. After a course of study, ordained candidates were presented with a diploma, *Hattarat Horaah* (permission to teach), signed by one or more scholars. This document contained the phrase *Yore, Yore, Yadin, Yadin* ('He may teach; he may render decisions'), and was granted after an examination by the teachers of the candidate or by an esteemed scholar from elsewhere.

After the Enlightenment in the 19th cent., the role of the rabbi significantly altered in Central and Western Europe. To meet the need for rabbis suited to deal with modern life, rabbinical seminaries were established to train candidates. In Eastern European Jewish communities, however, the pattern of traditional yeshivah (Jewish academy) education continued to flourish. In the USA, rabbinical training varies widely from the traditional Eastern European Orthodox pattern to modernist rabbinical programmes offered by Reform seminaries. Across the religious spectrum, candidates are granted the title 'rabbi', and in recent years women have been ordained within the non-Orthodox movements. Among the Orthodox, the priesthood continues to exist, but is the result of hereditary descent rather than ordination. Priests in Judaism are not necessarily religious leaders in the synagogue.

The Hebrew Scriptures served as the basis for the tradition of Christian ordination. In the New Testament, Jesus is conceived as priest, prophet, and king by the consecrating act of God, and through him the Church is given the authority to carry on his mission. In assigning leadership and prophetic ministry, it was the practice to lay on hands and invoke God's Spirit on those who were ordained. The *Apostolic Tradition* by Hippolytus (3rd cent.) is the first major witness to public rituals of ordination. In this work, the term begins to be restricted to the ministry of deacon, presbyter, and bishop. Placement into other orders (such as penitents, catechumens, and widows) is referred to by other names.

In the 3rd cent., the deacon was the administrative assistant to the bishop; the presbyterium was a largely ceremonial collegial body; the bishop was high priest and public embodiment of the Church. The 4th cent. saw the emergence of the presbyter-priest, who presided at the Eucharist. Other ministers (including the deacon) were subsumed under the priesthood. By the Middle Ages, there were four minor orders (exorcist, porter, acolyte, lector) and three major orders (sub-deacon, deacon, and priest). At the very least, ordination to these offices involved presentation to the bishop, congregational prayers for the Holy Spirit, and the laying on of hands. In the 16th cent., Reformation communities adopted a different conception of Church order and ministry. Ordination was not seen as a sacrament; rather, it was viewed as a licence to preach and teach. Nonetheless, the licensing ceremony generally continued to involve presentation, prayer, and the laying on of hands. In recent times, there has been considerable debate about the ordination of women. Within Protestant Christianity, women have generally been accepted for ordination in the interests of justice and equal opportunity, but this move has been vehemently resisted by the Roman Catholic and Orthodox Churches. Despite the acceptance of the biblical concept of ordination in both Judaism and Christianity, there are important differences between the varying traditions. Within at least the Catholic and Orthodox Churches, the laying on of hands at ordination is seen primarily as a sacramental act of God's calling and appointment. For Jews, as for many Protestants, on the other hand, ordination is understood as a process of a conferring of a formal position within the religious community which entails responsibilities for teaching and preaching.

Within traditional Christianity, a sharp line is drawn between those who have been ordained (the clergy) and other Christians (the laity). Specific religious duties, such as celebrating the Eucharist, can only be undertaken by those in orders. In Judaism, however, because ordination is not perceived sacramentally, religious responsibilities, such as leading the service, can be performed by any male Jew. Among the Orthodox, however, every man is in effect a religious leader in his own household, and potentially one also in the synagogue. The Reform Movement gives equal rights to women, and in their synagogues lay women can also have ritual responsibilities.

Original sin

Gen. 2–3 records how Adam and Eve ate the forbidden fruit; were expelled from the Garden of Eden; and work, pain, and death became part of human destiny. This story was given different interpretations in the different traditions. The rabbis taught that death was the direct result of Adam's disobedience, but in general they did not teach a doctrine of original sin. Nonetheless, they accepted that 'the wickedness of man was great in the earth, and that every imagination of the thoughts of his heart was only evil continually' (Gen. 6.5), and explained this by positing the existence of the evil inclination (*yetzer ha-ra*). This was paralleled by the good inclination (*yetzer ha-tov*), which was identified with the Torah (God's law). Through Torah, the evil inclination, which is with a person from birth, can be subdued and transformed.

In the epistle to the Romans and elsewhere, Paul taught that sin came into the world through Adam and 'one man's trespass led to condemnation for all men' (Rom. 5.18). This was explained by Augustine of Hippo (4th–5th cent.) to mean that Adam's guilt was transferred to all his descendants through sexual procreation, and that therefore all human beings are, of their very nature, essentially corrupt and totally depraved. Later, medieval theologians such as Anselm (11th–12th cent.) argued that original sin was not transferred through 'concupiscence' but by the privation of righteousness, and that through disobedience humanity lost its supernatural endowment. The Protestant reformers followed the old Augustinian line; they stressed the complete depravity of human beings, which they believed could only be transformed by the grace of God in Jesus Christ. From the 18th cent., the influence of rationalism and secularism has tended to undermine the idea of original sin. Darwin's (19th cent.) theory of evolution by natural selection in particular has encouraged the belief in natural progress. Nonetheless, there has been a revival of the doctrine in the 20th cent., especially among Roman Catholics and the neo-Orthodox. There is a general agreement that humanity is out of harmony with the will of God and that sin is all-pervasive. Thus, nowadays, Christians and Jews are not far

apart in their beliefs in this area. Although Jews do not accept the idea of inherited guilt, the concept of the inherent evil inclination is very similar to the Christian notion of the inherent sinfulness of the human race.

Orthodoxy

Orthodox Judaism refers to the rabbinic tradition as it developed through the ages. All Orthodox Jews are united in their adherence to the belief that the Torah (Written Law) is of divine origin and that the Oral Law is also authoritative. On this basis, Orthodoxy opposed the Karaites (8th–12th cent.), who adhered to Scripture but rejected the Oral Law. In modern times, the word 'Orthodoxy' has been used to designate the religious beliefs and practices of Jews in Central and Western Europe who have opposed the reforms to Jewish life brought about by the Enlightenment (*Haskalah*). As Jews gained social acceptance, many drifted away from traditional patterns of Jewish existence – religious obligations and customs were regarded as socially burdensome, and the Orthodox mode of worship was seen as aesthetically unacceptable. In these changed circumstances, a large number of Jews were sympathetic to the ideology of the Reform Movement, which pressed for halakhic (legal) and liturgical change.

Believing these challenges would undermine the Jewish way of life, traditionalists rejected the ideals of the Enlightenment, issued a ban of excommunication against Reformers, and urged congregants to resist modern tendencies. Such Orthodox leaders as Moses Sofer of Pressberg led a campaign against Reform Judaism, and the virtues of the traditional Jewish way of life were upheld by the Eastern European Jewish masses as well as Hasidic communities. Other Orthodox leaders such as Samson Raphael Hirsch and Azriel Hildesheimer promoted 'neo-Orthodoxy', which attempted to harmonize traditional Judaism with the values of the modern world. Their views characterized modern Orthodoxy as it developed from the end of the 19th cent.

In 1880–1920, millions of Jews emigrated from Eastern Europe to the USA, settling in New York and other metropolitan centres. By the 1930s, many of these immigrants had moved out of Jewish ghettos in these cities, simultaneously abandoning the Orthodox way of life. Despite this transformation,

Orthodoxy experienced a revival as a result of the arrival in the 1930s and 1940s of European scholars, heads of yeshivot (rabbinic seminaries), and Hasidic leaders. These immigrants infused new life into the already existing Orthodox institutions of the USA. Elsewhere, traditional Judaism retained its hold on Jewish communities, and in Israel it was established as the official religion of the State.

The word 'Orthodoxy' does not appear in the New Testament. In place of credal formulations, there are brief confessional formulae about Jesus. In his epistles, Paul speaks about the teaching he received and handed on: 'I commend you because you remember me in everything and maintain the traditions even as I have delivered them to you' (1 Cor. 11.2). In Gal., he similarly referred to the preaching of the faith, implying that it is a doctrine to be passed on (Gal. 1.23). The pastoral letters also express a concern with soundness of doctrine. Here the word 'teaching' (*didaskalia*) is used repeatedly to differentiate correct from incorrect teaching. In post-biblical Christianity, heterodox teachers were castigated by such writers as Ignatius of Antioch (1st–2nd cent.), and the word 'Orthodoxy' was employed by such 4th-cent. theologians as Eusebius of Caesarea, Julius I, Athanasius, and Basil.

In time, the Church issued proclamations of Christian belief that crystallized into official creeds such as the Apostles' Creed, the Nicene Creed, and the Athanasian Creed. In this way, the Church was able to proclaim official teaching in opposition to heterodoxy or heresy. Viewed as a pure tradition, following in a direct line from Jesus and the apostles, these credal formulations were understood as correct expressions of the true faith. From the 4th to the 9th cent., Greek writers applied the term 'Orthodox' to such areas as the interpretation of Scripture, the faith of the Church, the Church's liturgical worship, ecclesiastical decrees, and theological opinions. Because of their emphasis on correct belief, the Eastern Churches became known as 'Eastern Orthodox', as in the 'Greek Orthodox' or 'Russian Orthodox' Church.

At the time of the Reformation, confessional statements were produced by reformers, and various Churches were anxious to define and justify their distinctive beliefs in order to explain their separate existence. Such confessions as the Anglican Thirty-Nine Articles, the Scots Confession, and the Westminster Confession defined the particular Protestant communities that issued them. Nonetheless, the Roman Catholic Church continued to view itself as the sole heir of the Christian tradition, representing true Orthodoxy. In the 20th cent., the writings of such theologians as Karl Barth ushered in a period of neo-Orthodoxy, an approach that has been adopted by a significant number of Christians across the religious spectrum. In addition, the modern evangelical movement has claimed to represent true biblical Orthodoxy and other theologians regard themselves as radically orthodox. It is clear then that Orthodoxy – understood as the acceptance of correct doctrine – has been a dominant feature of both Judaism and Christianity through the centuries to the present day. For Jews, the belief that the Written and Oral Law were received by Moses on Mt Sinai has served as the theological fulcrum of belief and practice. In Christianity, on the other hand, doctrinal issues concerning God in Christ and the role and function of the Church have been of central importance in defining who is within and who outside the bounds of salvation.

Our Father *see* Lord's Prayer

P

Pacifism

(War): Peace is an important ideal in Judaism. The prophet Micah (7th cent. BCE) looked forward to a time when 'nation shall not lift up sword against nation, neither shall they learn war any more' (Mic. 4.3). This tradition was continued by the rabbis, very many liturgical prayers end with a petition of peace (shalom). Nonetheless, there is no tradition of pacifism in Judaism. War is recognized as a necessity in the face of national oppression and injustice, even though it is the duty of every Jew to work for the condition of peace. However, a distinction is made between obligatory wars that are commanded by God, or are the result of enemy aggression, and optional wars of political significance. Even the last category is not regarded as illegitimate in certain circumstances.

In the Sermon on the Mount, Jesus commended

peacemakers (Matt. 5.9) and told his followers to turn the other cheek (Matt. 5.39) and to love their enemies (Matt. 5.44). Some early Church Fathers, such as Tertullian (2nd–3rd cent.), forbade Christians to take part in military service, but others, such as Augustine of Hippo (4th–5th cent.), argued that war was justifiable as a last resort. Increasingly, moral theologians distinguished between just wars, in which it was legitimate to fight, and unjust wars. Thomas Aquinas (13th cent.) laid down three conditions for a just war: it must be authorized by the sovereign; it must be for a rightful cause; and the participants must be fighting with the intention of stopping evil or furthering good. Francisco de Vitoria (16th cent.) added the additional proviso that it must be fought by proper means. However, some Christians have maintained the position of absolute pacifism and have rejected all physical violence on principle; examples include the Mennonites, the Quakers, and the Anabaptists. The development of modern weaponry has added a further dimension to the debate, some authorities arguing that modern wars are inevitably unjust because they are not fought by legitimate means. However, there is no universal consensus on the morality of warfare in the Christian Churches.

Paganism

(Heathenism) (Idolatry): In the ancient world the worship of images made of wood, stone, or metal was widely practised. Such idolatry was specifically forbidden in the decalogue: 'You shall have no other gods before me. You shall not make for yourself a graven image, or any likeness of anything that is in heaven above, or that is in the earth beneath, or that is in the water under the earth; you shall not bow down to them or serve them' (Exod. 20.3–5). Similarly, in the Shema prayer ('Hear, O Israel'), warning is given about such abhorrent behaviour: 'Take heed lest your heart be deceived, and you turn aside and serve other gods and worship them' (Deut. 11.16). Among laws concerning idolatry are prohibitions against planting an *asherah* (tree used for worship by the Canaanites) near the altar and establishing pillars for worship.

According to tradition, idolatry, along with incest and murder, constitute the three major sins: they must not be transgressed even if loss of life is involved. In the Talmud, the tractate *Avodah Zarah*

deals with regulations concerning the treatment of idolaters. Included are laws forbidding business dealings with those who practise idolatry, associating with them, using their images, and benefiting from their wine.

Despite such stipulations, the Jewish people were prone to idolatrous worship in ancient times. In their wandering in the desert, the nation worshipped a golden calf made by Aaron in response to the request for a god to lead them when they awaited Moses' return from Mt Sinai (Exod. 32.1–4). Again, when the ancient Israelites entered the land of Canaan, they continually engaged in idolatrous practices and were rebuked by Judges and Prophets. In the northern Kingdom, in particular, idolatry was a common feature of Israelite worship where bulls were set up in the sanctuary. However according to the Talmud, the Men of the Great Assembly stamped out idolatry after the destruction of the first Temple (6th cent. BCE). In the Jewish faith, Christians were not viewed as idolaters, yet their use of images and their belief in the doctrine of the Trinity were understood as compromising monotheism. Muslims, on the other hand, were seen as pure monotheists.

The Christian faith shared the Jewish attitude to idolatry. Yet unlike almost all Jews, Christians through the centuries have felt obliged to engage in missionizing heathen peoples. From the beginning, missionary enterprise was one of the central tasks of the Church. Thus in Matt. 28.19, Jesus declared, 'Go therefore and make disciples of all nations, baptizing them in the name of the Father and of the Son and of the Holy Spirit.' Such a task was undertaken by Paul, the apostles, and early Christian leaders. This evangelization spread from east to west and north to south. In the medieval period, efforts were made to convert the remaining heathen tribes in Europe, and missionary work was also extended among Muslims, as well as further afield among Tartars, Chinese and Indians.

During the Reformation, this missionary activity was overshadowed by internal disputes within Christendom. However, the Counter-Reformation gave rise to a rebirth of the missionary enterprise. Dominicans, Franciscans, Augustinians, and Jesuits engaged in such activity in the Americas, India, Japan, China, and Africa. Such missionizing waned in the 18th cent., but was reactivated in the

19th cent. by Roman Catholic foreign missions. During this period, Christians engaged particularly in missionizing and educational work. In this century, the Roman Catholic Church has laid particular stress on the need to understand sympathetically non-Christian peoples and cultures.

Alongside such missionary work in the Roman Catholic Church, reformed Protestant Churches also encouraged the propagation of the gospel among heathen peoples. Beginning in the 17th cent., a number of societies to promote this activity were founded, and the evangelical revival in the 18th cent. added new stimulus to these efforts. As with Roman Catholicism, new directions have been taken in the missionary enterprise in this century, yet the quest to spread the gospel has continued to be of pivotal importance within Protestantism. Thus through the ages the Christian response to paganism has been one of outreach, whereas Judaism teaches that in order to avoid idolatry, Jews must separate themselves from the heathen. While the Jewish community enacted laws to prevent association between Jew and pagan, Christians felt impelled to serve as divinely appointed emissaries to bring knowledge of God and the promise of salvation to those deprived of the true faith.

Papacy

The jurisdiction of the Bishop of Rome over the Western Church was recognized by the Council of Sardica in 343 CE. The Pope is thought to have inherited the spiritual authority and office of the apostle Peter, who was martyred in Rome. Peter (*Cephas* in Greek) was described by Jesus as the rock (*Cephas*) on which the Church would be built; and he went on to say, 'I will give you the keys of the kingdom of heaven, and whatever you bind on earth shall be bound in heaven, and whatever you loose on earth shall be loosed in heaven' (Matt. 16.19). On this basis, the Pope has traditionally claimed the leadership of the Universal Church. This was never fully accepted by the Eastern Orthodox Churches who had their own patriarchs, and it was unequivocally rejected by the Protestant reformers, some of whom identified the Pope with the antichrist (1 John 2.18). In recent years, attitudes have modified. On the one hand, non-Roman Catholic Church leaders have generally been willing to visit and confer with the Pope and, on the

other, since the Second Vatican Council (mid-20th cent.) the emphasis has been on the 'collegiality' of all Roman Catholic bishops rather than the domination of the papacy.

Parable

In the Bible, no distinction is made between parable, allegory, and fable – they are all forms of comparison (*mashal*). The story parable is told in terms of ordinary experiences. Examples include Nathan's parable (2 Sam. 12.1–5), the parables of the surviving son (2 Sam. 14.5–7), the escaped prisoner (1 Kings 20.39–40), and the disappointing vineyard (Isa. 5.1–6). In contrast, the allegory parable is more artificial in character. Typical allegories include the laments of the lioness (Ezek. 19.2–9), the transplanted vine (Ezek. 19.10–14), the stories of the harlot sister (Ezek. 23.2–21), and the cooking pot (Ezek. 24.3–5). Another type of parable is the fable where animals or inanimate objects speak and act like human beings – Judg. 9.8–15 and 2 Kings 14.9–10 are examples. A riddle is a type of parable whose point is deliberately obscured – such as Samson's riddle (Judg. 14.14). Other biblical forms of parable include prophetic oracles, extended personifications, and revelatory dreams and visions.

In rabbinic literature, parables were frequently used as a method of teaching. Frequently, the parable is introduced by the phrase 'A parable: to what can this matter be compared' (*Mashal: le-mah ha-davar domeh le*). One of the most frequent motifs used was that of a leader, and is usually presented as a ruler with humanity as his subjects; a father with Israel as a sometimes wayward but beloved son; the husband with Israel as the wife; and the monarch of whom Israel is the favourite subject. Parables were also taken from the animal world, especially fox fables. Aspects of nature and plants were also made the subject of parables, as were details taken from everyday life. Medieval writers also utilized parables in their works; thus Bahya ibn Paquda and Judah Ha-Levi used the standard parable of the king. In addition, Hasidic literature contains numerous parables, and parables became characteristic of the method of preaching of various Hasidic figures. Jesus in his preaching made frequent use of parables, employing standard rabbinic patterns of teaching. There are 31 parables in the

New Testament, some of which are found in rabbinic sources in a somewhat different form. For example, the parable of the labourers in the vineyard (Matt. 20.1–16) parallels the parable by Zeira (2nd cent.) in his funeral oration on the death of Avin, the father of Hiyya. However, unlike the rabbis, through his use of parables Jesus wished his hearers to recognize God's activity and acknowledge that the Kingdom of God is at hand. The parables of Jesus were primarily concerned with the coming of the Kingdom of God, and their original meaning was directly related to the immediate situation of his ministry.

Many of these parables imply that the rule of God has already broken into ordinary life. Some are naturalistic and only minimally narrational (such as those dealing with the mustard seed, the lost coin, etc.). Others are concerned with human relationships – the unjust judge, the prodigal son, the wicked husbandman, the labourers in the vineyard, and the good Samaritan. Further parables imply that the ways of the conventional world are not the ways of God. Thus in the parable of the great feast, conventionally worthy guests are overshadowed by unconventional ones: '"Go out quickly to the streets and lanes of the city, and bring in the poor and maimed and blind and lame". . . . For I tell you, none of those men who were invited shall taste my banquet' (Luke 14.21, 24). Still other parables imply that their significance can only be grasped as listeners apply the stories to their own personal lives, such as the parable of the sower (Mark 4.3–9). Jesus' parables thus serve as powerful teaching devices, persuading listeners to ponder their own situations. They are one of the most distinctive features of Jesus' ministry, yet, unlike the parables of the rabbis, their main purpose was to proclaim the inbreaking of the Messianic Kingdom and God's imminent rule on earth.

Paradise *see* Heaven

Parental duties

According to the Jewish tradition, the primary purpose of marriage is to create a family. Thus God decrees in Gen.: 'Be fruitful and multiply' (Gen. 1.28). Within the context of family life, both children and parents have responsibilities and duties.

Biblical law stipulates that children must honour and respect parents: 'Honour your father and your mother, that your days may be long in the land which the Lord your God gives you' (Exod. 20.12); 'Every one of you shall revere his mother and his father' (Lev. 19.3). The rabbis stipulated that these commandments imply that both parents should be equally honoured and revered. Honour is traditionally interpreted to mean feeding, washing, dressing, and helping parents in and out of the house. The requirement to feed and care for the parent is to be undertaken at the parent's expense; in cases where this is not possible, care of parents takes precedence over all other charitable obligations. Respect is understood as not sitting in a parent's seat or contradicting them in conversation. The obligation of children to care for their parents continues beyond the parent's lifetime – it is the custom for the son to say the Kaddish prayer after the death of a parent, and both sons and daughters are to observe the anniversary of a parent's death.

In general, parental responsibilities devolve upon the father and include the child's basic needs. A father is obliged to circumcise a male child, provide him with a Jewish education, teach him a trade, redeem him if he is the first-born, and see to his marriage. For girls, the father is obliged to provide a sufficient dowry to ensure that she is marriageable. In the case of divorce, child custody is based on the welfare of the child. For children under the age of six, maternal care is crucial; afterwards, boys are to be in the custody of the father because of their need for religious instruction. Girls, however, normally remain with their mothers. Nonetheless, the father is obliged to support those children in the mother's custody unless she has agreed to do so.

Following the Jewish tradition, Jesus emphasized the importance of family life. In Mark 10.7–8 he declared: 'For this reason, man shall leave his father and mother and be joined to his wife, and the two shall become one flesh.' For Paul, marriage symbolized the union of Christ and the Church (Eph. 5.32), and he encouraged fathers to bring up their children in the Christian faith: 'Fathers, do not provoke your children to anger, but bring them up in the discipline and instruction of the Lord' (Eph. 6.4). In accordance with biblical teaching, children are told to honour and obey their parents: 'Children, obey your parents in everything, for this pleases the Lord' (Col. 3.20).

The early Church expressed its concern for the child in its opposition to abortion and infanticide, and from the earliest period Christians were obligated to rear children in the Christian faith. Children were baptized under the new covenant, and nurtured in the religion of their parents. Parents were obligated to teach the child obedience, respect for adults, and reverence for God. The early Christians sent their children to pagan schools but, with the break-up of the Roman Empire, learning was preserved through the monasteries and medieval universities. Formal educational facilities were thus restricted to only a small minority of Christian children. However, in the modern period, Christian education has become widespread, taking place largely through Church institutions as well as in the home. In both Judaism and Christianity, then, the duties of both parents and children are of fundamental importance in the context of family life. Drawing on biblical traditions of duty and respect, parents are to care for their offspring, and children are to honour and revere both their mother and father who nurtured them.

Parousia *see* Second coming

Paschal lamb *see* Lamb of God; Passover

Passover

(*Aphikoman*) (*Matzah*) (Paschal Lamb) (Pesah) (Seder) (Unleavened Bread): According to Exod. 23.14, Jews were commanded to make pilgrimage to the Temple three times a year, on the Feast of Weeks (Shavuot), Tabernacles (Sukkot) and Passover (Pesah). The festival of Passover is celebrated for eight days in the Dispersion and seven in Israel (and among non-Orthodox Jews), starting on 15 Nisan. It commemorates both the start of the barley harvest and the liberation of the Israelites from slavery in Egypt. The word 'Passover' recalls how the angel of death 'passed over' the houses of the Jews when he slew the first-born of the Egyptians. Every Israelite family was commanded to slaughter a lamb and sprinkle some of its blood on the door-posts of their houses as a sign to the angel. When Pharaoh did release the Jewish slaves in

response to the death of the first-born, they were in such a hurry to leave Egypt that they did not wait for their bread to leaven or rise.

Today, the celebration of Passover in Orthodox households requires considerable preparation. The house is completely cleaned and all leaven is removed. This includes all products containing wheat, barley, rye, or oats and, for the Ashkenazim (Eastern European Jews), rice, peas, and beans. During the whole holiday period, unleavened bread (*matzah*) is eaten, and no cutlery, china, or utensils that have previously been used for leavened goods may be employed. The Seder (Order) is the home ritual, which is observed on the first two nights (one by the non-Orthodox and by those living in Israel). Ritual food is placed on the table including an egg (a reminder of the festival sacrifice), a bone (for the paschal lamb), bitter herbs (signifying the bitterness of slavery), haroset (a mixture of apples, nuts, and wine symbolizing the mortar used by the Israelite slaves), a green vegetable (supposedly intended to keep alive the interest of the children), and salt water for the tears of the Jewish slaves. In response to the question, 'Why is this night different from all other nights?' the head of the household relates the story of the Exodus together with traditional expositions and interpretations. The whole ritual is set out in the Haggadah (narration) and involves the eating of unleavened bread (*matzah*), bitter herbs, and vegetables. Four cups of wine are drunk and an additional cup is poured for the Prophet Elijah who, it is believed, will return to earth to herald the 'great and terrible day of the Lord' (Mal. 4.5) during a Passover season. A custom has arisen of hiding a piece of *matzah* (*aphikoman*) during the course of the Seder to arouse the curiosity of the children present. When it is found, it is shared out at the end of the meal. The Seder also includes blessings, prayers, and songs, and a wide variety of traditions are followed by different communities and even by different families. Festival services are also held in the synagogue. On the Sabbath of the Passover week, the Song of Songs is read and this reflects the agricultural element of the festival.

According to the Synoptic Gospels (Matthew, Mark, and Luke), Jesus' Last Supper with his disciples appears to have been a Passover meal. Here he is described as transforming the symbols of bread and wine; they became his body and blood which were about to be sacrificed to establish a new covenant between God and humanity. The old Passover celebrated freedom from slavery to the Egyptians; the new sacrifice of Jesus ensured release from bondage to spiritual death, which is the just consequence of sin. In the Fourth Gospel, Jesus is actually crucified on the eve of Passover just as the paschal lambs were being sacrificed in the Temple. It is in that Gospel that Jesus is earlier described as the 'Lamb of God, who takes away the sin of the world' (John 1.29), and this designation is incomprehensible without an understanding of the Jewish Passover.

In the Middle Ages and later, Jews were frequently accused of using the blood of Christians to manufacture unleavened bread. This was the excuse for periodic outbreaks of anti-Semitism, and in the past Passover was frequently a time of terror for the Jewish community.

Peace

(Shalom): The Hebrew word 'shalom', meaning peace, indicates wholeness, completion, perfection. Thus when Jews pray for peace, they are not merely looking for the absence of war, but for a state of complete cosmic harmony. According to the rabbis, it is the duty of every Jew to love and pursue shalom, and very many liturgical prayers conclude with a petition for peace. Harmony will be the essential characteristic of the age of the Messiah when the nations 'shall beat their swords into ploughshares, and their spears into pruning hooks' (Mic. 4.3), and the traditional Hebrew greeting is *Shalom aleikhem* – 'Peace be unto you'.

The same emphasis is to be found in Christianity. Several of Paul's epistles end with a message of peace (for example, Eph. 6.23 and Gal. 6.16), and from the earliest days of the Church it has been customary to exchange a kiss of peace during the Eucharist service. Christians believe that through Jesus' death, final harmony is restored; as Paul wrote in his epistle to the Colossians, 'For in him all the fullness of God was pleased to dwell, and through him to reconcile to himself all things, whether on earth or in heaven, making peace by the blood of his cross' (Col. 1.19–20). Yet although this harmony is implicit in the life and work of Jesus, because the fullness of God's rule on earth has not

yet been realized, complete peace has not yet been fully established in the here and now. Christians, therefore, as well as Jews, look forward to the end of this era when the order of this world will at last reflect the perfect integrity of heaven.

Penance *see* Atonement

Penitence *see* Atonement

Pentateuch *see* Bible; law books

Pentecost

(Shavuot) (Weeks, Feast of) (Whitsunday): One of the three Pilgrim Festivals, the others being Passover (Pesah), and Tabernacles (Sukkot). The name Pentecost comes from the Greek term for 50, and the feast was so called because it occurs 50 days after Passover. Its Hebrew name 'Shavuot' (Weeks) comes from the biblical instruction to count seven weeks from the Passover barley celebration (Deut. 16.9–10). Pentecost commemorates the offering of the first ripe fruits in the Temple (Num. 28.26), and also the giving of the Law to Moses on Mt Sinai. Thus Pentecost is the culmination of the harvest season which began at Passover, and is also the climax of the Exodus story which God initiated with the slaughter of the first-born and the 'passing over' of the angel of death. Nowadays, synagogues are decorated with flowers, dairy foods are traditionally eaten, and the prescribed readings include the Ten Commandments and the Book of Ruth. Because the festival is connected with the giving of the Torah, it is usual to begin a child's Jewish education at this time of year, and in many communities this is also when religion school classes graduate.

According to the Acts of the Apostles (2.1), the Holy Spirit first descended on Jesus' disciples at the time of Pentecost. This was perceived as a fulfilment of prophecy (Joel 2.28) and a sign of the new Messianic era. From then on, the 12 dedicated themselves to the spreading of the Christian gospel to the world. Thus in the same way as the Jewish Pentecost is the fulfilment of the activity of God at Passover, the Christian Pentecost is the completion of the Easter story with the benefits of Jesus' resurrected life being poured out on to his followers. Just as the giving of the law on Mt Sinai marks the beginning of the Jewish religion, so the gift of the Holy Spirit initiates the spread of the Christian movement from Jerusalem 'to the ends of the earth' (Acts 1.8). The Christian Pentecost is popularly called Whitsunday and has been kept as a major Church festival since at least the 4th cent.

People of Israel *see* Israel

Peot *see* Ear-locks

Persecution *see* Martyrology

Pesah *see* Passover

Phylacteries

(Tephillin): The Book of Deuteronomy (6.8) commands that the laws should be bound 'as a sign upon your hand, and they shall be as frontlets between your eyes'. Phylacteries (tephillin) are small boxes that contain four biblical passages which adult male Jews bind on their arms and on their foreheads during the week-day services. The boxes are engraved with the Hebrew letter *shin*; the headstrap is tied with a knot in the shape of a *dalet* and the armstrap knot is like a *yad*. Thus the three letters, *shin, dalet, yad*, spell out one of God's names, *Shaddai*. The biblical passages are Exod. 13. 1–10, 11–16 and Deut. 6.4–9, 13–21, and the act of binding symbolizes being bound to the service of God. Because phylacteries were thought to have pagan origins, they were rejected by 19th-cent. Reformers, and until recently had no part in Reform liturgy. However, they have been taken up by some Jewish feminists on the grounds that a few women have worn tephillin in the past.

Phylacteries have no part in Christian worship and Matthew's Gospel records Jesus condemning the religious leaders of his day for their ostentatious flaunting of the phylacteries in order 'to be seen by men' (Matt. 23.5).

Pidyon Ha-Ben *see* Redemption of the first-born

Pilgrim festivals

According to Deut. 16.16, every male Jew is expected to make pilgrimage to Jerusalem three times a year on the festivals of Passover (Pesah), Weeks (Shavuot) and Tabernacles (Sukkot). All three feasts have both agricultural and historical significance. Passover celebrates the barley harvest and the liberation from Egyptian slavery; Weeks is the festival of the first fruits and the giving of the Torah on Mt Sinai; and Tabernacles is a harvest thanksgiving and a commemoration of the 40 years' wandering in the wilderness. Pilgrims were expected to offer sacrifice in the Temple, but, since 70 CE when the Temple was destroyed, special prayers and ceremonies are observed at home and in the synagogue.

Although the festivals of Passover and Weeks have been transformed by the Christian Church into Easter and Pentecost (Whitsunday) and most congregations observe a harvest celebration, none of them is regarded as a pilgrim festival. They are celebrated with various customs and liturgies, but there is no requirement to make regular pilgrimage. This may be because Christians, unlike Jews, do not regard themselves as a single nation, and therefore there is no need to meet in an earthly capital city. Although the whole Christian life is regarded by some as a pilgrimage, the ultimate destination is not in this world.

Pilgrimage

(*Aliyah*) (Holy Places): In ancient times, the Hebrew term *aliyah* (going up) has been used to refer to pilgrimage to Jerusalem for the three pilgrim festivals: 'Three times a year all your males shall appear before the Lord your God at the place which he will choose: at the feast of unleavened bread (Pesah), at the feast of weeks (Shavuot), and at the feast of booths (Sukkot)' (Deut. 16.16). During the time of the Judges, pilgrims went to Shiloh (1 Sam. 1.3), but after the Temple had been built in Jerusalem the Temple site became the focus of pilgrimage. The injunction to make pilgrimage was not construed as mandatory, yet multitudes descended on Jerusalem during these festivals. The pilgrims arrived in Jerusalem several days early and stayed either in the capital, in adjoining villages, or in tents erected in surrounding fields. During their sojourn, they engaged in the study of the Torah and participated in common festival meals.

In the second Temple period, thousands of pilgrims from within Israel as well as from the

Dispersion continued to make their way to the Temple at each of the three festivals. After the Temple was destroyed in 70CE, pilgrimages to Jerusalem continued, although the occasion was marked by sorrow, and this practice continued throughout the Middle Ages. After the Holy Land was conquered by Muslims under Saladin (12th cent.), Jews were allowed to visit holy places freely, and pilgrims came from Damascus, Babylonia, and Egypt. Following the expulsion of Jews from Spain in 1492, the number of pilgrims increased significantly. The most famous pilgrimage to the land of Israel by early Hasidic leaders was that of Nahman of Bratslav at the end of the 18th cent. In modern times, Moses Montefiore (19th cent.) made numerous journeys to the Holy Land, providing financial support for the Jewish settlement (*yishuv*). With the rise of Zionism, Jewish settlement in Palestine greatly increased and, after the State of Israel was founded, floods of Jews from throughout the world travelled to the Jewish homeland. Following the Six Day War and the unification of Jerusalem, the Western Wall of the Temple re-emerged as the focus of Jewish pilgrimage. (In addition, pilgrimages are made to the tomb of Simeon bar Yohai on the festival of *Lag Ba-Omer*, and on 14 Iyyar the tomb of Meir Baal Ha-Nes in Tiberius is also visited.)

From the 4th cent., Christian pilgrimage to Israel became an established institution. As the cradle of Christianity, the Holy Land was associated with the life of Jesus and the apostles. Nevertheless, Jerusalem was not conceived as the centre of Christianity as it was in Judaism. Rather, the city was interpreted in a symbolic, mystical sense. Many early Church Fathers discouraged pilgrimage but, in time, journeys to the Holy Land became an important feature of Christian life, and sites connected with the origin of Christianity, such as Bethlehem and Capernaum, were sanctified. During the Middle Ages, the Crusades were essentially a pilgrimage of armies intent on liberating holy places from the Muslims. In subsequent centuries to the present day, Christians have continued to travel to the land of Israel because of its religious associations.

Christians also made pilgrimages to other spiritual centres. For Western Christians, the journey to the East was exceedingly difficult, but since Rome was associated with Peter, Paul, and lesser saints, pilgrimages were frequently made there. Other popular shrines included St Martin at Tours, St James at Compostella, and St Thomas at Canterbury. During the 16th cent., the Protestant reformers discouraged this practice, but the growth of popular piety during the Counter-Reformation led to a revival of pilgrimage. In modern times, Lourdes has become a central place of pilgrimage, and the restoration of shrines to the Blessed Virgin Mother at Walsingham, England, has attracted numerous Anglicans, Roman Catholics, and Orthodox believers. In Christianity, then, the act of pilgrimage has been a central feature of the faith – primarily, it is conceived as an act of devotion to obtain supernatural help or as a means of expressing penance and thanksgiving. Within Judaism, on the other hand, the journey to Jerusalem was a biblically sanctioned commandment connected with the three pilgrim festivals, which was subsequently associated with historical memories and religious longing for the ancient Temple.

Pilpul *see* Casuistry

Pious

(Hasidim): In the Jewish faith, the term 'piety' refers to reverence for God with particular emphasis on the devout observance of the commandments. Hebrew terms used to describe the pious individual include *hasid* (the pious), *yere shamayim* (one who fears God), and *tsaddik* (the righteous). In the history of Judaism there were a number of groups who were known as Hasidim. During the second Temple period, such individuals (known as *Hasideans* from the Greek transliteration of the Hebrew Hasidim) appear to have joined the rebellion against Antiochus Epiphanes, and later joined the forces of Mattathias the Hasmonean. In the Midrash and the Talmud they are referred to as the Hasidim Rishonim (the early pietists). As a distinct group they disappeared during the Hasmonean period, but they seem to have influenced the Pharisees and the Essenes.

During the 12th–13th cent., a movement of Hasidim – the Hasidei Ashkenaz (the pious of Eastern European Jewry) – emerged in Germany. These individuals concentrated on the cultivation of inner piety through asceticism, humility, strict morality, and meticulous use of prayer formulae. Influenced by the literature of Jewish mystics of the Talmudic period, they believed that God manifested himself through his Glory (*Kvod*), and it is to this personification of Divine majesty that all anthropomorphic references in Scripture apply. The most important work of ethics to emerge from the school of these mystics was the *Sepher Hasidim* (The book of the Pious), written largely by Judah He-Hasid (12th–13th cent.). This work covers all aspects of a person's life – family relationships, education, the attitude towards non-Jews, prayer study, and social relationships.

In the 18th cent., a popular revivalist movement was founded by Israel ben Eliezer (known as the *Baal Shem Tov*) in Podolia. Initially the movement was a revolt against scholastic intellectualism, focusing instead on prayerful joy and intense religious enthusiasm. Guided by religious leaders known as *Tsaddikim* (the righteous), ordinary Jews were able to attain spiritual heights. According to Hasidic teaching, the *tsaddik* is a channel through which Divine grace flows. By observing the *tzaddik*, the believer can learn how God is to be worshipped. In Hasidism God is viewed as imminent throughout creation; Hasidim are thus to have God constantly in mind in everything they do. Although opposed by traditionalists, Hasidism spread throughout Eastern Europe and eventually became a world-wide religious community.

Parallel with the emergence of Hasidism, pietism arose among German Protestants in the 17th and 18th cent. as an alternative to the arid scholasticism of Lutheran Orthodoxy. Grounded in works of Lutheran mysticism, this movement was founded by Philipp Jakob Spener (17th–18th cent.), a Lutheran pastor at Frankfurt. In 1670 he established twice-weekly meetings of lay persons for Bible study. According to Spener, Lutheranism had ceased to be a living faith; in his *Pia Desideria* he urged devotional study of the Bible, the realization of the doctrine of the priesthood of all believers, emphasis on charitable aspects of Christianity, and the transformation of theological studies to encourage devotion to God.

Although pietism aroused considerable opposition (as did Hasidism in Judaism), its intense personalism and millenarian hope for the downfall of the papacy and the realization of God's Kingdom encouraged a series of revival movements.

Under Spener's disciple A. H. Francke (17th–18th cent.), the new University of Halle and Francke's Orphan House became focal points of mission and education. In time, the pietist movement served to encourage heterodox elements within the Enlightenment. Hostile to the confessional emphasis on doctrine, the movement encouraged practical experience and educational reform, and this attitude attracted numerous rationalist sympathizers. In various forms, pietism has continued into the present century, affecting a number of similar movements including Methodism. Thus in the modern period both Judaism and Christianity developed pietistic tendencies – though of a very different nature – in response to the aridity of religious intellectualism that sought to infuse new life into their respective traditions.

Platonism

Philosophical system based on the writings of Plato (4th cent. BCE). In Alexandria, Philo (1st cent. BCE–1st cent. CE) attempted to harmonize the Torah with Platonism by interpreting Scripture allegorically. In the Middle Ages, neo-Platonism, based on the writings of Plotinus (3rd cent.) and filtered through Islamic commentators, had a significant impact on Jewish thought. For a number of such writers, God was understood as the Form of the Good, the source of the intelligible world of ideas and the lower forms of being. According to Jewish neo-Platonists, the higher realm is the Throne of Glory to which the human soul longs to return. The goal of intellectual and contemplative activity is to bring about this reunification.

In the 9th–10th cent. Isaac Israeli argued that such ascent to the divine realm takes place through various stages, culminating in the angelic transformation of the soul. Similarly, Solomon ibn Gabirol (11th cent.) maintained that the end of human existence is the conjunction of the soul with the supernal world. The study of philosophy, he believed, offers liberation from death. In the late Middle Ages, Plato's *Republic* became known through the writings of the Arab philosopher Averroes. In the 14th cent., the *Republic* was translated into Hebrew by Samuel ben Judah of Marseilles and had an important impact on Jewish philosophy.

In the 15th cent., Judah Abravanel wrote a philosophical work, *Dialoghi di Amore*, modelled on the Platonic dialogues in which God is identified as love. Two centuries later Moses Mendelssohn explored the immortality of the soul in his *Phaedon*, which was based on Platonic thought. Alongside this philosophical development, neo-Platonism also exerted a powerful impact on Jewish mystical speculation, particularly kabbalistic (mystical) thought in the 13th cent.

Plato's dialogues were also of special interest to Christian theologians. A number of writers appealed to Plato for evidence of God as the Logos, the heavenly realm, creation, free will, final judgement, and the immortality of the soul. For Clement of Alexandria (2nd–3rd cent.) and Origen (2nd–3rd cent.), control of the body and its passions could be gained by cultivation of the mind. Thus secular studies, philosophy and the study of the Bible were espoused to encourage meditation on moral and spiritual ideas. In the 4th cent., Methodius of Olympus wrote a work, *Banquet of the Ten Virgins*, modelled on Plato's *Symposium*. Eusebius (4th cent.) collected Platonic texts to support Christian doctrine, and in the same century Gregory of Nyssa provided a manual of theology, *Sermo Catecheticus*, which influenced the views of Plato.

The works of the neo-Platonist Plotinus influenced a number of Christians such as Augustine (4th–5th cent.). It was Plato's works that convinced him that there is a non-spatial, eternal reality. He criticized Platonists, however, for ignoring the incarnation, the doctrines of the resurrection of the body, and subscribing to a belief in reincarnation. In his writings, Dionysius the Aeropagite imitated the triadic theology of the later Platonists. During the Middle Ages, Plato's works were lost, apart from a Latin version of the *Timaeus*. Nonetheless, the thought of Augustine and Dionysius continued to have an impact on Christian thought. In the 16th cent., Platonic scholarship revived in England, and later influenced the Cambridge Platonists. In the modern period, however, Platonism has ceased to exert an important influence on Christian thinking. Thus through the ages, the writings of Plato, as translated and interpreted by various writers, exerted an important influence on the development of theology in both Judaism and Christianity.

Pointer

(*Yad*): Because of its great sanctity, Jews are forbidden to touch the Torah scroll, and a pointer (*yad*, literally 'hand' in Hebrew) is used to keep the place while reading the weekly portion. It generally takes the form of a rod ending with a pointing hand, and it is usually hung on a chain from one of the Scroll rollers. Pointers have been in use since the 16th cent., and they are often highly artistic objects. Among the Sephardim (Oriental Jews), the fringes of prayer shawls are also used to point to the text. Pointers are not normally used when reading from the Bible in Christian churches, and there is no prohibition against touching the printed text. The reverence that Jews feel for the Torah is more likely to be held by Christians for the consecrated bread and wine of the Eucharist.

Polygamy *see* Marriage

Prayer

(Amen) (Worship): The Bible contains a wide variety of prayers of an impromptu and formalized nature. Initially, prayers were not stipulated for regular worship but, until the destruction of the second Temple, prayer was institutionalized through sacrifices and offerings. During the Babylonian exile, communal prayer in synagogues took the place of sacrifice and, after 70CE (when the second Temple was destroyed), the rabbis regularized daily prayer services. The set formula of worship is traditionally attributed to the Men of the Great Assembly, and congregational prayer expanded to include the morning benedictions, the Shema ('Hear O Israel') and its accompanying blessings, the *Amidah*, and the reading of the law. In addition, a liturgical pattern for daily, Sabbath and holiday worship was established. Through the ages, other prayers were added to the formal worship service. A quorum (minyan) of 10 male adults is required for the recitation of the *Berekhu*, *Kaddish*, and *Amidah* prayers (as well as other statutory liturgies); without this number, these elements of the worship service must be omitted.

The tradition asserts that it is vital to attain the correct frame of mind (kavvanah) while praying. Thus Moses Maimonides (12th cent.) maintained that prayer without devotion is no prayer at all. According to medieval mystics, such devotions (*kavvanot*) were identified as meditations on the divine mysteries that are hidden in the liturgy. From the 18th cent. Hasidim have regarded prayer as a central religious dimension through which communion with God can be attained. During the same period, Reform Judaism altered sections of the liturgy that were viewed as anachronistic, irrelevant or religiously unacceptable (such as prayers for the restoration of the sacrificial system and the return to Zion). This process of liturgical revision has also been undertaken by other non-Orthodox movements as well as by Jewish feminists.

In the New Testament, the early Church was a worshipping community. Arising out of Jewish traditions in the Temple and the synagogue, many forms of prayer were taken over by Christians (such as the blessing of God as Creator and Sustainer of life, and the response 'Amen' meaning 'so be it'). Yet these forms were infused with new meaning relating to God's saving purposes in Christ. Christians in the apostolic period believed they were living in the time of eschatological fulfilment, and this conviction shaped all aspects of Christian worship. Thus prayers were offered in Jesus' name, hymns were sung in his honour, and the characteristic liturgical act was the solemn meal of bread and wine taken in remembrance of him. In addition, the shift from the Jewish Sabbath to the eighth day of the new creation was made in recognition that Jesus rose from the dead on Sunday. The Jewish rite of baptism was also transformed in Christianity to become a symbolic act of purification and renewal into the new covenant.

From the earliest times, Christians gathered in churches or in improvised surroundings for prayer. In most corporate acts of Christian worship, a number of common features are found: (1) a preparation consisting of a general confession of sin (often followed by a declaration of absolution); (2) the ministry of the word – the reading of scriptural lessons and the sermon; (3) the singing of psalms or hymns, and (4) prayers of intercession. In many Christian communities these acts of devotion are followed by a celebration of the Lord's Supper (known as 'Holy Communion', 'Mass', 'Eucharist'). In addition, there are other forms of worship designed for special occasions (such as baptism, marriage, and burial). In both faiths, then, worship is seen as fundamental to the religious life.

Rooted in biblical traditions in the Temple and the synagogue, both Judaism and Christianity have sought through prayer to provide for the ordinary believer access to God's presence.

Prayer books

(Siddur): Written prayer books did not appear until relatively late in the history of Judaism. Prayers were memorized and handed down from generation to generation. The first prayer book was compiled by Amram Gaon in the 9th cent. and contained the statutory prayers for the whole year and reflected the customs of Spanish Jewry. Another siddur (prayer book) was produced by Saadiah Gaon in the 10th cent. for the Jews of Egypt, and the *Mahzor Vitry* (The Cycle of Prayers from Vitry) of the 11th cent. was a record of the French rite. Once printing was invented in the 15th cent., prayer books became available for every individual Jew. The *Siddur Katan* (small prayer order) published by Nathan Soncino in 1486 reflects the Italian practice, and the first Ashkenazi (Eastern European) prayer book was printed in 1512 in Prague. The prayer books contain the regular synagogue services for week-days, Sabbaths, and festivals, as well as prayers for use at home. In addition, liturgical poetry (*piyyutim*), benedictions, songs (*zemirot*), psalms, and penitential prayers (*selihot*) are included. Different communities still use different prayer books; the non-Orthodox movements in particular have made various changes to the traditional services, translating the Hebrew into the vernacular and altering the prayers in accordance with modern sentiments. Various creative liturgies have also been produced in recent years for experimental settings, including inter-faith services. A number of Jewish feminists have also produced alternative prayer services.

The missal that contained the liturgy for the celebration of the Eucharist in the Western Church throughout the year appeared first in the 10th cent. The breviary, which recorded all the prayers, hymns, readings, and psalms to be included in the Western Divine Office, appeared in the 11th cent. The eight daily services were formalized and the annual pattern of prayers and readings was set. The breviary was reformed in 1568; a new breviary was issued in 1911, and another was produced in 1971 after the Second Vatican Council. The Protestant reformers produced their own prayer books which reflected their theology, the most famous in the English world being the Book of Common Prayer which was finally completed in 1662. It has since been revised in 1929, and revised service books have been produced periodically from 1965. It is notable that traditional Christian prayer books are essentially for use in church. Unlike the Jewish community, literacy was not widespread among Christians until the 19th cent., and home prayers tended to be restricted to a few well-known liturgical prayers such as the 'Our Father' and individual extempore prayers. Since the middle of this century, as in Judaism, there has been a move within the churches towards creative liturgies, and there is a free borrowing of prayers from other denominations – and even other traditions as appropriate.

Prayer shawl

(Tallith): According to Num. 15.38, Jewish males are commanded to put fringes on their garments. Orthodox Jews fulfil this commandment in two ways: first, by wearing fringes (tallith Katan or *tsitsit*) on an undergarment, and secondly by wearing a prayer shawl (*tallit gadol*) in the synagogue during morning service, on the afternoon of 9 Av, and for all the services on the Day of Atonement. It is also always worn when reading from the Scroll of the law. The prayer shawl is generally made of wool or silk with fringes of the same material. It should be large enough to cover the head and upper body, and a special blessing is said before it is put on.

Lay Christians do not wear special clothing for prayer, but clergy often put on distinctive garments. In particular, a stole is often worn, which is a long narrow strip of silk. It is worn by deacons over the left shoulder and fastened under the right arm. Priests wear it round the neck with the ends falling straight in front. It is used when the Eucharist is celebrated, when the consecrated bread and wine is touched, when administering the other sacraments, and when preaching. Thus, in both traditions, it is felt necessary for the celebrants at a sacred service to don a special vestment which separates them from their everyday activities.

Preaching *see* Sermon

Predestination *see* Providence

Pre-existence

In rabbinic literature there are frequent references to the Torah as pre-existent, dwelling in heaven prior to creation. This view is based on Prov. 8.22–31 concerning the personification of Wisdom: 'The Lord created me at the beginning of his work, the first of his acts of old. Ages ago I was set up, at the first, before the beginning of the earth' (Prov. 8.22–23). In the Midrash, the Torah is viewed as the blueprint of the universe which God consulted in creating the world. For Philo (1st cent. BCE – 1st cent. CE) and others influenced by Platonic thought, such doctrines were based on Plato's conviction that ultimate reality consists of the world of ideas of which the sensible world is merely a reflection. In kabbalistic (mystical) literature, the theory that the Torah was pre-existent was related to the doctrine of divine emanation. Some kabbalists also maintained that the entire Torah is made up of names of God, and that these letters can be reordered to produce other divine names. This doctrine provided the basis for discovering hidden meanings in Scripture.

For Christians it is not the Torah, but Christ himself, who is pre-existent. Thus in Phil. Paul wrote: 'who, though he was in the form of God, did not count equality with God a thing to be grasped, but emptied himself, taking the form of a servant, being born in the likeness of men' (Phil. 2.5–7). Again, the author of Col. asserted: 'He is the image of the invisible God, the first-born of all creation; for in him all things were created, in heaven and on earth, visible and invisible . . . He is before all things, and in him all things hold together' (Col. 1.15–17). Similarly, the writer of the Fourth Gospel declared: 'In the beginning was the Word, and the Word was with God, and the Word was God. He was in the beginning with God . . .' (John 1.1–2). The early Church Fathers developed this doctrine up to the time of the Arian controversy (4th cent.). The theory of pre-existence was supported by Arians since a pre-existent being in history relieved God of direct involvement in human affairs. In response to this heretical view, most writers abandoned any attempt to trace the activity of the pre-existent Christ in biblical history. In modern times, the Logos doctrine has been used by a number of theologians in explaining the nature of the incarnation. In both faiths, then, the concept of pre-existence was utilized to serve very different ends. For Jews, the pre-existence of the Torah highlighted the eternal significance of God's revealed Law, whereas for Christians the pre-existence of Christ was seen as indicating Jesus' cosmic importance.

Presence of God *see* Theophany

Priesthood

(*Cohen*): In biblical times, priests, who were male descendants of Aaron, were responsible for the sacrificial system. In addition, they were to be teachers of the people. Four special garments were worn by priests, consisting of a tunic, sash, headdress, and breeches. Four others were also worn by the High Priest: the ephod (over-tunic), the breastplate, the robe of the ephod, and the plate (crown) hanging in front of the mitre (turban). During the period of the first Temple, High Priests were anointed with oil and had a status similar to the king.

Since the priests did not own land, they were dependent on gifts from the people. Each Israelite was obligated to give a fraction of his crop as a sacred donation. This offering (*terumah*) could only be eaten by the priest and his immediate family. Priests were also given parts of the meat of certain sacrifices, meal offerings, the first shearing of the wool, the first-born of the flock, and part of any dough that had been kneaded. The priests were organized into 24 divisions, each of which served in the Temple for a week at a time. Their duties included the daily sacrifices each morning and evening, taking care of the lamp (menorah), the burning of incense, and examining those suspected of leprosy.

According to biblical law, a priest (*cohen*) is forbidden to marry a divorcee, a harlot, a woman who has undergone the ceremony exempting her from Levirate marriage (*halitsah*), or a proselyte. If such a marriage takes place, the sons of the union are disqualified from the priesthood. Priests are also not allowed to come into contact with the dead; only in the case of the deaths of any of seven close relatives (the priest's father, mother, brother, never-married sister, son, daughter, and wife) may a priest become ritually impure.

Since the destruction of the second Temple in AD 70, sacrifice has ceased and, as a result, priests were no longer needed in a cultic context. Nonetheless, the priesthood as a hereditary position has continued to the present day, and rabbinic law continues to require such individuals to be shown a certain degree of respect. Although they have no formal duties and nowadays the knowledge of their descent is largely based on folk memory, a priest should be the first person called to the reading of the law and, if a priest is present, he should be invited to lead the grace after meals. Priests also have a special role in the ceremony of the redemption of the first-born and in blessing the people. Within Reform Judaism, however, the rules and restrictions relating to priests have been abolished. The duty of leading a congregation now falls to the rabbis (teachers), and every household head is responsible for officiating at the home ceremonies.

In the New Testament, the biblical concept of the priesthood was transformed in line with the message of the gospel. In the epistle to the Hebrews, Jesus is viewed as the High Priest: 'So also Christ did not exalt himself to be made a high priest, but was appointed by him who said to him: "Thou art my Son, today I have begotten thee . . . ; Thou art a priest for ever, after the order of Melchizedek"' (Heb. 5.5, 10). Through his own sacrifice, Jesus reconciled God to humankind, and in this sacrifice Christ is both priest and victim. According to the Church, a Christian priesthood was implied in his teaching, particularly in relation to the Eucharist.

Nonetheless, it was not until the 2nd cent. that the term 'priest' was applied to Christian ministers. Initially, only bishops were referred to in this way, but, with the spread of Christianity, presbyters (elders) adopted more fully the priestly functions of a bishop. A letter of Innocent I sent to Decentius in the 5th cent. specified that in towns the Eucharist is to be consecrated only by the bishop and sent to parish priests, but in outlying districts the priests are to consecrate it themselves. In time, the parish priest came to be the normal celebrant of the Eucharist and was invested with the power to pronounce absolution.

In the Middle Ages, the priesthood of the clergy was understood almost exclusively in relation to the Mass. During the Reformation, however, this view was rejected by reformers who repudiated the idea that the Eucharist was a re-enaction of the sacrifice offered on Calvary. In place of the term 'priest', 'minister' was generally used to refer to religious leaders (with the exception of the Church of England where the title 'priest' was retained for traditional reasons as well as to emphasize that deacons have no authority to celebrate Holy Communion). In both faiths, then, the institution of the priesthood occupies a central role in the religious life of the people. The concept of the hereditary priesthood in biblical Judaism was reformulated in Christianity, and linked to the celebration of the sacrificial death of Christ as commemorated through the Eucharist. In Judaism, on the other hand, the role of the priesthood has receded in significance as cultic sacrifice disappeared, and in practical terms the rabbinate has taken its place.

Principles of *see* Creeds

Profanation of God's name

(Blasphemy): Taking God's name in vain is forbidden by the third commandment (Exod. 20.7) and, according to Lev. 24.10–16, anyone who blasphemes the name of God should be put to death. In fact, by the time the Mishnah was compiled (3rd cent.), capital punishment was only employed for profanation of the tetragrammaton and, since it had to be confirmed by two witnesses, it was hard to prove. Once the community lost the political power to inflict the death penalty, the usual punishment was excommunication (*herem*). Nonetheless, the rabbis regarded blasphemy as a serious sin, and even Gentiles who were outside Jewish law were expected to avoid it if they wanted to inherit the world-to-come.

Jesus described blasphemy against the Holy Spirit (Matt. 12.31–32) as the unforgivable sin, and the Church has continued the Jewish tradition of deploring any form of insult to God. Blasphemy was made a capital offence at the Council of Aachen in 818CE, and in many countries it remained a serious crime. In the Middle Ages, in particular, Christians often accused Jews of blasphemy, and used the accusation as an excuse for popular programmes against them. However, in post-Enlightenment society, blasphemy ceased to be punishable as an offence against God; rather, it was seen as destructive of good social order and as such was regarded far less seriously.

Promised land *see* Israel

Prophecy

In biblical times, prophets were charismatic figures who were able to receive and communicate messages revealed to them by God. A number of prophets were reluctant to take on this role (such as Moses, Jeremiah, and Jonah), yet the prophet was obligated to serve as God's spokesman. Frequently, prophets prefaced their utterances with the expression, 'Thus says the Lord'. The second section of the Hebrew Scriptures is called *Neviim* (Prophets). The first part of this is referred to as 'Former Prophets' consisting of the Books of Joshua, Judges, Samuel and Kings; these historical works contain accounts of the pre-classical prophets, including Nathan, Elijah, and Elisha. The second part – the 'Later Prophets' – consists of the Books of the three Major Prophets (Isaiah, Jeremiah, and Ezekiel), and the 12 Minor Prophets (Hosea, Joel, Amos, Obadiah, Jonah, Micah, Nahum, Habakkuk, Zephaniah, Haggai, Zechariah, and Malachi).

The early prophets were sometimes referred to as 'seers'. During the period up to the 8th cent. BCE, there were schools of prophets who gathered together to engage in prophetic experience. Thus 1 Sam. records: 'When they came to Gibeah, behold, a band of prophets met him; and the spirit of God came mightily upon him [Saul], and he prophesied among them' (1 Sam. 10.10). Some of the pre-classical prophets criticized the rulers for their iniquity. For example, Nathan rebuked David for his wrongdoing in the matter of Bathsheba (2 Sam. 12), and Elijah condemned Ahab for the murder of Naboth and the confiscation of his vineyard (1 Kings 21).

The period of classical prophecy extended from Amos to Malachi (mid-9th–mid-5th cent. BCE). Coming from all sectors of society, these prophets reproved the leaders of the nation, and as a result were sometimes persecuted and subjected to hardship. Often they employed symbolic acts to illustrate their message. Although the prophets accepted the Temple cult, their criticisms were directed at those who were meticulous in performing ritual but failed to live up to the moral law. According to tradition, prophecy ceased after the time of Haggai, Zechariah, and Malachi.

In the Middle Ages, Jewish philosophers gave two different explanations to the phenomenon of prophecy. Rationalistic thinkers (such as Abraham ibn Daud (12th cent.), Maimonides (12th cent.), and Gersonides (13th–14th cent.)) argued that a prophet was endowed with perfection of reason, imagination, and moral character. Inspired by the Active Intellect, the faculties of reason and imagination were activated, culminating in prophetic experience. Other writers such as Judah Ha-Levi (11th–12th cent.) and Hasdai Crescas (14th–15th cent.) maintained that prophecy is a divine supernatural gift. The intellectual qualifications of a prophet are thus irrelevant.

In the New Testament, the concept of prophecy is rooted in the Hebrew Scriptures, but is also related to Jesus, his proclamation of God's Kingdom, and his triumph over the power of evil. Throughout his ministry Jesus saw himself as fulfilling biblical prophecy, and similarly the evangelists believed that in his life he fulfilled the traditional prophecies about the coming of the Messiah. According to Acts, after Pentecost the apostles saw the realization of biblical passages in Christ's resurrection, ascension, and coming of the Holy Spirit (Acts 2). Paul in his epistles also reminded Christian communities that Christ died for sin in accordance with Scriptures (1 Cor. 15.3). In Christian literature from the Church Fathers onward, a similar appeal was made to prophecy in the Hebrew Scriptures to demonstrate the truth of the gospel.

In the early Church there appears to have been a special group of 'prophets'. Thus Paul wrote: 'And God has appointed in the church first apostles, second prophets, third teachers' (1 Cor. 12.28). Paul here appears to place great emphasis on the gift of prophecy, involving the knowledge and communication of spiritual truth. Such utterances in all likelihood consisted of edifying discourses.

In the *Didache*, the Church is admonished to respect prophetic figures as long as they are not false prophets, and such writers as Justin Martyr (2nd cent.) discussed the problem of false prophecy. With the emergence of Montanism also in the 2nd cent., the Church began to distinguish between prophetic insights that conflict with the tradition as received from the apostles and those prophecies that are contained in Scripture. By the 3rd cent., the term 'prophecy' was limited to the prophetic portions of Scripture, and teachers took the place of prophets within the Church. As catechists and apologists, such teachers attacked false doctrine and supported the exposition of the true faith by appealing to Scripture. Yet despite this development, a number of Christians through the ages have claimed prophetic inspiration including contemporary Pentecostalists. Christianity has thus embraced the biblical concept of prophecy, extending its scope to include Christ's redeeming activity and the teaching of early Christian evangelists. Judaism, however, has insisted that prophetic inspiration ended with the post-exilic prophets.

Protestantism *see* Reform movements

Providence

(Fate) (Predestination): According to the Bible, human beings have been given freedom of the will despite the fact that God is viewed as involved in human history. Thus in the Garden of Eden Adam and Eve are instructed not to eat forbidden fruit: 'You may freely eat of every tree of the garden; but of the tree of the knowledge of good and evil you shall not eat, for in the day that you eat of it you shall die' (Gen. 2.16–17). When they disobeyed this decree, God punished them for their sinfulness. In Deut., Moses continually encouraged the people to choose good rather than evil: 'See, I have set before you this day life and good, death and evil' (Deut. 30.15). In line with this view, medieval theologians maintained that human beings have the capacity to act freely.

Nonetheless, the Bible attests to God's participation in human affairs. In Scripture, God's creative activity is described in detail. There is, for example, God's creative and sustaining activity as he upholds humanity and the world. Further, the Bible frequently depicts God's action through the natural order (general providence). In addition, God is depicted as speaking through a prophet or working through some specific action (special providence). Finally, there is what came to be called 'miracles', actions that defy any purely natural explanation. Some Jewish thinkers argued that Divine providence is exercised over animal and plant life as well as human history; other thinkers subscribed to the view that God's providence relates only to human affairs; a few writers believed that providential care governs the destiny of humanity as a whole, rather than the lives of individual persons.

Despite such divergent interpretations, the Jewish liturgy for the New Year and the Day of Atonement contains the *Un-Netanneh Tokef* prayer which states: 'On the New Year it is decreed and on the Day of Atonement it is sealed who shall live and who shall die . . .' This belief in divine predestination has given rise to a number of philosophical perplexities. If God knows what human beings will do in the future, how can they have free will? Again, if all things happen according to God's decree, how is it possible to account for the fact that the wicked prosper and the righteous suffer? To escape from these difficulties, a number of medieval theologians limited divine providence so as to allow for human responsibility; others asserted that the righteous and the wicked will be rewarded and punished in an afterlife. In the modern period, it has been widely recognized that human beings are influenced by heredity and environment. Nevertheless, the Jewish faith has continued to affirm the reality of human freedom along with the religious conviction that God is concerned with the fate of all.

Following biblical teaching, Jesus claimed that God cares for his children (Matt. 10.29–31), answers prayers (Luke 11.9–13), forgives sins (Matt. 6.14–15), and calls human beings to eternal life (John 6.40). In the writings of the early Church Fathers the term 'divine providence' was used to express the sense of God's fatherly love and care. In time, it came to denote God's plan for creation. Thus in the *City of God*, Augustine (4th–5th cent.) wrote: 'Divine Providence alone explains the establishment of human kingdoms.' He believed that predestination was linked to the conception of Divine providence and taught that God foreknows the gifts he decides to confer on those predestined for salvation: 'This and nothing else is the predestination of the saints, God's foreknowledge and preparation of his benefits whereby whoever is liberated is most certainly liberated. The whole human race is condemned to eternal punishment because of Adam's fall, yet God freely chooses some individuals by his gracious benefits and predestines them to eternal life.'

In the 7th–9th cent., John Damascene distinguished between the antecedent and consequent will of God. The antecedent intends and makes possible salvation for everyone; the consequent condemns those who remain unrepentant. The consequent plan is thus that aspect of God's antecedent plan which he puts into operation in view of human free choice. In the 13th cent., Thomas Aquinas described providence as the order of the world as this order pre-exists in the mind of God who causes it. Like John Damascene, he subscribed to a form of contingency planning in which human freedom cancels out God's antecedent plan.

The Protestant reformers adopted Augustine's teaching about predestination. Thus John Calvin (16th cent.) wrote: 'Predestination we call the eternal decree of God, by which He has determined in Himself what He would have become of every human individual. For they are not all created with a similar destiny; but eternal life is foreordained for some and eternal damnation for others.' Modern Christian thinkers have similarly struggled to make sense of providence and the possibility of human freedom. In Christianity, then, as in Judaism, the belief in divine providence poses numerous theological and philosophical difficulties. In different ways, both Jewish and Christian thinkers have attempted to reconcile the conception of an infallible, all-knowing Deity with the belief that human beings have free choice.

Psalms

The biblical Book of Psalms contains 150 sacred poems. The word 'psalm' comes from the Greek for a stringed instrument; the Hebrew title is *Tehillim* (meaning 'hymns of praise'). Traditionally, many of the psalms are ascribed to King David (11th–10th cent. BCE), and they were used as part of the Jewish liturgy by the time of the second Temple (5th cent. BCE). Technical instructions survive that illustrate that individual psalms were used in Temple worship. For example, the Song of Ascents (Ps. 120–134) may refer to the fact that they were performed on the steps between the women's and men's court. The impact of psalms on Jewish religious thought has been enormous, and they were taken over by the Church for use in Christian services. Psalms such as number 23 ('The Lord is my shepherd'), 121 ('I lift up my eyes to the hills'), and 137 ('By the waters of Babylon') are well known to every practising Christian or Jew, and are universally acknowledged to be a part of a shared cultural heritage. The influence of the psalms owes much to their spirit of unshakeable trust in God's grace and love, whatever suffering or adversity may be found in human history.

Pulpit *see* Dais

Punishment

(Retribution): According to biblical law, a wide range of penalties are prescribed for those who transgress the law. The central purpose of such punishments is to purge evil from the midst of the people (Deut. 17.7). This action is not so much directed against the offender, but is a demonstration of disapproval. By legislating judicial punishment, such conduct is condemned. Punishment is thereby inflicted on the offender not so much for his own sake, but to deter others. Thus Deut. 21.22 decrees that an offender should be impaled on a stake after having been put to death so as to proclaim the execution. In addition, Jewish law sought to ensure that the individual offender would be prevented from committing further crimes. Finally, punishment was executed to bring about the restoration of the status quo by inflicting on the criminal the same injury as he had caused.

Capital punishment was prescribed for a series of crimes including kidnapping, murder, idolatry, desecration of the Sabbath, blasphemy, adultery, incest and other sexual offences. Two forms of capital punishment are mentioned in Scripture: stoning and burning. In Talmudic times (2nd–5th cent. CE), two additional forms of execution – slaying by a sword and strangling – were added. Nonetheless, Talmudic law severely circumscribed the court's ability to convict those accused of criminal offences. Capital crimes can only be tried by a court of 23; conviction can only be obtained on the testimony of two eye-witnesses; circumstantial evidence and hearsay are inadmissible; witnesses related to each other or the accused by blood or marriage are disqualified; and conviction can not be made unless the accused has been warned in advance.

The Bible also prescribes flogging as a punishment for transgression of a negative biblical command, as well as for a person who refuses to fulfil a positive commandment. A maximum of 40 lashes is stipulated (which the rabbis expected to be no more than 39). In Talmudic times, sages levied fines as a substitute for penalties prescribed by Scripture. The court could also confiscate property as a means of ensuring compliance with the law. Although imprisonment was not decreed by Scripture, a person could be held in custody until the court could ascertain punishment. Rabbinic courts were also able to excommunicate those who gravely violated Jewish law or failed to comply with the decrees of local rabbis.

In New Testament times, the Jewish view of punishment was widely accepted, and capital punishment appears to have been accepted as legitimate by the Church. Thus Paul in Rom. 13 seems to recognize its validity. In the 3rd–4th cent., Lactantius was one of the few Church Fathers to oppose it, and he was subsequently followed by a minority within the Church. As in Judaism, corporal punishment was also accepted as a valid penalty for transgression, and flogging was inflicted for such crimes as robbery with violence and sexual assault. Since the Church acknowledged that civil government was a necessary institution for society, the structures for punishing transgressors were embraced by the Church. From the time of Constantine (4th cent.) through the Middle Ages, Church and State were united into one commonwealth; the distinction between them was to be seen largely in their separate hierarchies and the systems of law they administered. After the schism between East and West, there were essentially two commonwealths of this kind, and at the Reformation the Western Church was divided into a variety of national Churches; yet there was a common acceptance throughout Christendom of the validity of civil legislation, and this attitude has endured to the present day.

Nonetheless, in modern times a number of Christians have expressed serious reservations about various aspects of punishment. Regarding capital punishment, some critics have argued that there is no substantial evidence to demonstrate that this form of punishment actually deters offenders. Further, if reformation is seen as a crucial justification for inflicting punishment, the death penalty does not allow for such change of heart to occur. Also, many Christians are critical of the concept of retribution in view of Christian teaching on forgiveness, and thus capital punishment cannot be justified on this count either. If crime is a sickness to be cured rather than punished, therapy rather than judicial proceedings are required. Corporal punishment as well as other forms of civil penalties are also attacked by a number of Christians along similar lines. Nevertheless, despite this shift away from the traditional understanding of punishment for transgression, Christianity has generally adopted a similar view to Judaism regarding the necessity of penalties in a civilized society. For both faiths, it is essential that the community is protected from crime, and that wrongdoers are brought to judgement.

Purgatory

The rabbis taught that the righteous would have a place in the world-to-come, while the wicked would be punished in *Gehinnom* (hell). This punishment has been interpreted in various ways; the Talmud has some graphic descriptions of the tortures that take place, while Moses Maimonides (12th cent.) interpreted *Gehinnom* as the denial of eternal life. However, the mystical text the Zohar (13th cent.) described *Gehinnom* as a place where the soul was purged of its evil. This is not dissimilar to the idea of purgatory, but speculation about the afterlife has never been very prominent in Judaism.

In contrast, both the Eastern and Western Churches have taught that those who have died in the grace of God, but have not fully expiated their sins, are sent to purgatory. Their sufferings can be alleviated through Christian prayer and almsgiving. Over the years, the doctrine developed and was officially defined in the Roman Catholic Church at the Councils of Lyons (1274) and Florence (1439). However, the idea of purgatory was rejected by the Protestant reformers, who argued that salvation is only available through faith in Christ; any work is irrelevant, and there is thus no point in expiation either in this life or the next. Prayers for the dead are seen as valueless. In recent times, with increased secularization, there has been less conjecture about the nature of the hereafter, but purgatory remains an official dogma of the Roman Catholic Church.

Purification, ritual *see* Purity

Purim *see* Lots, festival of

Purity

(Purification Ritual): In the Bible, a person had to be ritually pure in order to participate in the Temple ritual, and the same applied to any utensil used in such a context. One who becomes impure must wait a prescribed period of time, bathe in a ritual bath (*mikveh*), and offer sacrifice. The primary sources of such uncleanliness are contact with dead bodies, leprosy, and issues from sexual organs.

Contact with a dead body (or even being in the presence of a corpse) can be purified by the person being sent out for seven days, immersing in a *mikveh*, and then being sprinkled by a priest with the ashes of the Red Heifer mixed with water. Impurity brought about by leprosy was to be diagnosed by a priest. Purification in such cases was achieved by the priest sprinkling on him the blood of a bird sacrifice mixed with water. Afterwards, the person was to immerse in a *mikveh*, wash his clothes, shave off his hair, and offer sacrifices.

With regard to impurities caused by an issue from sexual organs, a woman is regarded as impure during her menstrual cycle. She must not engage in marital relations, and she can transfer her uncleanliness to others as well as material objects. Purification is achieved by waiting seven days after the cessation of bleeding, and then bathing in a *mikveh*. Other impurities from sexual discharge require waiting either until evening or for seven days, offering a sacrifice, and immersing in a *mikveh*. It was also possible for inanimate objects as well as food to become unclean. With the destruction of the Temple, ritual purity connected with the Temple cult ceased to be relevant; however, the concept of purity retained its importance and Orthodox Jews still bathe in a *mikveh* to rid themselves of impurity. In modern times, the whole category has been rejected by the Reform Movement.

In the Christian Church, biblical legislation regarding ritual purity was set aside. In place of the Temple cult, the Church envisaged Jesus' death as the ultimate sacrifice. He is the paschal lamb, and the community of Christians is the new Temple. His sacrifice is a free gift that is offered independently of the ritual worthiness of the recipient. Thus although Christian faith is rooted in biblical

Judaism, Christians have felt at liberty to reject those aspects of the tradition that had ceased to retain spiritual significance in the light of Jesus' life, death, and resurrection.

R

Rabbinate

From approximately the 2nd cent. BCE, the title 'rabbi' (my teacher) was used as an expression of respect; in the 1st cent., it became the title of ordained members of the Sanhedrin (Great Assembly). The ceremony of ordination (*semikhah*) could take place only in the land of Israel; in Babylonia, the more limited title of *rav* was used instead. Although such ordination ceased in the 4th cent., the title 'rabbi' continued to be used to designate an individual who was expert in Jewish law, and a limited form of ordination emerged primarily among Ashkenazi (Eastern European) communities. Examinations for candidates for the rabbinate were supervised either by authoritative rabbis or yeshivot (rabbinical academies).

Through the centuries, rabbis served communities on a voluntary basis but, from the 15th cent., the rabbinate became a paid profession. Preeminent among the rabbi's duties were to give decisions in matters of Jewish law, head a yeshivah (rabbinical academy), and supervise ritual slaughter and the *mikveh* (ritual bath). Generally, he also preached sermons on Sabbaths preceding Passover and the Day of Atonement. It was often the case that the rabbi of major communities exercised jurisdiction over a larger area, and in some communities chief rabbis were appointed.

The Enlightenment in the 18th cent. constituted a major challenge to the traditional role of the rabbi. Jewish communities in Eastern Europe were largely unaffected by these changes, and yeshivot continued to flourish in the traditional manner. However, in neo-Orthodox communities, rabbis felt impelled to acquire secular knowledge in addition to Jewish learning, and a number of seminaries were established to meet this need. In Western Europe and the USA, non-Orthodox movements developed their own seminaries and rabbinical associations with different standards of rabbinic training and practice. As a result of these developments, the role of the rabbi came to resemble that of Christian ministers, and across the Jewish religious spectrum modern rabbis have come to be responsible for religious, pastoral, educational, social, and inter-faith activities of their congregations.

In the New Testament, Jesus is referred to as 'rabbi' ('Jesus turned, and saw them following, and said to them, "What do you seek?" And they said to him, "Rabbi" (which means teacher), "where are you staying?"' John 1.38), but this term was in all likelihood used simply to express respect. For the early Church, Christ was conceived as the minister par excellence, and the Christian ministry was modelled on his example. A minister was ordained to serve his congregation, to provide an example of moral rectitude and spiritual leadership. In time, three main orders developed in the Church (bishop, priest, and deacon), and this tripartite form has been retained by the traditional episcopal Churches. In the West since the 16th cent., several other types of leadership have emerged as well.

Candidates for the ministry are ordained and thereby established in ministries of service and leadership. In Churches that have a prescribed episcopacy, the orders of deacon, priest, and bishop are conferred through a bishop. Other orders of ministry are usually assigned through a local overseer or governing body. Traditionally, those who have been ordained are viewed as called by God and commissioned to serve the community as a whole. In the Roman Catholic and Eastern Orthodox Church, only those who have been ordained may exercise certain ministries, especially the celebration of the Eucharist. In Reformation theology, on the other hand, such special ministries are not absolutely restricted. Thus ministry in Christianity, though shaped by the biblical concept of assigning leadership, is far removed from the institution of the rabbinate. Whereas rabbis through the ages have acted as scholars and teachers, Christian ministers have primarily modelled themselves on Christ's example of service and spirituality. In contemporary society, the role of the rabbi and the Christian minister share many common features, but traditionally there is a profound difference in their self-understanding.

Rabbinical law *see* Law

Racism

(Anti-Semitism): Anti-Jewish attitudes were prevalent in classical times, but with the advent of Christianity anti-Semitism became a constant threat to Jewish life. Regarding itself as the new Israel, Christianity accused the Jewish people of the death of Jesus. According to Christian thinkers, the Jews had been rejected by God, and the law of Judaism was replaced by the new covenant. In the Muslim world, Jews were also viewed as second-class citizens, but they were never subjected to the same animosity and persecution that existed in Christian lands. Although classified as infidels, they (along with Christians) were regarded as 'People of the Book'.

During the Middle Ages, those Jewish communities that lay in the path of the Crusaders who made their way to the Holy Land were frequently massacred. In addition, during this period Jews were accused of ritually murdering Christian children to use their blood in the preparation of unleavened bread (matzah) for Passover. Jews were also accused of desecrating ritual objects, particularly the host. Under Christian rule, Jews were forbidden to own land or belong to guilds, and often they were subjected to arbitrary taxation. Frequent attempts were made to convert Jews to the Christian faith, and in some instances forced conversions were instituted. Jews were also compelled to engage in religious disputations with Christian scholars; events that led to widespread persecution. In the late Middle Ages, ghettos were established in many cities to isolate and restrict the movement of the Jewish community. From the 14th cent., the Christian Inquisition relentlessly hounded down converted Jews and their descendants (Marranos), who were regarded as guilty of heresy since many had reverted to Jewish belief and practice. This institution was established in the kingdoms of Castile, Aragon, and Navarre by Ferdinand and Isabella and lasted for nearly 350 years. Approximately 30,000 such individuals were sentenced to be burned at the stake, while another 16,000 were punished *in absentia* by being burned in effigy. Coupled with the Inquisition, wholesale slaughters of Jewish communities for religious and economic reasons took place for many centuries.

In the 19th cent., anti-Semitism underwent a significant transformation. In the past, the persecution of Jews was motivated by religion but, under the influence of pseudo-scientific theories, Jews were regarded as a pernicious racial element that needed to be eliminated from Western civilization. In 1879, the German anti-Jewish propagandist Wilhelm Marr coined the term 'anti-Semitism' to describe such racial hatred. This ideology was used to justify the Nazi Holocaust in which 6 million Jews were put to death. Although the end of the Second World War brought about a decline in overt anti-Jewish sentiment, the Soviet Union encouraged anti-semitism, and the Arab world fostered anti-Semitism chiefly in reaction to the conflict in the Middle East. Yet in recent times the Church has officially condemned anti-Jewish attitudes (for example, the Second Vatican Council decree *Nostra Aetate* of 1965), and steps have been taken to modify anti-Jewish teaching in Christian textbooks, catechisms, and liturgy. In addition, numerous associations (such as the International Council of Christians and Jews) have been created to foster Jewish Christian understanding and harmony.

Beside anti-Semitism, prejudice against black people has also had a long history in the Christian Church. The devil was often portrayed as black and Bede (7th–8th cent.) believed that the Ethiopian eunuch's skin colour was changed at his baptism (Acts 8.26–39). Both the apartheid policy of South Africa and the institution of Negro slavery in the USA has been justified by biblical texts such as the curse of Ham (Gen. 9.24–27), and many Christians still believe that the Church should restrict itself to spiritual concerns and not involve itself in campaigns for racial equality. However, Christians were associated with the fight against apartheid in South Africa, with the 19th-cent. abolition of slavery, and with the civil rights campaign in the USA. Despite the deep-seated racism of many societies, in recent years the Christian Church has generally condemned all forms of discrimination on the basis of race or colour. Being on the white side of the racial divide, Jews in the USA and South Africa have also contributed both to racist segregational policies and to anti-racist programmes.

There has been a community of black Jews in Ethiopia since the early years of the Christian era.

Until the early 20th cent., they were almost completely isolated from world Jewry, and it was only with the founding of the State of Israel that real interest in them was taken. Despite their devout practice of their form of Judaism, they were not immediately accepted as Jews for immigration purposes by the Israeli government. Only after 1975 were full rights bestowed, and since then several thousand Ethiopian Jews (Falashas) have been brought to Israel. However, the chief rabbinate insisted on symbolic conversion if they wished to be married in Israel; this caused deep offence to the Falasha community because it called into question the validity of their personal status. This demand has not been made of any other national group in Israel.

Reconstructionism

A 20th-cent. Jewish movement founded by Mordecai Kaplan. Kaplan believed that Judaism is a human creation expressive of a particular nation's culture and traditions. Although he abandoned the idea of a transcendent God and divine revelation, he maintained the value of traditional practices as an affirmation of Jewish peoplehood. Thus he viewed Judaism as a religious civilization, which he insisted should evolve in step with modern ideas and sentiments. The movement founded by Kaplan has engendered a network of synagogues in the USA, a rabbinical college (which accepts women as well as men), and various publications.

Ideas similar to those of Kaplan can be found among Christian thinkers, although no ecclesiastical movement has emerged as a result. Friedrich Nietzsche (19th cent.) argued that God is dead because man has killed him, and that human beings themselves must become supermen. In the 1960s, the 'death of God theologians' maintained that modern humanity must understand religion in secular terms, and the English thinker Don Cupitt practises and teaches a non-supernatural form of Christianity.

Redemption

In the Bible, the Hebrew terms for redemption (*padah; gaal*) were applied to the redemption of ancestral land from another to whom it had been sold (Lev. 25.25–26); financial redemption of a member of one's family from servitude to another (Lev. 25.48–49); and the redemption of a home,

field, ritually impure animal, or agricultural tithe dedicated to the sanctuary (Lev. 27). The term *gaal* was also applied to a deceased relative who dies childless – his brethren were obligated to redeem the name of the deceased by providing offspring. The meaning of the word *yasha* is to deliver from distress caused by enemies.

These terms were extended to apply to God's redeeming power. He is viewed as the Redeemer par excellence; it is he who takes care of the orphan and the widow, and the poor and the oppressed. In the Bible, deliverance from Egypt is seen as the paradigmatic example of such redeeming activity and, in time, national redemption became the primary concern of the people. In the prophetic books, it is stressed that military defeat and foreign rule resulted from infidelity to the divine covenant; thus the prophets attempted to draw the nation back to God's law. National repentance was viewed as crucial to this process. Throughout the prophetic writings, God is viewed as the Deliverer who preserves the saving remnant, brings about the ingathering of the exiles, restores the people to their former glory, and ushers in the era of universal harmony. Within this redemptive scheme, the Messiah is to play a pivotal role, but ultimately redemption will centre on God himself.

The destruction of the second Temple in 70CE led to the development of apocalyptic aspirations. Yet as the centuries passed, the rabbis of the Mishnah and the Talmud envisaged redemption within a national-political context; they looked forward to a time in which the Israelite monarchy would be restored, the nation would be liberated from foreign domination, the exiles would be ingathered, the Temple would be re-established, and humanity would undergo spiritual regeneration. In medieval times, a number of Jewish philosophers portrayed such a redemptive process in supernatural terms; other writers conceived of personal redemption in terms of developing the intellect and spirit. In kabbalistic (mystical) texts, a number of thinkers viewed redemption as a miraculous event unrelated to human initiative, whereas among the followers of Isaac Luria (16th cent.) redemption depends on human activity. For several modern Jewish philosophers, the initiative of personal redemption is the means by which national and universal redemption can be achieved. This perception was also shared by the Reform Movement, which saw redemption in terms of social reform. In recent times, many believers have viewed Zionism as the fulfilment of the divine call for national redemption, which will eventually lead to the redemption of all humanity.

The New Testament interprets Jesus' ministry, death, and resurrection as constituting the process of redemption that liberates humanity from the powers of evil and sin. Jesus regarded his healing of the sick, casting out of devils, and reviving the dead as signs of this redemptive action. Thus in Mark 10.45 he stated: 'For the Son of Man also came not to be served but to serve, and to give his life as a ransom for many.' Following this theme, Paul insisted that God regarded Christ's crucifixion as a means of expiation: 'they are justified by his grace as a gift, through the redemption which is in Christ Jesus, whom God put forward as an expiation by his blood, to be received by faith' (Rom. 3.24–25). For the early Christians, the traditional understanding of redemption was continued and developed. Some Church Fathers viewed Christ's teaching as a new message that liberates human beings from ignorance; another tradition related redemption to a transformation of human nature; other writers interpreted Jesus' redemption with the emancipation of human beings from the power of the devil.

In the Middle Ages, Anselm (11th–12th cent.) argued that since Jesus is God, he alone can offer a supererogatory satisfaction for human sin. Redemption is thus conceived as the restoration of the order of creation that has become distorted. In the same century, Abelard argued that Christ's promulgation of the love of God leads to a response of love; it is this love that liberates human beings from the servitude of sin. For Thomas Aquinas (13th cent.), all the activities and mysteries of Jesus' life are redemptive. God is the cause of human redemption, but Christ's human nature is its instrument. During the Reformation, emphasis was placed on the representational or substitutional role of Jesus. Christ suffered punishment on behalf of all; in exchange, human beings share in his righteousness. In modern theology, traditional notions of vicarious satisfaction and representation have been set aside in favour of the role of Christ in relation to the human individual and the Church. For a number of writers, Jesus' redemptive activity is

connected with his effect upon the Christian community. In recent years, the awareness of human exploitation has led to a conception of redemption in relation to oppressive political and economic structures. Despite the variety of interpretations of redemption within Christianity, there has been a universal recognition that God is at work in Christ and that his life and death have initiated a new spiritual order. In Judaism, on the other hand, the process of redemption has yet to be fulfilled. Within traditional Judaism, scriptural prophecies about the redemption of both the nation and humanity as a whole await the coming of a Messiah who will bring about a transformation of earthly life and human history.

Redemption of the first-born

(*Pidyon Ha-Ben*): Traditionally in Judaism the first-born is dedicated to God (Num. 3.13). According to Num. 18.15, 'Everything that opens the womb of all flesh, whether man or beast, which they offer to the Lord, shall be yours; nevertheless the first-born of man you shall redeem.' The price of redeeming the first-born is five shekels (Num. 3.44–51). The custom of dedicating the first-born to God may have originally been adopted from the Canaanites, who sacrificed their first-born sons; the story of the binding of Isaac should probably be understood in this context (Gen. 22.1–4). The Mishnah contains detailed regulations concerning the *Pidyon Ha-Ben* (redemption of the first-born). It only applies to male first-born children where the mother has not previously had a miscarriage, stillbirth, or daughter, or has not been delivered by Caesarean section. Traditionally, on the 31st day after the birth, the presiding priest (*cohen*) gives the father the choice of giving up his child to God or buying him back for five shekels. The father pays the redemption price and recites two blessings, one concerning the fulfilling of the commandment, and the other thanking God for bringing the family to this time. The priest symbolically returns the child, and recites the blessing over a cup of wine and the priestly benediction. Then there is usually a party.

St Luke's Gospel records Jesus, as the first-born of Mary, being redeemed in the Temple (Luke 2.22–38). Despite this, Christianity does not observe the custom of differentiating between first-born sons and other children. All Christians through their baptism are equally dedicated to God, and it is Jesus who provides the price of redemption through his sacrificial death (Eph. 1.7). Thus the ceremony of the redemption of the first-born has no meaning in Christianity.

Reform Judaism *see* Reform movements

Reform movements

(Reform Judaism) (Protestantism): With the rise of the Enlightenment in the 18th cent., Jews began to look beyond the narrow confines of traditional Judaism. Initially, reformers were primarily motivated by a desire to modify the liturgy. At the beginning of the 19th cent., Israel Jacobson organized a progressive Jewish school and synagogue in Sessen, Westphalia; subsequently he moved to Berlin where he continued to advocate Jewish reform. In 1818 a synagogue (called a 'Temple') was built in Hamburg, where prayers were chanted in the vernacular, the service was shortened, the sermon was preached in German, musical instruments were used, and the ceremony of confirmation was introduced into the calendar.

In response to these reforms, the Orthodox Jewish community attempted to ban this new movement. Yet despite such an attack, Reform Judaism attracted numerous adherents. These Jews insisted on making alterations to both the beliefs and practices of Orthodoxy. In place of ritual requirements, this new movement stressed the prophetic and ethical dimensions of the faith. This revision of Judaism aroused the hostility both of Orthodox Jews as well as many conservative reformers. As a consequence, the community split into radical reformers and conservatives like Zecharias Frankel (19th cent.).

Many of these reformers were distinguished scholars who contributed to the scientific study of Judaism (*Wissenschaft des Judentums*). Although initially a German development, Reform Judaism attracted followers in France, Germany, the USA and elsewhere. Prominent among these early reformers was Isaac Mayer Wise (19th cent.), who founded the Union of American Hebrew Congregations in 1873, and the Hebrew Union College in 1875. In 1889 he also organized the Central Conference of American Rabbis. During this period, a group of 19 rabbis met under the leadership of Kaufmann Kohler (19th cent.) in Pittsburgh to formulate the principles of the movement. As a result of their deliberations, the Pittsburgh Platform was created; this set out the principles of the movement. In 1917 the Columbus Platform reformulated a new ideology of the movement. Within contemporary Reform there has been an increased emphasis on Hebrew, traditional customs and ceremonies, and the State of Israel. Nonetheless, Reform Judaism has insisted on adopting radical positions concerning the ordination of women as rabbis, the acceptance of the criterion of paternal descent as a basis for Jewish identification, and the acceptance of homosexual rabbis. Within the Jewish fold, other reform groups also emerged in the 19th–20th cent. In England, Liberal Judaism was founded as a parallel movement to American Reform. A less extreme reform movement, Conservative Judaism, emerged under the influence of Zecharias Frankel in the 19th cent. and has become a major force in American Jewish life. Reconstructionist Judaism (an offshoot of Conservative Judaism) has also attracted a considerable number of adherents as has Humanistic Judaism and the Jewish Renewal Movement. Although these various reform groupings differ from one another over various aspects of belief and practice, they are united in their rejection of many of the tenets of Orthodoxy.

Within Western Christianity, religious reform occurred during the 14th–15th cent. Prior to Martin Luther's (15th–16th cent.) protest against the corruption of Rome, similar attacks had been made upon the hierarchical and legislative structure of the Church which had been suppressed. In 1517, however, Luther nailed to the door of the Castle Church in Wittenberg his 95 theses; these criticized the sale of indulgences and the materialism of the Church. Several years later, the Swiss theologian Ulrich Zwingli (16th cent.) carried out anti-papal, and anti-hierarchical, anti-monastic reforms in Zurich. In the same century, John Calvin in Geneva published *Institutio Christianae Religionis*, which promulgated doctrinal reform regarding the concept of election and redemption. In each case, the reformers broke away from the authority of the Roman Catholic hierarchy and established their own independent religious movements.

In addition to the Lutheran and Calvinist

traditions that emerged in the 16th cent., there were numerous other radical groups. Some of these reformers called for the baptism of adult believers and resisted compromise with the state. The most important surviving community of these persecuted Churches are the Mennonites. In assailing the medieval system, these various reform movements based their teaching on biblical authority, the use of the vernacular, and the doctrine of justification by faith which was rooted in Paul's theology. A new emphasis was placed on exegetical preaching, and the laity were encouraged to participate in singing. In these ways, the Reformation brought the Christian faith to the common people.

In response to these reforms, the Roman Catholic Church launched the Counter-Reformation. Nonetheless, the Protestant Reformation continued to attract followers, and pietistic and missionary developments flourished in subsequent centuries. In the Americas, Puritan settlers sought to be liberated from religious persecution and pressure in Europe, and became the core of Protestant America. In England, the Anglican revival under John Wesley (18th cent.) revitalized the Churches. In the USA, Methodists and Baptists eventually became the predominant Protestant movements, but Anglicanism and Lutheranism have become the largest Protestant communities world-wide. Religious reform has thus been a prominent feature of both Judaism and Christianity in recent centuries. In the Jewish community it was associated with the quest to revitalize the Jewish tradition in response to modernity; with Christendom, however, it was initially a Protestant movement against abuses in the Roman Catholic Church. Nonetheless, both movements called into question the authority of the traditional hierarchy and both put considerable emphasis on the conscience and judgement of the individual.

Repentance *see* Atonement

Responsa literature

Rabbinic sources, known as *Sheelot u-Teshuvot* (questions and answers), were issued by leading legal authorities through the centuries. This literature can be divided into three main periods. Beginning in the 7th cent., the Gaonic period lasted until the 11th cent. Initially, Gaonic Responsa consisted of the brief communications, but gradually they became more substantial. The subject-matter ranged from requests for advice about various aspects of Jewish practice to queries about both Jewish and secular learning. These questions were directed to the heads of the Babylonian academies (*geonim*), whose replies were recognized as authoritative.

During the next period (12th–15th cent.), early respondents (known as *Rishonim*) based their rulings directly on the Talmud. Prominent among the *Rishonim* were Meir of Rothenberg in Germany (13th cent.), Asher ben Jehiel of Germany and Spain (13–14th cent.), Solomon ben Adret of Barcelona (13th–14th cent.), Isaac ben Sheshet (14th cent.), and Simeon ben Tzemah Duran of Algiers (14th–15th cent.).

In the third period (16th cent. to the present), later scholars (*Aharonim*) took into consideration both the Talmud and earlier Responsa. Important *Aharonim* were Joseph Colon of Italy (15th cent.), and Israel Bruna of Germany (15th cent.). In recent centuries, the best-known collections of Responsa include works by Ezekiel ben Judah Landau of Prague (18th cent.), Moses Sopher of Pressburg (18th–19th cent.), and Israel Elhanan Spektor of Kovno (19th cent.). Responsa in the 20th cent., which rely on previous authorities, deal with the problems faced by Jews in the modern world. As in the past, these works treat all aspects of contemporary Jewish life, and they are consulted by Orthodox, Conservative, and Reform scholars.

Within Christianity, the tradition of canon law parallels this development in Judaism. These laws originate from the early Church practice of convening councils to settle matters of theological and ethical dispute. The importance of these councils determined the degree of authority of the canons that were issued. Thus the decrees of the Council of Nicaea (335) possessed great significance. In addition to these councils, individuals issued canon law as well. Thus Dionysius of Alexandria (3rd cent.), Gregory Thaumaturgus (3rd cent.), Basil of Caesarea (4th cent.), and Amphilochius of Iconium (4th cent.) issued canonical letters, and special authority was given to papal letters beginning with Pope Siricius (4th cent.). There was also the work of anonymous and fictitious authors such as the volume known as the *Apostolic Canons*.

With the *Decretum* of Gratian (12th cent), a

dividing line was drawn between *ius antiquum* (old law) and *ius novum* (new law) – all canons issued after the Council of Trent (1545–63) are called *ius novissimum* (very new law). The authority given to Gratian's *Decretum* led to its supplementation by later collections; this work came to be known as the *Corpus Iuris Canonici* (The Body of Canon Law) and served as the authoritative legal code for the Roman Catholic Church. In 1904 it was overhauled and recodified. The standard text is now the *Codex Iurus Canonici* (The Codex of Canon Law). Together with this corpus, local canons have also been used to provide a basic canonical guide. Thus in both Judaism and Christianity there has been an evolution of responses to legal matters. From apostolic times, the Church found it necessary to introduce laws over and above the teaching of Jesus; similarly, in Judaism rabbinic authorities felt compelled to extend biblical, Mishnaic and Talmudic enactments in the light of changing circumstances. However, Christian canon law does not concern itself with every detail of everyday life, as does Jewish Responsa.

Resurrection

(Immortality): The belief that the dead will arise and embark on some sort of heavenly existence. This doctrine emerged within Judaism possibly under Persian influence, and is found in the Book of Daniel: 'Many of those who sleep in the dust of the earth shall awake, some to everlasting life, and some to shame and everlasting contempt' (Dan. 12.2). During the period of the second Temple, the Pharisees viewed this belief as central to the Jewish faith, and they utilized various proof texts from Scripture (interpreted by means of Midrashic methods of exegesis) to justify its validity. The Sadducees (priestly caste), on the other hand, denied its Mosaic authority.

In the liturgy, the resurrection of the dead is mentioned in the second paragraph of the *Amidah* prayer, and it has come to be regarded as a central tenet of the Jewish religion. According to Moses Maimonides (12th cent.), it is one of the 13 principles of the Jewish faith. Most sages conceived of resurrection in a literal sense, although some writers such as Maimonides adopted a different interpretation. According to Maimonides, resurrection would take place, but it will not be a permanent state; instead, he assumed that the soul rather than the body would be immortal. Such a view was in accord with the conception of eternity as spiritual perfection rather than continued life in a material body.

In the presentation of the doctrine of resurrection in rabbinic Judaism, three eschatological beliefs were combined: resurrection, immortality, and the Messiah. According to mainstream Judaism, the soul continues after death, and after the coming of the Messiah the body will be resurrected and united with it. Among medieval philosophers, differing explanations of these events were given, and numerous difficulties troubled Jewish thinkers: Would righteous Gentiles as well as Jews be resurrected simultaneously? Will both the wicked and the righteous be revived? Will bodily imperfections disappear? Will resurrection take place before or after the coming of the Messiah? How is the resurrection of the dead related to final judgement? In the Middle Ages, a number of Jewish writers wrestled with such issues. During this period, kabbalists (mystics) maintained that the soul reappeared after death and entered a new body, and this belief in the transmigration of the soul continued into the early modern period. In recent times, however, non-Orthodox Jews have largely rejected the belief in physical resurrection, and instead have subscribed to the belief in the immortality of the soul.

Jesus' teaching about resurrection was primarily concerned with predictions that he would rise from the dead: 'And he began to teach them that the Son of Man must suffer many things, and be rejected by the elders and the chief priests and the scribes, and be killed, and after three days rise again' (Mark 8.31). In his confrontation with the Sadducees, Jesus defended the doctrine of resurrection (Mark 12.18–27), and the Fourth Gospel describes his teaching about the general resurrection: 'Do not marvel at this; for the hour is coming when all who are in the tombs will hear his voice and come forth, those who have done good, to the resurrection of life, and those who have done evil, to the resurrection of judgement' (John 5.28–29).

In the apostolic period, the belief in resurrection of the dead became a certainty because of the Easter story, and the proclamation that Jesus had risen from the dead became a focus of preaching. If the resurrection of the dead is connected with the coming of the Messiah, Jesus' resurrection confirms his Messiahship. According to Paul, Jesus' resurrection guarantees the efficacy of the atonement and the certainty of resurrection of believers in the future: 'Now if Christ is preached as raised from the dead, how can some of you say that there is no resurrection of the dead? . . . If Christ has not been raised, then our preaching is in vain' (1 Cor. 15.12–14).

The belief in Jesus' resurrection continued to be a cardinal feature of the Christian faith. Belief in the resurrection of the body is enshrined in the creeds, and through the ages Christians have asserted that at the Second Coming of Christ departed souls will be restored in a bodily life. The righteous will then enter heaven, while the wicked will endure punishment for their sins. However, in modern times, New Testament scholars have emphasized the difficulties in the Gospel accounts of the resurrection, and some liberal theologians have argued that the story of Christ's resurrection arose from subjective visions of women at the tomb as well as that of other disciples. On this account, Jesus' resurrection must not be understood literally; rather, the resurrection should be seen as a symbolic myth. In addition, with the growth of scientific knowledge, many Christians have replaced the concept of physical resurrection with the idea of the immortality of the soul.

Thus in Judaism and Christianity the belief in resurrection has served as a mainstay of the religion through the centuries. Both traditions connect the doctrine with the coming of the Messiah. For Jews, hope of re-embodiment after death will take place in the future and is related to the keeping of God's law; Christianity, on the other hand, teaches that the Messiah has already come and was vindicated by his resurrection from death; Jesus is perceived as the first fruits or forerunner of a general resurrection which will take place when he returns to judge the earth. However, in modern times, numerous adherents of both traditions have tended to envisage the hereafter in spiritual terms in which personal identity would reside in the continuation of the soul rather than the body.

Revelation

In the Bible, God is depicted as revealing himself through nature and history. In the account of the flood and the Tower of Babel, God made himself manifest; later he delivered the Israelite people out of Egypt, guided them in the wilderness, revealed the law on Mt Sinai, and led them to the Promised Land. By means of such divine acts, God disclosed various aspects of his nature, as well as his plan for Israel and for all human beings. Once the nation was established in its own land, God revealed himself to the prophets whom he used as spokesmen – at times he appeared to these individuals in dreams, but his most characteristic manner of revelation was through the spoken word. For this reason, the prophets frequently added the expression 'Thus sayeth the Lord' to their utterances.

According to rabbinic literature, divine communication is referred to as the 'coming to rest of the Shekinah' (indwelling presence), and the spirit of prophecy is conferred only upon those individuals who possess moral and spiritual qualities. For the rabbis, this process ceased in the 5th cent. BCE with the death of Haggai, Zechariah, and Malachi. Although new laws continued to be promulgated, this was not due to a direct revelation from God. God's presence could be experienced, but the rabbis were compelled to draw out the implication of the law through the application of exegetical principles to scriptural texts.

In medieval times, a number of Jewish theologians discussed the nature of the prophetic experience. For Moses Maimonides (12th cent.), prophecy should be understood as the natural connection between the human imagination and intellectual faculties and a cosmological entity referred to as the 'Active Intellect'. According to Maimonides, prophecy occurs as the result of the perfection of certain natural faculties, but whether a person becomes a prophet is dependent on the divine will. Judah Ha-Levi (11–12th cent.), on the other hand, viewed revelation as a supernatural event that individuals cannot attain on their own; it results from an infusion of the divine presence coupled with the religious emotion of love of God. Yet despite these different interpretations, it was a cardinal principle of the Jewish faith that the Torah was given by God to Moses and that he revealed himself through the prophets of Israel.

In modern times, considerable debate has taken place within Jewish circles about the concept of revelation. Although Orthodox thinkers have interpreted the process of revelation in varying ways, they have universally held that the Five Books of Moses are inerrant, and that Scripture is the result of divine inspiration. Both Conservative and Reform Judaism, however, have rejected the belief in *Torah MiSinai* (the revelation of the Torah on Mt Sinai). Instead, the Hebrew Scriptures are viewed as the product of divine inspiration filtered through human reflection. Reconstructionist and Humanistic Jews, on the other hand, have entirely rejected any supernatural view of revelation. There is thus a considerable range of opinion about the nature of God's communication to human beings, despite the fact that the belief in God's revelation has served as the foundation of the religious tradition through the ages.

Although the term 'revelation' is occasionally used in the New Testament in connection with the communication of divine knowledge, it generally refers to a future event in which God will disclose himself. This occurrence has already been effected in Jesus' ministry, and the early Christians found the definitive disclosure of God's love in Jesus' salvific activity. Yet revelation in the absolute sense will only take place at the end of the age (parousia). As Paul wrote: 'For now we see in a mirror dimly, but then face to face. Now I know in part; then I shall understand fully, even as I have been fully understood' (1 Cor. 13.12). Once the canon of Scripture was closed, revelation came to be thought of as contained in the words of the Bible. As in Judaism, the Church held that the scriptural text contains a written revelation, and the task of Christian theologians was conceived as providing a systematic treatment of biblical concepts.

During the Middle Ages, it was assumed that there were two types of divine knowledge. The task of natural theology was to formulate the truths about God that could be discovered by reason unaided. Yet it was widely believed that this does not provide a full basis for human life. What is required is 'saving knowledge' which embraces the doctrine of the Trinity, the incarnation, and redemption. Such information can only be conveyed through the divine word since human beings are limited; humanity thus stands in need of divine grace and a revelation that supplements natural knowledge.

At the Reformation, theologians minimized the value of natural theology; the Bible, they believed, contains all revelational truth. Such a view was reaffirmed by Karl Barth (19th–20th cent.) and his followers. Other modern theologians maintained that all knowledge is divinely inspired. General revelation is given to all people, but this needs to be supplemented by God's special revelation which was manifest in the history of Israel and culminated in Christ. God is thus conceived as revealing himself to all people, although his decisive revelation is manifest in the mighty acts of history as found in both the Old and New Testaments. In both Judaism and Christianity, then, the doctrine of revelation serves as the cornerstone of faith. For Orthodox Jews, God's word is contained in Scripture – the Torah is the tree of life to those who hold fast to it. Within Christianity, it is the Word made flesh who constitutes God's full disclosure. In the past, both faiths subscribed to the belief in the inerrancy of the biblical text, but in modern times liberal Jews as well as many Christians have come to regard Scripture as containing divine revelation as mediated through human reason and reflection.

Righteousness

(*Tzaddik*): The quality of righteousness is ascribed to God in the Hebrew Scriptures. In the Book of Deuteronomy, he is described as 'A God of faithfulness and without iniquity, just and right is he' (Deut. 32.4), and the writer of Ps. 145.7 declared that '[men] shall pour forth the fame of thy abundant goodness, and shall sing aloud of thy righteousness'. The prophets insisted that righteousness was what God wanted from humanity; so Amos wrote, 'let justice roll down like waters, and righteousness like an everflowing stream' (Amos 5.24). Similarly, rabbinic and medieval Jewish sages stressed the importance of righteousness as a state of spirituality and piety. In particular, the righteous man (*tzaddik*) was commended; according to Talmudic legend, it is the existence of 36 righteous men in each generation that saves the world from destruction. The Hasidic (pious) sects of the 18th cent, named their leaders *tzaddikim*, and believed they were a channel of communication between God and the people. The title was hereditary, being passed from father to son, and even today the *tzaddik* of a Hasidic sect is regarded by his followers as having supernatural powers.

137

Righteousness is also an important concept in Christianity. Jesus told his followers that their righteousness should exceed that of the scribes and Pharisees (Matt. 5.20), and he indicated that it was not enough just to keep the letter of the law. Christians should have righteous intentions, and those who genuinely 'hunger and thirst for righteousness' are promised satisfaction (Matt. 5.6). Following the Jewish tradition, the Fourth Gospel describes Jesus as addressing God as 'righteous Father' and this is associated with 'the love with which thou hast loved me' (John 17.25–26). Paul stressed that no human being was truly righteous (Rom. 3.10), and it is only through faith in the saving death of Jesus that humanity can be justified and be accounted righteous (Rom. 5.1). In the Christian liturgy, Jesus himself is identified with the 'sun of righteousness' promised by the prophet Malachi (Mal. 4.2). Instead of the world being saved by 36 righteous men, Christians believe it is redeemed by the one Jesus.

Thus righteousness is an admired ideal in both Judaism and Christianity. Judaism, however, teaches that it is attainable through dedication and piety, whereas the Christian Church, following Paul, stresses that people cannot make themselves righteous; only through the free gift of Jesus can righteousness be obtained. In both traditions, righteousness is an attribute of God and the Christian Church has extended it to Jesus.

Rosary

Among Roman Catholics it is customary to recite 15 decades of the Hail Mary Prayer, each decade preceded by the Lord's Prayer and concluded with the Gloria. While these prayers are being recited, the joyful, the suffering, and the glorious mysteries of Jesus' life are pondered. As an aid to this exercise, the Christian fingers beads as he or she prays. Rings with 10 small knots are sometimes used or a chaplet (string of beads) as an alternative to the conventional rosary, which has a crucifix on a string of five beads attached to a circlet of 50 beads. The existence of the rosary goes back at least to the 12th cent. in monastic orders, and Pope Pius V (16th cent.) established the order of prayer as it is practised today. In general, Protestants do not make use of rosaries in prayer – probably because rosaries are particularly associated with the worship of the Virgin Mary.

Phylacteries (tephillin) are a similar aid to concentration in prayer. However, the duty of donning phylacteries is compulsory for all adult male Jews and dates back to ancient times, while the use of the rosary is relatively recent and is entirely voluntary.

Rosh Hashanah *see* New Year

S

Sabbatarianism *see* Sabbath

Sabbath

(Sabbatarianism) (Saturday) (*Shabbat*) (Sunday): The Jewish Sabbath (*Shabbat*) is Saturday, the seventh day of the week. According to the creation account in Genesis, God rested on the seventh day (Gen. 2.1–3). When the Israelites were travelling in the wilderness to the Promised Land, they were commanded to gather a double portion of manna on the sixth day in preparation for the Sabbath, the day of rest (Exod. 16.23). When the Israelites received the Ten Commandments, the Fourth Commandment was to keep the Sabbath day holy; according to Exodus, this is because God rested on the seventh day (Exod. 20.11). The Deuteronomic version justified it on the grounds that 'you were a servant in the land of Egypt and the Lord your God brought you out from there with a mighty hand and an outstretched arm' (Deut. 5.15). The Sabbath is also described as a sign of the covenant between God and the Israelites (Exod. 31.13–16).

From the time of Ezra (5th cent. BCE), rules for the observance of the Sabbath began to be systematized and, by the time of Jesus, 39 different types of work had been defined and forbidden. However, Sabbath prohibitions can be superseded in times of danger, childbirth, or in order to save a life. The Sabbath is a day of joy and peace and is celebrated with special meals, study, and rest. The Sabbath begins on Friday evening just before sunset when the Sabbath candles are lit by the mother of the household with the traditional blessing. The evening service in the synagogue welcomes the Sabbath with the Sabbath hymn 'Lekhah Dodi' ('Come my beloved'). At home, the children are blessed, a Kiddush (sanctification over wine) recited, the hands washed, and a blessing is said over the plaited loaves (*hallah*). Normally there are two loaves, reminiscent of the double portion of manna. After the meal, hymns are often sung and the ceremony concludes with the grace after meals. On the following morning, the service in the synagogue includes the reading of the Torah portion for the week, and often the rabbi preaches a sermon. The rabbis ruled that three meals should be eaten on the Sabbath day, and pious Jews also attend afternoon services. The Sabbath concludes with the *Havdalah* (dividing) ceremony, which generally takes place at home. This includes smelling spices, lighting the *Havdalah* plaited candle, and plunging it into a cup of wine.

Reform Jews do not feel the need to refrain from all the forbidden work, and very often the major service of the week is not on Saturday morning, but on Friday night, which sometimes even includes a Torah reading. Orthodox Jews continue to keep the Sabbath very seriously. They do not smoke or drive a car because this would constitute kindling a fire; they will read but not write; admire a flower but not pick it; and, in a very traditional household, the electric lights will be on a time-switch.

Jesus is described as being highly critical of his Pharisee contemporaries' attitude to the Sabbath; he seems to have believed that they placed ritual correctness above human need (Mark 2.23–3.6). In fact, this is a misreading of the rabbis' attitude to the Sabbath, but it has coloured Christian attitudes to Jewish practice. In the early days of the Christian Church, the seventh day continued to be kept as a day of rest, but because the resurrection of Jesus and the coming of the Holy Spirit had occurred on the first day of the week, Christians began to observe Sunday as the Sabbath. Paul and the Christians of Troas gathered together for the breaking of bread on the first day of the week (Acts 20.7), and in the first epistle to the Corinthians the new converts are advised to put away something for charity on the first day (1 Cor. 16.2). Traditionally, Sunday was the pagan day of the sun, but, through the association of Jesus with the sun of righteousness (Mal. 4.2), it became the Lord's Day. From the 4th cent. CE, ecclesiastical legislation

began to be drawn up concerning the observance of Sunday, but the abstention from work was never so strictly enforced as in Judaism. Roman Catholics are expected to attend Mass and abstain from servile work. Protestants have shown a greater inclination towards Sabbatarianism (the excessive observance of the Day of Rest) and, for example, in the 17th cent. in Scotland all books and music that were not strictly religious were forbidden. Even today, such pressure groups as the Lord's Day Observance Society endeavour to keep Sunday special, but, in general, although few people work on a Sunday and services are held in the churches, Sabbath observance is not strictly followed in Christianity.

Sacrament

Initially the word 'sacramentum' meant a soldier's oath of allegiance; in Christian usage it is the equivalent of the Greek *musterion* (mystery), in that its meaning is disclosed only to believers. Augustine (4th–5th cent.) defined a sacrament as the 'visible form of invisible grace' or 'as a sign of a sacred thing', and applied the term to formulae such as the creeds and the Lord's Prayer. This application was maintained until the Middle Ages but, in the 12th cent., Hugh of St Victor enumerated 30 sacraments in *De Sacramentis Christinae fidei*. In the same century, Peter Lombard listed seven sacraments that have come to be regarded as traditional: baptism, confirmation, the Eucharist, penance, extreme unction, orders and matrimony. This list was formally affirmed in 1439 at the Council of Florence and in 1545–63 at the Council of Trent, which asserted that these seven sacraments were instituted by Christ. This sevenfold classification has also been accepted by the Eastern Church. From the earliest period, baptism and the Eucharist were viewed as having special significance.

The theological importance of the sacraments lies in the fact that they exhibit the principle of the incarnation – they embody in material form a spiritual reality. In addition, they serve as the means whereby the union of God in man is perpetrated in Christ's mystical body of the Church. According to traditional Catholic theology, the right matter, the right form, and the right intention are necessary conditions of the validity of the sacrament.

Sacraments do not convey grace to the recipients unless they are correctly disposed; without faith and repentance, an impediment can be put in the way of the grace that would otherwise flow from sacramental acts.

In modern times, emphasis has been put on the sacraments as deepening the union of the recipient with the Church. Christ as the expression of the Word, and the Church as his body, are viewed as primordial sacraments on which all the enumerated sacraments depend. Baptism, confirmation and orders are understood as imprinting an abiding character on the soul. Protestants, Quakers and the Salvation Army make no use of sacraments but, in other denominations, baptism and the Lord's Supper are considered of primary importance.

In the Jewish faith there is no sacramental theology; nonetheless, the notion of sanctification or holiness (*kedushah*) plays a vital role. Holiness is understood as an attribute of God; human beings can become holy in so far as they imitate God's nature: 'You shall be holy; for I the Lord your God am holy' (Lev. 19.2). As a consequence of the covenant, Israel became a holy people, dedicated to following God's commandments. Priests were viewed as a holy caste responsible for Temple ritual, and the Sabbath as well as festivals were observed as Holy Days. If the nation failed to fulfil its divinely sanctioned ceremonial obligations, this caused a state of imperfection that required cultic ritual to bring about rectification. Stress was also placed on ethical purity, and in biblical times the prophets frequently castigated the nation for its waywardness.

In rabbinic sources, the sagas were anxious to sanctify all aspects of human life. The profane in this context was conceived of as that which desecrates and pollutes the sacred. In rabbinic theology, holiness is defined as separateness, and is equated with abstinence from all that is unconsecrated. Nonetheless, separateness does not imply withdrawal from the world; rather, Jews are to remain separate from contamination while living in the world. Although it is not possible to enumerate a list of sacraments in the Jewish faith, parallels can be drawn between the traditional Christian sacraments and particular Jewish rites (baptism/ritual immersion; confirmation/bar mitzvah; the Eucharist/Kiddush (sanctification over wine);

penance/acts of supplication for forgiveness; extreme unction/the final Shema ('Hear, O Israel') prayer; orders/*semikhah* (ordination); matrimony/Jewish marriage). But these practices and institutions are simply part of the Jewish way of life, the whole of which is a sanctified existence through which spiritual purity can be attained.

Sacrifice

(Sin Offering): In the Bible, Cain and Abel offered sacrifices to the Lord, as did Noah and the patriarchs. When the sanctuary existed in the wilderness, sacrifice only took place there, but after the Israelites entered Canaan a permanent sanctuary was located at Shiloh. Eventually, Solomon's Temple was established in Jerusalem.

The Bible stipulates that sacrifices should consist of either animals or grain. All sacrifices had to be brought to the Temple. Animal sacrifices are of four types: the *orlah* was a burnt offering; 14 types of sacrifice were included in this category, including the daily morning and afternoon sacrifice. Only male animals (bulls, rams, or he-goats) could be used, but fowls could be of either gender. The entire animal was burned on the altar, but the hide belonged to the priests.

Shelamim were peace offerings which could be of either sex. Certain parts of the innards of the animal were burned, and the meat was eaten. Such sacrifices consisted of community peace offerings, festival peace offerings, pledged offerings, and offerings brought by a Nazarite at the end of his term. In the case of community peace offerings, the priests ate the meat, whereas the other sacrifices were eaten by the person making the offering.

Hatat were sin offerings brought when a person or an entire community transgressed a commandment through negligence. Depending on the sacrifice involved, a bull aged two or three, a year-old he-goat, a year-old female sheep or goat, or a fowl was offered. If the sin offering atoned for a sin committed by a high priest or by the community, the animal or fowl was burned outside the Temple; in other cases, the meat was given to the priests.

The fourth type of animal sacrifice was an *asha*, consisting of six types of guilt offerings. In all such cases, the animal had to be male and was given to the priests. In addition to animal sacrifices, grain offerings were presented at the Temple. Most were made with fine wheat flour and were composed of grain, oil, and frankincense. A different form of sacrifice was that of first fruits – when a person brought such offerings to the Temple he had to make a declaration before a priest (Deut. 26.5–10).

The purpose of sacrifice in ancient Israel was to create a bond between the believer and God. Sacrifice was viewed as a form of thanksgiving and a means of seeking forgiveness. However, after the destruction of the second Temple in 70CE, the practice of sacrifice was eliminated; only when the Messiah comes will Jews be permitted to rebuild the Temple and reinstitute the sacrificial system. In the meantime, prayer must take its place. The Orthodox liturgy retains prayers for such a restoration of the Temple cult, although Reform Judaism views the institution of sacrifice as an outmoded form of worship and has eliminated such prayers from its liturgy.

In Christian theology, the concept of sacrifice has been transformed through its application to Jesus' atoning death. According to Paul, Jesus is the paschal lamb: 'For Christ, our paschal lamb, has been sacrificed' (1 Cor. 5.7); he is the sin offering ('For our sake he made him to be sin who knew no sin, so that in him we might become the righteousness of God' (2 Cor. 5.21). Paul frequently refers to Jesus' ministry in sacrificial terms, and he repeatedly emphasizes that Christians are the new Temple where sacrifices of the new covenant are to be made: 'Do you not know that you are God's temple and that God's Spirit dwells in you? . . . For God's temple is holy, and that temple you are' (1 Cor. 3.16–17).

From the earliest period, Jesus' death and the Christian life were seen in sacrificial terms. Sacrifice in the Temple was spiritualized and given new meaning. For the Church Fathers, the uniqueness of the sacrifice resides in the fact that Jesus was a voluntary victim of infinite value, and also himself the High Priest. Within this context, the Eucharist offering was referred to as a sacrifice in virtue of its relationship to the sacrifice of Christ. For Thomas Aquinas (13th cent.), the Mass is an immolation in so far as it is an image of the Passion.

Jesus has thus been understood as the full, perfect, and sufficient sacrifice for the sins of the world. He is the eternal heavenly High Priest as well as the freely offered sacrifice. Through an obedient sacrifice of love, he undertook the work of atonement. Christ died for all people and, through this act, God's reconciling love is made manifest to all. Christianity has thus refashioned the biblical concept of sacrifice to suit its own religious purposes. Christ's death is understood as a replacement and fulfilment of the cultic ritual of the Temple, and his death is linked with the atonement of sin. Within the Christian faith the Jerusalem Temple thus ceased to have any function. Once the second Temple was destroyed in 70CE, cultic worship disappeared from Judaism as well, and prayer took the place of the sacrificial system. Nevertheless, traditional Jews continued to pray for the restoration of the Temple and the practice of sacrifice when the Messiah comes, and this longing became a central feature of the liturgy of the synagogue.

Sacrilege *see* Profanation of God's name

Sainthood

Veneration of the saints has been a feature of Christian worship from early times. The apostles, Jesus' mother, and the various martyrs of the early Church were perceived as being particularly close to God, although sharing in human nature and sympathetic to human need. The Book of Revelation describes the martyrs being given white robes (Rev. 7.14–17) and praying before God's throne (Rev. 6.9). When Paul (1st cent.) described the Church as the body of Christ, every individual was understood as having a particular role, including the saints (Rom. 12.4–8); new converts are 'no longer strangers and sojourners, but you are fellow citizens with the saints and members of the household of God, built upon the foundation of the apostles and prophets, Christ Jesus himself being the cornerstone' (Eph. 2.19–20). The custom grew of making pilgrimage and praying at the death-place of martyrs and preserving relics of their lives. By the 3rd cent., Origen was teaching that the faithful should imitate the lives of the saints and their prayers would be answered. The cult of the saints grew speedily, and the Church frequently found it necessary to curb the excess of hysteria and superstition that surrounded its practices. The Protestant reformers in particular condemned the invocation of the saints as a human invention and a pointless activity. Nonetheless, the custom has continued in Orthodox, Roman Catholic and Anglican circles and, even today, after a lengthy process of investigation, new saints are canonized within the Church.

There is no formal doctrine of the saints in Judaism, but the rabbis did teach that the merits of particularly pious people benefit their descendants and the nation as a whole. In particular, the patriarchs Abraham, Isaac, and Jacob have lasting merit, and their tombs near Hebron are a favourite place of pilgrimage. In the Second Book of Maccabees in the Apocrypha, Judas Maccabeus sees Onias and Jeremiah calling down blessings on the Jewish people (2 Macc. 15.12), and this is clearly similar to the Christian idea of the invocation of the saints. Similarly, the rabbis taught that the prayers of a *tzaddik* (righteous man) could avert disaster; and, according to the Talmud, in each generation there are 36 righteous individuals (*Lamed Vav Tzaddikim*) whose existence prevents the destruction of the world. This belief has been sustained particularly in kabbalistic (mystical) and Hasidic circles, and traditionally the Hasidim refer to their hereditary leader as a *tzaddik*, regarding him as a model for their behaviour. Pilgrimages are also made to the tombs of such sages as R. Simeon bar Yohai (2nd cent. CE) and R. Meir Ba'al Ha–Nes. Thus although there is no official doctrine of sainthood, Judaism does encourage the veneration of saintly figures.

Salvation

In the Bible, salvation is conceived in this-worldly terms. Individuals are to be rewarded or punished in this life, and no hint is given of an afterlife where God's justice is to be meted out. However, under Persian and Greek influence, Jews came to believe in a world-to-come where the righteous would inherit eternal life. This doctrine is based on the belief in physical resurrection and the reunion of the body and the soul before judgement.

According to the rabbis, the afterlife is divided into several stages. First there is the time of Messianic redemption. The Talmud states that the Messianic age is to take place on earth after a period of decline and calamity, and will result in a complete fulfilment of every human wish. Peace will reign throughout nature; Jerusalem will be rebuilt; and at the close of this era, the dead will be resurrected and restored with their souls, and a final judgement will come upon all human beings. Those who are judged righteous will enter into heaven (*Gan Eden*) whereas those who have violated God's laws will be everlastingly punished in *Gehinnom* (hell).

This eschatological scheme incorporating reward in heaven and punishment in hell was a serious attempt to explain God's ways. Israel is the chosen people and had received God's promise of reward for keeping his law. Since this did not happen on earth in this life, the rabbis believed it must occur in the world-to-come. Thus the individual who had died without seeing the justification of God would be resurrected to see the ultimate victory of the Jewish people. And just as the nations would be judged in the period of Messianic redemption, so would each person. In this way, the vindication of the righteous was assumed despite all the suffering on earth.

This scheme of salvation sustained the Jewish people through the centuries, but in modern times various aspects of traditional rabbinic eschatology have ceased to retain their hold on Jewish consciousness. Though Orthodox Judaism continues to subscribe to a belief in the coming of the Messiah, Reform Jews have tended to interpret Messianic redemption in worldly terms involving liberation from political and social oppression. Jews across the religious spectrum have found it increasingly difficult to believe in heavenly reward and everlasting punishment, and the doctrine of the resurrection of the dead has been generally replaced in both Orthodox and non-Orthodox Judaism by a belief in the immortality of the soul. Personal salvation thus continues to be an important feature of the Jewish faith, but it is largely disassociated from traditional rabbinic eschatology. As far as other religions are concerned, Jews have held the view that righteous Gentiles who subscribe to a belief in the laws given to Noah will receive a reward in the world-to-come.

In the New Testament, the concept of salvation is applied both to Jesus' ministry and to the redeeming acts of his Second Coming (parousia). In Matt. Christ is described as the one who saves his people from their sins: 'she will bear a son, and you shall call his name Jesus, for he will save his people from their sins' (Matt. 1.21). Further, in many of the healing miracles, restoration to health is viewed as a sign of salvation. Following rabbinic teaching, Paul believed that salvation also refers to a future event when God will judge the world, destroy the wicked, and establish his Kingdom on earth. Thus in Rom. he declared that the parousia and the Last Judgement were near at hand: 'For salvation is nearer to us now than when we first believed; the night is far gone, the day is at hand' (Rom. 13.11–12). For Paul, Jesus is the Saviour who is to bring about this transformation; 'we await a Saviour, the Lord Jesus Christ, who will change our lowly body to be like his glorious body, by the power which enables him even to subject all things to himself' (Phil. 3.20–21). Here and elsewhere Paul contends that eternal salvation has been made available through the death of Christ.

As the prospect of the immediate return of Jesus receded, this concept of salvation often came to be understood in spiritual and other-worldly terms. Rather than bringing about an earthly transformation of the human condition, Christians frequently envisaged salvation in heavenly terms as something that only happens completely in the future. In this connection, Christian theology elaborated complex doctrines of purgatory, heaven, and hell. In addition, salvation was perceived to be exclusive to Christianity. It was thus an urgent task to convert non-Christians to the true faith since only in this way could such individuals be saved. Although many Christians today still subscribe to these beliefs, there are some who find it increasingly difficult to believe in an exclusivistic conception of the afterlife reserved only for those who have accepted Christ. Thus within both faiths, salvation has been a central dimension of the religious tradition. In rabbinic Judaism, the belief in eternal life was conceived in relation to Messianic redemption, judgement, reward, and punishment. Rooted in this tradition, Christian thinkers expounded the salvific aspects of Christ's ministry, the fulfilment at his Second Coming, and they also looked forward to the promise of eternal salvation some time in the future.

Sanctification

God is the source of all holiness and the Jewish people are commanded to be holy because God is holy (Levi. 19.2). Thus the imitation of God is the first duty for a pious Jew, and the rabbis explained that this was to be attained through practising moral purity and being fearful of sin. Everyday life was to be sanctified by a strict observance of the teachings of the Torah. Jews are not required to withdraw from the world and pursue asceticism, but life in the world can be made holy through obedience to the commandments of God. Thus the dietary laws, the wearing of fringes, and the law of fixing a mezuzah (parchment scroll) to the door-post are all acts of sanctification by which a Jew dedicates himself to the way of the Lord.

Christians are also called to imitate the holiness of God (1 Pet. 1.15). However, unlike Judaism where sanctification is to be achieved through human effort, according to Christian teaching holiness is a free gift of God. As Paul put it in 1 Cor.: 'Do not be deceived; neither the immoral, nor idolaters, nor adulterers . . . will inherit the kingdom of God. And such were some of you. But you were washed, you were sanctified, you were justified in the name of the Lord Jesus Christ and in the Spirit of our God' (1 Cor. 6.9–11). Only through the transforming power of the Holy Spirit and the grace made available through the Church's sacraments can holiness be achieved. Paul, as a previously observant Jew, acknowledged the holiness of Jewish law: 'We know that the law is spiritual; but I am carnal, sold under sin' (Rom. 7.14). He had found it impossible to achieve holiness through the law, and Christians have followed his teaching that it can only be achieved through God's grace.

Sanctuary

In the Bible, the sanctuary (*mishkan*) was a portable shrine that the Israelites transported in the desert. It was built in accordance with God's instructions contained in Exod. 25–27. It stood in an open courtyard 100 cubits by 50 cubits. A fence around the courtyard consisted of wooden pillars placed every 5 cubits, from which a cloth curtain was hung. The middle 20 cubits of one of the short sides served as an entrance.

The sanctuary was in the eastern wall of the courtyard and was 30 cubits by 10 cubits. Three of its sides were made of acacia wood covered with gold; the other side had no wall. The boards were bound together by silver sockets; each board contained gold rings through which acacia wood bars covered with gold were placed. The Holy of Holies was located at the end of the sanctuary – it was separated from the rest of the sanctuary by a veil (on which were woven cherubs) suspended on five wooden pillars. The Ark was inside the Holy of Holies and contained two tablets with the Ten Commandments. A large cloth, which also had cherubs woven on it, extended from near the bottom of one of the two large sides of the sanctuary, over the top, and down to the other side. The front of the sanctuary had a similar covering with cherubs woven into it.

Inside, before the Holy of Holies, stood the table for shewbread, the incense altar, and the menorah (seven-branched candlestick). Another altar as well as a brass *laver* (wash basin) stood in the outer courtyard. This structure was eventually replaced by the Temple in Jerusalem which incorporated its numerous features. The Temple itself consisted of the Holy of Holies which housed the ark of the covenant; the Holy Place containing the altar of incense, the table of shewbread, and the menorah; and the court on the east containing the sacrificial altar. Surrounding the Temple were various buildings related to the cult. In 70CE the second Temple was destroyed, and the synagogue became the central religious institution in Judaism – it reflected in its contents various aspects of both the sanctuary and the Temple. The ark in the eastern wall contains the scroll of the law; a curtain hangs in front of the ark and there is often a menorah.

The earliest places for Christian worship were the houses of believers, but in time the community felt the need for buildings set apart for worship. These structures reflected various features of the sanctuary, which were adapted to Christian religious practice. Initially, there were relatively simple buildings, but after the Edict of Milan (313) churches came to be modelled on the basilica (a Roman building which served as a law court). The bishop's throne was placed in the apse (curved east end) and was surrounded by the seats of the clergy. In front stood the altar, below which were often housed the remains of a saint. Beyond this was the nave (from the Latin for 'ship'), the main part of the building for the congregation. In time, the altar became more distant from the laity. In the East, it was customary to separate the altar from the rest of the church by an iconostasis (a screen adorned with icons of the saints). In the West, the basilica plan was retained, but the church was divided by a screen. The chancel (for the clergy on the eastern side of the screen) contained a high altar. The nave (on the western side for the laity) held a pulpit, and sometimes a second altar. The chancel area became identified with the sanctuary because, like the Temple in Jerusalem, it contained the main altar and was thought of as the most sacred area of the building.

At the Reformation, church buildings were adapted in various ways: the screen was removed or made into a solid wall so that the entire community could worship in one room; the pulpit was placed on one of the long sides; the altar was removed and long tables were set up where the Lord's Supper was celebrated. A bracket was attached to the pulpit, which held the basin for baptism. In addition, some churches adopted a circular plan. With the romantic revival in the 18th–19th cent., the Gothic plan for church building was widely adopted. Despite evolution of architectural style, churches through the ages continued to echo certain features of the ancient sanctuary and, in addition, the Christian community adopted the biblical notion of refuge for fugitives in the altar of the sanctuary (1 Kings 1.50; 2.28). Traditionally, the altar in the Jerusalem Temple was considered a place of refuge similar to the cities of refuge mentioned in Deut. 19.1–7. Christian sanctuaries were first recognized by Roman law in the 4th cent. and canon law later permitted sanctuary in church to persons guilty of crimes of violence.

Sanhedrin *see* Courts; Synod

Satan *see* Devil

Saturday *see* Sabbath

Scapegoat

On the Day of Atonement it was customary in the Temple for the High Priest to draw lots over two male goats. One was sacrificed and the other, the scapegoat, was sent into the wilderness carrying all the sins of the Jewish people with it. The ritual is described in Lev. 16.

Jesus' crucifixion is understood by many Christians as an act of penal substitution. According to 1, Pet. 2.24, 'He himself bore our sins in his body on the tree.' Although the Jewish scapegoat ritual ended with the destruction of the Temple in 70 CE, the idea has survived in this interpretation of the atonement which was achieved through Jesus' suffering and death.

Scholasticism

The term is derived from the word for 'school', and Scholasticism literally refers to the educational traditions of the medieval schools. It has come to mean the medieval attempt to use philosophical ideas to understand Christian doctrine. Augustine (4th–5th cent.) taught his students that they should believe in order that they would understand. Following this precedent, Anselm (11th cent.) constructed the ontological argument for the existence of God and worked out a particular theory of the atonement on the basis of *fides quaerens intellectum* (faith seeking understanding).

Other influential theologians of this period include Abelard (11th–12th cent.), Peter Lombard (12th cent.), and Thomas Aquinas (13th cent.), whose *Summa Theologica* is regarded as the crowning achievement of Scholastic theology. By the 13th cent., the works of Aristotle had been translated from the Greek and Arabic and were enormously influential; Aquinas himself presented his doctrine in terms of argument, counter argument, and solution, and he distinguished clearly between faith and reason, showing their connection and complementarity. Scholasticism continued to be taught in Roman Catholic seminaries up until the present day, but has been less central to the Church's theological thinking since the Second Vatican Council (mid-20th cent.).

The Jewish philosopher Moses Maimonides (12th cent.) holds a similarly significant position in the history of theology as that of Thomas Aquinas. In his *Guide for the Perplexed*, he attempted to reconcile Aristotelian ideas with the teachings of rabbinic Judaism. Like Aquinas, he was concerned with such problems as the existence of God, the nature of good and evil, and divine providence, and he believed that spirituality could be fully integrated with reason. Thus both Jewish and Christian medieval theology were influenced by the intellectual currents of the time, and theologians of both traditions confronted the problem of reconciling faith with reason.

Screen

(*Mehitsah*): In Judaism, women have traditionally prayed in a separate area from men. In the Temple in Jerusalem there was a women's court (*Ezrat Nashim*), and this practice was retained in the synagogue. Either women sit in a gallery, curtained from view, or sometimes in a separate annex. When women and men sit on the same level, a screen (*mehitsah*) of metal, wood, or cloth is placed between the two areas. In Sephardi (Oriental) synagogues, the screen is sometimes pulled back for the reading of the Torah scrolls. The non-Orthodox movements, which insist on the complete equality of the sexes, do not have screens and in their synagogues families sit together.

Men and women do not sit separately in Christian churches, but very often churches have screens. These are to divide the choir or chancel where the priests sit, from the nave which is the place for the laity. In monastic churches, the screen was often impenetrable so that the common people could not even see the monks at prayer; but in Protestant churches, which have a less exalted view of the clergy, a screen is unusual.

Thus both Judaism and Christianity have felt a need to preserve a barrier in their places of worship. In Judaism the division is between men and women and in Christianity it is between priests and laity.

Scroll of the law

The Five Books of Moses, Genesis, Exodus, Leviticus, Numbers and Deuteronomy are hand-written on a large scroll (*Sepher Torah*), which is kept in the ark of a synagogue. From there it is taken out to be read each Sabbath, Monday and Thursday. There are many laws connected with the writing of the scroll – it must be on parchment from a ritually clean animal; the ink must be black and made to a traditional formula; each column of writing can have between 45 and 60 lines; and there are rulings on the precise shape of the letters used. Once the scroll is written, it is mounted on two rollers and covered with a sash and cloth mantle or with a wood or metal cover. The whole is then adorned with metal finials, a decorated breastplate, and a crown.

If a mistake is found in the scroll, it may not be used again until the error is corrected. The scroll is the most venerated of all Jewish ritual objects. The actual parchment may not be touched with the hand, and is read with a pointer. The congregation stands when it is brought out of the ark, and as the scroll is carried passed them, worshippers will touch it with their prayer shawls (tallit), and then kiss the prayer shawls. Before or after it is read, the open scroll is raised high so the congregation can see it. If a scroll is dropped on the ground, the whole congregation should fast, and once the scroll is too old for use it should be buried or stored in a special storage room (genizah).

Many ritual objects are accorded similar veneration in Christianity. The Eastern Church lays down a precise formulation for the painting of icons (religious pictures) to which genuflections (bowing the knee) are made and incense offered. Congregations stand for the entry of the cross, and the Roman Catholic and Anglican Churches use crucifixes (models of the cross with an image of Jesus hanging on it) for both public and private devotion. Relics of saints are also venerated. Similarly, when the Gospel is read at the Eucharist in the Roman Catholic Church, it is taken down in procession, and the book is censed before reading. It is usual to bow or genuflect before the cross on the altar, and kissing icons or the statues of the saints is a frequent practice. After the bread has been consecrated at the Eucharist, it is raised in much the same way that the Torah scroll is raised. Thus both Christians and Jews express their devotion to their central ritual objects in a similar manner.

Second Coming

(Parousia): Christians believe that Jesus will return to earth in glory to judge both those who have died and those who are still alive, and to establish God's Kingdom forever. The early Church thought that this event, the parousia (meaning 'presence'), was about to occur in the very near future, and the belief in the imminence of Judgement Day has been revived from time to time throughout the history of the Church, particularly among millenarian groups. The expectation is based on the recorded words of Jesus (e.g. Mark 8.38), and on the teachings of such apocalyptic books as Revelation.

Jews, who do not believe in the Messiahship of Jesus, do not accept that he will return to earth. They look for the second coming of Elijah who will 'turn the hearts of fathers to their children and the hearts of children to their fathers' (Mal. 4.6). Elijah will be the forerunner of the Messiah. It is the Messiah who will bring in an era of peace and harmony after which the dead will be raised, and judged on the great and terrible Day of the Lord. Thus both Jews and Christians look forward to a future judgement and the final era of God's Kingdom. For the Christians, it will occur with Jesus' second appearance, while Jews connect it with the first coming of the Messiah.

Secularism

The word 'secular' is derived from the Latin *saeculum*, meaning an era. The word came to refer to the institutions of the present era and was used to differentiate between worldly organizations and religious ones. Since the 19th cent., both the synagogue and the church have very largely been relegated to a narrow area of personal piety and religious influence. Most Jews and Christians send their children to secular schools, are employed by secular businesses, and participate in the secular political process. Even such spheres as care of the poor, counselling the unhappy, or punishing the wicked have been taken over by secular agencies such as the social services, the practitioners of psychiatric medicine, and state, and national correctional facilities.

Among a few Hasidic Jewish and extreme Christian sects there have been attempts to isolate adherents from the institutions of the contemporary world, but the influence of the modern mass media makes such effort highly problematic. Even in the State of Israel where the religious establishment has control of matters of personal status and whose religious parties are of necessity influential in forming coalition governments, the majority of the people ignore the laws of traditional Judaism. Outside Israel, secularism manifests itself in the Jewish community by increased assimilation and intermarriage. Similarly, the Church has far less influence in the lives of ordinary people than in the past, and in many countries church attendance even on festival days is the exception rather than the rule.

Seder *see* Passover

Semikhah *see* Ordination

Septuagint *see* Bible

Sermon *see* Homiletics

Sexual morality

(Adultery) (Chastity) (Homosexuality): In the Jewish tradition, legislation connected with sexual morality was enacted to hallow man's sexual instincts. The writers of the Hebrew Scriptures viewed sex as a central component of marriage; to marry and have children is the first commandment in Gen.: 'Be fruitful and multiply' (Gen. 1.28). It is thus the duty of all men to marry. Fidelity is viewed as a cardinal virtue, and modesty and restraint are to be exercised in sexual relations. Although the sexual drive is considered to be an expression of the evil inclination (*yetzer ha-ra*), it is bad only if uncontrolled.

Because sexuality is bound up with the creation of a family, any sexual acts that take place outside of marriage are forbidden. Thus according to Lev., homosexuality is viewed as a capital crime: 'If a man lies with a male as with a woman, both of them have committed an abomination; they shall be put to death' (Lev. 20.13). Bestiality is similarly condemned: 'If a man lies with a beast, he shall be put to death; and you shall kill the beast. If a woman approaches any beast and lies with it, you shall kill the woman and the beast' (Lev. 20.15–16). Again, adultery is castigated in similar terms: 'If a man commits adultery with the wife of his neighbour, both the adulterer and adulteress shall be put to death' (Lev. 20.10).

Also biblically forbidden are such acts as incest (Lev. 20.11–12), relationships with male or female prostitutes (Deut. 23.18), masturbation (Gen. 38.8–10), and wearing clothes of the opposite sex (Deut. 22.5). Such legislation sought to foster the ideal of holiness. Through the centuries rabbinic

sources stressed the centrality of such teaching, and these attitudes have continued until modern times. Nonetheless, in contemporary society some Reform rabbis have sought to modify such traditional prescriptions in the light of modern psychology and liberal thought.

As inheritors of the biblical tradition, the Christian community viewed relations within marriage as the only valid form of sexual intimacy. In the New Testament, this mutual relationship is understood as a reflection of the union of Christ and the Church. Thus Paul wrote: '"For this reason a man shall leave his father and mother and be joined to his wife, and the two shall become one flesh." This mystery is a profound one, and I am saying that it refers to Christ and the church' (Eph. 5.31–32). Through the ages, Christianity has endorsed heterosexual, monogamous, procreative marital relationships.

Since Christianity was influenced by Platonism, Stoicism, and Gnosticism, the faith absorbed a degree of suspicion about human sexuality. This is reflected in the espousal from the earliest times of chastity (understood as abstention from sexual intercourse). Following biblical teaching, sins against nature were viewed as those that interfere with the natural process of insemination (such as masturbation, sodomy, contraception, and bestiality). In addition, sins in accordance with nature but that violate moral norms (such as fornication, adultery, rape, and incest) were severely condemned. Procreation came increasingly to be seen as the primary purpose of sex, whereas the fostering of love was relegated to a position of secondary importance.

In the modern period, a number of Christian thinkers have advocated a more permissive approach to sexual ethics. For those who espouse a situation ethics, what is of central concern is whether a loving relationship exists between consenting partners – abstract rules are not to serve as the deciding factors in determining a course of action. Within this framework, it is possible to make a case for a more tolerant approach to such issues as pre-marital sex and homosexuality. Thus in both Judaism and Christianity, biblical teaching has been of central importance in determining standards of sexual behaviour through the centuries. However, in modern times, a more permissive approach to sexual ethics has been advocated by a number of liberal-minded members of both faiths.

Shabbat *see* Sabbath

Shalom *see* Peace

Shatnes *see* Clothing

Shavuot *see* Weeks, festival of

Sheitel *see* Clothing

Shekinah *see* Theophany

Shema *see* 'Hear O Israel'

Shiva *see* Funeral rites

Shofar *see* Trumpet

Shul *see* House of worship

Shulhan Arukh *see* Law books

Siddur *see* Prayer books

Sin

In the Bible, sin is understood as a transgression of God's decree. In Biblical Hebrew the word *het* means 'to miss' or 'to fail'. Here sin is understood as a failing, a lack of perfection in carrying out one's duty. The term *peshah* means a 'breach'; it indicates a broken relationship between man and God. The word *avon* expresses the idea of crookedness. Thus according to biblical terminology, sin is characterized by failure, waywardness, and illicit action. A sinner is one who has not fulfilled his obligations to God.

According to rabbinic Judaism, sins can be classified according to their gravity as indicated by the punishments prescribed by biblical law: the more serious the punishment, the more serious the offence. A distinction is also drawn in rabbinic texts between sins against other human beings (*ben adam la-havero*) and offences against God alone (*ben adam lap-Makom*). Sins against God can be atoned for by repentance, prayer, and giving charity. In cases of offence against others, however,

such acts require restitution and placation as a condition of atonement.

Rabbinic literature teaches that there are two tendencies in every person: the good inclination (*yetzer ha-tov*), and the evil inclination (*yetzer ha-ra*). The former urges individuals to do what is right, whereas the latter encourages sinful acts. At all times, a person is to be on guard against assaults of the *yetzer ha-ra*. It is not possible to hide one's sins from God since the Omnipresent knows all things. In the words of the Mishnah, 'Know what is above thee – an eye that sees, an ear that hears, and all thy deeds are written in a book.' Thus, God is aware of all sinful deeds, yet through repentence and prayer it is possible to achieve reconciliation with him.

In the New Testament, sin is recognized as rooted in human nature. Paul recognizes the impossibility of human behaviour being perfect and acceptable to God (Rom. 7.19). For Paul, sin is a breach of natural law written in the heart of man: 'When Gentiles who have not the law do by nature what the law requires, they are a law to themselves, even though they do not have the law. They show that what the law requires is written on their hearts' (Rom. 2.14–15). Unlike the legislation contained in the Torah, this law is universal. What is required of believers is to obey Christ; repentance comes from accepting the truth, love, and disclosure of God in Christ's ministry and death.

In the 2nd cent., Irenaeus (as against the teachers of dualistic heresies) defended the doctrine that evil came into the world through Adam's sin. Later, Methodius (4th cent.) argued that the full effects of the Fall are to be seen in human beings' inherent corruptibility. Didymus of Alexandria (4th cent.) believed that the transmission of the stain of original sin occurred through natural propagation. According to Augustine (4th–5th cent.), Adam's guilt is transferred to his descendants by concupiscence. In the Middle Ages, the doctrine of original sin became a central tenet of the faith, although varying opinions were expressed about its nature and transmission.

During the medieval period, personal sinfulness tended to be seen as a transgression that could be overcome through proper penance. Under the impact of Protestant teaching, however, such an external view of sin was largely rejected and the doctrine of justification by faith gained wide acceptance. In later centuries, those influenced by secularism tended to see sin in a moral rather than a religious setting. None the less, Christian theologians through the ages to the present day have been united in their conviction that obedience to Christ constitutes the true remedy for sin. Thus in both traditions sin is understood as a transgression of God's will: for the Jew these prescriptions are enshrined in the words of the Torah, whereas within Christianity they are manifest in the life and teaching of Jesus Christ.

Sin offering *see* Sacrifice

Skull cap *see* Clothing

Slavery

Servitude of one person to another. The Bible differentiates between a Hebrew and a Canaanite slave. A Hebrew became a slave because he was sold by a law court to repay a debt he could not otherwise repay, or because he could not support himself or his family. A Hebrew sold by a law court could not serve for more than seven years, but at the end of this period he could choose to remain a slave until the Jubilee Year. Such servitude was symbolized by the piercing of the slave's ear.

According to tradition, certain conditions must be fulfilled by the master of a slave. The sale of the slave must not take place in public, nor should he be obliged to do unlimited work, labour of no value, or demeaning activity. Jewish slaves must be supplied with the same quality of food and drink as the master, as well as the same type of living accommodation. A Hebrew slave who returns to his family must be given a grant by his former master: 'And when you let him go free from you, you shall not let him go empty-handed; you shall furnish him liberally out of your flock, out of your threshing floor, and out of your wine press' (Deut. 15.13–14).

A female can only become a slave if she is sold by her father. However, he should not undertake such a transaction unless he has no land or movable possessions. Yet in such cases, the father should redeem his daughter as soon as possible. A girl can only be sold while she is a minor; she is freed by the onset of puberty. The Torah protects her honour

– the master is to marry her or give her to his son in marriage. If this does not occur, she can go free without having to pay for the privilege (Exod. 21.11). Unlike a male slave, she cannot extend her service by having her ear pierced.

A Canaanite slave is bought for all time: 'you may buy male and female slaves from among the nations that are round about you ... You may bequeath them to your sons after you, to inherit as a possession for ever; you may make slaves of them' (Lev. 25.44–46). Nonetheless, if the slave is circumcised, he is to be treated as a member of the family. Slaves are required to rest on the Sabbath and observe the same commandments as women. It is possible for a foreign slave to be redeemed, or if the slave suffers a permanent injury through the action of his master, he is granted the right of freedom. Even though the Canaanite slave is the property of his master, he should not be mistreated. A Canaanite slave who has been freed can subsequently become a Jew. Despite the fact that the institution of slavery is legitimized in Scripture, the practice of slavery disappeared among Jews in the Middle Ages, and in modern times it is regarded as abhorrent and an offence against humanity.

In the New Testament, the proclamation of God's Kingdom was viewed as a blessing upon the poor – the meek are to inherit the earth. Thus Jesus brought the good news of the release of all who are enslaved: 'he has anointed me to preach good news to the poor. He has sent me to proclaim release to the captives and recovering of sight to the blind, to set at liberty those who are oppressed' (Luke 4.18). For Paul, Christ ushers in a new era in which there is no distinction between the free man and the slave: 'There is neither Jew nor Greek, there is neither slave nor free; there is neither male nor female; for you are all one in Christ Jesus' (Gal. 3.28). Slave and master are thus brothers and sisters in Christ.

Despite such teaching, the Church did not seek to abolish the institution of slavery. Jesus and Paul were both understood to be referring to spiritual slavery. In fact, as Christianity became established in the Roman Empire, the Church itself became a slave owner. Nonetheless, Augustine (4th–5th cent.) argued that slavery was a consequence of sin. Paradoxically, such a view tended to condition Christians to expect slavery to continue until the consummation of the Kingdom of God. In time, slavery was superseded by serfdom in a feudal order, and the exploration of Africa led to a large slave trade. During the Enlightenment, however, Christians became increasingly critical of slavery. As in Judaism, Christianity in the modern period has been fiercely critical of any form of slavery, despite the fact it is sanctioned in the Hebrew Scriptures.

Son of Man

In the Hebrew Scriptures, the term 'son of man' usually means 'a normal man', as in 'what is man that thou art mindful of him, and the son of man that thou dost care for him?' (Ps. 8.4). In the Book of Daniel, however, the writer states: 'behold, with the clouds of heaven there came one like a son of man . . . And to him was given dominion and glory and kingdom, that all peoples, nations, and languages should serve him' (7.13–14). Both Jews and Christians have interpreted Daniel's vision as a reference to the Messianic era.

Jesus frequently described himself as the Son of Man, as for example in, 'the Son of man came eating and drinking, and they say, "Behold, a glutton and a drunkard"' (Matt. 11.19). On other occasions, he talks of the Son of Man as if he is speaking of someone else, as in 'For whoever is ashamed of me and of my words in this adulterous and sinful generation, of him will the Son of man also be ashamed when he comes in the glory of his Father' (Mark 8.38). Some scholars argue that the title had a communal meaning and referred to the whole Messianic community. This interpretation takes into account the fact that the chapter in the Book of Daniel that mentions the 'Son of Man' goes on to say, 'the saints of the Most High shall receive the kingdom, and possess the kingdom for ever' (Dan. 7.18). Attempts have also been made to connect the Son of Man with the idea of the second Adam as found in Paul's first letter to the Corinthians (Ch. 15). Traditionally, however, the Church has explained Jesus' use of the title as an indication of his humble humanity in contrast with the glory of his nature as the second Person of the Trinity. In contrast, the rabbis taught that the 'Son of Man' was not an exalted title. Commenting on Num. 23.19 ('God is not man, that he should lie, or a son of man, that he should repent'), Rabbi Abbahu (4th

cent.) wrote, 'If a man says, "I am the Lord", he lies; if he says "I am the son of man", he will repent.'

Soul

Hebrew terms such as *nefesh, ruah*, and *neshamah* are usually translated as 'soul', but they do not refer to disembodied entities. Rather, they depict the animating spirit of the person. In rabbinic literature, however, the soul is understood as separate from the body. It is that element which is given by God to each individual which designates selfhood and departs from the body at death. In the words of the morning prayer: 'My God, the soul which you gave me is pure. You did create it. You did form it. You did breath it into me. You preserveth it within, and You will take it from me, but will restore it to me hereafter . . . Blessed are You, Lord, who restore souls to the dead.'

In the Middle Ages, Jewish theologians integrated such Jewish teaching with neo-Platonism, and Islamic concepts. According to Saadiah Gaon (9th–10th cent.), the soul was created together with the body; after death, it separates, but will eventually be reunited before the final Judgement. Moses Maimonides (12th cent.) asserted that the soul expresses itself according to five different faculties: nutritive, sensitive, imaginative, emotional, and rational. The first four aspects perish at the time of death, but individuals can attain immortality by developing the rational capacity. Ultimate reward was understood by Maimonides as the immortality of the soul with God, whereas punishment was viewed as complete extinction. Judah Halevi (12th cent.) and Hasdai Crescas (14th–15th cent.), on the other hand, taught that the development of the soul towards immortality depends upon moral actions and the love of God rather than intellectual activity.

During the medieval period, kabbalists (mystics) subscribed to the belief that the soul reappears after death and enters a new body. According to the *Bahir* (an early mystical work), God gives human beings another opportunity to atone for their sins and attain salvation after spending a first life as a wicked individual. In the 16th cent., the author of *Galya Raza* (another mystical work) stressed that the process of the transmigration of souls is a means of punishing sins. In the writings of Hayyim Vital (16–17th cent.), every one of the five parts of the soul migrates individually from body to body. Every soul is thus an amalgam of elements that have lived separately in the past in different locations. Related to these notions is the idea of the attachment of an evil soul to a living person (*dibbuk*). According to legend, a *dibbuk* is an evil spirit inside a person which speaks through his throat and causes the person great distress. Ceremonies to exorcise *dibbuks* are described in various mystical sources. In modern times, both Orthodox and non-Orthodox Judaism have tended to conceive of the hereafter in terms of the immortality of the soul rather than the resurrection of the body.

Following Jewish teaching, the early Church laid stress on the doctrine of the resurrection of the dead. After death, all human beings will be resurrected to a fully personal life with Christ in God. According to Paul, individuals will be raised in spiritual bodies: 'What is sown is perishable, what is raised is imperishable . . . It is sown as a physical body, it is raised a spiritual body' (1 Cor. 15.42,44).

In the patristic period, Platonic views of the soul exerted an important influence on Christian thought. Origen (2nd–3rd cent.), for example, believed that all spirits existed with God from eternity, and the Fall occurred before the world was created. The physical world was thus established as a testing-place for fallen souls. Although there was little agreement about the nature of the soul, Boethius' (5th–6th cent.) definition gained wide acceptance: 'An individual substance of rational nature' (*naturae rationalis individual substantia*).

Thomas Aquinas, in the 13th cent., utilized Aristotelian categories to describe the concept of the soul as an individual spiritual substance that is the form of the body. This will be united with the body after the general resurrection of the dead. In the modern period, there has been considerable debate about the idea of disembodied existence, yet many Christians of all denominations (as in Judaism) have tended to view the after-life in terms of the immortality of the soul rather than physical resurrection, although belief in the resurrection of the body is specified in the creeds. In both Judaism and Christianity, then, the doctrine of the soul has been a central feature of the faith, and has become increasingly important as the belief in physical resurrection has become more difficult to sustain in the light of scientific knowledge and secular thought.

Speaking in tongues

On the first Whitsunday when the disciples of Jesus received the Holy Spirit, in their joy they were heard speaking in many different languages (Acts 2.4–11). This phenomenon of speaking in tongues is also mentioned by Paul in his first letter to the Corinthians as one of the gifts of the Holy Spirit. The early Church saw it as a fulfilment of the prophecy of Joel concerning the Messianic age: 'I will pour out my spirit on your flesh; your sons and daughters shall prophesy' (Joel 2.28). Speaking in tongues still occurs in the Church, particularly at times of religious revival. It is a common part of worship among charismatic Protestant groups, but it occurs among adherents of all the Christian denominations. It is generally considered to be a form of ecstatic utterance; it is not understood by the speaker, but it is believed to be of particular spiritual benefit. Paul, however, stressed that comprehensible prophecy, although less dramatic, was a higher spiritual gift (1 Cor. 14.23, 24, 39).

Ecstatic utterance is also recorded in the Hebrew Scriptures – for example, by the recently anointed King Saul (1 Sam. 10.10). However, it was believed that the Holy Spirit ceased to inspire human beings after the last of the biblical prophets. Nonetheless, it was accepted that the Holy Spirit rests on pious Jews in every generation. As in Christianity, possessing the Spirit does not necessarily result in prophecy or speaking in tongues. Yet a similarly ecstatic phenomenon can be observed on the Festival of Rejoicing in the Law (*Simhat Torah*), which takes place on the ninth day of the festival of Tabernacles (Sukkot). It is traditional that day to sing, dance, and rejoice in thanksgiving for the gift of Torah. Among the Hasidim (a modern pious sect), in particular, the manifestation of their ecstatic joy is akin to that of a charismatic Christian speaking in tongues.

Spirituality

Spirituality is a fashionable term in both Judaism and Christianity for the beliefs, practices, and attitudes that inspire and express people's deepest concerns. Within both religions there are many different traditions of spirituality and, particularly at times of religious revival, there is a tendency to draw from the different strands to evolve a new tradition of prayer and ritual. Thus, for example, both

151

Jewish and Christian feminists seek to uncover within classic Jewish and Christian writings a recognition of the importance of the feminine principle in such fundamental concepts as God, personhood, wisdom, and creation. By rediscovering and reviving forgotten traditions, a new, uniquely feminist spirituality is forged. Similarly, with the growth of Christian–Jewish understanding and dialogue, individual Christians and Jews have found their own spiritual life deepened by sharing in joint services, by studying each other's spiritual classics, and by observing each other's customs.

Star of David *see* Symbolism

Suffering

In the Bible, the existence of suffering was generally viewed as a punishment for sin. Yet the existence of innocent suffering posed serious problems. Thus Habakkuk proclaimed: 'Why dost thou look on faithless men, and art silent when the wicked swallows up the man more righteous than he?' (Hab. 1.13). The Book of Job deals with this problem in detail. Job's friends subscribed to the traditional Jewish view: Job's suffering must be punishment from God for unwitting deviation from the Torah. However, the author maintains that Job was a righteous man. God's ways cannot be explained and God's questioning of Job points to human ignorance of the Divine plan: 'Where were you when I laid the foundation of the earth? Tell me, if you have understanding. Who determined its measurements – surely you know!' (Job 38.4–5).

During the Middle Ages, most Jewish thinkers adopted the Platonic view that evil is not an independent entity – rather, it is simply the absence of good. Kabbalists (mystics), on the other hand, believed in the reality of evil which they conceived as a residue of the primeval world. God created evil in order to challenge human beings to overcome it. Despite this debate as to the nature of evil, Jews through the centuries were convinced that reward for the righteous and punishment for the evil will take place in the hereafter. Thus the Mishnah declares: 'The world is like an antechamber to the world-to-come; prepare yourself in the antechamber so that you may enter into the hall.' This concept of a two-stage human existence helped Jews to make sense of God's ways. Suffering was

seen as a means for spiritual growth and development. In their reflections about the nature of ultimate reward and punishment, the rabbis referred to *Gan Eden* (heaven) as the place of reward, and *Gehinnom* (hell) as the place of punishment. Heaven was for those members of the community who had followed the way of Torah (law), whereas hell was for those Jews who had rejected it.

These ideas have served as the mainstay of the Jewish faith until the present day, when it has become increasingly difficult for Jews to believe in an afterlife. In the place of traditional rabbinic eschatology many Jews have looked to the State of Israel to provide a basis for survival in the modern world. Rather than believing in a heavenly protector who will safeguard the interests of his chosen people, Jewry has increasingly put its faith in the Holy Land as a bulwark against anti-Semitism. Thus in modern times there has been a significant shift away from traditional theological explanations of human suffering to politically oriented solutions to the problem.

Drawing on the Jewish view that God himself suffers through the tribulations of Israel, the New Testament viewed Jesus as the suffering servant of God who endured hardship for all people. As the Son of God, his suffering is Divine suffering, providing a vicarious atonement for the sins of the world. As Paul explained in the epistle to the Romans: 'since all have sinned and fall short of the glory of God, they are justified by his grace as a gift, through the redemption which is in Christ Jesus, whom God put forward as an expiation by his blood' (Rom. 3.23–25). Jesus' death on the cross serves as the means whereby all can be reconciled to God: 'For in him all the fullness of God was pleased to dwell, and through him to reconcile to himself all things, whether on earth or in heaven, making peace by the blood of his cross' (Col. 1.20).

Through the centuries, Christian theologians (like Jewish thinkers) have sought to make sense of the theological difficulties posed by the existence of evil. In the patristic period, a number of writers such as Irenaeus (2nd cent.) and Augustine (4th–5th cent.) followed the Platonic line and argued that evil is simply a privation of good. Such a view continued to influence Christian theologians in the Middle Ages. During the Reformation,

Protestant thinkers tended to view evil as part of God's providential plan – it serves to bring about good, and in the end will be overcome. In modern times, Christians have continued to wrestle with the problem of theodicy, and various conflicting theories have been propounded to reconcile God's goodness with the existence of human suffering.

Despite such variety of views about theodicy, Christians have been united in their conviction that both the righteous and the wicked will be judged in a future life. Adopting eschatological beliefs based on Jewish precedent, they have looked to the world-to-come as a source of compensation for the ills endured in this life. Both traditions therefore have grappled with the problem of suffering, and in general have offered similar theological explanations. Yet for Christians it is Christ's self-giving love that is fundamental to the understanding of God's relationship with humanity, whereas Jews rely on their adherence to the way of Torah as the means by which God's loving justice is ultimately revealed.

Suffering servant

In the second part of the Book of Isaiah, a servant of God is described who is not recognized by his own people, who suffers in silence for the sins of others, and who is ultimately vindicated by the Lord (see Isa. 42.1–4; 49.1–6; 50.1–11; 52.13–53.12). Jewish commentators have explained these passages by understanding the servant as a collective symbol for the Israelite nation. Throughout history the Jews have suffered, but through their obedience God is glorified (Isa. 49.3). Christians, on the other hand, have insisted that these verses are a prediction of the suffering and death of Jesus. Through his crucifixion, as Peter wrote in his first epistle: 'He himself bore our sins in his body on the tree, that we might die to sin and live to righteousness. By his wounds you have been healed' (1 Pet. 2.24). Thus both Jews and Christians understand the servant passages as looking to the future, but they have a different understanding as to whom they refer.

Suicide

Because a human being is not his own creator, suicide is strictly forbidden in both the Jewish and Christian traditions. Although there are instances of mass suicide in Jewish history – such as on the fortress of Masada in 72CE or the martyrs of York in 1190 – in general, people are not permitted to end their own lives. Rather than commit murder, adultery, or idol worship, however, Jews are to submit to being killed, but they should not actively destroy themselves. Traditionally, those who die as a result of suicide are buried separately in a Jewish cemetery.

The Christian Church has been equally disapproving. Augustine (4th–5th cent.) described suicide as self-murder, and Thomas Aquinas (13th cent.) condemned suicide as contrary to natural law. It was in effect rejecting the life that was given by God. As in Judaism, suicides were buried separately, traditionally outside consecrated ground.

In recent years, with increased knowledge of psychology, a more tolerant view of suicide has been taken by both Christians and Jews. In general, suicide is seen to be the result of a mental illness or overwhelming sense of failure, and is thus a cause for pity rather than condemnation.

Sukkot *see* Tabernacles, feast of

Sunday *see* Sabbath

Superstitions

(Witchcraft): The Bible decrees that the Israelites are not to engage in the superstitious practices of the nations whose land they are to inherit: 'When you come into the land which the Lord your God gives you, you shall not learn to follow the abominable practices of those nations. There shall not be found among you any one who burns his son or his daughter as an offering, any one who practises divination, a soothsayer, or an augur, or a sorcerer, or a charmer, or a medium, or a wizard, or a necromancer' (Deut. 18.9–11). Similarly, in the prophetic books, superstition was vigorously denounced. Thus Jeremiah declared: 'So do not listen to your prophets, your diviners, your dreamers, your soothsayers, or your sorcerers' (Jer. 27.9).

The Mishnah also deals with various forms of punishment for witchcraft. According to the Talmud, such practices are mostly prevalent among women, as exemplified by Simeon ben Shetah's decree that 80 witches be executed on the same

153

day. The Talmud stipulated a variety of superstitious actions that are punishable by whipping: 'Reading things into certain occurrences, telling fortunes from sands and stones, astrological forcasts, and reciting formulas to promote healing.'

Despite these prescriptions, superstitious practices continued into the Middle Ages with the use of divine names in remedies, charms, and amulets. Under kabbalistic (mystical) influence, mystics engaged in a wide variety of magical activities, and in the 17th–18th cent., wonder-workers began to appear in Eastern Europe who practised popular medicine and used amulets to drive away demons. By the knowledge of secret names they were supposedly able to unmask thieves, find lost property, and purify homes from evil spirits. In addition, they were able to exorcise the spirits of the dead who were believed to reside in human persons (*dibbuk*), and create robot-like creatures (*golem*). In modern times, however, such superstitious practices have lost their hold on Jewish consciousness – probably as a result of the rise of modern science.

In the New Testament, Paul refers to the practice of sorcery in Gal. 5.20, and in the patristic age a number of Church Fathers believed in the efficacy of such actions. However, it was opposed by some figures such as Hippolytus (2nd–3rd cent.), John Chrysostom (4th–5th cent.), and Caesarius of Arles (5th–6th cent.). In the early Middle Ages, Charlemagne (8th–9th cent.) prevented the persecution of witches, and in the following centuries a number of bishops wrote against such persecution. In the 11th cent., Gregory VII forbade the killing of women for allegedly causing such events as storms and epidemics.

In the Middle Ages, popular superstition was given a new impetus by Jewish and Islamic magical practices. During this period, Pope Alexander IV (13th cent.) and John XXII (14th cent.) allowed the Inquisition to deal with cases of witchcraft if they were linked to heresy. In Germany, secular courts also punished such crimes with exile as well as burning. In 1484, Innocent VIII encouraged inquisitions to take severe actions against witches. In the same century, the publication of *Malus Maleficarum* prescribed such activities as witches' Sabbaths, intercourse with the devil, transmigration into animals, and malicious spells cast on human beings and cattle. During the Reformation, Protestants adamantly opposed all superstitious acts, and in England a large number of women were hanged for witchcraft during the Commonwealth period. With the influence of the Enlightenment, the persecution of witches lessened; and in the modern period, superstitious folk beliefs have virtually disappeared from Christian life. Thus in Judaism and Christianity, magic and superstition have played a significant role in the history of both religions, but in contemporary society they have generally disappeared.

Symbolism

(Cross) (Crucifix) (Magen David) (Star of David): The Book of Exodus records God's instructions to Bezalel the craftsman: 'I have filled him with the Spirit of God, with ability and intelligence, with knowledge and all craftsmanship, to devise artistic designs, to work in gold, silver, and bronze, in cutting stones for setting, and in carving wood, for work in every craft' (Exod. 31.3–5). Yet despite this positive attitude to artistry, Scripture forbids any violation of the second commandment: 'beware lest you act corruptly by making a graven image for yourselves, in the form of any figure, the likeness of male or female, the likeness of any beast that is on the earth, the likeness of any winged bird that flies in the air, the likeness of anything that creeps on the ground, the likeness of any fish that is in the water under the earth' (Deut. 4.16–18).

The interpretation of this biblical prohibition has varied widely through the centuries. At times, the most strict interpretation was adopted, while in other periods a much more liberal stance became dominant. In the Greco-Roman period, a variety of symbols including the palm (*lulav*), citron (*etrog*), ram's horn (*shofar*), ark of the law, and the menorah (seven-pronged candlestick) were used in synagogues and for funerary objects. In addition, biblical scenes, figures of biblical heroes, and animal figures have been found in early synagogues.

In medieval times, Moses Maimonides (12th cent.) argued that the prohibition against making images for decorative purposes refers only to the human figure. For this reason, it is not permitted to fashion a human figure in wood, plaster, or stone. However, this applies only to figures in the round; if they are sunken, painted on a board, or woven in tapestry, it is allowed. Such a view was subscribed to by a number of prominent authorities of this period.

From the Middle Ages onwards, Jewish artists devoted attention to ritual objects, spice boxes, wine cups, Hanukkah candelabra, Torah scroll covers, the Passover Haggadah, marriage contracts, the scroll of Esther, the Prayer Book and the Bible. From the 18th cent., the Star of David, or Magen David (six-pointed star which was said to be the device on King David's shield), has been used as a unifying symbol of the Jewish people. In modern times, Jewish works of art of different kinds have been encouraged within the various branches of the religious establishment.

Following Jewish practice in the Hellenistic world, Christians decorated the walls of their worship places and catacombs with figures representing the Good Shepherd, Jonah and the whale, and other biblical scenes in a style derived from pagan Roman imagery. During the Byzantine period, sumptuous colours were used in Christian decoration to portray the Kingdom of God on earth. Figures with large eyes, schematized trees, and animals with ornamental colours were frequently utilized.

In the 8th cent., iconoclastic tendencies began to curtail Christian art; Celtic monasticism meanwhile produced decorative manuscript art containing plants, flowers, and allegorical beasts. By the Middle Ages, sculptured human figures appeared in church exteriors, and craftsmen worked with the basic plan of a cross to fashion churches and cathedrals of enormous proportions. The interior of these buildings were filled with pietà sculptures, murals, and stained glass portraying scenes related to the Bible and the Christian life. During the Renaissance, biblical stories, madonnas, annunciations, and adorations became the subject-matter of countless artists, and this tradition has continued into the modern world.

In the history of Christian art the crucifix (paralleling the Star of David in Judaism) served as the dominant symbolic motif of the Christian faith. In the 6th cent., Jesus was portrayed as victorious, reigning from the tree. From the 10th cent., realism in Christian art began to replace symbolism, culminating in an emphasis on Christ's suffering and death. In the Eastern Church, however, there was an aversion to sculptured portrayals, and art was restricted to the icon (holy picture). Thus in Judaism and Christianity the artistic expression of biblical history as well as religious motifs was a constant feature through the centuries, despite the warnings of the second Commandment. Religious truths were conveyed through architecture, sculpture, and painting. However, within the Christian world the affirmation of Jesus' Messiahship and Divinity led to a range of symbolism not found in the Jewish tradition.

Synagogue *see* House of worship

Synod

(Sanhedrin): The Great Sanhedrin (Council) in Jerusalem, which flourished at the time of the second Temple (3rd cent. BCE–1st cent. CE), was a legislative body to which lesser Sanhedrins in each city submitted questions. By the time of King Herod the Great (1st cent. BCE), its authority was purely religious. When the Temple was destroyed in 70CE, the Sanhedrin moved to Yavneh and subsequently to other towns. It continued to interpret the law and issue religious decrees and ordinances. So great was its prestige in its heyday that its authority spread far beyond the land of Israel. It was eventually dismantled in the 5th cent. by the Romans.

There have been various attempts to revive the Sanhedrin. When Napoleon convened a Jewish Assembly in 1807, it was called the Sanhedrin; and, with the foundation of the State of Israel in 1948, the re-establishment of a central rabbinic council with ultimate religious authority over the Jewish world was suggested. As yet, this idea has received little support, even from the Orthodox.

Similarly, Acts 15 describes the calling of a council, and this tradition was continued in the Christian Church. Periodically, a formal meeting of bishops or Church leaders was called to define doctrine or establish matters of Church discipline. Seven councils are generally agreed to be ecumenical (i.e., pertaining to the whole world). The last one, the Second Council of Nicaea, took place in 787CE. As a result of the growing schism between the Eastern and Western Church (9th cent. onwards), a general council of the whole Church was no longer possible, although the Roman Catholics recognize 14 other ecumenical councils.

Traditionally, the decrees of an ecumenical council are considered to have the highest possible authority in the Church. Local councils or synods are still called regularly within the various branches of the Church, but they only have local authority.

Thus in the past, both Judaism and Christianity looked to a council as its supreme authority on matters of doctrine or religious practice. In both cases, however, universally authoritative councils have not met for well over 1,000 years because of political pressure and internal disagreement.

T

Tabernacle

According to Exod. 25–27, when the Israelites were travelling in the wilderness on their way to the Promised Land, Moses made a portable shrine, known as the sanctuary or tabernacle. It stood in the centre of the camp in a large open courtyard. At the eastern end of the courtyard, a structure was built of three walls and one open side. Inside stood the Holy of Holies, hidden by a long curtain. The ark of the covenant containing the two tables of the Ten Commandments were kept in the Holy of Holies. In front of the Holy of Holies stood the menorah (candelabrum), the altar for incense, and the table for shewbread. This tabernacle was finally superseded when King Solomon (10th cent. BCE) built the Temple in Jerusalem where the ark was lodged permanently. The original tabernacle was thought to embody God's presence among the travelling Israelites. Probably it was the same as the tent of meeting, which is described in Exod. 33.7–10. It is reported that the pillar of cloud descended on this when Moses entered it, and Moses spoke to God 'face to face, as a man speaks to his friend' (Exod. 33.11).

Christians describe the ornamental case which is used in the Roman Catholic Church for housing the blessed sacrament (the consecrated bread and wine) as a tabernacle. Normally it is kept on the altar, covered with a veil, and a light burns in front of it. Here the faithful come to pray. Because Roman Catholics believe that the bread and wine become in substance the body and blood of Christ,

the tabernacle does in effect contain the presence of God. Thus the Jewish tabernacle in the wilderness and the Christian tabernacle in churches both embody the presence of God among his faithful people.

Tabernacles, feast of

(*Etrog*) (*Lulav*) (*Sukkot*): The Jews celebrate the festival of Tabernacles (Sukkot) for eight days beginning on 15 Tishri. Outside Israel, the first day is celebrated twice, while the eighth and ninth day are also holidays; the intermediate days have a special liturgy, but work is allowed. Tabernacles is one of the three pilgrim festivals (the other two being Passover and Weeks) when it was traditional to go to the Temple in Jerusalem. Like the other pilgrim festivals, the feast has both an agricultural and an historical dimension. It is the major harvest festival, and it commemorates the Israelites' 40-day sojourn in the wilderness when they lived in tabernacles. To remember this time, Jews are instructed to 'dwell in booths for seven days . . . that your generations may know that I made the people of Israel dwell in booths when I brought them out of the land of Egypt' (Lev. 23.42–43).

Today this commandment is observed by building a temporary structure at home. Traditionally, it is open to the sky, decorated with fruit and flowers, and all meals are eaten there unless it is too cold or wet. During the synagogue service, the four species, the citron (*etrog*), palm (*lulav*), myrtle and willow are waved in every direction to indicate God's universal rule over the world, and the Book of Ecclesiastes is read. Every day the congregation walks in procession around the synagogue, and on the seventh day the circuit is made seven times. On the eighth day (*Shemini Atseret*), a prayer for rain is said and on *Simhat Torah* (the Day of Rejoicing in the Law), the annual Torah reading cycle is concluded, and the new one begins. *Simhat Torah*, the eighth day of Tabernacles in Israel and the ninth day elsewhere, is a time of great rejoicing. The scrolls of the law are taken out of the ark and are carried in procession seven times round the synagogue accompanied by music and dancing. At the morning service it is customary to call up every man in the congregation to read from the Torah.

There is no equivalent festival in Christianity, although most churches do hold an unofficial harvest thanksgiving service. This takes place at about the same times as the festival of Tabernacles (September or October). Like the temporary Jewish tabernacles, churches are decorated with flowers and fruit, and these are subsequently given to charity. Special hymns are sung, and prayers are said to give thanks to God for the produce of the earth.

Tallit *see* Prayer shawl

Talmud *see* Law books

Tanakh *see* Bible

Targum *see* Biblical interpretation

Temple *see* House of worship

Ten commandments

(Decalogue): The Ten Commandments were spoken by God to Moses after the Israelites had escaped from slavery in Egypt. Subsequently, they were inscribed on two tablets of stone. They are recorded twice in the Hebrew Scriptures (in Exod. 20.2–17 and Deut. 5.6–21), and among the 613 commandments of the Pentateuch they are regarded as of central significance. They were kept in the ark of the covenant in the sanctuary and the Jerusalem Temple. Nowadays, when they are read in the synagogue, the congregation stands and the reader connects them together with a special cantilation (chanting). The rabbis taught that the two tables on which they were inscribed were prepared even before the creation of the world, and so the Ten Commandments have universal application beyond space and time.

The Commandments enjoin (1) that no other god but God should be worshipped; (2) that no idol should be made or worshipped; (3) that God's name should not be used falsely or lightly; (4) that the Sabbath day should be kept holy; (5) that parents should be honoured; (6) that murder is forbidden; (7) that adultery is forbidden; (8) that theft is forbidden; (9) that falsehood against neighbours is forbidden; and (10) that coveting the possessions of others is forbidden.

Jesus himself taught the Ten Commandments (Matt. 19.17–19), and commented on them in the Sermon on the Mount (Matt. 5.21–37). They remained an integral part of Christian teaching, and since the time of Augustine (4th–5th cent.) were used in the instruction of new converts. Many churches have them written up above the altar, and they are as familiar and important to practising Christians as they are to pious Jews.

Ten days of repentance *see* Days of awe

Tephillin *see* Phylacteries

Tetragrammaton *see* Jehovah

Theism *see* Monotheism

Theocracy

In the Bible, Samuel objected to the institution of kingship on the grounds that this would displace God's sovereign rule: 'the thing displeased Samuel when they said: "Give us a king to govern us." ... And the Lord said to Samuel, "Hearken to the voice of the people in all that they say to you; for they have not rejected you, but they have rejected me from being king over them"' (1 Sam. 8.6–7). Throughout the history of ancient Israel, the prophets criticized monarchs for abandoning God's law and, in the 1st cent. CE, the Zealot rebellion was motivated by the belief that God alone should rule over the people. From the time of the destruction of the second Temple CE, 70, Jewish life was dominated by the rabbinate which controlled the community through Halakah (Jewish law) – in this sense, the people were ruled by God's decree. Subsequently, Jewish autonomy was replaced by the authority of the state, but in modern Israel the Orthodox have sought to subject Israelis to religious legislation.

Despite the political realities of Jewish existence through the centuries, Jews have longed for the establishment of God's Kingdom on earth. References to divine Kingship are found throughout the liturgy, and the standard opening of every benediction is: 'Blessed art Thou, O Lord, our God, King of the Universe'. In the liturgy of the festivals, the sovereignty of God is a predominant theme. Thus on the New Year, the enthronement of God as King is a central motif, and the concluding blessing of the *Malkhuyyot* (prayers for God's Kingdom)

('Reign Thou in glory over the whole Universe, that . . . whatever hath breath in its nostrils may say, "The Lord God of Israel is King and His dominion ruleth over all . . . Blessed art Thou, O Lord, King over all the earth"') has been incorporated into the daily service.

In his teaching, Jesus both claimed he was establishing God's rule on earth (Luke 11.20) and instructed his followers to look forward to it in the future (Mark 13.32–37). When the early Christian community became a separate body of believers, it had to consider its relationship to dominant political powers. In the New Testament, there are contrasting attitudes. Paul in Rom. 13 argued that Christians should be obedient to the state: 'Let every person be subject to the governing authorities. For there is no authority except from God, and those that exist have been instituted by God' (Rom. 13.1). Yet in the Book of Revelation, the view is expressed that Roman rule is soon to be destroyed by God's judgement (Rev. 13. 17–18). With the conversion of Constantine (3rd–4th cent.), and the establishment of Christianity as the religion of the Empire by Theodosius (4th cent.), the Christian faith reached an accommodation with secular authority. In the Byzantine period in particular, Christianity was subject to imperial regulation and intervention.

Medieval Europe, however, became a Christian society in which ecclesiastic leaders exercised political authority. From the 11th cent, onwards, the papacy engaged in a sustained struggle with the Holy Roman Empire as well as with the kings of Western Europe. From the time of the Reformation, royal control was exerted over Christian institutions; in England, for example, Henry VIII was declared supreme head of the Church. Yet during this period, attempts were also made to create Christian commonwealths, as in the case of England after the Civil War, Calvinist Geneva, and Puritan Massachusetts. In addition, a number of Christian radicals and sectarians attempted to develop voluntary communities removed from the exercise of political power. With the rise of the Enlightenment in the 18th cent., the way was paved for religious toleration as enshrined in various political constitutions. In the modern period, the affirmation of religious liberty has led to the separation of Church and State in most countries. Thus, over the centuries, Christians have expressed considerable uncertainty about the precise relationship between the Christian faith and political power. Yet, as in Judaism, there has been a constant longing for God's reign – the Messianic promises were concerned with a King who would usher in a new order on earth and, obeying Jesus' command, Christians continue to pray for the coming of God's Kingdom on earth (Matt. 6.10).

Theodicy

(Evil): Vindication of God's justice. According to the Jewish faith, God exercised both justice and mercy in creating the universe. In the Jewish liturgy, he is portrayed as the ultimate Judge. On week-days within the context of the *Amidah* prayer, God is addressed in terms of the attributes of justice and mercy: 'The King who loves charity and justice.' During the High Holy Days (New Year, Day of Atonement, and the intervening Days of Penitence), God judges the people of Israel. Given such affirmations about God's nature, Jewish thinkers have been preoccupied with the question why the innocent suffer and the wicked prosper. Thus in the Bible Jeremiah asked: 'Why does the way of the wicked prosper?' (Jer. 12.1). In the Book of Habakkuk, the prophet lamented: 'O Lord, how long shall I cry for help, and thou wilt not hear? Or cry to thee "Violence!" and thou wilt not save? . . . so the law is slackened and justice never goes forth. For the wicked surround the righteous, so justice goes forth perverted' (Hab. 1.2–4).

In Scripture, various answers are given. Amos asserted that because of God's special relationship with Israel, more is expected of his chosen people: 'You only have I known of all the families of the earth; therefore I will punish you for all your iniquities' (Amos 3.2). The suffering servant passages in Isa. 53 have been interpreted as implying that Israel suffers in order to bring about atonement for the sins of others. In the Book of Job, suffering is presented as a test of faith. Yet in the same book, God declares to Job that his divine plan cannot be comprehended by human reason.

In rabbinic sources, the sages maintained that in the hereafter individuals will receive their true reward or punishment. Thus the Talmud declares that since there is no reward in this world for keeping God's commandments, this must take place in a future life. In their reflections about the hereafter, the rabbis depicted *Gan Eden* (Garden of Eden) as the place of reward, and *Gehinnom* (Gehenna) as the place of punishment. Earthly existence was conceived as an antechamber to the world-to-come: Jews are to prepare themselves in this life so that they might be accorded a place in eternity.

In the Middle Ages, a number of Jewish philosophers discussed the nature of reward and punishment. According to Saadiah Gaon (9th–10th cent.), the souls of the righteous and the wicked are kept separate until the resurrection of the dead, which will take place after the coming of the Messiah. Once bodies and souls are reunited, judgement will occur and the righteous will be rewarded and the wicked punished in the world-to-come. Moses Maimonides (12th cent.) asserted that resurrection will take place after the advent of the Messiah. For the righteous, reward will consist of a purely spiritual existence in the presence of God, but the wicked will undergo extinction. In modern times, this traditional eschatological scheme has come under critical scrutiny, and the problem of theodicy has become increasingly acute, especially in the light of the Holocaust.

Within Christianity, theologians have adopted a number of approaches to the problem of evil. Privation theories, associated with Augustine (4th–5th cent.) and Thomas Aquinas (13th cent.), assert that evil is not something in itself; rather, it is the absence of good. Evil (as the privation of good) is thus viewed as entering the world through sin – it is not willed by God, but brought about by those who do evil. The responsibility for such privation does not lie with God; he simply permits people to choose to do evil. A second group of theories explains the existence of evil by demonstrating what purposes it serves. Inspired by Irenaeus (2nd cent.), these writers maintain that pain, suffering, and sin are necessary for human beings to grow spiritually. Each person's life is a journey, and evil is seen as a necessary part of this process of personal development. Human suffering is thus viewed as the means to make persons better, worthy to participate in the Divine life. A third group of theodicies redefine traditional theological categories to eliminate the problem of evil. Modern Process theologians, for example, have understood God's omnipotence as omni-persuasive rather than

all-powerful: he has the power to persuade rather than control human beings. Evil enters the world when human beings resist God's will.

Despite such theological reflection, Christians through the centuries have embraced the doctrine of the afterlife as a way of making sense of God's justice. Following Jewish patterns of thought, Christians subscribed to a belief in the final fulfilment of human existence in the world-to-come. For Christians, heaven means the decisive communication of God and the transformation of self in his presence; hell is conceived as the dwelling place of the damned. Christians have formulated a variety of conceptions of these realms. Nevertheless, through the ages, Christians of all denominations have subscribed to the belief that since the righteous did not receive their just reward in this life, God's justice would be meted out in a future existence. Thus both Jews and Christians have been preoccupied with the question of God's just rule, yet both faiths have ultimately looked to eternal reward and punishment as the way of making sense of suffering in this world.

Theology

Systematic study of religious belief. The Bible contains little theological reflection; it is a record of the history of the religious experience of the ancient Israelites. Theological views are expressed throughout the Talmud, but they are not presented systematically. Often the opinions and arguments of the sages are compressed into epigrams, parables, or brief stories. Rather than formulate the contents of the Jewish faith into a set of dogma, religious principles were left fluid. Nevertheless, the rabbis subscribed to a belief in a providential Lord of history who has guided his chosen people on earth, and will inaugurate a new era in the world-to-come.

Under the influence of Hellenistic thought, Philo (1st cent. BCE–1st cent. CE) attempted to reconcile the Jewish tradition with Greek philosophy. By applying an allegorical mode of exegesis to Scripture, he developed the concept of the Divine Logos (or Wisdom of God), which he identified with God's attributes of justice and mercy as well as with the angelic realm. The desire to engage in theological speculation did not re-emerge until the Middle Ages when Jews came into contact with

Islamic-Arabic civilization. During this period, Jewish theologians strove to defend rabbinic Judaism against attack from the Karaites (who acknowledged only the authority of the Bible) and Islamic and Christian scholars.

Medieval Jewish theology began with Saadiah Gaon's (9th–10th cent.) *Book of Beliefs and Opinions*, which provided a rational defence of the basic concepts of Judaism. In the 11th cent., Solomon ibn Gabirol worked out a metaphysical system along neo-Platonic lines in his *Fountain of Life*. In the next century, Bahya ibn Pakuda's *Duties of the Heart* was written to intensify the inner religious experience. In the same century, Judah Halevi composed the *Kuzari*, a philosophical work in the form of a dialogue between the king of the Khazars and a Jewish scholar. Abraham ibn Daud's (12th cent.) *The Exalted Faith* was based on Aristotle, as was Moses Maimonides' (12th cent.) *Guide for the Perplexed*. In the 14th cent., Levi ben Gershom produced *Wars of the Lord*, a scholarly discussion of central problems of religious philosophy. During this period, Hasdai Crescas analysed the basic doctrines of Judaism in *Light of the Lord*, and in the following century Joseph Albo also discussed the dogmas of Judaism.

The period of the Enlightenment produced such figures as Moses Mendelssohn (18th cent.), who sought to defend the Jewish religion on philosophical grounds. In the 19th cent., a number of German scholars (including Solomon Ludwig Steinheim, Samuel Holdheim, and Abraham Geiger) attempted to present a theology of Judaism consistent with contemporary thought. In the same century, Samson Raphael Hirsch, the founder of neo-Orthodoxy, defended traditional Judaism. In recent times, such thinkers as Herman Cohen (19th–20th cent.), Mordecai Kaplan (19th–20th cent.), Franz Rosenzweig (19th–20th cent.), and Martin Buber (19th–20th cent.) presented various interpretations of Jewish theology in the light of contemporary thought. Most recently, a number of writers (including Richard Rubenstein, Eliezer Berkovits, and Emil Fackenheim) have struggled with issues connected with the Holocaust.

In the New Testament, Jesus directed his teaching to those without formal education; he taught the good news of the Kingdom of God rather than formal theology. For Paul, God's revelation in Christ rather than a series of propositions about religious truth was what was important. In his first letter to the Corinthians he wrote: 'Greeks seek wisdom, but we preach Christ crucified' (1 Cor. 1.22–23). Despite such a view of theological speculation, the early Church sought to defend doctrines about Christ in rational terms. In the 2nd cent., Irenaeus wrote at length against Gnostic heretics, and Hippolytus (3rd cent.) engaged in the same debate. In the same century, Tertullian coined the theological vocabulary that became standard for the Latin-speaking Church.

During this early period, Alexandrians such as Clement (2nd–3rd cent.) and Origen (2nd–3rd cent.) developed a particular tradition of philosophical theology. Like Philo, they utilized allegory in interpreting Scripture. In the 4th cent., the Arian controversy led to the first ecumenical Council of Nicaea, and determined the course of theology for the next century and a half. During this period, John Chrysostom (4th–5th cent.) preached influential sermons dealing with theological issues, and Cyril of Alexandria (5th cent.) engaged in various Christological controversies. In the West, such figures as Jerome (4th–5th cent.), Ambrose (4th cent.), Augustine (4th–5th cent.), and Gregory the Great (6th cent.) made major contributions to Latin theology.

In the Middle Ages, Christian theology underwent a major transformation as exemplified by Anselm's teaching: *Credo ut intelligam* ('I believe that I may understand'). Specific questions were introduced by a dialectical opposition of objection, response, and resolution. In the 12th cent., Peter Abelard initiated the method of *Sic et Non*, in which contradictory statements of Church Fathers were juxtaposed. During this period, Albert the Great (13th cent.) was concerned with questions of natural philosophy, and Bonaventure (13th cent.) was preoccupied with the individual's relation to God. Pre-eminent among Scholastic thinkers was Thomas Aquinas (13th cent.), who utilized the dialectical method in his *Summa Theologica*, arguably the major achievement of Christian theology in the Middle Ages. Aquinas' approach was later criticized by Duns Scotus (13th cent.) and the Scholastic approach to theology became less influential.

The 17th cent. witnessed the beginning of scholarly research into the Fathers and early Church history. In the next century, the intellectual climate of the Enlightenment had a profound effect on Christian thought – a number of theologians sought to reinterpret Christian doctrine along rationalist lines. In the 19th and 20th cents, a range of new developments occurred in Christian theology, including the emergence of neo-Scholasticism, neo-Orthodoxy, Christian Existentialism, and liberation theology. Thus in Judaism and Christianity, theological speculation has undergone a wide variety of transformations in the history of both traditions.

Theophany

(Presence of God) (Shekinah): In the Bible, God is depicted as appearing to patriarchs and prophets. Such appearances are described using various degrees of anthropomorphism. Thus in Gen. 3.8, God is portrayed as walking in the Garden of Eden: 'And they heard the sound of the Lord God walking in the garden in the cool of the day.' Alternatively, he is represented by messengers: 'And the Lord appeared to him [Abraham] by the oaks of Mamre, as he sat at the door of his tent in the heat of the day. He lifted up his eyes and looked, and behold, three men stood in front of him' (Gen. 18.1–2). Again, in Exod. 19.18, God appeared to Moses in a natural phenomenon: 'And Mount Sinai was wrapped in smoke, because the Lord descended upon it in fire.'

In some instances, such a divine disclosure takes place in a dream; in other cases, God appears directly to individuals. Yet the Bible insists that except in the case of Moses (Deut. 34.10), it is not possible to have a direct sensory experience of God's presence. For this reason, various circumlocutions are frequently used to describe God's manifestation. Thus in Gen. 33 Moses asks God to show him his Glory (*kavod*). In later rabbinic literature, the term used for God's presence is 'Shekinah'. This term is derived from scriptural passages that depict God's dwelling in the midst of Israel. According to the rabbis, God dwells wherever there is domestic peace, and among those who gather in prayer. Sin and injustice, however, drive God's presence from the world. In kabbalistic (mystical) literature, the Shekinah is the tenth *sephira* (emanation of the Divine) and represents the feminine aspect of divinity. According to kabbalistic doctrine, the separation of the Shekinah from God can be repaired by loyalty to the Torah. For medieval philosophers, the Shekinah is seen as a divine entity separated from God – from Saadiah Gaon (9th–10th cent.) onwards, Jewish thinkers identified it with the Divine Glory and conceived it as God's first creation.

According to Christian doctrine, God made himself manifest by coming among human beings as a person: Jesus is the incarnate Word. Such a view is held to be implicit in the New Testament, and was refined over the first five centuries of the Christian era, culminating in the ecumenical councils of Nicaea (4th cent.), Constantinople (4th cent.), Ephesus (5th cent.), and Chalcedon (5th cent.). These various councils rejected a number of heretical beliefs: Arianism (the denial of the Son's eternal divinity), Apollinarianism (the denial of Christ's human spirit); Nestorianism (the denial that the divine-human Christ could be conceived as a single Person), Eutychianism (the denial of Christ's two natures); and Monotheletism (the denial of the human and divine will in Christ). Instead, the Church insisted on the full humanity and divinity of Christ.

The doctrine of the incarnation implies that the gap between man and God has been closed; by revealing himself to human beings in Christ, God has disclosed his self-sacrificial love. Through Christ's death, he has subjected himself to the conditions of human life. Further, the model of the divine involvement in suffering and sin became the pattern for Christian ethical commitment. Parallel with the formulation of the doctrine of the incarnation, Christians were anxious to formulate a theory of the Godhead which would account for the presence and action of God in the world in Jesus Christ. In the 4th cent., at the Council of Nicaea and at Constantinople, the dogma was defined in its simplest terms. Against competing heresies, the co-equality and co-eternity of the three Persons were affirmed. The Persons differ only in origin in that the Father is ungenerated, the Son is generated by the Father, and the Holy Ghost proceeds from the Father through the Son. In the West, the procession of the Holy Ghost was attributed to the Father and the Son. In the history of the Church these doctrines of the incarnation and the Trinity have undergone numerous developments, yet through the centuries Christians have universally affirmed their belief that God's ultimate manifestation on earth was his presence in Christ – through such a disclosure, the promise of salvation is offered to all. For Jews, on the other hand, it is the Shekinah that constitutes the true presence of God in the world.

Tithe

According to Lev. 27.30, 'All the tithe of the land, whether of the seed of the land or of the fruit of the trees, is the Lord's'. Traditional Jewish law stipulates that a minimal amount from each crop be given as a heave-offering (*terumah*) to the priest. After the separation of the *terumah*, one-tenth of the remainder had to be given to the Levites. The Levites were the one Israelite tribe who had no land. Their duty was to teach Torah, and in return they were supported by the other 11 tribes. Then the Levites were expected to give one-tenth of what they received to the priests of the Temple. No tithes were given every seventh year, because then the land was expected to lie fallow. After the destruction of the second Temple in 70CE, the laws of tithing fell into disuse, but even today very observant Jews living in Israel continue to practise the separation of *terumah*. Many Jews, however, continue to donate up to one-tenth of their income to charity.

The Christian Church in many countries has maintained the system of tithing until recent times. It was organized in different ways, but the principle was that the local clergy were entitled to a tenth part of all the produce of the land. Although this custom has long since died out, many Christians continue to give a tenth of their income to the Church or, like many Jews, give an equivalent amount to charity.

Torah *see* Law

Trinity

From the earliest period, Christians stressed that there is no inconsistency between Trinitarian doctrine and the belief in one God. According to Christian exegetes, the doctrine of the Trinity is contained implicitly in Scripture in the appearance of the three visitors to Abraham (Gen. 18), and in the declaration 'Holy, holy, holy is the Lord of hosts' in Isaiah's vision (Isa. 6.3). The tradition also maintains that it is taught in the New Testament in such passages as Matt. 28.19: 'Go therefore and make disciples of all nations, baptizing them in the name of the Father and of the Son and of the Holy Spirit.'

This teaching was preached by the early Church and formulated in creeds and doxologies as well as individual confessions of martyrs. At the Councils of Nicaea (325) and Constantinople (381), the doctrine of the Trinity was defined. Against various heretical views (including Sabbelianism, Arianism, and Macedonianism), the co-equality and co-eternity of the three Persons (Father, Son, and Holy Ghost) were affirmed. According to Orthodox doctrine, the three Persons differ only in origin: the Father is ungenerated, the Son is generated from the Father, and the Holy Ghost proceeds from the Father through the Son. The procession thus resembles a straight line. In the West this doctrine took a different form. The procession of the Holy Ghost was attributed both to the Father and the Son – thus the Trinitarian symbol was not a line, but a triangle.

In the Latin Church, the chief patristic exponent of Trinitarian doctrine was Augustine (4th–5th cent.), who in *De Trinitate* compared the two processes of the Divine life to human self-knowledge and self-love. His views were subsequently taken over by medieval Scholasticism, and the classical exposition of the doctrine of the Trinity was undertaken by Thomas Aquinas (13th cent.). From medieval times to the present day, the doctrine of the Trinity has undergone numerous developments, yet it has remained the central teaching of the Church about the nature of the Godhead.

In the Hebrew Scriptures, the Israelites experienced God as the Lord of history. The most uncompromising affirmation of his unity is the Shema prayer: 'Hear, O Israel: The Lord our God is one Lord' (Deut. 6.4). According to Scripture, the universe owes its existence to the one God, the creator of heaven and earth, and since all human beings are created in his image, all men and women are brothers and sisters. Thus the belief in monotheism implies for the Jewish faith that there is one God, one humanity, and one world.

Jewish biblical theology stressed that God alone

is to be worshipped, and the struggle against polytheism continued into the rabbinic period. The Talmud contains numerous prescriptions against idolatry (*avodah zara*). In particular, the rabbis were concerned about the threat of dualism, and Christianity was attacked for its apparent dualistic character. According the the rabbis, the doctrine of the incarnation implies that there are two powers in heaven: the Father and the Son.

In the Middle Ages, Jews were anxious to refute Trinitarian claims. Christian exegetes during this period frequently interpreted the three references to God in the Shema as applying to the Trinity. Jewish scholars, however, declared that this was a misreading of the verse, and that there is only one God and not three Persons in the Godhead. The mystical work, the Zohar, asserted that the three names of God in the Shema represent three powers in the Godhead (the three *sephirot* (emanations) of loving kindness, judgement, and beauty); on this basis, Christian kabbalists (mystics) read into the Zoharic interpretation the doctrine of the Trinity. Such a reading, however, was firmly refuted by Jewish apologists. According to medieval Jewish philosophy, there can be no multiplicity in God's being – he is absolute simplicity. From medieval times to the present day, Jews of all persuasions have insisted on the correctness of this view – Judaism rejects any form of dualistic or Trinitarian doctrine, no matter how such beliefs are reconciled with the concept of monotheism.

Trumpet

(Shofar): The traditional trumpet (shofar) is made from a ram's horn, and in biblical times was used for proclaiming the Jubilee Year (Lev. 25.9) or at the anointing of a new king (1 Kings 1.34). So powerful is the sound, that when the priests all blew their rams' horns round the city of Jericho, and the people shouted, the walls collapsed (Josh. 6.20). Nowadays, the ram's horn is blown in the synagogue only during the High Holy Days' services. In particular, a complex order of sounds has been devised for the New Year (Rosh Hashanah) rituals, and it is also blown at the end of the Day of Atonement (Yom Kippur). Moses Maimonides (12th cent.) explained the message of the ram's horn to be one of rousing from slumbers. The New Year was the time to remember God and turn to

him. In the modern State of Israel, the ram's horn is blown on secular occasions such as the swearing in of a new president. In Orthodox neighbourhoods, it is also blown to greet the arrival of the Sabbath.

Neither rams' horns nor modern brass trumpets have a particular ritual use in Christianity, although trumpets may be part of a conventional orchestra accompanying church music. However, following Paul's description of the resurrection of the dead in 1 Cor. 15.51–52, it is generally believed that the final Day of Judgement will be accompanied by the sound of the trumpet ('in a moment, in the twinkling of an eye, at the last trumpet. For the trumpet will sound, and the dead will be raised imperishable, and we shall be changed'). This is very much in the Jewish tradition of understanding the blast of a trumpet as God's call to repentance, but modern Christians almost certainly visualize a modern brass trumpet rather than a traditional ram's horn.

Truth

In the Bible and rabbinic literature the Hebrew word *emet* does not refer to the theological truth; rather, it denotes honesty, truthfulness, and integrity. Thus in Zech. 8.16, it is used to refer to correct judgements: 'Speak the truth to one another, render in your gates judgments that are true.' In Jer., it is used to indicate God's faithfulness: 'the Lord is the true God' (Jer. 10.10). According to the Psalms, God's precepts are morally worthy: 'the ordinances of the Lord are true, and righteous altogether' (Ps. 19.9).

In both the Bible and the Talmud, truth is regarded as one of the central virtues of the faith. Thus Ps. 15 declares that only the person who speaks truth from his heart shall dwell in God's holy mountain. Similarly, in the daily morning service, worshippers are told: 'At all times let a man fear God secretly as well as publicly, acknowledge the truth in his heart.' In the Mishnah Simeon ben Gamaliel (1st cent. CE) maintained that truth is one of the three pillars on which the world rests. The Talmud proclaims that truth will ultimately triumph, and that the Divine Presence does not abide with liars.

Nonetheless, rabbinic literature emphasizes that in certain situations other concerns should be allowed to override the necessity of telling the truth. The sages stated that it is proper to modify the truth for the sake of domestic harmony. Aaron the brother of Moses, for example, as a lover of peace, sometimes told a 'white lie' if peace could be restored. Thus in the biblical and rabbinic period the word *emet* was used in a fluid way to designate loyalty and moral correctness; only later in medieval theological literature was it employed to denote logical, eternal, or revealed truth in a philosophical sense. During this period, Jewish thinkers accepted the Greek notion of truth as correspondence with reality. In subsequent centuries, the term has generally been used in much the same way as in biblical and rabbinic times.

In his epistles, Paul utilized the same notion of truth as found in the Bible and rabbinic sources. Christians are exhorted to speak truthfully in love: 'Rather, speaking the truth in love, we are to grow up in every way into him who is the head, into Christ' (Eph. 4.15). Here truth is construed as truthfulness. Also in the New Testament, truth is understood in a second sense: Jesus himself is viewed as the truth – 'I am the way, and the truth, and the life' (John 14.6). This assertion is a claim about the veracity of Christ himself: as the Son of God, he is the Word made flesh, the true revelation of God to humanity.

Through the centuries, Christians have asserted that Jesus is the promised Messiah, the incarnation of God, the second Person of the Trinity. These claims were refined through time and Christian theology has undergone numerous changes. Yet despite this evolution of thought and despite the divisions within the Church, Christians have viewed their faith as embodying everlasting truths. In this respect, Christianity has been viewed by its adherents as the fullest expression of God's truth, and traditionally this has meant that anyone outside the Church cannot be saved. Thus the Council of Florence in the 15th cent declared that 'no one remaining outside the Catholic Church, not just pagans but also Jews or heretics or schismatics, can become partakers of eternal life'.

This has been the official teaching of the Church until modern times, but increasingly Christians across the religious spectrum have come to recognize the validity of other faiths. A number of 20th-cent. theologians such as Karl Rahner have argued that salvation is open to adherents of other world religions as well. For some writers such as

John Hick, Christianity should lay no claim to superiority. Rather, the Divine is manifest in the various religions of the world, and no tradition should assume that it is the final embodiment of God's revelation. Truth understood in the correspondence sense of conforming with reality has thus been a pivotal notion in Christianity through the ages. In Judaism, particularly in the medieval period, the same concept has also been found. Yet for Jews, the notion of religious truth has preeminently been one of loyalty, integrity, and truthfulness.

Tsitsit *see* Clothing

Tzaddik *see* Righteousness

U

Unity of God *see* Monotheism

Unleavened bread *see* Passover

Unwritten law *see* Law

Usury
According to Lev. 25.35–37, it is forbidden for a Jew to charge a resident alien interest on a loan. Deut. 23.20–21, however, permits charging interest from a foreigner.

The Church also forbade usury. This made the conduct of commerce very difficult indeed but, because Jews were permitted to charge Gentiles interest, the Western Church at the Fourth Lateran Council (1215) formally decreed that practising usury was allowed to them. In most countries in the Middle Ages, Jews were not permitted to own land, and thus money-lending was one of the few occupations open to them. From this, it was a short step to the Christian stereotype of the grasping avaricious Jew which was the source of so much persecution.

With the rise of capitalism, the prohibition against usury became totally impractical and, increasingly, civil law provided for the moderate charging of interest. Nowadays, the term 'usury' is only used for excessive interest rates.

V

Vestments

Traditionally the priests of the Jerusalem Temple wore four garments: the coat, girdle, turban, and breeches. In addition, the High Priest wore the apron (ephod), breastplate (*hoshen*) that was inscribed with the names of the 12 tribes, a robe of blue wool, and a gold headplate. The priestly vestments were stored in a special room in the Temple and were never taken outside the Temple area.

Once the Temple was destroyed in 70CE, the role of the priesthood largely disappeared in Judaism, and priestly garments were no longer worn. However, all observant male Jews continue to wear fringes (*tsitsit*) on a special tunic worn underneath their shirts in obedience to the commandment in the Book of Num. 15.38, and they cover their heads. Also, adult male Jews wear a prayer shawl (tallith) for every synagogue morning service and every additional service except on 9 Av. On the Day of Atonement, the shawl is worn for all five services, and is worn by the reader at the afternoon and evening service. It is obviously in some sense a holy vestment because when someone not wearing a prayer shawl is called up to read from the Torah, he must put one on before reciting the appropriate blessing.

In many branches of the Christian Church, priestly vestments are still worn. The custom arose between the 4th and 9th cent., and by the 10th cent. was fully established. Priests wear the alb (a long white tunic) covered by a chasuble (a decorated overtunic) or cope (semicircular cloak) and stole (thin shawl) for celebrating the Eucharist. In addition, bishops wear a mitre (a head-dress not unlike the Jewish priests' turbans), carry a shepherd's crook, and wear a ring often engraved with a signet. For other services, clergy frequently wear a long gown or cassock covered by a white surplice (short tunic). Outside church, a special round collar is worn as a sign of their clerical calling, rather as Jewish men wear a fringed undergarment and cover

their heads as a sign of their membership of the covenant. Although both the Catholic and Orthodox Churches use vestments, the Protestant clergy tend to wear a simple scholar's gown or ordinary dress. This is because they do not regard themselves as priests in the traditional sense of offering sacrifice; instead, they see themselves primarily as ministers to their congregations.

Thus both Jews and Christians have made use of priestly vestments. Once the sacrificial system ended with the destruction of the Temple, Jews restricted vestments to a single shawl worn by men for prayer and a simple undergarment, again only worn by men, put on every day as a reminder that they belong to a holy nation. Through the Eucharist, on the other hand, Christians have continued to offer sacrifice, and the tradition of priestly vestments has continued. As in the Jerusalem Temple, they are only worn by celebrants during services, although many priests continue to wear distinctive clothing as a sign of their vocation. Even these, however, have largely been discarded by those branches of the Christian Church that do not have a sacramental view of the clergy.

Vows *see* Oaths

Vulgate *see* Bible

W

War *see* Pacifism

Washing *see* Immersion

Wealth

The Bible asserts that since poverty will always exist, all Jews have an obligation to the poor: 'For the poor will never cease out of the land; therefore I command you, You shall open wide your hand to your brother, to the needy and to the poor, in the land' (Deut. 15.11). In prophetic literature the nation was exhorted to heed the cry of the destitute and champion their rights. The Prophets attacked those who oppressed and exploited those at the bottom of society.

Wealth thus brings its obligations. According to Scripture, landowners are to leave the edges of their fields for the needy as well as the olives, grapes, and sheaves of grain that are left over from harvesting. A sabbatical year is prescribed every seventh year; the fields are to lie fallow, and the poor are permitted to eat from them. The Bible also stipulates that tithes are to be given to the poor just as they are to be distributed among the priests and those dedicated to God's service.

In rabbinic literature, this attitude of caring for the disadvantaged continued, and by the 3rd cent., the principle of anonymous giving was institutionalized. In rabbinic times, community institutions collected and distributed charity: a charity fund was created to provide food and clothing; a soup kitchen was instituted to support transients; a dowry society provided dowries for poor brides; and a poorhouse and asylum provided for the old and sick as well as strangers.

Through the centuries, communal responsibility for the downtrodden has continued to be a central feature of Jewish life. Although a number of ascetic moralists (such as Bahya ibn Pakuda (11th cent.)) and mystics (in such medieval works as the *Sepher Hasidim* and the *Zohar*) viewed poverty as a virtue, this attitude was a minority opinion. Poverty was generally regarded as a misfortune. God's blessing is meant to include prosperity; material reward is the result of following his law. Wealth is understood as part of the Divine plan.

In the New Testament, however, poverty is extolled. Thus Jesus declared: 'Blessed are you poor, for yours is the kingdom of God' (Luke 6.20). In the Synoptic Gospels, he exhorted his disciples to abandon property: 'Sell your possessions, and give alms; provide yourselves with purses that do not grow old, with a treasure in the heavens that does not fail, where no thief approaches and no moth destroys. For where your treasure is, there will your heart be also' (Luke 12.33–34).

In the early Church, a life of poverty and simplicity was praised, and this was carried to an extreme by ascetic hermits. In the 4th–5th cent., Benedict decreed that monks should have no property; nonetheless, it was not unusual for monastic communities to have considerable corporate wealth. Responding to such a situation, Francis of Assisi (12th–13th cent.) advocated both personal and corporate poverty. Protestantism, however, has generally taught the correct stewardship of wealth rather than complete renunciation.

Despite such an exalted view of poverty, the Church (like the synagogue) has stressed the importance of alleviating the situation of the poor. This has been a constant theme of Christian history, and in modern times has been particularly emphasized by Christian liberation theologians who advocate the emancipation of the oppressed. Thus although both Jews and Christians seek to relieve human suffering as a result of a lack of material resources, there are important differences between their attitudes to wealth. Within Judaism, material prosperity is seen as a sign of God's favour, despite the recognition of the dangers of misusing wealth. For Christians, on the other hand, poverty is frequently extolled as a virtue, and many believers have attempted to serve their Lord by following his exhortation to live lives of utter simplicity.

Weeks, festival of

(Shavuot): This festival, the second Jewish pilgrim festival, takes place seven weeks after Passover. During these weeks, the omer (sheaf of barley) is counted and, after a week of weeks (49 days), the festival is celebrated as the conclusion of the barley harvest in accordance with Lev. 23.15. Like Passover and Tabernacles (the other pilgrim festivals), Weeks is associated with an historical event – in this case, the giving of the Torah (law) to Moses on Mt Sinai. In the synagogue, the Book of Ruth is read, partly because of its connection with barley harvests, and partly because Ruth was a convert to Judaism who accepted the Torah. The synagogue is often decorated with greenery, and it is customary to eat dairy produce rather than meat. As with most festivals, it is celebrated for two days outside the land of Israel.

It was on the festival of Weeks that Jesus' 12 disciples received his promised Holy Spirit, which gave them the power to preach the Christian gospel to all nations (Act 2). Thus Christians also celebrate the festival of Weeks, calling it Whitsun or Pentecost. The two festivals clearly echo each other. Weeks celebrates the giving of the Torah, God's final revelation to Israel, while Whitsunday commemorates the gift of the Spirit which animates and inspires God's new Israel, the Church.

Whitsunday *see* Pentecost

Wigs *see* Clothing

Wine

Wine has traditionally been used in Jewish religious rituals. It was found on the altar as a libation to accompany the sacrifices (Num. 28–29), and mourners were given a cup of wine (Prov. 31.6). After the destruction of the Temple, wine continued to be used; a blessing was pronounced over it ('Blessed art Thou Lord God King of the Universe ... who createst the fruit of the vine') at Sabbaths and festivals (the kiddush), and wine is part of the *Havdalah* (ending of the Sabbath service). At a circumcision one cup is drunk; at a wedding two cups are used, from which both the bride and groom drink; at Passover four cups of wine are served; and, in Talmudic times, 10 cups were given to mourners in their seven-day period of mourning. It is still regarded as almost a duty to be slightly intoxicated on Purim (the festival of Lots), although on other occasions the rabbis warned against over-indulgence.

According to the Gospels, Jesus transformed the traditional benedictions over bread and wine so that the elements symbolized his body and blood. The different denominations differ in their understanding of precisely the relationship between Jesus and the bread and wine, but in almost all Churches the Eucharist service is regarded as the central act of Christian worship. Some Christians, however, disapprove of the drinking of wine, having seen the effects of alcoholic excess; for their sake, in some churches unfermented grape juice is used as a substitute.

Wisdom

According to Scripture, when other nations learn about the statutes of the Torah, they will say: 'Surely this great nation is a wise and understanding people' (Deut. 4.6). In Wisdom literature (Job, Proverbs, Psalms, and Ecclesiastes), wisdom is repeatedly extolled. Thus Prov. 7.4 declared: 'Say to wisdom, "You are my sister," and call insight your intimate friend.' In the rabbinic tradition, the highest Jewish ideal has been that of a wise scholar (*talmud hakham*) embued with knowledge of the Torah. Conversely, an ignorant person (*am ha-*

arets) has been viewed with contempt, largely because he does not have the knowledge to fulfil the commandments correctly.

Although wisdom is of central importance in Judaism, it must be tempered with fear of God. Thus Ps. 111.10 proclaims: 'The fear of the Lord is the beginning of wisdom.' Again, the Mishnah cautions: 'A man whose fear of sins is greater than wisdom – his wisdom will endure; and the man whose wisdom exceeds his fear of sin – his wisdom will not endure.' Wisdom is a gift from God, and it must be used in his service: 'Let not the wise man glory in his wisdom ... but let him who glories glory in this, that he understands and knows me, that I am the Lord who practise steadfast love, justice, and righteousness in the earth; for in these things I delight'. (Jer. 9.23–24).

According to rabbinic theology, wisdom is identified with the Torah, and Prov. 8.22–23 was used as a proof-text for the belief in the doctrine of the Torah's pre-existence: 'The Lord created me [wisdom] at the beginning of his work, the first of his acts of old. Ages ago I was set up, at the first, before the beginning of the earth.' During the Middle Ages, wisdom was also viewed as one of God's attributes and, in kabbalistic (mystical) sources, the term *hokhmah* (wisdom) refers to one of the 10 *sephirot* (emanations of the Divine). Thus from biblical times the concept of wisdom has been of central importance in defining human ideals as well as in understanding the nature of God and his relation to the world. In the New Testament, divine wisdom is viewed as incarnate in Christ. For Paul, Jesus is the wisdom of God: 'For Jews demand signs and Greeks seek wisdom, but we preach Christ crucified, a stumbling block to Jews and folly to Gentiles, but to those who are called, both Jews and Greeks, Christ the power of God and the wisdom of God' (1 Cor. 1.22–24). It is in Jesus that are hid all the treasures of wisdom and knowledge (Col. 2.3). At the same time, wisdom is associated with the Holy Ghost: 'To one is given through the Spirit the utterance of wisdom' (1 Cor. 12.8).

Amongst the Church Fathers, wisdom was used as a synonym for the incarnate Word, or Logos. Yet some writers, such as Theophilus (2nd cent.) and Irenaeus (2nd cent.), equated wisdom with the third Person of the Trinity. In Gnostic thought, wisdom was viewed as a divine emanation, and a cause of both creation and redemption. In various Gnostic systems, it was conceived as the spouse of the Logos, or the mother of the demiurge (creative spirit).

In the modern period, a number of Russian authors such as Vladimir Solovieff (19th cent.) and Sergius Bulgakov (19th–20th cent.) have reflected upon the nature of wisdom in connection with the deity; in their writings, they distinguish between a created and an uncreated wisdom, which together form God's unity and the world. In their teaching, it is connected with the Platonic World-Soul, the *Theotokos* (mother of God) and the Holy Ghost. Thus in both Judaism and Christianity the concept of wisdom has been important in understanding the nature of the Divine. Yet in Christianity it is directly related to the doctrine of the incarnation and the Trinity.

Witchcraft *see* Superstitions

Women, position of

In the creation account in Gen., woman is viewed as a valuable counterpart to man: 'It is not good that the man should be alone; I will make him a helper fit for him' (Gen. 2.18). Both man and woman are created in the image of God (Gen. 1.27): 'in the image of God he created him; male and female he created them'. In rabbinic times, women continued to be honoured. Jewish legislation recognized their equality: men and women were subject to the same injunctions, prohibitions, and penalties; women were allowed to offer sacrifices in the Temple; and mothers were to be accorded the same respect as shown to fathers. The four matriarchs (Sarah, Rebecca, Leah, and Rachel) were respected, and a number of women were recognized as having played a prominent role in Jewish history (such as Miriam, Huldah, Deborah, Hannah, and Ruth).

Nonetheless, in various spheres men and women have different roles. In marriage and divorce, the man is the active party (he gives a ring to his wife and recites the legal formula of divorce; the woman, on the other hand, is a passive recipient). Similarly, inheritance and particular property rights are invested in men. Further, women are not allowed to hold ecclesiastical positions or assume any authoritative function, nor are they permitted to be witnesses in court. Although they are theoretically allowed to act as ritual slaughterers and circumcisers, this has rarely occurred. Moreover, although women are legally entitled to read the Torah, a rabbinical enactment forbade this so as to maintain public decorum. The primary duty of women is in the house, and therefore they are exempted from the performance of positive precepts that occur at a particular time, and until modern times women's education has been generally neglected.

In the 20th cent., many Jewish women have been critical of the patriarchal nature of the Jewish faith. Encouraged by the women's liberation movement, they have advocated the improvement of women's status. In response, the Reform, Reconstructionist and Conservative movements have ordained women as rabbis, accepted women as cantors, and have encouraged women to take a more active part in Jewish life. Orthodoxy, however, has been less responsive to such demands; and, as a consequence, some Orthodox women have organized their own prayer and study groups.

Following the Jewish tradition, Christianity has upheld the view that women are equal with men on the basis of the creation account in Gen. Nevertheless, throughout the history of the Church until modern times, women were excluded from the ordained ministry and higher theological education. Further classical Christian theology embodied a negative anthropology of women, which has influenced Christianity's teachings about God, sin, grace, Christology, redemption, and ecclesiology. The female principle was identified with flesh in contrast to spirit, and with earth as against heaven. Through the first woman, Eve, sin took root in the world, and many of the early Church Fathers saw women as the gateway of temptation.

As in Judaism, modern Christian feminists have been anxious to criticize the masculine bias of Christian thought. Feminist criticism highlights such patriarchal attitudes in Scripture as well as in patristic, medieval, and modern Christian thought. A central concern of these writers is to discover alternative historical traditions that emphasize the personhood of women and their inclusion in leadership roles both in the Church and in society. In their quest, these feminists have attempted to uncover the meaning of central theological concepts and use them as a critique of male domination.

Further, among these women, early Christianity has been perceived as a counter-cultural movement reacting against traditional hierarchical relationships. What is required, these feminists argue, is a reformulation of the Christian tradition incorporating the insights of women and making use of their particular contributions.

Within feminist theology there is debate about the usefulness of traditional feminine motifs within the Church (Mother Church, Mariology, etc.). Some women wish to expand these symbols; others are critical of their traditional representations. There are also those who are seeking an alternative tradition. Believing that Christianity is inherently patriarchal, such post-Christian feminists wish to abandon the Christian faith and return to ancient religions that embody female symbols of the divine. Thus in both contemporary Judaism and Christianity there has been a growing awareness of the subordination of women, and a significant attempt is being made to reorient the two faiths so as to include the experience and contribution of women.

Worship *see* Liturgy

Written Law *see* Law books

Y

Yad *see* Pointer

Yahrzeit *see* Funeral rites

Yarmulka *see* Clothing

Yeshiva *see* Education

Yom Kippur *see* Day of Atonement

Yom Tov *see* Festivals

Z

Zion *see* Jerusalem

Zionism

The desire to return to Zion (as a synonym for Jerusalem and, by extension, to the entire land of Israel) was first expressed by those who had been exiled to Babylonia after the destruction of the first Temple. After the destruction of the second Temple in 70CE, the longing to return to Zion became a central factor in Jewish life and was expressed in rabbinic literature and the liturgy. So, for example, the Passover Seder (service) concludes with the words 'Next Year in Jerusalem!'

The ideology of the modern Zionist movement drew on these numerous religious strands, altering the Messianic and religious dimensions to a secular ideology. The emergence of nationalism in 19th-cent. Europe prompted Jews to seek a political solution to the problem of anti-Semitism. Theodor Herzl's (19th cent) political Zionism was at first opposed by Orthodox Jews, who claimed that the creation of a Jewish state should only be inaugurated through divine intervention as well as by the Reform Movement – which believed it to be a betrayal of the religious mission of the faith. Subsequently, particularly in the light of the events of the Holocaust, Zionism was embraced by nearly all sectors of the Jewish world as a primary objective of Jewish life.

For Christians, there has not been an equivalent longing to return to Zion. Although the history of the Christian faith begins with Christ's ministry, crucifixion, and resurrection in the Holy Land, Christians have not shared the Jewish attitude to statehood. Over the centuries, Christians have made pilgrimages to Israel to venerate the holy sites of the Christian faith, yet within Christianity Jerusalem is understood as a heavenly rather than earthly domain, a place of spiritual redemption rather than political and social emancipation. The longing for Zion exists in Christianity, but it is not for the geographical city of Jerusalem, but for the celestial city in heaven.

Zohar *see* Mysticism

Further Reading

Bayfield, Tony and Braybrooke, Marcus (eds), *Dialogue With a Difference*, London: SCM Press, 1992. Collection of essays by British Jewish and Christian scholars focusing on important issues in Jewish–Christian dialogue.

Beck, Norman A., *Mature Christianity in the 21st Century: The Recognition and Repudiation of the Anti-Jewish Polemic of the New Testament*, New York: Crossroad, 1970. This work explores the most pressing of Christian agenda. The author argues that the Church needs consistent help from New Testament specialists in order to reach a new consensus and disseminate its findings to those responsible for liturgy and worship.

Bemporad, Jack and Shevack, Michael, *Our Age: The Historic New Era of Christian–Jewish Understanding*, New City Press, 1996. This book, written by two rabbis, depicts the efforts by Catholic and Protestant Churches to refute the falsehoods of the past.

Berkovits, Eliezer, *Faith after the Holocaust*, New York: Ktav, 1973. An important discussion of the Holocaust by a leading Orthodox theologian who uses the free-will argument to explain the tragedy of the Nazi era.

Boys, Mary C., *Jewish–Christian Dialogue: One Woman's Experience*, Mahwah, NJ: Paulist Press, 1997. This work explores the contribution of a serious and sustained encounter with another religious tradition as one of the most important factors in forming healthy religious commitments.

Boys, Mary C., *Has God Only One Blessing? Judaism as a Source of Christian Self-Understanding*, Mahwah, NJ: Paulist Press, 2000. This book explains why commitment to the way of Jesus cannot come at the expense of deprecating the Jewish people.

Bradshaw, Paul F. and Hoffman, Lawrence A., *The Making of Jewish and Christian Worship*, Notre Dame, IN: University of Notre Dame Press, 1992. In this work two scholars explore the origin and growth of Christian and Jewish liturgies from the first century.

Braybrooke, Marcus, *Time to Meet: Towards a Deeper Relationship between Jews and Christians*, London: SCM Press, 1990. A leading British Christian theologian explores the nature of Jewish–Christian encounter in the modern world.

Braybrooke, Marcus, *Christian–Jewish Dialogue: The Next Steps*, London: SCM Press, 2000. This work surveys the changing relationship between Judaism and Christianity reflected by Jewish scholars' interest in Christianity and Christian scholars' appreciation of Judaism.

Burrell, David and Laundau, Yehezkel (eds), *Voices from Jerusalem: Jews and Christians Reflect on the Holy Land*, Mahwah, NJ: Paulist Press, 1992. A Jewish–Christian dialogue concerning the Holy Land.

Cargas, Harry James, *Shadows of Auschwitz: A Christian Response to the Holocaust*, Notre Dame, IN: University of Notre Dame Press, 1987. A Catholic scholar considers the Nazi era from a Christian perspective.

Charlesworth, James H. (ed.), *Overcoming Fear Between Jews and Christians*, New York: Crossroad, 1992. This series of essays focuses on the courage demanded for Jewish–Christian encounter.

Cohn-Sherbok, Dan, *Holocaust Theology*, London: Lamp 1991. An examination of significant theological responses to the Holocaust by a number of Jewish writers.

Cohn-Sherbok, Dan, *The Crucified Jew: Twenty Centuries of Christian Anti-Semitism*, London: HarperCollins, 1993. A history of the development of Christian anti-Semitism through the centuries.

Cohn-Sherbok, Dan, *Holocaust Theology: A Reader*, Exeter: University of Exeter Press, 2002. A collection of the writings of Jewish and Christian thinkers who explore the religious impact of the Holocaust.

Cracknell, Kenneth, *Towards a New Relationship: Christians and People of Other Faith*, London: Epworth, 1986. The author seeks to present a Christology and spirituality for inter-faith encounter.

Croner, Helga (ed.), *Stepping Stones to Further Jewish-Christian Dialogue*, Mahwah, N J: Stimulus, 1977. A collection of key documents from Catholic and Protestant sources dealing with Jewish–Christian encounter.

Croner, Helga (ed.), *More Stepping Stones to Further Jewish–Christian Dialogue: An Unabridged Collection of Christian Documents*, Mahwah, N J: Stimulus, 1985. An important collection of sources.

Croner, Helga and Cohen, Martin A. (eds), *Christian Mission – Jewish Mission*, Mahwah, N J: Stimulus, 1982. This book consists of a collection of essays providing an overview of the varied uses and meaning of the term mission for Jews and Christians.

Eckhardt, A. Roy, *Elder and Younger Brothers: The Encounter of Jews and Christians*, New York: Schocken, 1973. The Methodist scholar Roy Eckhardt expresses disillusionment that the Christian Churches had for twenty years remained silent about the Holocaust and continue to dismiss contemporary Jewish existence.

Eckhardt, A. Roy, *Jews and Christians: The Contemporary Meeting*, Bloomingto, IN: Indiana University Press, 1986. A stimulating attempt to depict and assess the contemporary encounter between Christians and Jews.

Eckhardt, Alice and Eckardt, Roy, *Long Night's Journey into Day: A Revised Perspective of the Holocaust*, Detroit, MI: Wayne University Press, 1987. This study reflects on the task now facing Christian theology in the light of the Holocaust.

Edwards, John, *The Jews in Christian Europe 1400–1700*, London: Routledge, 1987. A survey of a critical period in the rise of anti-Semitism.

Ellis, Marc, *Faithfulness in an Age of Holocaust*, Amity House, 1986. The author argues that Holocaust theology has failed because of its inability to analyse the modern use of power.

Ellis, Marc, *Beyond Innocence and Redemption: Confronting the Holocaust and Israeli Power*, London: Harper & Row, 1991. In this work, the author criticizes various themes within Holocaust theology including suffering and empowerment, innocence and redemption, and specialness and normalization.

Evans, Craig and Copan, Paul (eds), *Who was Jesus? A Jewish–Christian Dialogue*, Louisville: Westminster John Knox Press, 2001. A collection of essays revolving around the discussion between Jewish New Testament scholar Peter Zaas and the Christian writer William Craig.

Fackenheim, Emil L., *The Jewish Return to History: Reflections in the Age of the Holocaust and a New Jerusalem*, New York: Schocken, 1978. Here the author seeks to interpret the significance of survival rather than the death camps. In his view, God and Israel are still in relationship.

Fackenheim, Emil L., *To Mend the World: Foundations of Future Jewish Thought*, New York: Schocken, 1989. A discussion of the theme that the Shoah has not undermined the Jewish faith experience.

Feld, Edward, *The Spirit of Renewal: Finding Faith after the Holocaust*, Woodstock, VT: Jewish Lights, 1994. The author argues that religious belief must be reconstructed in a post-Holocaust world.

Fisher, Eugene J., *Homework for Christians: Preparing Christian–Jewish Dialogue*, New York: National Conference of Christians and Jews, 1989. A study guide for small groups which address the New Testament, conversion and persecution, the crucifixion, anti-Semitism and the Holocaust.

Fisher, Eugene J., *Faith Without Prejudice: Rebuilding Christian Attitudes Toward Judaism*, New York: Crossroad, 1993. A book designed for Christians to help them translate the spirit of *Nostra Aetate* and other statements into action.

Fisher, Eugene J., *Interwoven Destinies: Jews and Christians Through the Ages*, Mahwah, NJ: Paulist Press, 1993. A collection of pairs of essays by four Jews and four Christians concerning Jewish–Christian relations through history.

Fisher, Eugene J. (ed.), *Visions of the Other: Jewish and Christian Theologies Assess the Dialogue*, Mahwah, NJ: Paulist Press, 1994. These essays illustrate that both Christians and Jews can come to terms with theological problems.

Fisher, Eugene J., Rudin, James and Tanenbaum, Marc (eds), *Twenty Years of Jewish–Catholic Relations*, Mahwah, NJ: Paulist Press, 1986. A collection of essays by Jewish and Catholic scholars concerning a range of topics including liturgy, Bible, Israel, and religious education.

Friedlander, Albert A., *A Thread of Gold: Journeys Towards Reconciliation*, London: SCM Press, 1989. An autobiographical account exploring the nature of Jewish–Christian dialogue and reconciliation.

Friedlander, Saul (ed.), *Probing the Limits of Representation: Nazism and the 'Final Solution'*, Cambridge, MA: Harvard University Press, 1992. An important study of Hitlerism by a leading Jewish scholar.

Fry, Helen (ed.), *Christian–Jewish Dialogue: A Reader*, Exeter: University of Exeter Press, 1996. An excellent collection of readings from a leading writer covering a range of central issues.

Gold, Judith Taylor, *Monsters and Madonnas: Roots of Christian Anti-Semitism*, Syracuse NY: Syracuse University Press, 1999. The author argues that the depiction of Jews in the Gospels is the result of Christian anti-Semitism.

Gager, John, *The Origins of Anti-Semitism: Attitudes Towards Judaism in Pagan and Christian Antiquity*, Oxford: Oxford University Press, 1983. This work by a leading New Testament scholar offers an extensive account of anti-Jewish attitudes prior to the emergence of the Church.

Hall, Stanley G., *Christian Anti-Semitism and Paul's Theology*, Minneapolis, MN: Fortress Press, 1994. A useful survey of the field.

Hargrove, Katharine T. (ed.), *Seeds of Reconciliation: Essays on Jewish–Christian Understanding*, Dallas, TX: D. & F. Scott Publishing, 1996. A collection of essays written by leaders in Jewish–Christian encounter.

Harrelson, Walter and Falk, Randall M., *Jews and Christians: A Troubled Family*, Nashville, TN: Abingdon Press, 1990. A positive evaluation of Jewish–Christian encounter by a Christian biblical scholar and a rabbi who explore a wide range of issues.

Hilberg, Raul, *The Destruction of the European Jews*, New York: Holmes and Meier, 1985. The first study to describe the events of the Nazi period.

Isaac, Jules, *The Teaching of Contempt: Christian Roots of Anti-Semitism*, Holt, Rinehart and Winston, 1996. A classic account of the Christian background to the development of Christian hostility towards Judaism.

Kessler, Edward, Pawlikowski, John T. and Banki, Judith H. (eds), *Jews and Christians in Conversation: Crossing Cultures and Generations*, Cambridge: Orchard Academic, 2002. This collection includes contributions from important theologians from the USA, Europe and Israel.

Klein, Charlotte, *Anti-Judaism and Christian Theology*, London: SPCK, 1975. This work by a German Roman Catholic nun who converted from Judaism reveals the ideas of those who contrast law and grace in Pauline theology.

Klenicki, Leon (ed.), *Toward a Theological Encounter: Jewish Understandings of Christianity*, Mahwah, NJ: Paulist Press, 1991. Contains contributions from Norman Solomon, Elliott Dorff, Walter Jacob, David Novak, Michael Wyschogrod and Daniel Breslauer.

Klenicki, Leon and Wigoder, Geoffrey, *A Dictionary of Jewish–Christian Dialogue*, Mahwah, NJ: Paulist Press, 1984. This volume contains brief articles on key theological concepts.

Langmuir, Gavin I., *History, Religion and Anti-Semitism*, Berkeley: University of California Press, 1960. A historical account which seeks to explain the oppression of the Jews in European history.

Lapide, Pinchas E., *Hebrew in the Church: the Foundations of Jewish–Christian Dialogue*, Grand Rapids, MI: Eerdmans, 1984. A work which examines attempts made by Christians to translate the New Testament and Christian liturgy into Hebrew for evangelistic purposes.

Lodahl, Michael E., *Shekhinah–Spirit: Divine Presence in Jewish and Christian Religion*, Mahwah, NJ: Paulist Press, 1992. The author wrestles with three theological difficulties: exclusivism, evil and eschatology.

Lohfink, Norbert, *The Covenant Never Revoked: Biblical Reflections on Christian–Jewish Dialogue*, Mahwah, NJ: Paulist Press, 1991. This collection contains a series of theses providing a new approach to the New Testament texts on Judaism.

Lubarsky, Sandra B., *Tolerance and Transformation: Jewish Approaches to Religious Pluralism*, Cincinnati, OH: HUC Press, 1990. The author elucidates the concept of veridical pluralism, the view that there is more than one tradition that conveys religious truth.

Maduro, Otto (ed.), *Judaism, Christianity and Liberation*, Maryknoll, NY: Orbis Books, 1991. This volume contains important essays by Jews and Christians about the theology of liberation.

Maybaum, I., *The Face of God after Auschwitz*, Amsterdam: Polak and van Gennep, 1965. The author sees God's providence in the events of the Nazi era.

McGarry, Michael B., *Christology after Auschwitz*, Mahwah, NJ: Paulist, 1977. According to the author the main condition for fruitful dialogue is the Christian repudiation of supercessionism.

McInnes, Val A. (ed.), *New Visions: Historical and Theological Perspectives on the Jewish–Christian Dialogue*, New York: Crossroad, 1993. This collection of essays focuses on the early centuries of Jewish–Christian encounter.

Merkle, John C. (ed.), *Faith Transformed: Christian Encounters with Jews and Judaism*, Collegeville Liturgical Press, 2003. This volume contains essays by Walter Harrelson, Alice L. Eckardt, Eva Fleischner, Franklin Sherman, Norman A. Beck, Clark M. Williamson, John T. Pawlikowski, Eugene J. Fisher, Michael McGarry, Mary C. Boys, and John C. Merkle.

Mussner, Franz, *Tractate on the Jews: The Significance of Judaism for Christian Faith*, London: SPCK, 1994. The author emphasizes the Jewishness of both Jesus and Paul and their relationship to the law.

Neusner, Jacob and Chilton, Bruce, *The Intellectual Foundations of Christian and Jewish Discourse*, London: Routledge, 1997. The authors argue that the Judaic and Christian heirs of Scripture adopted Greek philosophical modes of thought and argument for their own ends.

Neusner, Jacob and Chilton, Bruce, *Jewish and Christian Doctrines: The Classics Compared*, London: Routledge, 1999. An introduction to the foundations of Judaism and Christianity.

Novak, David, *Jewish–Christian Dialogue: A Jewish Justification*, Oxford: Oxford University Press, 1992. A Jewish scholar argues for the theological validity and necessity of dialogue between Christians and Jews.

Oberman, Heiko A., *The Roots of Anti-Semitism in the Age of the Renaissance and Reformation*, Minneapolis, MN: Fortress Press, 1981. Written by a Dutch scholar, this work summarizes the finding of much detailed research.

Oesterreicher, John M., *The New Encounter Between Christians and Jews*, New York: The Philosophical Library, 1985. Contains Roman Catholic perspectives on Jewish–Christian dialogue.

Parkes, James, *The Conflict of the Church and Synagogue: A Study in the Origins of Anti-Semitism*, New York: Athenaeum, 1969. An important study of the conflict between Christianity and Judaism.

Pawlikowski, John T., *What Are They Saying about Christian–Jewish Relations?*, Mahwah, NJ: Paulist Press, 1980. The author treats the central issues concerning Jewish–Christian dialogue.

Pawlikowski, John T., *Christ in the Light of the Christian–Jewish Dialogue*, Mahwah, NJ: Paulist Press, 1982. The author reformulates Christology and mission in the light of Jewish–Christian encounter.

Pawlikowski, John T and Wilde, James A., *When Catholics Speak about Jews: Notes for Homilists and Catechists,* Chicago: Liturgy Training Publications, 1987. A helpful resource which provides detailed suggestions for teaching, preaching, writing and praying.

Peck, Abraham J. (ed.), *Jews and Christians after the Holocaust*, Minneapolis, MN: Fortress Press, 1982. This collection contains contributions by leading Jewish and Christian theologians.

Pulzer, Peter, *The Rise of Political Antisemitism in Germany and Austria*, London: Peter Halban, 1987. An appraisal of the extent of Christian responsibility for the Final Solution.

Rahner, Karl and Lapide, Pinhas, *Encountering Jesus – Encountering Judaism: A Dialogue*, New York: Crossroad, 1987. A leading Christian theologian and a Jewish writer discuss Jesus' life and work.

Rausch, David A., *Fundamentalist-Evangelicals and Anti-Semitism*, Harrisburg, PA: Trinity Press International, 1993. The author argues that theological triumphalism and supersessionism foster contempt for Judaism.

Rubenstein, Richard, *After Auschwitz: Radical Theology and Contemporary Judaism*, Indianapolis: Bobbs-Merrill, 1966. An important work which argues that the traditional concept of God must be jettisoned in the light of the events of the modern period.

Rubenstein, Richard and Roth, John, *Approaches to Auschwitz*, Louisville, KY: John Knox, 1987. A collection of material summarizing most of the positions discussed in treatments of the Holocaust.

Rudin, A. James and Wilson, Marvin R. (eds), *A Time to Speak: the Evangelical–Jewish Encounter*, Grand Rapids, MI: Eerdmans, 1987. The evangelical position is treated in this discussion. Topics include scripture, theology and history.

Ruether, Rosmary Radford, *Faith and Fratricide: The Theological Roots of Anti-Judaism*, New York: Seabury, 1974. The author argues that anti-Jewish attitudes in the New Testament were related to the development of anti-Semitism.

Sanders, Jack, *The Jews in Luke-Acts*, London: SCM Press, 1987. The author argues that Luke-Acts represents the most serious polemic against the Jews.

Sandmel, Samuel, *We Jews and Jesus*, Oxford: Oxford University Press, 1965. A contemporary understanding of New Testament research about Jesus.

Saperstein, Marc, *Moments of Crisis in Jewish–Christian Relations*, London: SCM Press, 1989. A rabbi's brief treatment of the central turning points in the history of Jewish–Christian relations.

Shermis, Michael and Zannoni, Arthur E. (eds), *Introduction to Jewish–Christian Relations*, Mahwah, NJ: Paulist Press, 1991. A collection of articles on key issues of dialogue. Basic essays on Scripture, Holocaust, Israel, anti-Semitism and Jesus.

Spong, John Shelby and Spiro, Jack, *Dialogue: In Search of Jewish–Christian Understanding*, St Johann Press, 1999. A discussion of Jewish–Christian relations by a rabbi and leading Christian thinker.

Standhal, Krister, *Paul among Jews and Gentiles*, Minneapolis, MN: Fortress Press, 1976. The author examines the New Testament in the light of his work and involvement with inter-faith relations.

Swidler, Leonard, *Bursting the Bonds: A Jewish–Christian Dialogue on Jesus and Paul*, Maryknoll, NY: Orbis Books, 1991. Contributions from leading thinkers about Jesus and Paul.

Thoma, Clemens, *A Christian Theology of Judaism*, Mahwah, NJ: Paulist Press, 1980. The author assesses biblical and systematic theology in the light of the Jewish–Christian dialogue.

Thoma, Clemens and Wyschogrod, Michael(eds.), *Understanding Scripture: Explorations of Jewish and Christian Traditions of Interpretation*, Mahwah, NJ: Paulist Press, 1987. Jewish and Christian biblical scholars consider issues raised by both their traditions' claim to the Hebrew Scriptures.

Thoma, Clemens and Wyschogrod, Michael (eds), *Parable and Story in Judaism and Christianity*, Mahwah, NJ: Paulist Press, 1989. A collection of essays about the art of storytelling common to Christians and Jews.

Uko, Hans, *Common Roots, New Horizons: Learning about Christian Faith from Dialogue with Jews*, Geneva: World Council of Churches, 1994. The author reflects on his world-wide experience.

van Buren, Paul M., *A Theology of the Jewish Christian Reality*, Lanham, MD: University Press of America, 1995. A systematic theology which reinterprets the Christian tradition to see Judaism and the Jewish people as partners on the same way.

von der Osten-Sacken, Peter, *Christian–Jewish Dialogue: Theological Foundations*, Minneapolis, MN: Fortress Press, 1986. The author envisions a transformation of Christian theology in light of its encounter with Judaism and the Jewish people.

Wigoder, Geoffrey, *Jewish–Christian Relations since the Second World War*, Manchester: Manchester University Press, 1987. The author surveys the development of Jewish–Christian relations since the Second World War.

Wiles, Maurice, *Christian Theology and Interfaith Dialogue*, London: SCM Press, 1992. A Christian scholar focuses on the central question of whether Christian theology is able to develop a positive view of other religions.

Williamson, Clark M., *A Guest in the House of Israel: Post Holocaust Church Theology*, Louisville, KY: Westminster John Knox Press, 1993. A work which discusses anti-Jewish teachings within the Church, and argues that Christians should reconsider the doctrines of the faith.

Zannoni, Alfred E. (ed.), *Jews and Christians Speak of Jesus*, Minneapolis, MN: Fortress Press, 1994. A stimulating collection of essays concerning Jesus.

Index: List of Entries